Elkouri & Elkouri

HOW ARBITRATION WORKS

Fifth Edition

1999 Supplement

Other BNA Books Authored by the ABA Section of Labor & Employment Law

Covenants Not To Compete: A State-by-State Survey

The Developing Labor Law

Discipline and Discharge in Arbitration

Employee Benefits Law

Employee Duty of Loyalty: A State-by-State Survey

Employment Discrimination Law

Equal Employment Law Update

The Fair Labor Standards Act

International Labor and Employment Laws

Labor Arbitration: A Practical Guide for Advocates

Labor Arbitration: Cases and Materials for Advocates

Labor Arbitrator Development: A Handbook

Occupational Safety and Health Law

The Railway Labor Act

Trade Secrets: A State-by-State Survey

Elkouri & Elkouri

HOW
ARBITRATION
WORKS

Fifth Edition

1999 Supplement

Editors-in-Chief

Edward P. Goggin
Professor Emeritus and Arbitrator
Northern Kentucky University

Alan Miles Ruben
Professor and Arbitrator
Cleveland State University

 Committee on ADR in Labor & Employment Law
American Bar Association
Section of Labor and Employment Law

The Bureau of National Affairs, Inc., Washington, D.C.

Copyright © 1999
American Bar Association
Chicago, IL

and

The Bureau of National Affairs, Inc.
Washington, DC

Library of Congress Cataloging-in-Publication Data

Elkouri, Frank.
  How arbitration works / Elkouri and Elkouri; co-editors, Edward
P. Goggin, Marlin M. Volz. — 5th ed.
          p. cm.
Includes index.
ISBN 0-87179-790-9
  1. Arbitration, Industrial--United States. I. Elkouri, Edna
Asper. II. Goggin, Edward P. III. Volz, Marlin M., 1917-
IV. Title
KF3424.E53 1997
344.73'0181943--dc21

                                                    96-40120
                                                    CIP

Published by BNA Books
1231 25th St. NW, Washington, DC 20037
International Standard Book Number: 1-57018-163-2
Printed in the United States of America

Edward A. Pereles
Arbitrator
Philadelphia, PA

Stephen B. Rubin
Arbitrator
Oak Park, IL

Gregory J. Schroedter
Bell, Boyd & Lloyd
Chicago, IL

Chapter 4

Steve Bierig
Attorney
Highland Park, IL

Chapter 4

Steve Bierig
Attorney
Highland Park, IL

Chapter 5

Joseph F. Gentile
Arbitrator
Los Angeles, CA

Chapter 5

Kristine Aubin
Previant, Goldberg, Uelmen,
    Gratz, Miller & Brueggeman,
    S.C.
Milwaukee, WI

Edna E.J. Francis
Arbitrator
Los Angeles, CA

Lynne L. Hicks
Hornbein & MacDonald
Denver, CO

Richard C. Hunt
Lane, Powell, Spears, Lubersky
Portland, OR

Naomi E. Soldon
Previant, Goldberg, Uelmen,
    Gratz, Miller & Brueggeman,
    S.C.
Milwaukee, WI

Scott D. Soldon
Previant, Goldberg, Uelmen,
    Gratz, Miller & Brueggeman,
    S.C.
Milwaukee, WI 53212

Chapter 10

Joseph C. D'Arrigo
Attorney
York Harbor, ME

Chapter 10

Hope K. Abramov
Thompson Coburn
St. Louis, MO

Aaron Baker
Descher & Scholz
St. Louis, MO

Arthur T. Carter
Haynes and Boone, L.L.P.
Dallas, TX

Frederick W. Cory
Attorney
Communications Workers of
    America
AFL-CIO, CLC
Washington, DC

Henri L. Mangeot
Arbitrator
Louisville, KY

Bruce N. Petterson
Attorney
Siemens Energy & Automation,
    Inc.
Alpharetta, GA

Robert T. Rosenfeld
Attorney
Cleveland, OH

Carrie L. Schierer
Thompson Coburn
St. Louis, MO

Chapter 11

Frances Asher Penn
Arbitrator/Mediator
Chicago, IL

Chapter 11

B. Frank Flaherty
Attorney
Garden City, NJ

John Kagel
Attorney
San Francisco, CA

Donald D. Slesnick, II
Slesnick & Casey
Miami, FL

David L. Gregory
Professor
St. John's University
Jamaica, NY

Chapter 14

Donald A. Romano
Carpenter, Bennett & Morrissey
Newark, NJ

Andrew M. Kofsky
Carpenter, Bennett & Morrissey
Newark, NJ

Chapter 14

J. Bruce Cross
Cross, Gunter, Witherspoon &
    Galchus
Little Rock, AR

Robin Shively Brown
Cross, Gunter, Witherspoon &
    Galchus
Little Rock, AR

Gust Callas
Black, McCuskey, Souers &
    Arbaugh
Canton, OH

Vito Carnevale
Carpenter, Cennett & Morrissey
Newark, NJ

Thomas Y. Mandler
Schwartz & Freeman
Chicago, IL

Chapter 15

Edwin R. Render
Professor
University of Louisville
Louisville, KY

Chapter 15

Keith E. White
Bose, McKinney & Evans
Indianapolis, IN

Rosemary A. Townley
Arbitrator/Mediator
Riverdale, NY

Judith A. LaManna
Arbitrator
Syracuse, NY

Chapter 17

Alan Miles Ruben
Professor/Arbitrator
Cleveland State University
Cleveland, OH

Chapter 17

John D. Dunbar
Daniels & Kaplan
Kansas City, MO

Carrie G. Donald
Professor
University of Louisville
Louisville, KY

Alan Kaplan
Morgan, Brown & Joy
Boston, MA

David Leightty
Attorney
Louisville, KY

Kevin McCarthy
Miller, Canfield, Paddock &
   Stone
Kalamazoo, MI

Glenn E. Dawson
Attorney
Boston, MA

Don Meade
Miller & Meade
Louisville, KY

Allyn Lebster
Attorney
Grand Rapids, MI

Susan Grody Ruben
Arbitrator
Cleveland, OH

Rachael L. Leonard
Schwartz & Freeman
Chicago, IL

Lionel Richman
Attorney
Toluca Lake, CA

Foreword to 1999 Supplement

Since 1945 the ABA Section of Labor and Employment Law has had as its stated purposes (1) to study and report upon continuing developments in the law affecting labor relations, (2) to assist the professional growth and development of practitioners in the field of employment and labor relations law, and (3) to promote justice, human welfare, industrial peace, and the recognition of the supremacy of law in labor-management relations.

Through the publication of books such as *How Arbitration Works,* and through annual and committee meeting programs designed to provide a forum for the exchange of ideas, the Section has pursued these stated goals. Gradually, the Section has built a library of comprehensive legal works intended for the use of the Section membership as well as the bar generally.

The Section of Labor and Employment Law is pleased to provide this supplement to the classic treatise on labor arbitration as part of its library of books published by BNA Books, a Division of The Bureau of National Affairs, Inc. The combined efforts of many individual authors from the Committee on ADR in Labor and Employment Law of the Section are reflected in this work.

The Section wishes to express its appreciation to the committee, and in particular to the editors-in-chief, Edward P. Goggin and Alan Miles Ruben. This group has tried to accomplish two primary objectives: (1) to be equally balanced and nonpartisan in their viewpoints, and (2) to ensure the book is of significant value to the practitioner, student, and sophisticated nonlawyer.

The views expressed herein do not necessarily represent the views of the American Bar Association, or its Section of Labor and Employment Law, or any other organization, but are simply the collective, but not necessarily the individual, views of the authors. Information on the affiliation of government employees who contribute to this work is for informational purposes and does not constitute any official endorsement of the information provided herein.

Max Zimny
Chair
Mark S. Dichter
Chair-Elect
Section of Labor and Employment Law
American Bar Association

September 1999

Preface

This First Supplement to the Fifth Edition of *How Arbitration Works* was conceived, planned, authored and edited by the ADR in Labor and Employment Law Committee, a standing committee of the Section of Labor and Employment Law of the American Bar Association. This Committee was responsible for the publication of the Fifth Edition, itself, and also was responsible for both supplements to the Fourth Edition of the Elkouris' well-known treatise.

The two individuals most responsible for this Supplement are its Co-Editors: Professor Edward P. Goggin of Salmon P. Chase College of Law, Northern Kentucky University; and Professor Alan Miles Ruben, Cleveland Marshall Law School, Cleveland State University. These two scholars provided effective leadership, not only in updating topics encompassed by the Fifth Edition, but also in expanding that work by incorporating developments in the emerging area of employment arbitration in the non-union sector.

This Supplement has been prepared so that it dovetails and correlates directly with the text of the Fifth Edition of *How Arbitration Works*. The Supplement text has its own footnotes, but uses the same topic headings as are found in the parent volume. The materials for each chapter in the Supplement follow the same order and topic sequence as in the original text, although not every topic or subtopic has been updated. Thus, for example, topics where no significant developments occurred are not treated in the Supplement. For the convenience of the reader, parallel page numbers of the Fifth Edition where topics and subtopics begin have been listed in the Supplement's Table of Contents. The Supplement covers arbitration awards found in Volumes 98 through 108 of the BNA Labor Arbitration Reports.

Professor Ruben wishes to acknowledge the valuable contributions of his secretary Mrs. Laura Gardner and his Research Assistant Mark Gardner. Also, Professor Goggin wishes to acknowledge the valuable contribution of his secretary Alice Carter and his Research Assistants James Kareth, Kellie Van Swearingen and Craig Wasson.

Lawrence J. Casazza, Management Co-Chair
Patricia T. Bittel, Neutral Co-Chair
Joseph D. Garrison, Plaintiffs Co-Chair
Lynne L. Hicks, Union Co-Chair

Summary Table of Contents

Detailed Table of Contents

Chapter 1

Arbitration and Its Setting

The Expanding Role of Arbitration in the Resolution of Statutory Employment Claims [New Topic]

Commentators have noted a growing tendency of collective bargaining agreements to incorporate by reference requirements to abide by statutes such as the Americans With Disabilities Act (ADA), the Age Discrimination in Employment Act (ADEA), and the Family and Medical Leave Act (FMLA); this, in effect, brings these statutory claims within the four corners of the agreement for an arbitrator's consideration and interpretation.[1] This trend is not limited to the collective bargaining context.

State and federal agencies charged with the enforcement of statutory employment laws have begun to offer alternative dispute resolution (ADR) options to parties litigating charges before their respective agencies. For example, the Massachusetts Commission Against Discrimination launched an ADR program in 1996 that offers voluntary arbitration of employment discrimination charges, and the New York State Human Rights Commission has offered voluntary arbitration since 1993.[2] The Department of Labor is also exploring the use of arbitration as a vehicle to resolve certain whistleblower, FMLA, and Office of Federal Contract Compliance Programs claims.[3]

---

[1]"Academy Board Endorses ADR Task Force Prototype," 104 Daily Lab. Rep. (BNA) A-4, A-5 (May 31, 1995).

[2]"Massachusetts Rights Agency Launches ADR Program to Arbitrate Bias Disputes," 33 Daily Lab. Rep. (BNA) A-1 (Feb. 20, 1996); "Lawyers Urged to Consider Arbitration as Alternative in Employment Disputes," 26 Daily Lab. Rep. (BNA) A-9, A-10 (Feb. 8, 1996); Evan J. Spelfogel, *Legal and Practical Implications of ADR and Arbitration in Employment Disputes,* 11 H Lab. L.J. 247, 256–57 (1993).

[3]"Lawyers Urged to Consider Arbitration as Alternative in Employment Disputes," 26 Daily Lab. Rep. (BNA) A-9, A-10 (Feb. 8, 1996).

A recent and controversial increase in the number of employers requiring nonunion employees to submit statutory employment claims to arbitration has been attributed to the Supreme Court's 1991 decision in *Gilmer v. Interstate / Johnson Lane Corp.*[4] In *Gilmer*, the Supreme Court held that an ADEA claim can be subjected to mandatory arbitration. The *Gilmer* case marked the first time that the Supreme Court had ruled on the arbitrability of an individual employee's statutory claims outside the collective bargaining context,[5] and it sparked the beginning of an ongoing national debate. Lower courts have relied on *Gilmer* to enforce employment agreements[6] requiring mandatory arbitration of claims brought under various federal and state employment statutes.[7]

Proponents of mandatory arbitration of statutory employment claims note its potential for reducing the high number of employment bias cases currently being litigated, its lower cost and speed as

---

[4]Gilmer v. Interstate/Johnson Lane Corp., 111 S. Ct. 1647 (1991); Van Wezel Stone, *Labor / Employment Law: Mandatory Arbitration of Individual Employment Rights: The Yellow Dog Contract of the 1990s,* 73 Denver U. L. Rev. 1017, 1036 (1996). For a more complete discussion of the *Gilmer* decision, see Chapter 10 of the Main Volume, under "U.S. Supreme Court Statements Regarding Arbitral Consideration of External Law."

[5]Brian K. Van Engen, Note, *Post-Gilmer Developments in Mandatory Arbitration: The Expansion of Mandatory Arbitration for Statutory Claims and the Congressional Effort to Reverse That Trend,* 21 J. Corp. L. 391, 401–02 (1996).

[6]There has been some disagreement among the courts regarding the applicability of *Gilmer* in the context of collective bargaining agreements. Most courts that have considered this issue have drawn a distinction between the enforceability of mandatory arbitration clauses contained within individual employment contracts and mandatory arbitration clauses contained within collective bargaining agreements. These courts have followed the reasoning of the Supreme Court in Alexander v. Gardner-Denver Co., 415 U.S. 36 (1974), to hold that arbitral remedies contained within collective bargaining agreements do not preclude individual employees subject to these agreements from bringing statutory employment claims in court in addition to or in lieu of arbitration. Bates v. Long Island Railroad Co., 997 F.2d 1028 (2d Cir. 1993), *cert. denied,* 510 U.S. 992 (1993); Ryan v. City of Shawnee, 13 F.3d 345 (10th Cir. 1993); Pryner v. Tractor Supply Co., 109 F.3d 354 (7th Cir. 1997), petition for cert. filed, 65 U.S.L.W. 3783 (U.S. May 16, 1997) (No. 96-1830), petition for cert. filed, 66 U.S.L.W. 3108 (U.S. July 18, 1997) (No. 97-123). *See also* Cole v. Burns Int'l Sec. Servs, 105 F.3d 1465 (D.C. Cir. 1997), for a comprehensive analysis in an opinion written by Chief Judge Harry Edwards in which in dictum he forcefully distinguishes between enforcement of a mandatory arbitration provision dealing with statutory claims contained in an individual employment agreement and enforcement of such a provision in a collective bargaining agreement. Nonetheless, some courts have expanded *Gilmer* to require individual employees to exhaust mandatory arbitral remedies contained within collective bargaining agreements before filing a statutory action in court. Austin v. Owens-Brockway Glass Container, Inc., 78 F.3d 875 (4th Cir. 1996), *cert. denied,* 117 S. Ct. 432 (1996); Reece v. Houston Lighting & Power Co., 79 F.3d 485 (5th Cir. 1996), *cert. denied,* 514 U.S. 864 (1996). On March 2, 1998, the U.S. Supreme Court granted certiorari in *Wright v. Universal Maritime Serv. Corp.,* a case from the Fourth Circuit involving this question. 41 Daily Lab. Rep. (BNA), AA-1 (Mar. 3, 1998).

[7]*Developments in the Law—Employment Discrimination,* 109 Harv. L. Rev. 1670, 1672, 1675–77 (1996); Richard A. Bales, *Compulsory Arbitration of Employment Claims: A Practical Guide to Designing and Implementing Enforceable Agreements,* 47 Baylor L. Rev. 591, 604–05 (1995); Christine K. Biretta, Comment, Prudential Insurance Company of America v. Lai: *The Beginning of the End For Mandatory Arbitration?,* 49 Rutgers L. Rev. 595, 596–600, 614–18 (1997); Van Wezel Stone, *supra* note 4, at 1033–34.

compared with litigation, and its potential to increase access to a system of dispute resolution for lower-income employees.[8] Critics of mandatory arbitration of statutory employment claims point to the procedural differences between arbitration and litigation—that is, the absence of discovery rules in arbitration—as potentially placing employees at a greater disadvantage than employers,[9] and they assert that even experienced arbitrators are not well versed in employment law.[10]

Critics of mandatory arbitration of employment claims include the Equal Employment Opportunity Commission (EEOC), the National Labor Relations Board (NLRB), the National Academy of Arbitrators (NAA), and the Commission on the Future of Worker-Management Relations (CFWMR).[11] The chairman of the NLRB questioned whether deference should be given by the NLRB to mandatory arbitration in nonunion settings because the system is set up and paid for by management.[12] The NAA released a statement opposing mandatory employment arbitration as a condition of employment when it requires waiver of direct access to either a judicial or administrative

---

[8]*Developments in the Law—Employment Discrimination,* 109 Harv. L. Rev. 1670, 1672–73 (1996).

[9]Id. at 1674. The National Academy of Arbitrators, the American Arbitration Association, and the American Bar Association have each published procedural guidelines to assist members who are appointed to hear individual claims alleging violations of federal and state employment statutes. "Arbitrators' Academy Votes to Oppose Mandatory Arbitration of Job Disputes," 103 Daily Lab. Rep. (BNA) A-3 (May 29, 1997); "National Academy of Arbitrators' Statement and Guidelines Adopted May 21, 1997," 103 Daily Lab. Rep. (BNA) E-1 (May 29, 1997); "NAA Opposes Mandatory Arbitration Restricting Statutory Rights," 1878 Lab. Arb. Awards (CCH) 3–4 (June 10, 1997); "American Arbitration Association Rules for Resolution of Employment Disputes," 102 Daily Lab. Rep. (BNA) E-17–E-26 (May 28, 1997); Biretta, *supra* note 7, at n.18.

[10]*Developments in the Law—Employment Discrimination,* 109 Harv. L. Rev. 1670, 1680 (1996).

[11]In August 1997, the National Association of Securities Dealers Inc. (NASD) voted to eliminate mandatory arbitration of statutory employment discrimination claims for registered brokers. Approval of the new rule by the Securities and Exchange Commission (SEC) possible in 1998. 153 Daily Lab. Rep. (BNA) AA-1 (Aug. 8, 1997); 62 Fed. Reg. 66, 164 (1997). Bills were introduced in both houses of the U.S. Congress to eliminate mandatory arbitration of federal employment discrimination claims. "Elimination of Mandatory Arbitration of Discrimination Claims Proposed by NASD." "Feingold Urges SEC to Advise Industry to End Mandatory Arbitration of Job Claims," 68 Daily Lab. Rep. (BNA) A-8 (Apr. 9, 1997); "Schroeder Bill Would Bar Enforcement of Mandatory Arbitration Contracts," 128 Daily Lab. Rep. (BNA) A-1–A-2 (July 3, 1996); Van Engen, Note, "Post-Gilmer Developments in Mandatory Arbitration: The Expansion of Mandatory Arbitration for Statutory Claims and the Congressional Effort to Reverse the Trend," 21 Iowa J. Corp. L. 391, 410–12 (1996); Biretta, Comment, "Prudential Insurance Company of America v. Lai: The Beginning of the End for Mandatory Arbitration?," 49 Rutgers L. Rev. 595, 597 (1997).

[12]NLRB Chairman Questions Impartiality of Arbitration in Nonunion Workplaces," 72 Daily Lab. Rep. (BNA), A-2 (Apr. 15, 1997); "NLRB Chairman Outlines Growing Use of Arbitration Among Nonunion Employers," 69 Daily Lab. Rep. (BNA) A-2, E-1–E-6 (Apr. 10, 1997).

forum for the pursuit of statutory rights.[13] The CFWMR emphasized in its 1995 Report and Recommendations to the Secretary of Labor that, while it strongly supports the expansion and development of ADR mechanisms in the workplace, it does not favor compulsory arbitration of employment claims as a condition of employment.[14]

---

[13]"Arbitrators' Academy Votes to Oppose Mandatory Arbitration of Job Disputes," 103 Daily Lab. Rep. (BNA) A-3; (May 29, 1997); "National Academy of Arbitrators' Statement and Guidelines Adopted May 21, 1997," 103 Daily Lab. Rep. (BNA) E-1, E-2 (May 29, 1997); "NAA Opposes Mandatory Arbitration Restricting Statutory Rights," 1878 Lab. Rep. Awards (CCH) 3–4 (June 10, 1997).

[14]"Report and Recommendations of the Commission on the Future of Worker-Management Relations (January 9, 1995)," reproduced in 6 Daily Lab. Rep. Supp. (BNA) S-42, S-48 (Jan. 10, 1995) (Special Supplement); Dunlop, "Employment Litigation and Dispute Resolution: The Dunlop Commission Report," Proceedings of the 48th Annual Meeting of NAA, 129 (BNA Books, 1996); "Dunlop Commission Panel Strongly Endorses Use of ADR, But Opposes Mandatory Arbitration," 6 Daily Lab. Rep. (BNA) AA-4 (Jan. 10, 1995).

Chapter 2

Legal Status of Arbitration

Federal Law: Private Sector

De Novo Litigation Following Arbitration

The Alexander v. Gardner-Denver Case. See "U.S. Supreme Court Statements Regarding Arbitral Consideration of External Law" in Chapter 10. Following the decision in *Gilmer v. Interstate Johnson Lane Corp.*, discussed in the Main Edition, the federal courts have been struggling to reconcile *Gardner-Denver* with *Gilmer* and to resolve a variety of issues related to arbitration of discrimination claims, in both the unionized and nonunionized workplace. A detailed discussion of the many decisions, sometimes conflicting, by the federal courts of appeal and district courts is beyond the scope of this work. For additional information on these decisions see recent volumes of the proceedings of the annual meetings of the National Academy of Arbitrators; editions of Seymour and Berish Brown, *Equal Employment Law Update*, Chapter 28 "Pre-Dispute Arbitration Agreements"; and Lindemann and Grossman, *Employment Discrimination Law, Third Edition* and supplements thereto, Chapter 32 "Election and Exhaustion of Remedies."

Other Supreme Court Decisions Affecting Arbitration

Meritor Savings Bank v. Vinson. In 1998 the U.S. Supreme Court recast the law of sexual harassment in *Burlington Industries, Inc. v. Ellerth*, 524 U.S. 742, 77 FEP Cases 1 (1998) and *Faragher v. City of Boca Raton*, 524 U.S. 775, 77 FEP Cases 14 (1998). The court held that employers may be held vicariously liable under Title VII if a supervisor demands that an employee submit to sexual advances or else suffer a tangible adverse employment action. Where the plaintiff does not suffer a significant tangible employment action, the Court held, an employer can avoid liability by affirmatively proving that (1) it had exercised reasonable care to prevent and promptly correct sexual harassment and (2) the employee unreasonably failed to take advantage of opportunities to prevent or avoid harm. See also Chapter 17 Employee Rights and Benefits under the headings "Protection Against Sexual Harassment" and "Same-Sex Harassment [New Topic]." For further information, see Seymour and Berish Brown, *Equal Employment Law Update*, Chapter 24, "Demands for Sexual Favors" and Chapter 25 "Hostile Environment"; and Lindemann and Grossman, *Employment Discrimination Law, Third Edition* and supplements thereto, Chapter 20, "Sexual and Other Forms of Harassment."

Legal Status of Arbitration in State-Sector Employment

This topic and its subtopics deal with collective bargaining and arbitration for employees of state or local government, pubic school boards, and public colleges and universities. Accordingly, as used below, the terms "state sector," "public sector," "public employees," "public employers," and "public employment" refer only to such employment and not to the federal sector.

Often labor relations problems of state and local government employees are not covered by federal statutes or regulations, and a constitutionality issue likely will arise whenever Congress moves to cover such employees by federal law. Many states and municipalities allow organizational, bargaining, and dispute-resolution activities by some or all public employees. However, employees in both the state and federal sectors generally continue to be restricted by the traditional prohibition against strikes by public employees.

The traditional prohibition against strikes by public employees is weakening in some quarters. At least 14 states now provide a right to strike in one variation or another for their employees. Alaska, Hawaii, Idaho, Illinois, Minnesota, Montana, Ohio, Oregon, Pennsylvania, Vermont, and Wisconsin[1] legislatively grant public employees the

---

[1]See "Public Employees Bargain for Excellence: A Compendium of State Public Labor Relations Law" (AFL-CIO), 1995); Alaska Stat. §23.40.200 (Michie 1997); Haw. Rev. Stat. §89-12 (1997); Idaho Code §44-1811 (1997); 5 Ill. Comp. Stat. 315/17 (West 1997); Minn. Stat. §179A.18 (1996); Mont. Code Ann. §39-32-110, 39-34-105 (1997); Ohio Rev. Code Ann. §4117.15–16 (Anderson 1997); Or. Rev. Stat. §243.726 (1996); 43 Pa. Cons. Stat. §1101.1001–1003, 1101.2201 (1997); Vt. Stat. Ann. tit. 21 §1730 (1997); Wis. Stat. §111.70(4)(cm)(6)(c) (1995–96). See generally Note, "Reinventing a Livelihood: How United States Labor Laws, Labor-Management Cooperation Initiatives, and Privatization Influence Public Sector Labor Markets," 34 *Harv. J. On Legis,* 557, 567 (1997).

right to strike. In California, Colorado, and Louisiana public employees have gained similar rights via judicial interpretation.[2] Writers have cautioned that "[t]he decentralized nature of public sector labor relations, as evidenced by the variety of legislation, court decisions, opinions of Attorney Generals and local ordinances and resolutions, makes the identification of patterns and trends most difficult."[3] However, the objective here is merely to present an overview of the legal status of bargaining and arbitration in state-sector employment, and to provide the reader with suggested sources of more detailed coverage of the subject as well as state statutory and decisional law.[4]

Sovereignty Doctrine

Sovereignty concepts,[5] such as the *nondelegable* responsibility of public officials to determine policy and to exercise official judgment and discretion in determining matters of government[6] originally led many public employers and courts (and probably some legislatures) to conclude that it would be improper and illegal to share such responsibility by collective bargaining and arbitration. Since 1960, however, the sovereignty doctrine has been eroded by the courts.[7]

---

[2]In County Sanitation Dist. No. 2 v. Los Angeles County Employees' Ass'n, 699 P.2d 835, 849–50, 119 LRRM 2433 (Cal. 1985), the California Supreme Court held public employees may not be prohibited from striking unless the strike would cause imminent danger for public health or safety. The Colorado Supreme Court held that "under the relevant statutes employees in the public sector have a qualified right to strike subject to explicit executive and judicial controls," Martin v. Montezuma-Cortez Sch. Dist. RE-1, 841 P.2d 237, 240 (Colo. 1992). The Louisiana Supreme Court refused to enjoin a teachers' strike, holding that a public employee strike was not 'per se' illegal; Davis v. Henry, 555 So. 2d 457, 461, 133 LRRM 2271 (La. 1990). For a discussion of the judicial determination of public employee rights to strike and particularly the Louisiana court's approach, see Rickey L. Babin, "Davis v. Henry: One More Piece to the Public Employee Strike Rights Puzzle," 51 La. L. Rev. 1271, 1271–78 (1991).

[3]Sinicropi & Gilroy, "The Legal Framework of Public Sector Dispute Resolution," 28 Arb. J. 1 (1973).

[4]See generally NAA Committee on Academy History, The National Academy of Arbitrators: Fifty Years in the World of Work (Gruenberg, ed., 1997).

[5]"The distinctive characteristics of State employment stem from two related factors. The first is the dual role of the State as employer and as government, which in a democratic system means it is accountable to the legislature for its actions. The second is the source of revenue for the services the State provides. Unlike private sector employers, which derive their revenue primarily from profit and are generally dependent upon maintaining a competitive position in the market in order to survive, the State derives its revenue predominantly from taxation." Morris & Frednian, "Is There a Public/Private Labor Law Divide?" 14 Comp. Lab. L. 115, 123 (1993).

[6]"State constitutional vesting clauses, which entrust certain branches of government with specified functions and powers, are the primary source of limitations on delegations. Nondelegation . . . clauses are often construed to mean that legislative powers may not be exercised by officials in other branches of government." Julie Huston Vallarelli, "Note: State Constitutional Restraints on the Privatization of Education," 72 B.U.L. Rev. 381, 391 (1992).

[7]Westbrook argues that the sovereignty doctrine "has almost no continuing influence" and that it "is no longer a significant factor" in public-sector bargaining cases. Westbrook, "The Use of the Nondelegation Doctrine in Public Sector Labor Law: Lessons from Cases That Have Perpetuated an Anachronism," 30 St. Louis U. L.J. 331, 353, 356 (1986).

Some states, no longer deterred by sovereignty concepts, have legalized collective bargaining and arbitration by public employers. Other states selectively apply the sovereignty doctrine to public employee collective bargaining. Finally, some states continue to apply the sovereignty doctrine without exception.[8]

State-Sector Collective Bargaining

The majority of the states have enacted statutes relating to collective bargaining in the public sector.[9] Some states limit the kind and extent of the bargaining rights of public employees; others limit the types of employees able to avail themselves of the stipulated rights. Some statutes mimic the National Labor Relations Act, some reflect the Federal Labor Relations Act to a greater degree, and others merely provide broad 'meet and confer' options that result in nonbinding memoranda of understanding. Both the coverage of and the nature of the obligation created by the statutes vary. Most states still prohibit strikes "to protect the public from the loss of essential public services."[10] These limitations are founded on the concept of sovereignty. The theory is "since there is no choice for the taxpayer in the market

---

[8]For a general history and critique of the demise of the nondelegation doctrine, see Schoenbrod, Power Without Responsibility: How Congress Abuses the People Through Delegation (1993). See also Matthew D. Adler, "Judicial Restraint in the Administrative State: Beyond the Countermajoritarian Difficulty," 145 U. Pa. L. Rev. 759 (April 1997). In County Sanitation Dist. v. Los Angeles County Employees' Ass'n, 699 P.2d 835, 842 (Cal. 1985), the court reasoned that

> [t]he sovereignty concept, however, has often been criticized in recent years as a vague and outdated theory based on the assumption that "the King can do no wrong." As Judge Harry T. Edwards has cogently observed, "the application of the strict sovereignty notion—that governmental power can never be opposed by employee organizations—is clearly a vestige from another era, an era of unexpanded government. * * * With rapid growth of the government, both in sheer size as well as in terms of assuming services not traditionally associated with the "sovereign," government employees understandably no longer feel constrained by a notion that ['] The [sic] King can do no wrong.' The distraught cries by public unions of disparate treatment merely reflect the fact that, for all intents and purposes, public employees occupy essentially the same position vis a vis the employer as their private counterparts.
> * * *
> [T]he use of this archaic concept to justify a per se prohibition against public employee strikes is inconsistent with modern social reality and should be hereafter laid to rest.

Id. See also Befort, "Public Sector Bargaining: Fiscal Crisis and Unilateral Change," 69 Minn. L. Rev. 1221 (June 1985).

[9]Partial lists of the relevant statutes are found and discussed in O'Reilly, "Collision in the Congress: Congressional Accountability, Workplace Conflict and the Separation of Powers," 5 Geo. Mason L. Rev. 1, 21 (1996); see also, by the same author, "More Magic with Less Smoke: A Ten Year Retrospective on Ohio's Collective Bargaining Law," 19 U. Dayton L. Rev. 1, 28 (1993).

[10]Dilts & Walsh, Collective Bargaining and Impasse Resolution in the Public Sector 162 (1988). For general information concerning public employee collective bargaining, see Aaron, Najita & Stern, Public Sector Bargaining (2d ed., I.R.R.A. Series, 1988); Benjamin Aaron, "Unfair Labor Practices and the Right to Strike in the Public Sector: Has the National Labor Relations Act Been a Good Model?" 38 Stan. L. Rev. 1097 (1986).

place, then there should be no choice for the public employees or their
unions in whether to offer their services during a labor dispute."[11]
Both North Carolina and Texas have a statute expressly prohibiting
collective bargaining by public employees.[12] Only the states of Ala-
bama, Arizona, Arkansas, Colorado, Louisiana, Mississippi, South
Carolina, and West Virginia have not passed statutes related to public employee collective bargaining. Nevertheless, in a number of these
states, some form of public employee collective bargaining is allowed.[13]
The courts are split as to whether statutory authority is required to
legalize public-sector collective bargaining. For example, the Virginia
Supreme Court has held that such authority is required.[14] Similarly,
although Arkansas has no statute, the Arkansas Supreme Court held
that "collective bargaining would in effect amount to strikes against
government."[15] However, the Colorado Supreme Court has held that
legislative authority is not required for a public entity to enter into
collective bargaining.[16]

Grievance Arbitration With and Without Statutory Authority

A majority of states have statutory provisions for establishment
of grievance and arbitration procedures in public-sector employment.[17]
Statutory support for grievance arbitration has even been found even
though the particular arbitration statute did not expressly cover the
class of public employees asserting arbitration rights.[18]

There is little reason to doubt the validity of binding grievance
arbitration in the public sector if authorized by statute.[19] Moreover,

---

[11]Dilts et al., supra note 10, at 162.

[12]N.C. Gen. Stat. §§95–97 to 100 (1993); Tex. Gov't Code Ann. §617.002 (West 1997).

[13]For example, in Arizona, a county may meet and confer with a nonexclusive representative of its employees. See Sachen, "Collective Negotiations in Arizona's Public
Schools: The Anomaly of Tolerated Illegal Activities," 28 Ariz. L. Rev. 15 (1986). Dilts et
al., supra note 10, at 18–19, provide a handy chart of the kinds of provisions available
for public employees in each state.

[14]Virginia v. County Bd. of Arlington County, 232 S.E.2d 30, 44 (Va. 1977).

[15]Czech v. Baer, 677 S.W.2d 833, 836 (Ark. 1984).

[16]Littleton Educ. Ass'n v. Arapahoe County Sch. Dist. No. 6, 553 P.2d 793, 795 (Colo.
1976). See also similar findings in Louisiana and West Virginia: St. John the Baptist
Parish Ass'n of Educators v. Brown, 465 So.2d 674 (La. 1985), and State, County &
Municipal Employees Council 58, Local 598 v. City of Huntington, 317 S.E.2d 167 (W.Va.
1984).

[17]See statutes listed, supra note 1. Also, see discussion and specific statutory descriptions in Schneider's Chapter 6 entitled "Public Sector Labor Legislation—An Evo-
lutionary Analysis" in Aaron et al., supra note 10, at 189–228.

[18]Providence Teachers Union, Local 958, American Fed'n of Teachers, AFL-CIO v.
School Comm. of City of Providence, 276 A.2d 762 (R.I. 1971). Also see Community
College of Beaver County v. Community College of Beaver County, Soc'y of the Faculty,
375 A.2d 1267, 1276, 96 LRRM 2375 (Pa. 1977); Gary Teachers Union, Local No. 4,
American Fed'n of Teachers v. School City of Gary, 284 N.E.2d 108, 113–14, 80 LRRM
3090 (Ind. Ct. App., 1972). Cf. Westly v. Salt Lake City Corp. Bd. of City Comm'rs, 573
P.2d 1279, 97 LRRM 2580, 2581 (Utah 1978).

[19]Examples of recent cases supporting public-sector grievance arbitration include
In re Professional, Clerical, Technical Employees Ass'n (Buffalo Bd. of Educ.), 683 N.E.2d
733 (N.Y. 1997); City of Bethany v. Public Employees Relations Bd. of Okla., 904 P.2d

significant judicial support has been expressed for its validity even in the absence of statutory authorization,[20] despite the delegation issues that are implicated. The Colorado Supreme Court has stated:

> When an arbitrator is required to interpret the provisions of an existing agreement, he acts in a judicial capacity rather than in a legislative one. . . . The authority to interpret an existing contract, therefore, does not constitute legislative authority, and the nondelegation principle is not implicated in grievance arbitration.[21]

Interest Arbitration Statutes

Many states provide by statute for use of mediation and/or fact-finding in the resolution of interest disputes (contract negotiation disputes) in public-sector employment,[22] and frequently these stat-

---

604 (Okla. 1995); Mayfield Hts. Fire Fighters Ass'n, Local 1500, I.A.F.F. v. DeJohn, 622 N.E.2d 380 (Ohio Ct. App. 1993); Board of Educ. of Community High School Dist. No. 155 v. Illinois Educ. Lab. Relations Bd., 617 N.E.2d 269 (Ill. Ct. App. 1993); Rowry v. University of Mich., 441 Mich. 1, 490 N.W.2d 305 (1992); Board of Educ. of Bloomfield v. Bloomfield Educ. Ass'n, 598 A.2d 517 (N.J. 1991).

[20]For cases supporting grievance arbitration in the absence of statutory authorization, see Anne Arundel County v. Fraternal Order, 543 A.2d 841 ((Md. 1988); Stratford v. Professional & Technical Eng'rs Local 134, 519 A.2d 1, 6, 125 LRRM 2052 (Conn. 1986) (an arbitration award that resulted from the consent of parties and not from statute upheld); Fire Fighters (IAFF) Local 5891 v. City of Newburgh, 116 A.D.2d 396, 501 N.Y.S.2d 369 (1986) (public policy does not exist disfavoring delegation of issues involving compensation for job-related injury or illness to an impartial third party, in this case a physician); Dayton Classroom Teachers Ass'n v. Dayton Bd. of Educ., 323 N.E.2d 714, 88 LRRM 3053 (Ohio 1975) (applying decisions from other states which upheld grievance arbitration without statutory authorization, including a Wisconsin Supreme Court decision that rejected the contention that "to require the city to submit to binding [grievance] arbitration is an unlawful infringement upon the legislative power of the city council and a violation of its home rule powers"); Danville Bd. of Sch. Directors v. Fifield, 315 A.2d 473, 476, 85 LRRM 2939 (Vt. 1974); but see School Bd. of Richmond v. Parham, 243 S.E.2d 468, 472 (Va. 1978) (striking down binding grievance arbitration agreement between local school boards and their employees on the ground that it removed from the local board and transferred to others a function that was essential and indispensable to the board's exercise of its power of supervision). It appears clear that such express statutory authorization of binding grievance arbitration would be required to legalize it in any state that does not permit collective bargaining by public employers. In the latter regard, also see City of Fairmont, 73 LA 1259, 1261–63 (Lubow, 1979). For reference to the allowance of grievance arbitration in the absence of statutory authorization, particularly when collective bargaining is nevertheless approved, see "Developments in the Law—Public Employment," 97 Harv. L. Rev. 1611, 1720–21 (1984). Although favor in the public sector for grievance arbitration grows, greater scrutiny is seemingly given to the award of an arbitrator in the public sector to ensure that it complies with his or her authority. See discussion in article by Lefkowitz, "The Legal Framework of Labor Arbitration in the Public Sector," *in* Labor Arbitration: A Practical Guide for Advocates (Zimny et al. eds., 1990), 30 et seq. For illustrative arbitration decisions in which the arbitrator concluded because of the scope of an applicable state statute or for some other related reason, the arbitrator lacked jurisdiction to hear a public employee grievance brought before him or her, see Springfield Bd. of Educ., 87 LA 16 (Feldman, 1986); City of Houston, 86 LA 1068 (Stephens, 1986); City of Elyria, Ohio, 84 LA 318 (Laybourne, 1985).

[21]Denver v. Denver Firefighters Local No. 858, 663 P.2d 1032, 1038–39 (Colo. 1983).

[22]For an up-to-date listing of statutory provisions regulating contract negotiations disputes and use of dispute resolution mechanisms for public-sector employees, see v. 1 & 2, State Laws section of LRRM (BNA).

utes provide for use of arbitration for disputes that have not been resolved by mediation or fact-finding.[23] In some states, there are also local ordinances and charter provisions dealing with use of mediation, fact-finding, and arbitration for interest disputes involving municipal employees.[24] Coverage of employees in these statutes and ordinances relating to interest disputes varies widely. Some apply only to limited classes of employees such as police and/or firefighters, teachers, hospital employees, or mass transit employees.[25] Others apply much more broadly, covering most employees of the state or municipality.[26] Some states have two or more statutes, with different coverage.

---

[23]For example, the Maine statute provides for final and binding arbitration for judicial employees on matters other than salary, pension, and insurance. On these topics, the arbitrator can make only advisory recommendations. 26 Me. Rev. Stat. Ann. tit. 26. §1285.4(B) (West 1996). By contrast, the Hawaii statute provides that the parties "may mutually agree" to submit their differences to final and binding arbitration if their impasse has lasted at least 30 days. Haw. Rev. Stat. Ann. §89–11(b)(3) (Michie 1996). In Illinois, "The parties may, by mutual agreement, provide for arbitration of impasses resulting from their inability to agree upon wages, hours and terms and conditions of employment to be included in a collective bargaining agreement." 5 Ill. Comp. Stat. Ann. 315/14(a) (West 1993). A statute specifically addressing security employees, peace officers and fire fighter disputes, provides: "If any dispute has not been resolved within 15 days after the first meeting of the parties and the mediator, or within such other time limit as may be mutually agreed upon by the parties, either the exclusive representative or employer may request of the other, in writing, arbitration, and shall submit a copy of the request to the Board.") 5 Ill. Comp. Stat. 315/7 et seq. (West 1997); Minn. Stat. §179A.16 (1996); Wash. Rev. Code Ann. §41.56.100 (West 1996). For a general discussion of interest arbitration, see Howlett, "The Kenneth M. Piper Lectures: Interest Arbitration in the Public Sector," 60 Chi.-Kent L. Rev. 815 (1984). See also Malin, "Public Employees' Right to Strike: Law and Experience," 26 U. Mich. J.L. Reform 313 (1993). For a discussion of one state's experience with fact-finding, see O'Reilly, "More Magic with Less Smoke: A Ten Year Retrospective on Ohio's Collective Bargaining Law," 19 Dayton L. Rev. 1 (1993). See also Martin, "Fixing the Fiscal Police and Firetrap: A Critique of New Jersey's Compulsory Interest Arbitration Act," 18 Seton Hall Legis. J. 59 (1993).

[24]For a general discussion of states that have statutory provisions expressly permitting local governments to adopt their own procedures, see Anderson & Krause, "Interest Arbitration: The Alternative to the Strike," 56 Fordham L. Rev. 153 (1987). For a discussion on how the provisions are applied to Ohio counties through the "municipal home rule" provisions, see White and Kaplan et al., "Ohio's Public Employee Bargaining Law: Can It Withstand Constitutional Challenge?," 53 U. Cin. L. Rev. 1 (1984). In contrast, the Oregon statute was reportedly "easily evaded by local government employers because the statute applied to them only if the local government had petitioned the newly-created Public Employee Relations Board (now the Employment Relations Board) for determination of a bargaining unit." Drummonds, "A Case Study of the Ex Ante Veto Negotiations Process: The Derfler-Bryant Act and the 1995 Amendments to the Oregon Public Employee Collective Bargaining Law," 32 Willamette L. Rev. 69 (1996).

[25]For example, see Illinois' laws. Although interest arbitration is required only for police, fire, and security personnel, it is available as a voluntary option to others. 5 Ill. Comp. Stat. 315/7 et seq. (West 1996). A discussion of Iowa's final offer arbitration provisions for educators is found in Hoh, "The Effectiveness of Mediation in Public Sector Arbitration Systems: The Iowa Experience" 39 Arb. J. 30 (1984).

[26]"Iowa is the first state to grant final and binding arbitration of interest disputes * * * to every nonsupervisory public employee of the state and its political subdivisions." Loihl, "Final-Offer Plus: Interest Arbitration in Iowa," Proceedings of the 31st Annual Meeting of NAA, 317, 318 (BNA Books, 1979). "The statute provides for mediation, fact-finding, and a modified form of final-offer-by-issue arbitration, with the fact-

Frequent and significant variations in features exist in interest arbitration statutes and ordinances from state to state (and indeed sometimes from statute to statute or ordinance within the same jurisdiction). Variations in features of statutes and ordinances include, but are not limited to, the following:[27]

1. Arbitration may be entirely voluntary, it may be made mandatory, or it may be required only in certain circumstances.[28]
2. Arbitration decisions may be (1) binding, (2) merely advisory, or (3) a hybrid of binding and advisory options. A number of statutes make interest arbitration both compulsory and binding.[29]
3. Arbitrators may make their award reflect their assessment of the equities or they may be confined to accepting the "final offer" of one party or the other. If "final offer" arbitration is specified, the arbitrators may be required to accept a single party's final offers as to all issues or they may be required to choose final offers on an "issue-by-issue" rather than "total package" basis.[30]

---

finder's recommendation an alternate selection for the arbitrator on each issue. The arbitration proceeding is moderately rigid and judicial, not permitting amendment of final offers or mediation by the arbitrator. The results (for the first three years) are encouraging, particularly when viewed as the first full-blown experiment with legislated arbitration for public employees other than those in the 'essential' services. Low usage of arbitration, particularly among teachers and other educational employees, has left a high proportion of voluntary settlements, although the time parameters have resulted in an overuse of mediation. Fact-finding shows a surprisingly high success ratio both in resolving disputes prior to arbitration and reducing the number of arbitrated issues. * * *" Id. at 340. For additional discussion of the Iowa program, see Hoh, "The Effectiveness of Mediation in Public Sector Arbitration Systems: The Iowa Experience," 39 Arb. J. 30 (1984).

[27]For publications listing states with interest arbitration statutes for public-sector employment, see Dilts & Walsh, supra note 10 at 18–19. See also Martin, supra note 23.

[28]For example, although the Illinois State Labor Relations Act mandates arbitration, it may successfully be avoided by prior successful mediation. Mediated resolutions are allowed even if the matter has officially gone to arbitration and can abort the arbitration procedure. 5 Ill. Comp. Stat. 315/14 (West 1997).

[29]For example, in Illinois the law provides that even when the arbitrator's decision is issued, it is not final and binding upon the parties until it has been accepted by the local governing authority of the public sector entity negotiating the contract. If the local board rejects the arbitrator's award, the matter goes back to arbitration. 5 Ill. Comp. Stat. 315/14 et seq. (West 1997). A different approach is taken in Iowa, where the parties "can, through joint agreement, formulate their own impasse procedure." Gallagher, "Interest Arbitration Under the Iowa Public Relations Act," 33 Arb. J. 30 (1978), quoted in Teple & Moberly, Arbitration and Conflict Resolution (1949).

[30]For discussion of "final offer" arbitration, see Feuille, "Final-Offer Arbitration and Negotiating Incentives," 32 Arb. J. 203 (1977). See Martin, supra note 23. A particularly flexible variety of final-offer compulsory arbitration exists under a New Jersey statute for police and firefighter interest disputes. See Weitzman & Stochaj, "Attitudes of Arbitrators Toward Final-Offer Arbitration in New Jersey," 35 Arb. J. 25 (1980). Evaluations of final-offer arbitration often reveal that it has potential utility but that both of its basic forms have problems and critics. For example, the total-package variety carries greater danger of unreasonable awards on some issues. Note, for example, the lament expressed on this score by Arbitrators Arvid Anderson in City of Oak Creek (Wisc) & Local 133, AFSCME (DPW Employees), 98 LA 325 (1991), and Stanley H. Michelstetter

4. Variations exist in procedural provisions such as those relating to hearings, use of transcripts, written findings of fact, and written opinions.

5. Specific criteria or standards may or may not be specified for consideration by the arbitrators or for their guidance.[31]

6. Safeguards against budgetary problems resulting from monetary awards may or may not be specified.[32]

7. The arbitration tribunal's membership may be tripartite (a common requirement in public-sector interest arbitration), or it may be limited to neutrals.

II in City of Manitowoc & IAFF, Local 386, 108 LA 140 (1997). The issue-by-issue variety reduces incentive to settle more issues prior to arbitration (a basic goal of final-offer statutes is less arbitration) since a party may believe a favorable award on favored issues will be more assured if the party offers additional issues that the arbitrators may resolve against it in formulating a balanced award on all issues. Perhaps the most novel approach to this problem is seen in the Minnesota statute. It allows parties to choose whether to limit the arbitrator to a choice between the total package or an issue-by-issue approach. Minn. Stat. §179A.16(7) (1996). See, for a discussion of this option, Anderson & Krause, supra note 24.

[31]It has been noted that virtually all statutes providing for interest arbitration include some guidelines for arbitrators. The most common major criteria include "comparability, ability to pay, cost of living changes, productivity changes, variations in job content or hazards, historical trends, equity and forces within the labor marketplace." Martin, supra note 23 at 68–69. See also the state-by-state compilation in Anderson & Krause, supra note 24, at 158–60, and the comments of Bornstein in "Interest Arbitration in Public Employment: An Arbitrator Views the Process," 83 Lab. L.J. 77 (1978).

[32]For example, Wisconsin's Municipal Employment Relations Act, Wis. Stat. §111.70(4)(cm)7 and 7g (1995), requires an interest arbitrator to give the greatest weight to the ability of the municipal employer to pay and to the economic conditions in the jurisdiction. Illinois, on the other hand, includes these factors in a list of eight different categories. 5 Ill. Comp. Stat. 315/14(h) (West 1997) provides in pertinent part:

[T]he arbitration panel shall base its findings, opinions and order upon the following factors, as applicable:

(1) The lawful authority of the employer.

(2) Stipulations of the parties.

(3) The interests and welfare of the public and the financial ability of the unit of government to meet those costs.

(4) Comparison of the wages, hours and conditions of employment of the employees involved in the arbitration proceeding with the wages, hours and conditions of employment of other employees performing similar services and with other employees generally:

(A) In public employment in comparable communities.

(B) In private employment in comparable communities.

(5) The average consumer prices for goods and services, commonly known as the cost of living.

(6) The overall compensation presently received by the employees, including direct wage compensation, vacations, holidays and other excused time, insurance and pensions, medical and hospitalization benefits, the continuity and stability of employment and all other benefits received.

(7) Changes in any of the foregoing circumstances during the pendency of the arbitration proceedings.

(8) Such other factors, not confined to the foregoing, which are normally or traditionally taken into consideration in the determination of wages, hours and conditions of employment through voluntary collective bargaining, mediation, fact-finding, arbitration or otherwise between the parties, in the public service or in private employment.

The statute also has specified limitations on the specific kinds of discretionary managerial determinations which the legislature believed constituted policy determinations. See 5 Ill. Comp. Stat. 315/14(I) et seq. (West 1997).

Constitutionality of Binding Interest Arbitration. Federal constitutional questions beyond delegability issues focus primarily on preemption questions, "exploring whether state laws regulating the workplace run afoul of the Supremacy Clause.[33] Binding interest arbitration has been challenged on state constitutional grounds in a number of states. The challenge has succeeded in some cases but more often has failed.[34]

In holding binding interest arbitration for firefighters to be unconstitutional, the Utah Supreme Court explained:

> [T]he act authorizes the appointment of arbitrators, who are private citizens with no responsibility to the public, to make binding determinations affecting the quantity, quality, and cost of an essential public service. The legislature may not surrender its legislative authority to a body wherein the public interest is subjected to the interest of a group which may be antagonistic to the public interest.
>
> Although it is not dispositive of the delegation issue, in this case the legislature failed to provide any statutory standards in the act or any protection against arbitrariness, such as, hearings with procedural safeguards, legislative supervision, and judicial review.[35]

Determining Arbitrability and Compelling Arbitration

In addition to constitutional issues raised by delegability and creating a private body to determine public policy, the constitutionality of public-sector interest arbitration statutes has been challenged because the statutes (1) provide inadequate arbitral standards or guidelines, (2) violate due process, and (3) violate equal protection mandates. Municipal home rule questions, frequently part of state constitutions, also should be considered in this context.[36]

---

[33]Michael H. Gottesman, "Labor, Employment and Benefit Decisions of the Supreme Court's 1995–96 Term," 12 Labor Law 325 (1997). For an overview and history of state approaches to interest arbitration, see Martin, supra note 23 at 68 et seq. See also the review of provisions in Lawlor's annotation "Validity and Construction of Statutes or Ordinances Providing for Arbitration of Labor Disputes Involving Public Employees," 68 A.L.R. 3d 855 (1976 & Supp. 1992).

[34]The range of views can be seen in the challenges to the Ohio statute shortly after it was passed in 1984. The Ohio Supreme Court found the Ohio Public Employee's Collective Bargaining Act unconstitutional to the extent it mandated binding arbitration of disputes on municipal safety employee wages and benefits because the provision conflicted with the city's constitutional right to local self-government. City of Rocky River v. State Employment Relations Bd., 530 N.E.2d 1, 129 LRRM 2975 (Ohio 1988). However, on reconsideration, the Ohio Supreme Court held that the Ohio Public Employee Collective Bargaining Act, Ohio Rev. Code ch. 4117, and specifically Ohio Rev. Code §4117.14(I), are constitutional as they fall within the General Assembly's authority to enact employee welfare legislation pursuant to §34, art. II, of the Ohio Constitution; the home-rule provision may not impair, limit, or negate the Act. City of Rocky River v. State Employment Relations Bd., 539 N.E.2d 103, 131 LRRM 2952, 2965 (Ohio 1989). See also O'Reilly, supra note 23, and Note, "Binding Interest Arbitration in the Public Sector: Is It Constitutional?" 18 Wm. & Mary L. Rev. 787 (1977).

[35]Salt Lake City v. International Ass'n of Firefighters, Locals 1645, 593, 1654 & 2064, 563 P.2d 786, 789, 95 LRRM 2383 (Utah 1977).

[36]The Pennsylvania Supreme Court addressed both the due process and equal protection issues when it upheld the constitutionality of the binding interest arbitration

For contractual impasses, the question of abitrability is one of statutory compliance. In such cases arbitrability depends on when the impasse occurs and whether the parties have complied with statutory preconditions such as whether the requisite efforts to mediate have been made and the appropriateness of the filing with the applicable state agency.[37]

For grievances arising under a contract, arbitrability in the public sector is usually handled similarly to arbitrability in the private sector: questions of substantive arbitrability are for the courts to determine unless the parties mutually agree to allow the arbitrator to address such questions,[38] and questions of procedural arbitrability are for the arbitrator, not the courts, to resolve.[39] The issue of when an arbitrability issue must be raised for the first time is a procedural question answerable by the arbitrator.[40] Some states allow arbitrability challenges to be raised directly in the courts while others give an administrative agency or board exclusive original jurisdiction to determine arbitrability.[41]

Because some substantive issues may be excluded from public employee bargaining and arbitration, a dispute over such matters

---

statutory provisions for police and fire personnel in Harney v. Russo, 255 A.2d 560 (Pa. 1969). But see City of Sioux Falls v. Sioux Falls Firefighters, Local 814, 234 N.W.2d 35 (S.D. 1975), holding similar provisions unconstitutional. Discussion of municipality prerogatives and problems with arbitrators' determining allocation of tax monies may be found in Hillsdale PBA Local 207 v. Borough of Hillsdale, 622 A.2d 872 (N.J. Super Ct. 1993). See generally Note, "Constitutionality of Public Sector Binding Interest Arbitration" in Teple & Moberly, supra note 29 at 485–487. For further discussions, see Anderson & Krause, supra note 24; Lawlor, supra note 33; and Rebecca Hanner White et al., "Ohio's Public Employee Bargaining Law: Can It Withstand Constitutional Challenge?" 53 U. Cin. L.Rev. 1 (1984).

[37]See American Metal Prods. Inc. v. Sheet Metal Workers Int'l Ass'n, Local No. 104, 794 F.2d 1452 (9th Cir. 1982); ACTION & AFSCME Local 2927, 78 LA 790 (Phelan, 1982).

[38]Abrams, "The Power Issue in Public Sector Grievance Arbitration," 67 Minn. L. Rev. 261 (1982). See also In re Denver Public Schools (Denver, Colo.) & Amalg. Transit Union, Div. 1563, 88 LA 507 (Watkins, 1986). Parties wanting to avoid circular trips through the courts to resolve such issues must specifically provide in their contract and/or submission agreement that the arbitrator is empowered to answer all arbitrability issues. See Kilanek v. Kim, 548 N.E.2d 598 (Ill. Ct. App. 1989).

[39]John Wiley & Sons, Inc. v. Livington, 376 U.S. 543, 84 S. Ct. 909 (1964). For example, as the Michigan Supreme Court noted, it "frequently looks to the federal courts' interpretation of the National Labor Relations Act in construing the PERA." Port Huron Educ. Ass'n v. Port Huron Area Sch. Dist., 452 Mich. 309, 550 N.W.2d 228 (1996) (citing Kaleva-Norman-Dickson Sch. Dist. No. 6 v. Kaleva-Norman-Dickson Sch. Teachers' Ass'n, 227 N.W.2d 500 (Mich. 1975)).

[40]This is true even under statutes that include detailed management rights clauses. See Department of Navy, Naval Base North Isl. San Diego & I.A.F.F. Local F-33, 38 FLRA 1509 (1991). See also Dick v. Dick, 534 N.W.2d 185 (Mich. Ct. App. 1995), holding that only the arbitrator can interpret the contract.

[41]The Illinois courts, for example, direct that such questions be handled by the Illinois Public Labor Relations Boards: Board of Educ. of Warren Township High Sch. Dist. 121 v. Warren Township High School Fed'n of Teachers, Local 504, 538 N.E.2d 524 (Ill. 1989).

may not be arbitrable.[42] In addition, it is possible to waive the right to arbitrate by participating in a judicial proceeding without raising the question of arbitrability.[43] Because of the delegability concerns, arbitrability claims are three times more likely to be raised in the public sector than in the private sector.[44] However, the presumption in favor of arbitrability in the public sector is very strong.[45]

Arbitrability issues in the public sector may reach court in the same ways as they do in the private sector; that is, one party asks the court to compel or enjoin arbitration, or to review an arbitration award that already has been issued.

Under federal law applicable to the private sector the question of substantive arbitrability is for the court unless the arbitration clause clearly specifies that the arbitrator shall make the determination; a similar rule applies in the public sector.[46] Also as in the private sector, questions of procedural arbitrability are for the arbitrator and not for the courts.[47]

The Supreme Court in *AT&T Technologies v. Communication Workers of America*,[48] reaffirmed the private-sector principle that substantive arbitrability—whether a collective bargaining agreement creates a duty for the parties to arbitrate a particular grievance—is

---

[42]As in the federal sector, some states have precluded arbitrability of questions relating to the negotiability of an issue, preferring that such questions go to the agency rather than the arbitrator. Ridgefield Park Educ. Ass'n v. Ridgefield Park Bd. of Educ., 393 A.2d 278, 284 (N.J. 1978). See also In re Board of Trustees of Univ. of Ill. at Chicago & Individual Grievant, 100 LA 728 (Goldstein, 1992), holding that the nondelegability doctrine precludes the arbitrator from deciding or reviewing matters involving a public entity's discretionary acts, even when they appear to be arbitrary.

[43]International Ass'n of Firefighters Local 23 v. City of East St. Louis, 571 N.E.2d 1198 (Ill. Ct. App. 1991).

[44]Naval Plant Rep. Office (West Palm Beach Cty, Fla.) & N.A.G.E., Local R1-143, 91 LA 964 (Abrams, 1988).

[45]Board of Educ. of Dover Union Free Sch. Dist. v. Dover-Wingate Teachers' Ass'n, 463 N.E.2d 32 (N.Y. 1984); see generally Roumell "Arbitration," 1995 Det. C.L. Rev. 281 (1995). Corcoran, "The Arbitrability of Labor Grievances That Arise after Expiration of the Collective Bargaining Agreement," 43 Syracuse L. Rev. 1073 (1992).

[46]In the past few years the U.S. Supreme Court has reinforced its prior rulings, insisting on deferral to arbitration for statutory claims (Gilmer v. Interstate/Johnson Lane Corp., 500 U.S. 20 (1991)), as well as contractual matters (AT&T Tech. Inc., v. Communications Workers of Am., 475 U.S. 643 (1986)). See *AT&T Technologies;* Glendale Professional Policemen's Ass'n v. City of Glendale, 264 N.W.2d 594, 599, 98 LRRM 2362 (Wis. 1978); Policeman's & Fireman's Retirement Bd. of City of New Haven v. Sullivan, 376 A.2d 399, 402, 95 LRRM 2351 (Conn. 1977) (the court said the parties may manifest their intent that the arbitrator determine arbitrability either by an express provision or by use of a broad arbitration clause); West Fargo Pub. Sch. Dist. No. 6 v. West Fargo Educ. Ass'n, 259 N.W.2d 612, 619, 97 LRRM 2361 (N.D. 1977). In Providence Teachers' Union Local 958 v. Providence Sch. Comm., 433 A.2d 202, 112 LRRM 2998, 2999–3000 (R.I. 1981), both private- and public-sector cases were cited by the court in stating that: "Courts should not equate the issue of arbitrability with the deference due the arbitrator's interpretation of the contract. . . . Rather, a reviewing court must decide the question of arbitrability de novo."

[47]See Duquesne City Sch. Dist. v. Duquesne Educ. Ass'n, 380 A.2d 353, 356, 97 LRRM 2011 (Pa. 1977); *West Fargo Pub. Sch. Dist.*, 259 N.W.2d at 618–19.

[48]106 S. Ct. 1415, 121 LRRM 3329 (1986).

an issue for the courts, unless the parties clearly and unmistakably provide otherwise. Some states, however, have given an administrative board exclusive original jurisdiction to determine arbitrability for purposes of collective bargaining agreement administration.[49]

A number of states have also adopted for public-sector arbitration a rule similar to the rule of presumptive arbitrability that applies to the private sector under federal law: doubts are to be resolved in favor of arbitrability.[50] But New York has held that for public-sector cases under the state's Taylor Law, the courts in determining arbitrability "are to be guided by the principle that the agreement to arbitrate must be express, direct and unequivocal as to the issues or disputes to be submitted to arbitration; anything less will lead to a denial of arbitration."[51]

---

[49]In School Dist. No. 42 of City of Nashua v. Murray, 514 A.2d 1269 (N.H. 1986), it was held that the Public Employee Labor Relations Board had exclusive original jurisdiction to determine arbitrability for purposes of collective bargaining agreement administration. Coles County Bd. of Educ. Dist. 1 v. Compton, 526 N.E.2d 149, 131 LRRM 2313 (Ill. 1988). See discussion of application of U.S. Supreme Court rulings regarding arbitrability in the states in Bethel, "Recent Supreme Court Employment Law Decisions 1990–91," 17 Dayton L. Rev. 33, 36 (1991).

[50]City of Muskogee v. Martin, 796 P.2d 337, 134 LRRM 3265 (Okla. 1990); State, County, & Mun. Employees Dist. Council 48 (Milwaukee) v. Milwaukee County, 388 N.W.2d 630 (Wis. App. 1986); St. Clair Prosecutor v. American Fed'n of State, County, & Mun. Employees, 388 N.W.2d 231 (Mich. 1986); Board of Trustees of Community Colleges Dist. 508 v. Cook County College Teachers Union, Local 1600, 487 N.E.2d 956 (Ill. Ct. App. 1986); Westbrook Sch. Comm. v. Westbrook Teachers Ass'n, 404 A.2d 204, 207–08, 102 LRRM 2396, 2398 (Me. 1979); Joint Sch. Dist. No. 10, City of Jefferson v. Jefferson Educ. Ass'n, 253 N.W.2d 536, 544, 95 LRRM 3117 (Wis. 1977); Kaleva-Norman-Dickson Sch. Dist. No. 6 v. Kaleva-Norman-Dickson Sch. Teachers' Ass'n, 227 N.W.2d 500, 505–06, 89 LRRM 2078 (Mich. 1975). But note that in the public sector some matters may be held excluded from public-employer bargaining and arbitration by statutes and public policy considerations; a dispute over such matters is not arbitrable, regardless of what the collective bargaining agreement says. See subtopic entitled "Statutory and Public Policy Limitations on Scope of Bargaining and Arbitration," infra.

[51]Acting Superintendent of Liverpool Central Sch. Dist. v. United Liverpool Faculty Ass'n, 369 N.E.2d 746, 747 96 LRRM 2779 (N.Y. 1977), where the court reasoned that because arbitration is not as well established and proven in the public sector as in the private sector, stronger proof of intent to arbitrate is required. In *Liverpool* the arbitration clause was narrow and the question whether the disputed matter fell within, or without, the clause was debatable. The court said the matter was not arbitrable since it did not fall "clearly and unequivocally within the class of claims agreed to be referred to arbitration." Id. at 750. Shortly after *Liverpool* was decided, the court upheld arbitrability in a case involving a broad arbitration clause, even though the clause did not specifically mention the particular matter in dispute. In New York Bd. v. Glaubman, 53 N.Y. 2d 781, 783, 439 N.Y. S.2d 907, the court stated: "Although we noted in [*Liverpool*] that the choice of the arbitration forum should be 'express' and 'unequivocal' we did not mean to suggest that hairsplitting analysis should be used * * * to discourage or delay demands for arbitration in public sector contracts * * *." See N.Y.C. Dep't of Sanitation v. MacDonald, 627 N.Y. S.2d 619 (N.Y. App. Div. 1995), where the court held that a broad interpretation is acceptable if the collective bargaining agreement gives a broad definition of arbitrability. But see Progressive Casualty Ins. Co. v. C.A. Reasegurador Nacional de Venezuela, 991 F.2d 42 (2d Cir. 1993), denying such an interpretation.

Court Review of Arbitration Awards

Because arbitration is used in the public sector, as in the private sector, to settle disputes between employers and employees without extended use of time and resources, it is not surprising that states have tended to view the matter of court review of arbitral awards along lines similar to the private-sector pattern.[52] It is apparent that the states by their statutes and by the decisions of their highest courts have tended to adopt a policy of only limited judicial review of arbitration awards in the public sector.[53]

The Minnesota Supreme Court, for example, has stated that "only when it is established that an arbitrator has clearly exceeded his powers under the agreement to submit to arbitration must a court vacate an award."[54] In reviewing a public-sector arbitration award, the Wisconsin Supreme Court explained:

> The standard of review of an award under both [the Wisconsin statute] and common law is substantially the same. The court will not relitigate issues submitted to arbitration. The parties contracted for the arbitrator's decision, not the court's. Under common law rulings, an award may be set aside for fraud or partiality or gross mistake by the arbitrator. . . . [The statute] sets forth similar standards. If these standards were not violated by the arbitrators' award, the trial court should confirm the award.[55]

---

[52]In their chapter on "Judicial Response to Arbitration" (Chapter 7) Joseph R. Grodin and Joyce M. Najita note "The language which the [state] courts use when asked to review arbitral awards is * * * generally in accord with federal principles, but the application of that language is in some cases highly dubious, reflecting a significantly greater tendency to substitute the court's judgment for that of the arbitrator." Aaron, Najita, & Stern, Public Sector Bargaining 10 (2d ed., I.R.R.A. Series, 1988).

[53]One observer has pointed out, for instance, that courts "rarely will overturn the factual conclusions of an arbitrator and they will accord contractual interpretations similar respect"; also, that "Remedial orders of arbitrators usually are accorded similar judicial respect." Craver, "The Judicial Enforcement of Public Sector Grievance Arbitration," 58 Tex. L. Rev. 329, 346–47 (1980). That observer concluded that "critical differences between grievance arbitration and interest arbitration militate in favor of a somewhat stricter standard of judicial review pertaining to interest arbitration awards." Craver, "The Judicial Enforcement of Public Sector Interest Arbitration," 21 B.C.L. Rev. 557, 571 (1980).

[54]Minnesota v. Berthiaume, 259 N.W.2d 904, 910, 96 LRRM 3240 (Minn. 1977), in which the Uniform Arbitration Act was considered equally applicable to the public and private sectors. Similarly, see City of Hillsboro v. Fraternal Order of Police, 556 N.E.2d 1186, 134 LRRM 2995 (Ohio 1990); City of Yukon v. Fire Fighters Local 2055, 792 P.2d 1176 (Okla., 1990); City of Madison v. Madison Professional Police Officers Ass'n, 425 N.W.2d 8 (Wis. 1988); Connecticut v. Connecticut Employees' Union, 440 A.2d 229 (Conn. 1981). Although Minnesota has reiterated that its courts will not interfere with the arbitration process pursuant to a collective agreement, it nonetheless recognizes the limitation that arbitrators may not decide constitutional issues regardless of the scope of the arbitration agreement. County of Hennepin v. Law Enforcement Labor Servs., Inc., 527 N.W.2d 821, 148 LRRM 2627 (Minn. 1995).

[55]Joint Sch. Dist. No. 10, 253 N.W.2d at 547. Awards are impeachable for manifest disregard of the law, including illegality, but not for mere errors of judgment as to law or fact: City of Hartford v. Local 1716, Council 4, AFSCME, 688 A.2d 882 (Conn. Super. Ct. 1996); City of Salamanca v. City of Salamanca Police Unit of Cattarangas County,

Of special interest is the fact that New York's high court, whose *Liverpool*[56] decision adopted a particularly cautious approach for determining arbitrability in public-sector cases, has subsequently reaffirmed the following rules of that state regarding court review of arbitration awards in the public sector:

1. "[O]nce the issue is properly before the arbitrator, questions of law and fact are merged in the award and are not within the power of the judiciary to resolve."

2. Reviewing courts are not to review the merits, for the "fact that a different result might have been reached had the dispute been resolved in the courts is of no moment and does not empower a court to substitute its judgment for that of the arbitrator."[57]

The court did say that "a small number of areas, interlaced with strong governmental or societal interests, restrict the power of an arbitrator to render an otherwise proper award.[58]

Even where arbitration of public-sector disputes has been made compulsory, the states have not generally tended toward broad judicial review of awards.[59] Some statutes actually deny any right to appeal from the award.[60] Several statutes are silent on the matter of

---

497 N.Y.S.2d 856 (N.Y. Sup. Ct. 1986). See Belanger v. Matteson, 346 A.2d 124, 138, 91 LRRM 2003 (R.I. 1975); Providence Teachers Union, Local 958 v. McGovern, 319 A.2d 358, 362, 86 LRRM 2899 (R.I. 1974) (Rhode Island Supreme Court held that lack of funds was no defense to the enforcement of an arbitration award requiring payment of severance pay by the public employer).

[56]Acting Superintendent of Liverpool Cent. Sch. Dist. v. United Liverpool Faculty Ass'n, 369 N.E.2d 746, 96 LRRM 2779 (N.Y. 1977).

[57]Binghamton Civil Serv. Forum v. City of Binghamton, 374 N.E.2d 380, 382–83, 97 LRRM 3070 (N.Y. 1978).

[58]In confirming the award, the court said the employer had bargained to arbitrate the question of just cause for discipline or discharge of the employee, and that "[t]he bargain, having been struck, must now be honored." Id. at 387.

[59]See Comment, "Compulsory Arbitration: The Scope of Judicial Review," 51 St. John's L. Rev. 604, 618–25 (1977), where some of the approaches are indicated: the statute may specify that compulsory arbitration awards are subject to the limited review associated with voluntary arbitration (Alaska is an example); an "arbitrary or capricious" standard of review may be specified (Washington is an example); or the statute may specify broader grounds for court review (Michigan is an example, making the award vulnerable if "unsupported by competent, material and substantial evidence on the whole record," or if procured by fraud, or if it exceeds the arbitrator's jurisdiction). See City of Moses Lake v. IAFF Local 2052, 847 P.2d 16, 142 LRRM 2922 (Wash. 1993). Generally, judicial review of the merits of an award is not available. Board of Trustees of Junior College Dist. 508, Cook County v. Cook County College Teachers Union, Local 1600, 422 N.E.2d 115 (Ill. Ct. App. 1981). Even when an award is ambiguous, Illinois courts have ruled that all questions must be construed in favor of enforcing the award. AFSCME v. Illinois, 529 N.E.2d 534 (Ill. 1988).

[60]See Pennsylvania State Police v. Pennsylvania State Troopers' Ass'n, 656 A.2d 83, 149 LRRM 2877 (1995). The U.S. Arbitration Act and many state statutes that mimic it, as well as those state public-sector bargaining statutes that incorporate an arbitration act by reference, direct that courts confirm arbitral awards "unless within the time limits hereinafter imposed grounds are urged for vacating or modifying or correcting the award." Robert A. Besner & Co. Lit Am., Inc., 574 N.E.2d 703 (Ill. Ct. App. 1991) (citing the Illinois Arbitration Act, 710 Ill. Comp. Stat. 5/11). Pennsylvania is an example, but the Pennsylvania Supreme Court nonetheless does recognize limited grounds for review.

judicial review of awards.[61] Although a New Jersey statute for compulsory and binding arbitration of interest disputes was silent regarding judicial review of awards, the New Jersey Supreme Court held judicial review to be implied; the court added that "because the arbitration process is imposed by law, the judicial oversight available should be more extensive than the limited judicial review had under [another statute for] parties who voluntarily agree to submit their dispute to binding arbitration."[62]

Limited judicial review is available in the public sector when an arbitration award is contrary to public policy. "Incantations of 'public policy' may not be advanced to overturn every arbitration award."[63] The public policy that obliges a court to refrain from enforcing an award must be clear and explicit: absolute.[64]

Although there is limited judicial review of arbitration awards in the public sector, courts will overturn an award contrary to an appropriate public policy.[65] However, the public policy that obliges the court to refrain from enforcement of the award must be clear and explicit. In one case, a court upheld an arbitrator's award reinstating a bus driver discharged for drunk driving where the discharge was based only on the odor of alcohol on his breath and not on a chemical test.[66] The court found no violation of a clear and explicit public policy.

---

[61]"[T]he absence of a specified provision usually will not prevent judicial review on grounds such as fraud, lack of impartiality or wrongful assumption of power by the panel." McAvoy, "Binding Arbitration of Contract Terms: A New Approach to the Resolution of Disputes in the Public Sector," 72 Colum. L. Rev. 1192, 1204 (1972). See also Charles B. Carver, "Public Sector Impasse Procedures," Kenneth M. Piper Lectures, 60 Chi.-Kent L. Rev. 779, 797 et seq. (1984); Note, "Public Sector Grievance Procedures, Due Process and the Duty of Fair Representation," 89 Harv. L. Rev. 752 (1976).

[62]Hillsdale PBA Local 207 v. Borough of Hillsdale, 622 A.2d 872, 873 (N.J. Super. Ct. 1993). In City of Buffalo v. Rinaldo, 364 N.E.2d 817, 818, 95 LRRM 2776 (N.Y. 1977), the New York Court of Appeals similarly held a right of judicial review to be implied under a compulsory and binding interest arbitration statute; that court reaffirmed the view that judicial review is limited to determining whether the award is "rational or arbitrary and capricious."

[63]To prevent enforcement of an arbitration award because it is against public policy it must be shown that (1) the agreement to arbitrate is against public policy and (2) the policy itself is both "well defined and dominant," i.e., not merely a general public interest consideration. Board of Educ. of Sch. Dist. U-46 v. Illinois Educ. Lab. Relations Bd., 576 N.E.2d 471 (Ill. Ct. App. 1991). See discussion in Mayes, "Labor Law—The Third Circuit Defines the Public Policy Exception to Labor Arbitration Awards—Exxon Shipping Co. v. Exxon Seamen's Union, 993 F.2d 357 (3d Cir. 1993)," 67 Temple L. Rev. 493 (1994).

[64]Baltimore County v. Mayor & City Council of Baltimore, 621 A.2d 864 (Md. 1993); In the Matter of Blackburne, 664 N.E.2d 1222, 151 LRRM 3032 (N.Y. 1996). Amalgamated Transit Union, Div. 1300 v. Mass Transit Admin., 504 A2d 1132, 121 LRRM 2894 (Md. 1986); Enlarged City Sch. Dist. of Troy v. Troy Teachers Ass'n, 508 N.E.2d 930 (N.Y. 1987).

[65]See also Paperworkers Int'l Union v. Misco, Inc., 108 S. Ct. 364, 126 LRRM 3113 (1987), where the Supreme Court further clarified the limits of judicial review of arbitration awards when public policy considerations are involved, and W.R. Grace & Co. v. Rubber Workers Local 759, 103 S. Ct. 2177, 2183, 113 LRRM 2641 (1983).

[66]Amalgamated Transit Union, Div. 1300 v. Mass Transit Admin., 504 A.2d 1132, 121 LRRM 2894 (Md. 1986).

Similarly, a court confirmed reinstatement of an auditor fired for dishonesty.[67] Errors of law or fact without more almost never justify vacating an arbitrator's decision.[68] An arbitrator's award will not be overturned for errors of judgment on the law unless "manifest disregard for the law" has occurred.[69]

Statutory and Public Policy Limitations on Scope of Bargaining and Arbitration

Regarding collective bargaining and arbitration in the federal sector, we have seen that under the Civil Service Reform Act significant limitations exist on permitted scope of bargaining and arbitration by virtue of the overriding status of (1) certain laws, rules, and regulations, and (2) certain areas of exclusive management rights.[70] In some states similar limitations exist on the scope of bargaining and arbitration in the public sector.[71]

In its *Liverpool* decision the New York Court of Appeals stated that two questions are to be answered in determining arbitrability in public-sector cases: (1) whether the law *permits* arbitration of the disputed matter, and, if so, (2) whether the parties have agreed to arbitrate the disputed matter.[72] The Maine Supreme Court also has stated two questions, to be considered in determining whether a matter is subject to public-sector interest arbitration: (1) "whether the

---

[67]State Office of State Auditor v. Minnesota Ass'n of Professional Employees, 504 N.W.2d 751, 144 LRRM 2102 (Minn. 1993). Cf. St. Paul v. AFSCME, 567 N.W.2d 524 (Minn. Ct. App. 1997).

[68]Sylvania City Sch. Dist. Bd. of Educ. v. Sylvania Educ. Ass'n, 121 LRRM 2346 (Ohio Ct. Com. Pls. 1985).

[69]City of Madison v. Fire Fighters (IAFF) Local 311, 394 N.W.2d 766, 768, 124 LRRM 2131, 2133 (Wis. Ct. App. 1986). Cf. Madison Landfills v. Libby Landfill Negotiating Comm., 524 N.W.2d 883 (1994).

[70]For a discussion of judicial review of federal sector arbitration and public policy, see Grodin & Najita, supra note 525, at 247 et seq. See also Rabban, "Can American Labor Law Accommodate Collective Bargaining by Professional Employees?" 99 Yale L.J. 689 (1990), and Befort, "Public Sector Bargaining: Fiscal Crisis and Unilateral Change," 69 Minn. L. Rev. 1221 (1985).

[71]See Note, "Taking the Public Out of Determining Government Policy: The Need for an Appropriate Scope of Bargaining Test in the Illinois Public Sector," 29 J. Marshall L. Rev. 531 (1996). Edwards, Clark & Craver, Labor Relations Law in the Public Sector, 693 (1979). Blair, "State Legislative Control Over the Conditions of Public Employment: Defining the Scope of Collective Bargaining for State and Municipal Employees," 26 Vand. L. Rev. 1 (1973).

[72]Acting Superintendent of Liverpool Cent. Sch. Dist. v. United Liverpool Faculty Ass'n, 369 N.E.2d 746, 749, 96 LRRM 2779 (N.Y. 1977). In connection with the first question the court spoke of "overarching and fundamentally nondelegable" responsibilities of elected representatives of the public. Id. In a subsequent decision the same court indicated a narrow scope for the public policy limitation on arbitration: "[A] small number of areas, interlaced with strong governmental or societal interests, restrict the power of an arbitrator to render an otherwise proper award * * *. In the public sector, this policy limitation has arisen with respect to school matters and is derived from the statutory scheme implicit in the Education Law * * *." Binghamton Civil Serv. Forum v. City of Binghamton, 374 N.E.2d 380, 383, 97 LRRM 3070 (N.Y. 1978).

matter is within the statutorily defined scope of bargaining," and, if so, (2) "whether the matter is limited by any other existing statutory enhancements."[73]

Mandatory, Prohibited, and Permitted Subjects of Bargaining. Matters that are mandatory subjects of bargaining in the public sector can ordinarily be made arbitrable by agreement of the parties. However, some subject matter may fall outside the legal bargaining authority of public-sector employers because either (1) a collective bargaining statute expressly removes it from the scope of bargaining, or (2) the subject matter is regulated by some controlling statutory law, preempting regulation by bargaining, or (3) public policy requires that responsibility over the matter, because of its nature, be exercised exclusively by the public employer. Such matters thus are not proper subjects of bargaining and in this sense may be classified as prohibited or nonnegotiable subjects. A matter is not arbitrable if it is not negotiable, regardless of whether or not the parties have agreed to arbitrate.[74]

As to still other matters, public-sector employees may be permitted but not required to bargain. Management can elect to retain control over such permissible subjects of bargaining merely by refraining from bargaining or agreeing on provisions that share management's control. If a public employer does elect to bargain on a permissible subject of bargaining and a clause on the subject is negotiated, grievances involving application of the clause may be made subject to arbitration.[75] But at least one state has not given general recognition to the "permissible subjects of bargaining" category for the public sector. New Jersey has held that in the public sector except for police and firefighters there are only two categories of issues, "mandatory negotiable terms and conditions of employment and nonnegotiable matters of governmental policy."[76]

---

[73]Town of Winslow Superintending Sch. Comm. v. Winslow Educ. Ass'n, 363 A.2d 229, 232, 93 LRRM 2398 (Me. 1976).

[74]Arbitrability in the public sector has been challenged on "scope of bargaining" grounds both in suits to compel arbitration and in suits to vacate arbitration awards. Primary issues raised are discussed in Note, "Developments in the Law-Public Employment [Part 2 of 2]" 97 Harv. L. Rev. 1611, 1676 (1984).

[75]See, e.g., Rochester City Sch. Dist. v. Rochester Teachers Ass'n, 362 N.E.2d 977, 982, 95 LRRM 2118 (N.Y. 1977). The Massachusetts Supreme Court has held that both mandatory and permissible subjects of bargaining may be submitted to interest arbitration, but educational policy matters cannot be arbitrated. Boston Sch. Comm. v. Boston Teachers Union, Local 66, 363 N.E.2d 485, 95 LRRM 2855 (Mass. 1977). But see School Comm. of Holbrook v. Holbrook Educ. Ass'n, 481 N.E.2d 484 (Mass. 1985), interpreting the scope of such policy matters.

[76]Ridgefield Park Educ. Ass'n v. Ridgefield Park Bd. of Educ., 393 A.2d 278, 287, 98 LRRM 3285 (N.J. 1978). The police and firefighter exception resulted from a 1977 statutory amendment and has been narrowly construed. Paterson Police P&A Local No. 1 v. Paterson, 432 A.2d 847, 854, 112 LRRM 2205 (N.J. 1981); Board of Educ. of City of Englewood v. Englewood Teachers Ass'n, 311 A.2d 729, 732, 85 LRRM 2137 (N.J. 1973).

Express Statutory Removal of Matter From Bargaining. Statutes providing for collective bargaining in the public sector often expressly remove some subject matters from the scope of bargaining, particularly specified areas of management rights.[77] When management rights are statutorily removed from the duty to bargain, procedures regarding the implementation of such subjects remain topics for bargaining.[78]

Contractual Terms Versus Statutory Law Covering Similar Matters. Collective bargaining statutes for the public sector vary regarding the relationship between contractual terms and statutory law covering similar matters. Some variations are as follows:

1. Often the collective bargaining statute is silent regarding the relationship between contract terms and statutory law covering the subject matter. This leaves to the courts the ultimate determination of any nonbargainable subject.[79]
2. The statute may provide that where the agreement conflicts with statutory law, the statutory law prevails.[80]

---

[77]For example, see Wisconsin State Employment Labor Relations Act, §§111.90, 111.91 (1995–96), prohibiting bargaining on various specified matters including listed management rights (except that management is permitted but not required to bargain on certain of the rights). Further discussed in Rabban, supra note 70, the Hawaii Act, which covers most public employees in the state, provides in §89-9(d) (1997) that: "The employer and the exclusive representative shall not agree to any proposal which would be inconsistent in merit principles or the principle of equal pay for equal work pursuant to [statute], or which would interfere with the rights of a public employer [to exercise any of the extensive list of management rights listed in the statute]."

[78]For example, see Hawaii Act, §89-(9)(d); Wisconsin State Employment Labor Relations Act, §111.91(1)(b)(1995-96).

[79]See Glendale Professional Policemen's Ass'n v. City of Glendale, 264 N.W.2d 594, 602, 98 LRRM 2362 (Wis. 1978). The parties may in the collective bargaining agreement prohibit the arbitrator from deciding whether a statute makes a term illegal in the contract, thereby leaving the question for the courts to decide. See Duluth Fed'n of Teachers, Local 692 v. Independent Sch. Dist. 709, 361 N.W.2d 834, 122 LRRM 3084 (Minn. 1985). Also see Ed. Krinsky, "Municipal Grievance Arbitration in Wisconsin," 28 Arb. J. 50, 58 (1973). In Jefferson Cty. Bd. of Educ., 69 LA 890, 895 (Render, 1977), a board of education contended that statutes vesting it with broad administrative discretion precluded arbitrability of a compulsory retirement grievance, to which the arbitrator responded: "The existence of statutes dealing with the same subject matter does not necessarily preclude an arbitrator from concluding that contractual violations may also exist. * * * If the Board was allowed to successfully forestall arbitration in this case, few, if any, Association complaints could ever be resolved through the contractual grievance procedure." Also see Leechburg Area Sch. Dist. v. Leechburg Educ. Ass'n, 380 A.2d 1203, 1206, 97 LRRM 2133 (Pa. 1977). It should be noted that where substantive provisions of a collective agreement are uncertain as to intent, arbitrators often do not hesitate to consider external law as an aid in determining that intent. Southern Tioga Educ. Ass'n v. Southern Tioga Sch. Dist., 668 A.2d 260 (Pa. Comm. W. Ct. 1995). See, e.g., Garner v. City of Tulsa, 651 P.2d 1325, 113 LRRM 3613, 3615 (Okla. 1982).

[80]An example is the Vermont State Employee Labor Relations Act, Vt. Stat. Ann. tit. 3 §904(a) (1997). In holding statutory authorization not to be required for school-employer bargaining, the Colorado Supreme Court stated that, in the absence of specific statutes to the contrary, collective bargaining agreements, "must not conflict with existing statutes concerning the governance of the state school system." Littleton Educ. Ass'n v. Arapahoe County Sch. Dist., No. 6, 553 P.2d 793, 797, 93 LRRM 2378 (Colo.

3. Some collective bargaining statutes specifically prohibit bargaining over specified subjects covered by statutory law.[81]
4. The collective bargaining statute may provide that the agreement shall prevail against statutory law insofar as areas of legal bargaining are concerned.[82]

Some Matters Sometimes Held Nonbargainable. In this section we will note some of the matters that might be held to fall outside the scope of bargaining. Many of the challenges relate to education, an area that has produced much of the litigation.[83]

Following are some of the matters that have been held outside the scope of bargaining by at least one state in public-sector litigation:[84]

1. Tenure—grant or denial (but procedural steps preliminary to employer's final action on tenure are ordinarily held bargainable and arbitrable).[85]

1976). *Cf.* Denver Classroom Teachers Ass'n v. Denver Sch. Dist. No. 1, 911 P.2d 690 (Colo. Ct. App. 1995). A similar limitation imposed by the Ohio Supreme Court was recognized by Arbitrator Cohen in Berea City Sch. Dist., 71 LA 679, 682, 685 (1978).

[81]Although those states that have comprehensive public-sector labor laws usually follow the NLRA in allowing bargaining for "wages, hours and other terms and conditions of employment," most also limit or prohibit bargaining regarding civil service provisions and certain management rights. Richard C. Kearney, Labor Relations in the Public Sector 83–84 (1992). See, for example, New Hampshire Public Employee Labor Relations Law, N.H. Rev. Stat. Ann. §273-A:3, ¶III (1987). Hill & Sinicropi, "Public-Sector Concerns/State Restrictions," *in* Management Rights: A Legal and Arbitral Analysis, 140-45 (BNA Books, 1986).

[82]For example, the Wisconsin State Employment Labor Relations Act, §§111.90, 111.91 & 111.93(3) (1995-96) specifically indicates areas of mandatory bargaining, areas of permissible bargaining, and areas where bargaining is prohibited. It provides: "If a labor agreement exists between the state and a union representing a certified or recognized bargaining unit, the provisions of such agreement shall supersede such provisions of civil service and other applicable statues related to wages, hours and conditions of employment whether or not the matters contained in such statutes are set forth in such labor agreement." See also Conn. Gen. Stat. §5-278(e)(1997).

[83]For related discussion, see Holden, "The Clash Over What Is Bargainable in the Public Schools and Its Consequences for the Arbitrator," Proceedings of the 31st Annual Meeting of NAA, 282–90 (BNA Books, 1979).

[84]See generally Dilts & Walsh, supra note 10, at 29–30; Martin Malin, "Implementing the Illinois Educational Labor Relations Act," 61 Chi-Kent L. Rev. 101 (1985); Turner & Feiley, "The Changing Landscape of School District Negotiations: A Practitioner's Perspective on the 1995 Amendments to the Oregon Public Employee Collective Bargaining Law," 32 Willamette L. Rev. 707 (Fall, 1996).

[85]A number of states have held that substantive tenure decisions or decisions not to renew a nontenured teacher's contract are both nonbargainable and nonarbitrable. Union County College v. Union County College Chapter of AAUP, 684 A.2d 511 (N.J. 1996); University Educ. Ass'n v. Regents of University of Minn., 353 N.W.2d 534 (Minn. 1984); School Comm. of Natick v. Education Ass'n of Natick, 666 N.E.2d 486 (Mass. 1996). See, for example, Moravek v. Davenport Community Sch.. Dist., 262 N.W.2d 797, 98 LRRM 2923 (Iowa 1978); Cohoes City Sch. Dist. v. Cohoes Teachers Ass'n, 358 N.E.2d 878, 94 LRRM 2192 (N.Y. 1976) (but procedural steps are bargainable and enforceable); Town of Winslow Superintending Sch. Comm. v. Winslow Educ. Ass'n, 363 A.2d 229, 93 LRRM 2398 (Me. 1976), discussing numerous other cases on the subject. But reaching the contrary result, Port Huron Educ. Ass'n v. Port Huron Area Sch. Dist., 550 N.W.2d 228, 158 LRRM 2997 (Mich. 1996); Riverview Sch. Dist. v. Riverview Educ. Ass'n, 639 A.2d 974, 145 LRRM 2964 (Pa. Commw. 1994). Danville Bd. of Sch. Directors v. Fifield, 315 A.2d 473, 85 LRRM 2939 (Vt. 1974). Also see Hawaii Supreme Court decisions covering

   2. Discharge of probation officers.[86]
   3. Right to inspect teacher personnel files.[87]
   4. Class size.[88]
   5. Curriculum (courses of study).[89]

---

three disputes, University of Haw. Professional Assembly v. University of Haw., 659 P.2d 717, 720, 729, 113 LRRM 3201, 3203 (Haw. 1983). Discharge of a teacher who *had* tenure could be submitted to arbitration in New York according to the court in Board of Educ. of Union Free Sch. Dist. No. 3 v. Associated Teachers of Huntington, Inc., 282 N.E.2d 109, 79 LRRM 2881 (N.Y. 1972), where the agreement authorized arbitration of tenured teacher discharge for misconduct or incompetency. The court said" "[This provision] assures teachers with tenure that no disciplinary action will be taken against them without just cause and that any dispute as to the existence of such cause may be submitted to arbitration. It is a provision commonly found in collective bargaining agreements in the private and public sectors and carries out Federal and State policy favoring arbitration as a means of resolving labor disputes." Id. at 113. For a discussion of tenured teacher discharge cases submitted to arbitration in New York, see Gross, "Standards of Behavior for Tenured Teachers: The New York State Experience," Proceedings of the 40th Annual Meeting on NAA, 181 (BNA Books, 1988). For a general discussion of discharge of tenured faculty in higher education, Kruft, *"McDaniels v. Flick:* Terminating the Employment of Tenured Professors—What Process is Due?" 41 Vill. L. Rev. 607 (1996).

   [86]In Int'l Ass'n of Firefighters Local 1383 v. City of Warren, 311 N.W.2d 702 (Mich. 1981), the court required judicial review of discharge of probation officers after finding the subject was not bargainable. Apart from special classes of employees, however, discharge of public employees is a proper subject of bargaining and arbitration. See Racine Educ. Ass'n v. Racine Unified Sch. Dist., 500 N.W.2d 379, 143 LRRM 3110 (1993).

   [87]Great Neck Union Free Sch. Dist., Bd. of Educ. v. Areman, 362 N.E.2d 943, 947–48, 95 LRRM 2165, 2169 (N.Y. 1977), holding that "a board of education cannot bargain away its right to inspect teacher personnel files and that a provision in a collective bargaining agreement which might reflect such a bargain is unenforceable as against public policy." However, the court cautioned that "any inspection must be related to legitimate board purposes and functions." LaRocca v. Board of Educ., 632 N.Y.S.2d 576 (N.Y. App. Div. 1995).

   [88]Kenai Peninsula Borough Sch. Dist. v. Kenai Peninsula Educ. Ass'n, 557 P.2d 416, 97 LRRM 2153 (Alaska 1977) (the court provided a list of nine nonnegotiable matters and a list of 38 negotiable matters). Also see National Educ. Ass'n—Topeka, Inc. v. Unified Sch. Dist. 501, Shawnee County, 592 P.2d 93, 98, 101 LRRM 2611 (Kan. 1979). But see West Hartford Educ. Ass'n v. DeCourcy, 295 A.2d 526, 537, 80 LRRM 2422 (Conn. 1972) (class size and teacher load held mandatory subjects of bargaining). New York has held that although class size is not a mandatory bargaining subject, if a school employer voluntarily contracts on the subject, a dispute over the provision may be arbitrable. Susquehanna Valley Cent. Sch. Dist. v. Susquehanna Valley Teachers' Ass'n, 339 N.E.2d 132, 90 LRRM 3046 (N.Y. 1975). The *impact* of class size as it bears on teacher workloads was held a mandatory subject of bargaining in City of Beloit v. Wisconsin Employment Relations Comm'n, 242 N.W.2d 231, 240–41, 92 LRRM 3318, 3325 (Wis. 1976). Under a "primarily related" test, the court classified the following subjects as mandatory subjects of bargaining: teacher evaluation procedures, teacher access to their personnel files, seniority in teacher layoffs (without restricting school employer right to determine curriculum and to retain teachers qualified to teach particular subjects), school calendar and in-service days, impact of class size, and impact of reading program. Id. at 236–42.

   [89]Board of Educ. of Rockaway Township Educ. Ass'n, 295 A.2d 380, 384, 81 LRRM 2462, 2465 (N.J. Super. Ct. Ch. Div. 1972). The court said that "if the contract is read to delegate a teacher or a teacher's union the subject of courses of study, the contract in that respect is *ultra vires* and unenforceable," and the court held nonarbitrable a grievance alleging interference with "academic freedom" (teacher was prohibited from conducting debate in seventh grade class on the subject of abortion) even though the agreement recognized that "academic freedom is essential to the fulfillment of the purposes" of the school. Following this case the New Jersey courts continued to hold that public-sector labor laws are superseded by and must give way to education law provisions if

6. Classification of students according to their abilities.[90]
7. Medical disqualification standards.[91]
8. Teacher evaluations.[92]
9. School calendar.[93]
10. Reclassification of teachers.[94]
11. Decision to abolish positions.[95]
12. Hours of work of teachers.[96]
13. Teacher transfers.[97]

---

and when they conflict. Board of Ed. of Neptune v. Neptune Township Educ. Ass'n, 675 A.2d 611, 615, 144 N.J. 16 (1996). See also the discussion of academic freedom as a policy issue in In re University of Med. & Dentistry of N.J., 677 A.2d 721, 152 LRRM 2606 (1996). In Joint Sch. Dist. No. 8 v. Wisconsin Employment Relations Bd., 155 N.W.2d 78, 82–83 (Wis. 1967), court dictum indicated that curriculum content would not be bargainable because it was within the scope of basic educational policy, citing with approval Blackhawk Teachers Fed'n Local 2308 v. Wisconsin Employment Relations Comm'n, 326 N.W.2d 247, 256 (1982).

[90]Rapid City Educ. Ass'n v. Rapid City Area Sch. Dist., 376 N.W.2d 562, 120 LRRM 3424 (S.D. 1985).

[91]A Pennsylvania court declared medical standards for bus drivers to be instruments promoting public policy in favor of promoting transportation safety: Southeastern Pa. Transp. Auth. v. Transport Workers' Union of Am., 525 A.2d 1, 125 LRRM 3051 (Pa. Commw. Ct. 1987).

[92]Wethersfield Bd. of Educ. v. Connecticut State Bd. of Labor Relations, 519 A.2d 41, 125 LRRM 2510 (Conn. 1986).

[93]Board of Educ. of Montgomery County v. Montgomery County Educ. Ass'n, 505 A.2d 905, 123 LRRM 2505 (Md. Ct. Spec. App. 1986), stating that the school calendar and reclassification of teachers are subjects only tenuously related to the mandatory subject of wages, hours, and working conditions and are management's prerogatives; but see to the contrary, City of Beloit v. Wisconsin Employment Relations Comm'n, 242 N.W.2d 231, 92 LRRM 3318 (Wisc. 1976). In accord, Racine Educ. Ass'n v. Wisconsin Employment, Relations Comm'n, 571 N.W.2d 887 (1997). Also see Burlington County College Faculty Ass'n v. Board of Trustees, 311 A.2d 733, 84 LRRM 2857 (N.J. 1973).

[94]See Ishpeming Supervisory Employees' Chapter of Local 128 v. City of Ishpeming, 400 N.W.2d 661, 124 LRRM 3182 (Mich. Ct. App. 1987), holding that there is no duty to bargaining over the loss of positions through reclassification although the impact of the elimination is a mandatory subject of bargaining. See also United Teachers of Flint v. Flint, Sch. Dist., 404 N.W.2d 637 (Mich. Ct. App. 1986). Similarly, the merging of academic departments has been held to be nonnegotiable: Dunellen Bd. of Educ. v. Dunellen Ed. Ass'n, 311 A.2d 737, 85 LRRM 2131 (1973).

[95]Old Bridge Township Bd. of Educ. v. Old Bridge Educ. Ass'n, 489 A.2d 159, 121 LRRM 2784 (N.J. 1985), holding that the decision to abolish positions is not negotiable but a provision for notice is.

[96]West Hartford Educ. Ass'n v. DeCourcy, 295 A.2d 526, 534, 80 LRRM 2422 (Conn. 1972) (held not a mandatory subject of bargaining, and the court's general discussion reasons that the legislature did not intend such matters to be subjected to bargaining). But hours of work of teachers was held bargainable in Board of Educ. of City of Englewood v. Englewood Teachers Ass'n, 311 A.2d 729, 85 LRRM 2137 (N.J. 1973).

[97]See Tippecanoe Edc. Ass'n v. Board of Sch. Trustees, 429 N.E.2d 967, 973 (Ind. Ct. App. 1981). In Minneapolis Fed'n of Teachers Local 59 v. Minneapolis Special Sch. Dist. No. 1, 258 N.W.2d 802, 806, 96 LRRM 2706 (Minn. 1977), the court held: "1. The decision to transfer a number of teachers is a managerial decision and not a subject for negotiation. 2. The adoption of the criteria by which individual teachers may be identified for transfer is a proper subject for negotiation, and, as such, is properly included in the collective bargaining contract. 3. To insure that individual teacher transfers conform to the negotiated contract, each individual transfer is a proper subject of grievance arbitration." Cf. School Comm. of Lowell v. Local 159, Service Employees Int'l Union, 679 N.E.2d 583 (Mass. Ct. App. 1997). A form of transfer of work, subcontracting out, has also been held nonnegotiable: IFPTE Local 195 v. New Jersey, 443 A.2d 187, 112 LRRM 2214, 113 LRRM 2535 (N.J. 1982). (But see discussion of subsequent statutory amendments intended to limit applicability of the 1982 decision found in New Jersey v. State Troopers Fraternal Ass'n, 634 A.2d 478, 145 LRRM 2564 (N.J. 1993).)

14. Faculty workload.[98]

15. Hiring of teachers.[99]

Relationship Between Contractual and Statutory Grievance Channels

Often statutory provisions for collective bargaining and arbitration in public employment are silent regarding the relationship between contractual grievance procedures and statutory procedures such as those under civil service laws.[100] Where a statute does deal expressly with the question, one possibility is that the employee will be given an option to use either the contractual grievance procedure or a statutory procedure.[101] However, some statutes make the contractual grievance procedure exclusive if it covers the grievance. For example, Massachusetts provides that if there is an applicable contract grievance procedure, such procedure shall "be exclusive and shall supersede any otherwise applicable grievance procedure provided by law."[102]

States that authorize collective bargaining and arbitration in the public sector generally permit employees to adjust their grievance with the employer without intervention of the union, but the adjustment must be consistent with the terms of the collective agreement, and the union is entitled to be present.[103]

---

[98]Tualatin Valley Bargaining Council v. Tigard Sch. Dist., 840 P.2d 657, 662 (Or. 1992). Also see Metropolitan Technical Community College Educ. Ass'n v. Metropolitan Technical Community College Area, 281 N.W.2d 201, 102 LRRM 2142, 2146 (Neb. 1979), stating that certain decisions of other states were distinguishable. The allocation of nonprofessional chores to teachers was held nonbargainable and nonarbitrable in Kenai Peninsula Educ. Ass'n v. Kenai Peninsula Sch. Dist., 628 P.2d 568, 569 (Alaska 1981).

[99]Bd. of Directors of Maine Sch. Admin. Dist. v. Teachers Ass'n, 428 A.2d 419, 110 LRRM 3361, 3364 (Me. 1981). Also see New Bedford Sch. Comm. v. New Bedford Educators Ass'n, 405 N.E.2d 162, 165, 108 LRRM 3201, 3204–05 (Mass. App. Ct. 1980). Cf. *School Comm. of Lowell,* 679 N.E.2d 583. A form of transfer of work, subcontracting out, has also been held nonnegotiable: *IFPTE Local 195 v. New Jersey,* 443 A.2d 187. (But see discussion of subsequent statutory amendments intended to limit applicability of the 1982 decision found in *State Troopers Fraternal Ass'n,* 634 A.2d 478.

[100]For general discussion of the subject, see Rabban, "Can American Labor Law Accommodate Collective Bargaining by Professional Employees?" 99 Yale L.J. 689 (1990); Hayford & Pegnetter, "A Comparison of Rights of Arbitration and Civil Service Appeals Procedures," 35 Arb. J. 22 (1980); Pegnetter & Hayford, "State Employee Grievances and Due Process: An Analysis of Contract Arbitration and Civil Service Review Systems," 29 S.C. L. Rev. 305 (1978).

[101]See Zelin, Annotation, "Rights of State and Municipal Public Employees in Grievance Proceedings," 46 A.L.R. 4th 912 (1996). For an example of the statutory provision, see Minnesota Public Employment Labor Relations Act, §179A.25 (1996).

[102]Mass. Gen. Laws Ann. ch. 150E, §8 (West 1989). Another example is the Maine State Employees Labor Relations Act, §979-K. In City of Ontario, Or.; 72 LA 1089, 1091–92 (Conant, 1979), the public employer was upheld in reprimanding an employee who bypassed the contractual grievance procedure, which was construed to provide the exclusive remedy, and carried his complaint to a city councilman; the arbitrator said that in public-sector labor relations, "'end-runs' to city officials can disrupt and impair the functioning of the bargaining process."

[103]For example, see Del. Code Ann. tit. 19, §1304(b) (1974), and Illinois State Labor Relations Act, 5 Ill. Comp. Stat. 315/6 (West 1997). See discussion in Svoboda v. Department of Mental Health & Developmental Disabilities, 515 N.E.2d 446 (Ill. Ct. App. 1987).

Chapter 3

Scope of Labor Arbitration

Interest Arbitration [New Topic]

It continues to be the law that interest arbitration clauses[1] are nonmandatory subjects of bargaining. The NLRB has now so indicated as well.[2] Thus, a union's insistence on bargaining to impasse on inclusion of an interest arbitration provision into a contract constitutes an unfair labor practice,[3] and a union cannot rely on an interest arbitration clause in an existing contract to require an employer to agree to a similar clause in a successor contract.

Arbitrator's Function in Rights Disputes

Unlike the arbitrator's quasi-legislative role in interest disputes, the arbitrator's function in rights disputes is limited to interpretation of the bargained-for agreement. Beginning with its *Enterprise Wheel*[4] decision, the Supreme Court limited the arbitrator's role in rights disputes to interpretation and application of the collective bargaining agreement. Along with the federal courts, "arbitrators are still the principal sources of contract interpretation."[5] The *Enterprise*

---

[1]"Interest arbitration is a method by which an employer and union reach agreement by sending the disputed issues to an arbitrator rather than by settling them through collective bargaining and economic force." Silverman v. Major League Baseball Players Relations Committee, Inc., 67 F.3d 1054, 1062 (2d Cir. 1995).

[2]See George Koch & Sons, Inc., 306 NLRB 834, 839 (1992).

[3]Id.

[4]United Steelworkers v. Enterprise Wheel & Car Corp., 363 U.S. 593 (1960).

[5]Litton Fin. Printing Div. v. NLRB, 501 U.S. 190, 202 (1991) (quoting NLRB v. Strong, 393 U.S. 357, 360–61 (1969)). See also, e.g., Conoco Inc. v. NLRB, 91 F.3d 1523, 1525 (D.C. Cir. 1996)) ("we have held that under federal labor laws, arbitrators, and the courts, rather than the [National Labor Relations] Board, are the primary sources of contract interpretation'" (quoting NLRB v. United States Postal Serv., 8 F.3d 832, 836 (D.C. Cir. 1993)).

Wheel Court held that although an arbitrator may look outside the contract for guidance, "he does not sit to dispense his own brand of industrial justice," and his award is therefore legitimate only insofar as it "draws its essence" from the collective bargaining agreement.[6]

The Supreme Court has continued to adhere to the *Enterprise Wheel* "essence" standard, as have the lower federal courts.[7] The Court has now recently reconfirmed the principle that "the arbitrator's award must draw its essence from the contract and cannot simply reflect the arbitrator's own notions of industrial justice. But as long as the arbitrator is even arguably construing or applying the contract and acting within the scope of his authority, that a court is convinced he committed serious error does not suffice to overturn his decision."[8] At the same time, the Supreme Court endorsed an exception, albeit a narrow one, to the usual judicial deference paid to arbitrators by the "essence" standard—when the award violates well-defined and dominant public policy.[9]

Even as the courts generally limit arbitrators to interpretation of the collective bargaining agreement, the arbitrator's authority to

---

[6]United Steelworkers v. Enterprise Wheel & Car Corp., 363 U.S. at 597.

[7]E.g., Upshur Coals Corp. v. UMW, 933 F.2d 225 (4th Cir. 1991) (confirming award that employer was required to provide accrued health benefits to laid off employees even after agreement expired); NCR Corp., E & M Wichita v. [Int'l] Ass'n of Machinists and Aerospace Workers, 906 F.2d 1499 (10th Cir. 1990) (confirming award that employer subcontracting violated agreement); Island Creek Coal Co. v. UMW, 29 F.3d 126 (4th Cir. 1994) (vacating award of punitive damages); Bruce Hardwood Floors, Div. of Triangle Pacific Corp. v. UBC, 103 F.3d 449 (5th Cir. 1997) (vacating award that mitigated discharge penalty where agreement expressly permitted discharge for immoral conduct); SFIC Properties, Inc. v. [Int'l] Ass'n of Machinists & Aerospace Workers, 103 F.3d 923 (9th Cir. 1996) (affirming award that implied a just cause discharge requirement); Excel Corp. v. United Food & Commercial Workers Int'l Union, 102 F.3d 1464 (8th Cir. 1996) (vacating award reinstating employees because it ignored plain language of agreement.). Amax Coal Co. v. UMW, 92 F.3d 571 (7th Cir. 1996) (vacating award because "an arbitrator cannot grant a remedy when he finds that there is no breach of the collective bargaining agreement"); Midwest Coca-Cola Bottling Co. v. Allied Sales Drivers, 89 F.3d 514 (8th Cir. 1996) (confirming award that ordered reinstatement of chronically absent and progressively disciplined employee).

[8]United Paperworkers v. Misco, 484 U.S. 29, 38 (1987).

[9]484 U.S. at 43. See generally D. Meltzer, *After the Labor Arbitration Award: The Public Policy Defense,* 10 Indus. Rel. L.J. 241 (1988); Harry T. Edwards, *Judicial Review of Labor Arbitration Awards: The Clash Between the Public Policy Exception and the Duty to Bargain,* 64 Chi.-Kent L. Rev. 3 (1988). See also, e.g., American Postal Workers Union v. United States Postal Serv., 52 F.3d 359, 362 (D.C. Cir. 1995) ("the Supreme Court has made clear that to overturn a labor arbitration award as contrary to public policy is a daunting task"); United Transp. Union Local 1589 v. Suburban Transit Corp., 51 F.3d 376, 382 (3rd Cir. 1995) (the public policy "exception is available only when 'the arbitration decision and award create an explicit conflict with an explicit public policy.'"); Pierce v. Commonwealth Edison Co., 112 F.3d 893 (7th Cir. 1997) (rejecting public policy argument); Exxon Corp. v. Baton Rouge Oil & Chemical Workers Union, 77 F.3d 850 (5th Cir. 1996) (public policy exception applies both to bar reinstatement of a drug-abusing employee and to bar an award to him of back pay); United Food Workers Int'l Union, Local 588 v. Foster Poultry Farms, 74 F.3d 169 (9th Cir. 1995) (rejecting public policy defense against reinstatement of drug-using drivers); Exxon Shipping Co. v. Exxon Seamen's Union, 73 F.3d 1287 (3d Cir. 1996) (and cases discussed therein) (reinstatement of transportation employee who refused drug test would violate public policy).

construe the agreement also depends upon the scope of the arbitration clause.[10] Broad arbitration clauses give an arbitrator expansive authority to decide a multitude of disputes. The lower courts have not hesitated to support arbitration of an issue (unless they are convinced that the contract specifically excludes that issue),[11] since the Supreme Court ruled that a broad grievance arbitration provision should be held to encompass all disputed matters not specifically excluded. "[Arbitration] should not be denied unless it may be said with positive assurance that the arbitration clause is not susceptible of an interpretation that covers the asserted dispute. Doubts should be resolved in favor of coverage."[12]

Moreover, the issue of arbitrability is to be resolved by the courts, not by an arbitrator.[13] In ruling on arbitrability, however, the court "is not to rule on the potential merits of the underlying claims"[14] In some cases, however, a determination that a dispute is or is not arbitrable is effectively a determination of the underlying dispute as well. The Court has strongly indicated that the judicial obligation to determine arbitrability must prevail even if it requires an interpretation of the agreement that would leave an arbitrator with virtually nothing to do. The Court stated" "Although doubts should be resolved in favor of [arbitrability], we must determine whether the parties have agreed to arbitrate this dispute, and we cannot avoid that duty because it requires us to interpret a provision of a collective bargaining agreement."[15] As one appellate court explained, "'[i]t appears that the rule that courts must decide arbitrators' jurisdiction takes precedence over the rule that courts are not to decide the merits of the underlying dispute. If the courts must, to decide the arbitrability issue, rule on the merits, so be it.'"[16]

---

[10]Safeway Stores' Inc. v. United Food & Commercial Workers Union Local 400, 621 F. Supp. 1233 (D.D.C. 1985) (arbitration is a matter of contract and arbitrator's authority is defined by agreement); see also Seafarers v. National Marine Servs., 639 F. Supp. 1283, 1290 (E.D. La. 1986) ("arbitration is a creature of contract with no life independent of its collective bargaining agreement").

[11]For an example of a contract that very specifically narrowed the scope of arbitration, see International Ass'n of Machinists & Aerospace Workers v. Caribe General Electric Prods., 108 F.3d 422 (1st Cir. 1997).

[12]AT&T Technologies v. Communications Workers, 475 U.S. 643, 650 (1986) (quoting United Steelworkers of America v. Warrior & Gulf Navigation Co., 363 U.S. 574, 582–83). "In the absence of any express provision excluding a particular grievance from arbitration, . . . only the most forceful evidence of a purpose to exclude the claim from arbitration can prevail." Warrior & Gulf Navigation Corp., 363 U.S. 574, 584–85 (1960).

[13]First Options of Chicago, Inc. v. Kaplan, 514 U.S. 938 (1995).

[14]AT&T, 475 U.S. at 649.

[15]Litton Fin. Printing Div. v. NLRB, 501 U.S. 190 (1991).

[16]International Brotherhood of Teamsters v. Hinckley & Schmitt, Inc., 76 F.3d 162, 165 (7th Cir. 1996) (quoting Independent Lift Truck Builders Union v. Hyster Co., 2 F.3d 233, 236 (7th Cir. 1993)).

Perhaps because it seems so at odds with their traditional, over-riding role as contract interpreters, a degree of controversy has emerged recently over the question of vesting the resolution of statu-tory discrimination charges with labor arbitrators. In 1974, the Su-preme Court stated that "the federal policy favoring arbitration of labor disputes and the federal policy against discriminatory employ-ment practices can best be accommodated by permitting an employee to pursue fully both his remedy under the grievance-arbitration clause of a collective bargaining agreement and his cause of action under Title VII."[17] However, in 1991, the Supreme Court held that the fed-eral courts would enforce private arbitration agreements to compel arbitration of Federal Age Discrimination in Employment Act claims.[18] Although this more recent decision did not arise in the context of a collective bargaining agreement's grievance-arbitration clause, it was not long before the lower federal courts faced such cases and badly splintered.[19]

Rights Arbitration Contract Clauses

Precontract and Postcontract Grievances

Even the Supreme Court has now noted the "substantial disagree-ment as to the proper application of our decision in *Nolde Brothers,*"[20] and this confusion led the Court to grant certiorari in *Litton Finan-cial* where the Court resolved questions over the rule announced in *Nolde* by stating as follows:

> We agree with the approach of the Board and those courts which have interpreted *Nolde Brothers* to apply only where a dispute has its real source in the contract. The object of an arbitration clause is to implement a contract, not to transcend it. *Nolde Brothers* does not announce a rule that postexpiration grievances concerning terms and conditions of employment remain arbitrable. A rule of that sweep in fact would contradict the rationale of *Nolde Brothers*. The *Nolde Brothers* presumption is limited to disputes arising under the contract. A

---

[17]Alexander v. Gardner-Denver Co., 415 U.S. 36, 59–60 (1974).

[18]Gilmer v. Interstate/Johnson Lane Corp., 500 U.S. 20 (1991).

[19]Compare Austin v. Owens-Brockway Glass Container, Inc., 78 F.3d 875 (4th Cir. 1996) (the arbitration pledge in a collective bargaining agreement precludes a union member from bringing a Title VII and ADA claim in federal court), with Pryner v. Trac-tor Supply Co., 109 F.3d 354, 363 (7th Cir. 1997) (workers' statutory rights are arbi-trable if the worker consents, but "the union cannot consent for the employee by sign-ing a collective bargaining agreement that consigns the enforcement of statutory rights to the union-controlled grievance and arbitration machinery created by the agreement", and with Varner v. National Super Markets, Inc., 94 F.3d 1209 (8th Cir. 1996), and with Martin v. Dana Corp., 155 LRRM 2525 (3d Cir. 1997).

[20]Nolde Brothers, Inc. v. Bakery & Confectionary Workers Union Local 358, 430 U.S. 243 (1977).

postexpiration grievance can be said to arise under the contract only where it involves facts and occurrences that arose before expiration, where an action taken after expiration infringes a right that accrued or vested under the agreement, or where, under normal principles of contract interpretation, the disputed contractual right survives expiration of the remainder of the agreement.[21]

For the time being, the Court's above-quoted *Litton Financial* decision has brought an end to the previous disputes concerning the arbitrability of postcontract grievances.

---

[21]501 U.S. at 205–206 (1991).

Chapter 4

The Arbitration Tribunal

"Temporary" or "Ad Hoc" Arbitrators

Advantages

In a presentation at the Fiftieth Annual Meeting of the National Academy of Arbitrators, Abe Rosner[1] discussed the unique process of handling disputes under the Canadian Railway System. Mr. Rosner highlighted the prearbitration process, which requires extensive prehearing preparation by the parties. At the hearing, each party arrives with a written brief that contains evidence, argument, and references to authorities. In addition, Mr. Rosner noted that over a 30-year period his union has relied on the arbitral skills of two "permanent" arbitrators.[2]

Tripartite Arbitration Board

A recent commentator challenged the use of tripartite arbitration panels within the context of the Federal Arbitration Act (FAA)

---

[1]National Representative, Canadian Auto Workers Union, Montreal, Quebec.

[2]*See* Ad Hoc Arbitration on Canadian Railways by Abe Rosner, *Arbitration 1997, the Next Fifty Years, Proceedings of the Fiftieth Annual Meeting, National Academy of Arbitrators,* BNA Books (1998) pp. 115–122, in which the author discusses the method in which grievances are arbitrated by the Canadian Auto Workers in the Canadian Railway System. In this discussion, Rosner points out the virtue of consistently naming the same group of ad hoc arbitrators in order to decrease the learning curve in the complicated railway industry. *See also* By Land and Air: Two Models of Expedited Grievance Procedure in *Arbitration 1997, The Next 50 Years, Proceedings of the Fiftieth Annual Meeting of the National Academy of Arbitrators,* BNA Books (1997). Specifically, see the Chapter 4 subparts which are:

 I. A Perspective on the Canadian Railways Office of Arbitration by Dennis W. Coughlin

 II. Ad Hoc Arbitrator's on Canadian Railways by Abe Rosner

 III. Moving from the Old to the New American Airlines Expedited Grievance Resolution Process by Judith A. Ladislaw

 IV. The New American Airlines Expedited Grievance Resolution Process by Jack P. Upchurch and the American Arbitration Association (AAA). While the article is written in a nonlabor context, it stated that the courts have shown too much deference to the advocacy which is part and parcel of the tripartite panel:

> In at least one form of dispute resolution sanctioned by the federal courts, neutrality and impartiality are not only ignored but denounced as hindering its effectiveness. In tripartite panels, under the rules of the American Arbitration Association (AAA), party-appointed arbitrators are permitted and even encouraged to be predisposed toward the position of their nominating party.
>
> The courts approach toward challenges to arbitral awards on the basis of arbitrator relationships or misconduct suggests an unwillingness to restrain, in any meaningful way, an arbitrators behavior. Rather, it denotes a willingness to apply a lesser standard of ethical behavior to arbitrators than is applied to judicial officers. This approach permits a court to use arbitration to reduce its docket while neglecting to monitor the arbitration process itself.[3]

Disadvantages

A recent commentator indicated that the ethical boundaries are stretched when dealing with tripartite panels. While courts are required to overturn arbitration awards if they find that there has been evident partiality, that is the very nature of two of the arbitrators of a tripartite panel:

> Maintaining the goals of arbitration speed, efficiency, and economy is hindered rather than helped by the participation of party-appointed arbitrators. Uncertainty exists as to what behavior the courts will tolerate from arbitrators as well as which relationships are taboo. It is clear, however, that federal appellate courts are not inclined to set aside arbitral awards for inappropriate arbitrator behavior for fear of creating a tide of continually relitigated cases [footnote omitted]. The judiciary's unwillingness to upset arbitral awards almost certainly leads parties and their counsel to push the limits of party-appointed arbitrator behavior as far as possible to assist the nominating parties in arising victoriously from the arbitration. Unfortunately, it is the repeat, experienced and more savvy users of arbitration who best realize how elastic the boundaries of accepted arbitrator conduct can be.[4]

Methods of Selecting Arbitrators

Many cases focus on the specific language of the collective bargaining agreement at issue. In a recent case, management argued that the union did not seek to strike arbitrators from a list provided

---

[3]Predisposed with Integrity: The Elusive Quest for Justice in Tripartite Arbitrations by Desiree A. Kennedy, *The Georgetown Journal of Legal Ethics, Vol. VIII,* No. 4, pp. 749–790.
    [4]*Id.*

by the Federal Mediation and Conciliation Service (FMCS). The collective bargaining agreement merely indicated that there was a mutual obligation to meet and select an arbitrator with no other obligations. The arbitrator rejected management's contention and indicated that where the collective bargaining agreement placed a mutual obligation on both parties to meet and select an arbitrator without any other specified obligations, without substantial evidence that the union had solely caused the arbitrator selection process to be tardy, the arbitrator could not find a procedural fault and ruled the grievance to be timely.[5]

In *Rhone Poulec Basic Chemicals Co.*[6] The union wrote a letter to the FMCS asking for a panel of arbitrators. However, the union did not send a copy of the letter to the company. No response was received from the FMCS within 4 months and 10 days. Again, the union wrote to the FMCS, but again did not copy the company. When the FMCS finally responded and sent a panel of arbitrators after 161 days, the company protested the delay. Because the union failed to copy the company on any of its requests, the arbitrator ruled that the matter was untimely and thus not arbitrable. However, in another case, the union unilaterally waited 4 months to request a list of arbitrators from the FMCS. Management claimed that this delay caused the grievance to be untimely. However, the arbitrator disagreed, indicating that the collective bargaining agreement in question set no specific deadline for requesting a panel from the FMCS. Since no specific deadline was required by the collective bargaining agreement, the delay was not a violation and thus the grievance was timely.[7]

Arbitrators and Their Qualifications

Background, Training, and Supply of Arbitrators

In a recent extensive unpublished study by Professor Anne Draznin of the University of Illinois, it was determined over an 8-year period, from 1987–1994, many gender factors had not changed dramatically. According to Professor Draznin's study, approximately 60% of arbitrators are attorneys. Further, the overwhelming majority of arbitrators continued to be male. This did not change significantly between 1987 and 1994, as the ratio of men and women in the field hovered around 90%:10%. Professor Draznin writes:

> Overall, the most striking point in the year by year review of arbitrator biographical; characteristics is therefore not the difference but the sameness of the look of the pool. It is remarkable because there was an

---

[5]Martin-Brower Co., 102 LA 673 (Dilts, 1994).

[6]103 LA 791, 793 (Darrow, 1994).

[7]Mercury Consolidated Inc., 101 LA 309, 314 (Schubert, 1993) *citing International Union of Operating Engineers, Stationary Local 39 and Mercury Consolidated,* Unpublished Decision (Kennedy 1988).

increase of approximately 300+ persons in the total numbers of arbitrators over this same eight year time span. In 1987, there were a total of 1145 active arbitrators [footnote omitted] in the pool, 1035 or 90.4% of which were men and 110 or 9.6% of which were women. By 1994, the total numbers had increased considerably. Of a total of 1457 active arbitrators nominated for appointment during the fiscal year, 1287 or 88.3% were men and 170 or 11.7% were women.[8]

---

[8]*Debunking the Myths about Gender Factors In Labor Arbitrator Selection,* Unpublished, Anne L. Draznin, Professor,University of Illinois, Springfield, paper presented before the ADR in Employment Law Committee of Labor and Employment Law Section of the American Bar Association, Midwinter Meeting, February 16, 1998 at pp. 12–13.

Chapter 5

Grievances—Prelude to Arbitration

Attitude of Parties to the Grievance Procedure

The attitude of the parties becomes clear as the grievance moves through the grievance machinery. The terms and provisions of the bargaining agreement may provide for full, partial, or no disclosure.[1] However, unless there are contractual prohibitions, both parties should make a complete disclosure of all the facts, positions taken, and provisions of the agreement relied upon at the earliest possible step in the grievance procedure.[2] For "[n]owhere in the relationship between Employer and Union is mutual good faith more important than in handling grievances. . . . Accordingly, settlements at the first steps of the grievance procedure will be facilitated by honest and open disclosure of each party's position and its basis."[3] The absence of such disclosure, with its inherent lack of good faith, is not only unfair but unwise.

---

[1]See e.g., Simmons Indus., Inc., 101 LA 1201 (Stephens, 1993) (employer that failed to furnish list of proposed witnesses and exhibits to Union as required by the collective bargaining agreement is prohibited from using such evidence at hearing).

[2]Michigan Dept. of Corrections, 103 LA 37 (Sugarman, 1994) (employer violated collective bargaining agreement by refusing to furnish union with requested information); Central PA Water Supply Co., 101 LA 873 (Talarico, 1993) (employee's grievance sustained due to Employer's lack of candor in providing inaccurate and false information during grievance proceeding). See also Comments of Arbitrator Hilgert in Spectrulite Consortium, Inc., 101 LA 1134, 1140 (1993) in holding that it was not unduly burdensome to reschedule an investigatory meeting before discharging the employee who had failed to appear, "employees should be afforded all due process that can reasonably be made available to them, even if this causes some inconvenience on the part of either or both parties."

[3]Central PA Water Supply Co., 101 LA 873, 876 (Talarico, 1993).

Abuse and Misuse of Grievance Procedure

An "irresistible impulse to file grievances" is not a dischargeable offense, though the purposeful filing of deliberately untruthful grievances may be.[4]

Failure to Comply Strictly With Technical Requirements of Grievance Procedure

A general presumption exists that favors arbitration over dismissal of grievances on technical grounds.[5] Applying this presumptions to a situation where the grievant did not testify in the preliminary stages of the arbitration, one arbitrator found a grievance arbitrable since the specific language of the contract surrounding the grievance procedure did not require such testimony and thus implied informality.[6]

However, where the parties' collective bargaining agreements contain specific language and requirements as to the filing of grievances, arbitrators will deny a grievance where the procedure is not followed.[7] Arbitrators will also sustain a union's grievance against an employer if the employer likewise fails to follow the proper grievance procedure.[8]

Finally, regardless of the procedure followed during the steps leading to arbitration, if a party does not timely object to the arbitrability of the grievance, but instead waits until the hearing or shortly before the hearing to object, the arbitrator will likely find that the party waived the objection.[9] Arbitrators also find waiver of an arbitrability argument where a party processes a grievance fully, including the selection of an arbitrator, and then argues for the first time at the arbitration hearing that the grievance is not arbitrable.[10]

Should Grievance Machinery Be Open to All Complaints?

The question of whether a complaint is subject to the grievance procedure may itself be processed through the grievance procedure

---

[4]National Lead Co. of Ohio, 37 LA 1076, 1079 (Schedler, 1962). Also illustrating the strong inclination of arbitrators to protect employees against reprisals for filing grievances. See Arbitrator Moore in Tyson Foods, Inc., 105 LA 1119, 1123 (1996) "[A]n employer may not unilaterally determine that a grievance was filed in bad faith and discipline an employee for doing so").

[5]Rodeway Inn, 102 LA 1003, 1013 (Goldberg, 1994).

[6]Id.

[7]Monroe Mfg., Inc., 107 LA 877, 879 (Stephens, 1996).

[8]USS, A Division of USX Corp., 107 LA 772, 775 (Neyland 1996); Wisconsin Tissue Mills, Inc., 102 LA 601, 605 (Jacobs 1994).

[9]Ardco, Inc., 108 LA 326, 330 (Wolff, 1997); Lincoln Technical Inst., 108 LA 158, 163 (Cohen, 1997); Stone Container Corp., 105 LA 385, 388–89 (Berquist, 1995).

[10]Masolite Concrete Prods., Inc., 103 LA 10, 14 (Keenan, 1994).

and arbitration. As a rule, grievance statements should not be too general in nature. However, failure to cite the relevant contract provisions in the grievance will not necessarily prevent an arbitrator from considering such provisions.[11]

An arbitrator may not, however, consider an employer's entire substance abuse policy, but rather only that provision of the policy that the grievant was subjected to, where the policy was part of the employer's final contract offer, the Union did not grieve the implementation of the policy as a whole, and the Union had not filed an unfair labor practice charge.[12]

Whether an arbitrator may decide an issue that raises a question under labor laws and employment laws depends on the nature of the issue and the underlying facts.[13]

Where the contract contains a nondiscrimination clause, an arbitrator may consider issues of discrimination based on race, national origin, disability, pregnancy, or religion.[14]

Sometimes former employees may utilize the grievance procedure for grievances based upon their previous employment status. One arbitrator allowed former employees to proceed with a grievance after examining the language in the collective bargaining agreement and finding that the definition of grievance was expansive enough to include the former employees' complaint.[15] However, another arbitrator denied a former employee access to the grievance procedure based on the fact that the employee had voluntarily resigned, finding

---

[11]Consolidated Drum Reconditioning, 108 LA 523, 524 (Richman, 1997) (union did not waive contention that employee was not in probationary status, even though union's grievance did not cite contract provision dealing with the employer's probation policy); The Motion Picture and Television Fund, 103 LA 988, 991 (Gentile, 1994) (union may discuss contractual article not cited in original grievance where article is subsumed in any consideration of management's policy at issue).

[12]Jefferson Smurfit Corp., 106 LA 306, 311–12 (Goldstein, 1996).

[13]Southern Bag Corp., 108 LA 348, 353–54 (Overstreet, 1997) (arbitrator will decide whether NLRA was violated when the six month statute of limitations for filing charge with NLRB has run); Arizona Opera Co., 105 LA 1126, 1130–31 (Wyman, 1995) (arbitrator has authority to decide violation of NLRA where union has not filed ULP charge); Steelworkers v. IUE, 105 LA 961, 963 (Lesnick, 1995) (arbitrator need not defer determination of issue pending NLRB decision where there is no showing that such decision will illuminate issue of whether contract violation occurred); cf. Smithfield Packing Co., 107 LA 503, 505 (Fraser, 1996) (arbitrator will not withhold award due to alleged NLRA violation which should be dealt with before NLRB); Swift Cleaning & Laundry, 106 LA 954 (Nelson, 1995) (arbitrator does not have authority to hear question of representation or appropriateness of unit); Norfolk Shipbuilding & Drydock Corp., 105 LA 529, 533 (Hockenberry, 1995) (Weingarten issue not reviewable by arbitrator where NLRB has not deferred on issue but rather settled matter without issuing complaint).

[14]Flamingo Hilton-Laughlin, 108 LA 545 (Weckstein, 1997) (disability); Champion Int'l Corp., 106 LA 1024 (Howell, 1996) (disability); Clallam County Public Hosp., 105 LA 609 (Calhoun, 1995) (religion); San Francisco Unified Sch. Dist., 104 LA 215 (Bogue, 1995) (disability); Motion Picture and Television Fund, 103 LA 988 (Gentile, 1994) (national origin); Minnegasco, Inc., 103 LA 43 (Bognanno, 1994) (pregnancy).

[15]Marion County, 108 LA 698, 701 (Downing, 1997).

that the employee was no longer an employee with any right to file a grievance under the collective bargaining agreement.[16]

Identification and Signature of Individual Grievants; Group Grievances

Arbitrators have found that a member of a bargaining unit does not have standing to file a grievance without showing a personal interest in the grievance's outcome, or indicating that the grievance is a class action grievance, or that the grievant is an official of the bargaining unit.[17] However, a union has standing to file a class action grievance that affects a significant portion of the bargaining unit.[18] Additionally, another arbitrator found that the grievance submitted by the union was arbitrable because although the contract did not expressly name the union a "grievant," the express provision allowing for group grievances implied that the union could be a grievant, especially because the alleged violation affected a class of bargaining unit members.[19]

Steps in Grievance Procedure

While some vacillation occurs in the enforcement of contractual time period requirements, they are usually strictly enforced where the parties have previously and consistently enforced such requirements. These grievances will either be refused a hearing or automatically sustained due to the employer's lack of compliance with such requirements.[20] However, these strict requirements were followed even where management had a history of lax compliance with the time guidelines.[21] Vacillation occurs in cases where no definite time period restriction is contained in the agreement or where the actual triggering date is difficult to determine.[22] Certain situations, however, are not subject to contractual time limits. When the subject of a grievance is an ongoing violation, time limit restrictions are lifted.[23] Time

[16]Chivas Prods. Ltd., 101 LA 546, 548 (Kanner, 1993).
[17]Cyprus Emerald Resources Corp., 101 LA 1053, 1055 (Ipavec, 1993) citing Arbitrator Marvin J. Feldman in case no. EMC/D 22-86-43.
[18]Id.
[19]Los Angeles Community College Dist., 103 LA 1174, 1178 (Kaufman, 1994).
[20]Huron Lime Co., 106 LA 997, 1003–4 (Bowers, 1996); Wisconsin Tissue Mills, Inc., 102 LA 601, 615 (Jacobs, 1994).
[21]Protection Tech. Los Alamos, 104 LA 23, 29–30 (Finston, 1994).
[22]Colwell Gen. Inc., 104 LA 1036, 1041 (Brunner, 1995) (grievance timely where collective bargaining agreement does not specify triggering event); Regional Transp. Dist., 107 LA 813, 819 (Finston, 1996) (although triggering data difficult to determine, grievance found timely by resolving doubts as to timeliness in favor of processing grievance).
[23]Municipality of Anchorage, 108 LA 97, 99 (Landau, 1997); Kuhlman Elec. Corp., 106 LA 429, 436 (Duda, 1996); Larry's Mkts., 105 LA 795, 799 (Lehleitner, 1995); Harding Galesburg Mkts., Inc., 103 LA 1158, 1163 (Daniel, 1994); U.S. Silica Co., 102 LA 342,

limits are also waived if the parties to a grievance allow the grievance to move from step to step in the procedure without making timeliness objections.[24]

Grievance Representatives

Right to Union Representation at Early Stage

Since the Supreme Court declared in 1975 that individual employees have a right to refuse to submit without union representation to investigatory interviews that they reasonably believe may result in discipline, the NLRB has continued to shape the "contours and limits of the statutory right" established in *Weingarten*.[25] For example, the Board recently found that *Weingarten* applies when an employee is being questioned by a grievance council consisting of nonsupervisory employees who have final authority to uphold, modify, or set aside the employer's discipline.[26] The NLRB found that *Weingarten* protections applied because the proceedings were investigatory in nature and that for the purposes of grievance adjustment the council was an agent of the employer who made the final determination as to discipline.[27]

Following its holding in *Baton Rouge Water Works Co.*[28] the NLRB continues to uphold the right of employers to deny union representation during noninvestigatory disciplinary meetings.[29] Further, evidence obtained from an employee in a meeting where his *Weingarten* rights were violated may not be used against that employee in imposing discipline.[30] On the other hand, the Board has held that when no nexus exists between an improper denial of representation and discipline imposed, the discipline stands.[31]

344–45 (Goodstein, 1994); Stone Container Corp., 102 LA 219, 220 (Thornell, 1994); Dyncorp Wallops Flight Facility, 101 LA 1033, 1036 (Jones, 1993); Hacienda Health Care, Inc., 101 LA 550, 552 (Levy, 1993).

[24]Ardco, Inc., 108 LA 326, 330 (Wolff, 1997) (employer who objected to timeliness of grievance for first time at arbitration hearing waived that objection); Georgia Pacific Corp., 107 LA 182, 184–85 (Cocalis, 1996) (employer waived timeliness defense which it did not raise until day before hearing). But compare Trinity Industries, Inc., 107 LA 417, 420–24 (Poole, 1996) (employer did not waive right to challenge timeliness of grievance despite one year delay in raising issue).

[25]NLRB v. Weingarten, 402 U.S. 251, 95 S. Ct. 959, 963, 88 LRRM 2689, 2691 (1975).

[26]Henry Ford Health Sys., 320 NLRB 1153, 1154, 152 LRRM 1033, 1033–34, (1996).

[27]Id. at 1154–55, 152 LRRM 1034–35.

[28]Baton Rouge Water Works Co., 246 NLRB 995, 103 LRRM 1056 (1979).

[29]American Arbitration Assoc., No. 13-CA-34009, 1997 NLRB LEXIS 194 at 8 (NLRB March 20, 1997).

[30]Frank v. Department of Transp. Federal Aviation Admin., 35 F.3d 1554, 1559–60 (Fed. Cir. 1994).

[31]U.S. Postal Serv., 314 NLRB 227, 146 LRRM 1222 (1994). See also Anchorage Hilton Hotel, 102 LA 55, 58 (Landau, 1993) (absent a showing of prejudice resulting from *Weingarten* violation, it is not appropriate to overturn disciplinary action, but rather more appropriate to take the violation into account as a mitigating factor in reviewing the disciplinary penalty imposed).

Weingarten and its progeny have gained general acceptance among arbitrators who typically find *Weingarten* protections implicit in the just cause standard contained in many collective bargaining agreements.[32] According to one arbitrator, employees in such cases are still entitled to "their day in court" where the employer must prove the agreement has been violated, and as a result, the employee shall not be denied basic procedural rights.[33] However, arbitrators will not decide *Weingarten* issues where the NLRB is involved and has not deferred to the arbitrator.[34]

Following the Board's lead, arbitrators have also found that where the contract is silent about union representation during predisciplinary investigations and interviews, an employee's right to representation may be limited to instances when the employee specifically requests union assistance and the meeting's purpose is not merely to inform the employee of disciplinary already decided upon. It should be noted, however, that even if discipline is not necessarily decided upon when an employee is working under a last chance agreement, *Weingarten* protections apply.[35]

Weingarten does not apply during a police interview in which the employer was not allowed to participate,[36] nor does the *Weingarten* doctrine allow employees to refuse to answer an employer's questions regarding the investigation.[37] However, an employee is allowed *Weingarten* representation if asked to sign documents that could possibly damage the employee's position, where the request to sign is accompanied by threats of discipline for failure to do so.[38]

Grievance Adjustment by Individual Employees

Much has been written concerning statutory rights in grievance adjustment and arbitration, and concerning the employee's right to fair representation.[39]

---

[32]Union Tank Car Co., 104 LA 699, 703 (Fullmer, 1995).

[33]Lenzing Fibers Corp., 105 LA 423, 428 (Sergent, 1995) (employees under last chance agreements are nevertheless entitled to their "day in court").

[34]Simkins Indus., Inc., 106 LA 551, 557–58 (Fullmer, 1996); Norfolk Shipbuilding & Drydock Corp., 105 LA 529, 533 (Hockenberry, 1995).

[35]Trendler Metal Prods., 101 LA 749, 756 (Green, 1993). See also Eaglebudd Enters., Inc., 106 LA 659, 661–62 (Franckiewicz, 1996). But compare S and J Ranch, 103 LA 350, 361–62 (Bogue, 1994) (language in contract expressly placed burden on employer to ensure union representative was present in appropriate cases, even if the employee does not specifically make a request).

[36]Briggs & Stratton Corp., 107 LA 1023, 1029–30 (Briggs, 1997).

[37]AT & T, 102 LA 931, 934–35 (Kanner, 1994).

[38]Ralphs Grocery Co., 101 LA 634, 638–39 (Ross, 1993).

[39]See e.g. Van Wezel Stone, "Mandatory Arbitration of Individual Employment Rights: The Yellow Dog Contract of the 1990s," 73 Denv. U. L. Rev. 1017 (1996); Ware, "Employment Arbitration and Voluntary Consent," 25 Hofstra L. Rev. 83 (Fall 1996).

Duty of Fair Representation

In decisions following *Bowen v. United States,*[40] various courts of appeal have continued to give union representatives considerable leeway in the processing and presentation of grievances.[41] However, where a union failed to interview and call the one witness who could have effectively and objectively corroborated the grievant's testimony on a vital matter, the court found that the union breached its duty of fair representation.[42]

Although the Supreme Court has not yet revisited *O'Neill's*[43] holding that *Vaca's* tripartite standard for finding a breach of duty of fair representation applies to contract negotiation as well as administration, lower courts have applied *O'Neill* using the *Vaca* tripartite standard to examine the union's handling of grievances,[44] contract negotiation,[45] the administration of union security clauses,[46] and even the implementation of an arbitral award.[47] However, one court has determined that the analysis used in *O'Neill* does not apply to the operation of a hiring hall.[48]

Privileges and Protection of Grievance Representatives

In order to facilitate the operation of the grievance machinery, labor agreements frequently give special privileges and immunities to union grievance representatives. Subject to restraints imposed by

---

[40]459 U.S. 212, 103 S. Ct. 588, 112 LRRM 2281 (1983).

[41]Pegump v. Rockwell Int'l. Corp., 109 F.3d 442, 444, 154 LRRM 2816, 2818 (8th Cir. 1997); Young v. UAW-LETC, 95 F.3d 992, 996–98, 153 LRRM 2198, 2200–02 (10th Cir. 1996); Ayala v. Union De Tronquistas De Puerto Rico, Local 901, 74 F.3d 344, 345–46, 151 LRRM 2298, 2299 (1st Cir. 1996); Conkle v. Jeong, 73 F.3d 909, 915, 151 LRRM 2065, 2067–68 (9th Cir. 1995); Cleveland v. Porca Co., 38 F.3d 289, 295–96, 147 LRRM 2385, 2388–89 (7th Cir. 1994); VanDerVeer v. United Parcel Serv., Inc., 25 F.3d 403, 405–06, 146 LRRM 2890, 2891–92 (6th Cir. 1994).

[42]Black v. Ryder/P.I.E. Nationwide, Inc., 15 F.3d 573, 585, 145 LRRM 2387, 2396–97, (6th Cir. 1994). See also Cruz v. IBEW, Local No. 3, 34 F.3d 1148, 1153–54, 147 LRRM 2176, 2181 (2d Cir. 1994) (union acted arbitrarily when it failed to conduct investigations into validity of complaints).

[43]Airline Pilots v. O'Neill, 111 S. Ct. 1127, 136 LRRM 2721 (1991).

[44]Young v. UAW-LETC, 95 F.3d 992, 153 LRRM 2198 (10th Cir. 1996); Black v. Ryder/P.I.E. Nationwide, Inc., 15 F.3d 573, 145 LRRM 2387 (6th Cir. 1994).

[45]Griffin v. Air Line Pilots Assn., Int'l, 32 F.3d 1079, 146 LRRM 3092 (7th Cir. 1994).

[46]Nielson v. International Ass'n of Machinists, Local Lodge 2569, 94 F.3d 1107, 153 LRRM 2161 (7th Cir. 1996), cert. denied, 520 U.S. 1165, 117 S. Ct. 1426 (1997), International Union of Electronic Workers v. NLRB, 41 F.3d 1532, 148 LRRM 2070 (D.C. Cir. 1994). See also California Saw and KnifeWorks, 320 NLRB 224, 151 LRRM 1121 (1995), modified on other grounds, 321 NLRB 731, 152 LRRM 1241 (1996).

[47]NIDA v. Plant Protection Ass'n. Nat'l, 7 F.3d 522, 144 LRRM 2530 (6th Cir. 1993).

[48]Plumbers Local No. 32 v. NLRB, 50 F.3d 24, 33–34, 148 LRRM 2833, 2837 (D.C. Cir. 1995) (finding that unions wield increased power when they are acting as employers in the operation of a hiring hall, the standard for determining whether a union acting as an employer breached its duty of fair representation should be lowered to "a high standard of fair dealing.").

courts and arbitrators, these contractual protections serve to ensure the union's ability to handle grievances and administer the contract. Some arbitration decisions also provide disciplinary immunity to grievance representatives for their performing grievance handling and administration.[49]

Superseniority

Although the underlying purpose of superseniority provisions is most often to assure the fullest possible union representation by experienced representatives, there is considerable arbitrable authority limiting superseniority benefits to rights and privileges clearly protected by the agreement.[50]

Furthermore, the Board's decisions in *Dairylea*[51] and *Gulton*[52] have limited the reach of superseniority provisions. *Dairylea* provides that provisions which are not on their face limited to layoff and recall are presumptively invalid, and the burden of rebutting that presumption rests on the party asserting their lawfulness.[53] *Gulton* provides that officers not involved in grievance processing or other on-the-job agreement administration should not have received superseniority.[54]

The presumed illegality of a superseniority clause not limited to layoff and recall may be rebutted by showing that having the same steward on the job furthers effective administration of the labor agreement.[55]

Arbitrators have, however, permitted layoff of union stewards where they would have been retained in an area they didn't previously represent,[56] or where they would have bumped a more senior employee from a different classification.[57]

---

[49]Comparable protections may exist for employer grievance representatives. However, union fines of member-supervisors with no collective bargaining or grievance handling responsibility do not violate the NLRA. NLRB v. Sheet Metal Workers, Local 104, 64 F.3d 465, 150 LRRM 2071 (9th Cir. 1995); Sheet Metal Workers, Local 33, 316 NLRB 504, 148 LRRM 1277 (1995).

[50]Matanuska Elec. Ass'n., 107 LA 402, 407 (Landau, 1996) (alternate shop steward not protected from layoff under contract provision that only allows for retention of one shop steward); Walker Mfg. Co., 106 LA 1075, 1080 (Dichter, 1996) (while considering the purpose of superseniority clauses, the arbitrator must look first and foremost to the provisions of the agreement). See also, Amerimark Bldg. Prods., 104 LA 1066, 1070 (Klein, 1995); Masolite Concrete Prods., 103 LA 10, 15 (Keenan 1994); USS-Fairless Works, 102 LA 810, 812–13 (Petersen, 1994).

[51]Dairylea Coop., Inc., 219 NLRB 656, 89 LRRM 1737 (1975), enforced sub nom. NLRB v. Milk Drivers, Local 338, 531 F.2d 1162 (2nd Cir. 1976).

[52]Gulton Electro-Voice, Inc., 266 NLRB 406, 112 LRRM 1361 (1983), enforced sub nom. Int'l Union of Electrical Workers, Local 900 v. NLRB, 727 F.2d 1184 (D.C. Cir. 1984).

[53]Dairylea, at 658, 89 LRRM at 1738–39.

[54]Gulton, at 409–10, 112 LRRM at 1364–65.

[55]Goodyear Tire & Rubber Co., 322 NLRB 1007, 154 LRRM 1119 (1997).

[56]Masolite Concrete Prods., 103 LA 10, 15 (Keenan, 1994).

[57]Walker Mfg. Co., 106 LA 1075, 1079 (Dichter, 1996).

Special Immunity

Many arbitrators have recognized that union stewards have some immunity against discipline for their actions in performing union duties, especially where great potential exists for disrupting labor-management relations.[58] Many disciplinary actions are set aside or reduced because the "cause" for the discipline (often abusive language in heated exchanges with supervisors) emerged from or was related to union steward duties.[59] However, many arbitrators uphold discipline against stewards in extreme situations, even though the basis for the discipline was related to the employee's conduct as steward.[60]

The cases considering disciplinary immunity for stewards are very fact specific, with various lines of arbitral thought. Arbitrators have been reluctant to uphold discipline of union stewards engaged in grievance representation if it interferes with the union's grievance handling responsibilities. Where an employer suspended an employee acting as a union representative for using profanity during a meeting as well as causing damage to a door by slamming it, the arbitrator found the suspension without just cause because the representative had not intended to damage the door and was merely expressing his adamant opposition to the company's position.[61]

While steward conduct in the course of union business is protected, the immunity is not absolute. One arbitrator upheld the termination of a union steward who had disobeyed his supervisor's direct orders, causing $2000 in damage to company machinery.[62] In another case the arbitrator reinstated a terminated union steward, but without back pay or benefits, finding that the employee's record

---

[58]Tennsco Corp., 107 LA 689, 692–93 (Nicholas, Jr., 1996) (Decisions of Arbitrators recognize that Union Stewards, representing fellow employees in grievance meetings, are entitled to equal stature with Management and may not be subjected to disciplinary action when using 'ungentlemanly' language in the course of their representation. . . . 'The very nature of the collective bargaining process is that an employee who is designated as Union representative must be free to discuss Union matters as though he were not a Company employee. Otherwise, an employee would be inhibited in the performance of his duties as a Union representative, by fear of discipline for the use of strong language.' . . . Undeniably, the use of 'liar' was a bad choice of words. However, I do not find that such choice of words was either egregious or malicious.").

[59]See Arbitrator Nicholas in Tennsco Corp., 107 LA 689, 693 (1996); Cipolla in P.Q. Corp., 106 LA 381, 384 (1996).

[60]See Arbitrator Brodsky in Converters Paperboard Co., 108 LA 149, 154–56 (1997); see Arbitrator Murphy in Mid-West Chandelier Co., 102 LA 833 (1994) (union steward/bargaining committee member properly suspended for statements to employees concerning management discriminatory motive even though steward was acting in committee member capacity by informing employees of status of negotiations where there was no support for statements nor evidence of anti-union animus); Cocalis in Overhead Door Corp., 101 LA 610, 612–13 (1993).

[61]P.Q. Corp., 106 LA 381, 384 (Cipolla, 1996).

[62]Bermuda Dunes Country Club, 104 LA 1082, 1086 (Darrow, 1995).

of absences warranted some discipline, and that steward status does not prevent discipline for nonunion activities.[63]

Pay for Grievance Time

Some arbitrators have held that past practice should determine whether grievance handling time is compensable where the agreement is silent or ambiguous.[64] One arbitrator held that past practice entitled the union representatives to compensation not only for time spent on processing grievances, but also for time spent conducting general union business, even though such compensation was not expressly authorized in the contract.[65]

Written Statement of Grievance

There are various reasons why the general practice is that grievances should be presented in writing at an early stage of the grievance procedure. The written complaint establishes a record of the grievance. By putting the grievance in writing, it is less likely to become distorted while being processed through the grievance procedure.[66] Additionally, written grievances without merit are often dropped.

The discussion of grievances not filed in writing when required by the labor agreement can waive the "written grievance" requirement.[67]

---

[63]Kasle Steel Corp., 107 LA 1006, 1009–1010 (Kerner, 1996). See also National Linen Supply, 107 LA 4 (Ross 1996); Sheridan Health Care Center, 106 LA 1125 (Draznin, 1996); Tyson Foods, Inc., 105 LA 1119 (Moore, 1996).

[64]Morton Salt, 104 LA 444, 446 (Fullmer, 1995); Motor Wheel Corp., 102 LA 922, 930–31 (Chattman, 1994).

[65]Motor Wheel Corp., 102 LA at 930–31 (1994).

[66]For a related discussion, see Chapter 7 topic entitled "Extent of Permissible Deviation from Prearbitral Discussion of Case."

[67]See Arbitrator Cohen in Western Textile Prods., 107 LA 539, 546–47 (1996); Jacobs in Wisconsin Tissue Mills, 102 LA 601, 604–05 (1994).

Chapter 6

Determining Arbitrability

[There were no significant developments relating
to this chapter.]

Chapter 7

Arbitration Procedures and Techniques

Source of Procedural Rules

Control of Arbitration Proceedings

In order to ensure a fair hearing, arbitrators have prohibited the admission of evidence when a party failed to furnish a list of proposed witnesses and exhibits sufficiently in advance of the arbitration as required by the collective bargaining agreement,[1] and have prohibited the admission of an affidavit tendered by a party after the arbitration hearing.[2]

The increasing number of arbitrations in the nonunion context has given rise to a corresponding increase in arbitration procedures where the grievant, and not a union, is the party in interest vis-à-vis the employer. Because the grievant's advocate in these proceedings is more likely than in traditional union-management arbitration to be inexperienced or an employee of the same employer, the arbitrator may need to take a more active role to ensure that the grievant is afforded due process under the proceedings.[3]

Professor David Rudenstine has suggested that the trend of submitting statutory claims to arbitration, such as those arising under Title VII of the Civil Rights Act of 1964, may make arbitration more costly, increase the length of time from when a demand for arbitration is submitted until the time of award, make arbitration more for-

---

[1]Simmons Indus., 101 LA 1201, 1204–05 (Stephens, 1993).

[2]Grace Indus. Inc., 1102 LA 119, 122–23 (Knott, 1993).

[3]Gerhart, "The Changing Competitive Environment and Arbitration," Proceedings of the 46th Annual Meeting of NAA, 24, 33 (BNA Books, 1994).

mal and adversarial, and subject arbitration awards to more searching judicial review.[4]

Initiating Arbitration: Submission Versus Arbitration Clause

The untimely selection of an arbitrator under the terms of a collective bargaining agreement has been held not to preclude arbitration where neither party was the sole cause of the tardy selection.[5] Use of the term "may" in connection with required timelines for submitting a case to arbitration has been held to apply to the fact that the parties have a choice as to whether they will submit a case to arbitration, not as to whether they must observe the mandatory timelines for such submission.[6] Arbitrators continue to recognize that when an agreement does not specifically require written notice of intent to arbitrate, oral notice is sufficient.[7]

Stating the Issue

Although the courts generally give the same deference to an arbitrator's interpretation of the scope of the issue submitted as they give to the arbitrator's interpretation of the collective bargaining agreement, they can and do decline enforcement of awards if the arbitrator exceeds his or her authority by arbitrating issues not submitted by the parties.[8]

Simultaneous Arbitration of Several Grievances

At least one arbitrator has held that if the parties intend that more than one grievance be arbitrated at a time, the agreement should provide for the arbitration of "disputes" rather than the arbitration of "a dispute."[9]

---

[4]Rudenstine, "The Impact on the Arbitration Process of Arbitrating Statutory Claims," Proceedings of New York University 46th Annual National Conference on Labor, 249–66 (Little, Brown, 1994).

[5]Martin-Brower Co., 102 LA 673 (Dilts, 1994).

[6]Trinity Indus., Inc., 109 LA 86, 94 (Oberstein, 1997).

[7]Id. at 95.

[8]Madison Hotel v. Hotel & Restaurant Employees Local 25, 128 F.3d 743, 156 LRRM 2801 (D.C. Cir. 1997).

[9]Heekin Can, Inc., 101 LA 130, 133–34 (Feldman, 1993) (although the agreement allowed no more than one grievance to be arbitrated at a time, it did not prohibit the same arbitrator from hearing the various grievances in succession).

Extent of Permissible Deviation From
Prearbitral Discussion of Case

Even where the collective bargaining agreement requires specific identification of the provision that covers the grievance, arbitrators will rarely hold that the grievance is not arbitrable because of the union's failure in this regard if the employer has not been misled as to the nature of the dispute.[10]

Representatives in Arbitration

The right of grievants to be represented in arbitration proceedings by persons of their own choosing has been held to include the right to choose a union representative in arbitrating a dispute with a nonunion employer.[11]

Privilege to Attend Hearing

Limiting Attendance by Witnesses

An arbitrator's order that witnesses at an arbitration hearing be sequestered requires only that they be absent from the hearing room during the testimony of other witnesses; it does not prevent the witnesses from meeting to discuss the case during breaks in the arbitration.[12]

Default Awards in Ex Parte Proceedings

Where the collective bargaining agreement provided for default in favor of the grievant if the employer failed to comply with the time limits in the grievance steps and if the remedy requested was legal and reasonable under the circumstances, the arbitrator held that even though the employer's actions were not timely, he could not make a determination on whether the remedy requested was legal and reasonable under the circumstances without a hearing on the merits.[13]

---

[10]Kliklok Corp., 102 LA 183, 185 (Frost, 1993). *But see* International Paper Co., 108 LA 758, 764–65 (Nicholas, 1997) (union prevailed on the merits but was denied consequential damages because they were not requested in the grievance as required by the collective bargaining agreement).

[11]Ogden Servs. Corp., 107 LA 696, 698–99 (Lipson, 1996).

[12]Anderson Concrete Corp., 103 LA 433, 438 (Kindig, 1994).

[13]Department of Veteran Affairs, VA Medical Ctr., 101 LA 731, 735 (Curry, 1993). The arbitrator also held "that the matter involved in the instant grievance is not the type of case that the parties intended when they provided for default winning in cases where time limits were violated. This case deals with a subject matter and allegations far too important to be resolved on [a] technical procedural basis." Id.

Court Enforcement of Default Awards

Where the arbitrator entered a default award in the union's favor and ordered reinstatement of employees replaced with those from another company represented by a different union, the district court order vacating the award was upheld because the affected employees were not covered by the collective bargaining agreement and the arbitrator accordingly had no power to adjudicate the dispute.[14]

When an arbitrator refused to hear evidence from an employer before rendering a decision, the award was vacated. Although the arbitrator initially concluded that the employer had willfully failed to appear, the employer notified the arbitrator one day after the hearing that it had not been given adequate notice. The arbitrator declined to reopen the hearing. The U.S. district court held that the arbitrator had violated the Federal Arbitration Act by refusing to hear "pertinent and material" evidence bearing on the issue of whether the employer had just cause to terminate the employee.[15]

When an arbitrator granted a default award in favor of the union due to the employer's refusal to attend the hearing, the court of appeals affirmed the district court's grant of summary judgment vacating the award upon finding that the collective bargaining agreement did not cover the employees of an independent contractor. The arbitrator had no power to adjudicate the dispute.[16]

Where the agreement conditioned default on finding that the requested remedy was "legal and reasonable under the circumstances," the determination required a hearing on the merits. The award was not sustained despite the employer's untimely response to the grievance since the subject matter was too important to be resolved on a technical procedural basis.[17]

The Ohio Court of Appeals affirmed the dismissal of a union's action for enforcement of grievances that the union argued was automatically granted because of the employer's failure to comply with various procedural requirements in the grievance process. The court held that the lower court lacked subject matter jurisdiction because the union had not proceeded to arbitration, and the default award could be enforced.[18]

---

[14]Bevona v. 820 Second Ave. Assocs., 27 F.3d 37, 146 LRRM 2673 (2d Cir. 1994).

[15]Kaplan v. Alfred Dunhill of London, Inc., 156 LRRM 2080 (S.D.N.Y. 1996).

[16]Bevona v. 820 Second Avenue Assocs., 146 LRRM 2673 (2d Cir. 1994). Compare Coca-Cola Bottling Co. of New York, Inc. v. International Bhd. of Teamsters Local Union 1035, 156 LRRM 2223 (D. Conn., 1997) (court upheld award finding that arbitrator did not exceed his authority because employee's falsification of documents was not just cause for dismissal).

[17]Department of Veteran Affairs, VA Medical Ctr., 101 LA 731 (Curry, 1973).

[18]Local Educ. Ass'n v. North Central Local Sch. Dist. Bd. Educ., 155 LRRM 2511 (Ohio Ct. App., 1996) (trial court lacked jurisdiction to confirm default award because grievance did not constitute arbitration award).

Withdrawal of Cases From Arbitration

Arbitrator's Charges When Cause Is Cancelled

Where the parties reached an oral settlement agreement and the union's attorney paid the arbitrator's cancellation fee, the arbitrator held that the settlement agreement was not binding because the union rejected the employer's written memorial of the settlement agreement and the union was not aware that its attorney had paid the arbitrator's cancellation fee.[19]

Split Hearings

Arbitrator's Express Retention of Jurisdiction

The practice by arbitrators of retaining jurisdiction to ensure that their awards are properly carried out and to resolve subsequent disagreements between the parties with respect thereto remains common.[20] At least one arbitral opinion has held that the arbitrator's retention of jurisdiction does not allow modification of a prior award unless reconsideration has been properly requested under governing statutes and the Arbitrator's Code of Professional Responsibility of Labor Management Disputes.[21]

Also, arbitrators can exceed the scope of their jurisdiction both by deviating from the issues submitted for arbitration and by issuing an award that does not draw its essence from the parties' agreement.[22]

Transcript of Hearing

Arbitrators will generally allow a party to tape-record the arbitration hearing over the other party's objection in the absence of any

---

[19]Williams Furnace Co., 107 LA 215 (Monat, 1996).

[20]See, e.g., Weyerhaeuser Co. Forest Prods., 108 LA 26, 32 (Levak, 1997) (arbitrator retained jurisdiction to resolve any disagreement between the parties concerning the amount of back pay or benefits due); Waukesha Engine Div., 103 LA 696, 700 (Redel, 1994) (arbitrator retained jurisdiction for a period of 30 days to implement his award if requested, despite union's statement that the parties could work out the remedy after arbitrator found a contract violation when the employer failed to pay first-shift maintenance employees for their 15-minute lunch period); Young's Commercial Transfer Inc., 101 LA 993 (McCurdy, 1993) (arbitrator who retained jurisdiction to resolve disputes arising from the calculation of back pay subsequently interpreted contract to require payment of pension contributions as part of back pay); Hexcel Corp., 101 LA 700, 703 (Silver, 1993) (arbitrator retained jurisdiction in the event the parties could not agree on the calculation of amounts due to employees as the remedy for the company's improper subcontracting of work).

[21]World Jai-Alai, 104 LA 1157, 1163 (Haemmel, 1995).

[22]Madison Hotel v. Hotel & Restaurant Employees Local 25, 154 LRRM 2031 (D.D.C., 1996).

contract provision barring the practice, where the tapes are not part of the record and duplicates of the tapes are made available to the objecting party.[23]

Settlements at Arbitration Stage

At virtually any point in the arbitration process one or both of the parties may invite the arbitrator to mediate. Whether or not the arbitrator mediates the dispute absent a contractual requirement depends on the noninviting party's agreement and the agreement of the arbitrator.[24]

Reopening the Hearing

One arbitrator held that in order to reopen a hearing to receive new evidence:

> [The] evidence must (a) be of a nature that is material to the outcome of the case, (b) [be] unavailable at the time of the hearing, (c) not seriously affect the rights of the other party, and (d) [show] that reasonable grounds existed for the nonproduction at the time of the hearing.[25]

The arbitrator applied these standards in denying the union's request to reopen the hearing to determine whether an employer's videotape admitted into evidence had been edited. The union had been furnished with a copy of the videotape when the grievance was initially filed and had it in its possession for several months prior to the three-day hearing. The videotape was played numerous times at the hearing and was the subject of meticulous direct and cross-examination by the union's attorney. There was a twelve-day recess between the second and third day of the hearing, but the issue of the tape's being edited was not raised until the union's posthearing brief was submitted 61 days after the hearing, and no explanation for the union's delay in raising the issue was given.[26]

Clarification or Interpretation of Award

After receiving a letter from the company's attorney asking him to reconsider and/or clarify his decision and award and receiving a

---

[23]See, e.g., Allsteel, Inc., 101 LA 1187, 1192 n.5 (Wolff, 1993).

[24]Kagel, "Mediating Grievances," Proceedings of the 46th Annual Meeting of NAA, 77 (BNA Books, 1994). John Kagel offers various suggestions and considerations for the arbitrator's acting as grievance mediator, with comments from management's perspective offered by Nancy Cornelius House and additional comments from Daniel Ish. Id. at 80–103.

[25]Tyson Foods, Inc., 105 LA 1119, 1121 (Moore, 1996).

[26]Id.

letter from the union's attorney asking for clarification on the compu-
tation of back wages, the arbitrator modified his prior award to include additional lost earnings to compensate the grievant for the
company's failure to forthwith reinstate her.[27]

Remedy Power and Its Use

Scope of Remedy Power

Many collective bargaining agreements leave a "gaping void" on
the topic of arbitral remedies.[28] One method of determining the appropriate remedy when an agreement does not address the arbitrator's
remedial power is through the application of gap-filling rules that
have developed over time. One such rule suggests that the arbitrator
assess remedial needs of the parties against the backdrop of the legal
context in which the agreement came into existence.[29] As noted by
Professor David Feller, another rule suggests that "unless the contrary is stated in the agreement . . . the primary authority implicitly
granted to the arbitrator is the authority to award specific performance of the provisions of the agreement.[30] In some instances the
arbitrator will remand the case to the parties for them to negotiate a
remedy.[31]

Arbitrators are generally not given contractual authority to order the discipline of supervisors or to award damages for pain and
suffering.[32] Arbitrators also generally do not have authority to grant
remedies that are in the nature of punitive damages.[33] Some collec-

---

[27]Democratic Printing & Lithographing Co., 103 LA 330 (Weisbrod, 1994).

[28]See generally Snow, "Informing the Silent Remedial Gap," Proceedings of the 48th
Annual Meeting of NAA, 150, 152 (BNA Books, 1996).

[29]Id. at 158 ("By taking into account the legal context in which the parties created
their agreement, an arbitrator comes closer to understanding expectations of the parties with regard to fashioning an appropriate remedy. The agreement emerged from the
parties' legal-economic relationship, and arbitral remedies should be fashioned within
that same context"). With respect to the application of external law to arbitration and
mediation, see Appendix B, "A Due Process Protocol for Mediation and Arbitration of
Statutory Disputes Arising Out of the Employment Relationship," Proceedings of the
48th Annual Meeting of NAA, 298–304 (BNA Books, 1996).

[30]Snow, supra note 28, at 161 (quoting Feller, "Remedies in Arbitration: Old Problems Revisited," Proceedings of the 34th Annual Meeting of NAA, 109, 116 (BNA Books,
1982)). Professor Feller characterizes arbitral monetary awards as compensation to the
grievant for the time gap between the contract breach and the award of specific performance requiring adherence to the contract's terms. Snow at 161–62; Feller at 116–18.

[31]See, e.g., Los Angeles County MTA, 108 LA 301, 304–5 (Gentile, 1997); American
Red Cross, 104 LA 68 (Garrett, 1995).

[32]See, e.g., Union Camp Corp., 104 LA 295, 300–02 (Nolan, 1995).

[33]See, e.g., Ralphs Grocery Co., 108 LA 718, 723 (Prayzich, 1997); Stone Container
Corp., 102 LA 219, 220 (Thornell, 1994). But see Tennessee Valley Authority, 101 LA
218, 226 (Bankston, 1993).

tive bargaining agreements provide that if the arbitrator finds a party had no reasonable grounds for its position in the arbitration, that party may be ordered to pay the arbitrator's fee.[34]

Reinstatement with back pay is a common remedy in discharge cases when the grievance is sustained. One arbitrator has held that the arbitrator's authority to order reinstatement with back pay also includes the authority to order lesser included remedies.[35]

Common Errors in Arbitration

Whether arbitration can or should be used for a "therapeutic" effect on the labor-management relationship, rather than simply to resolve a labor dispute pursuant to contract, is hotly debated.[36]

---

[34]H. Meyer Dairy Co., 105 LA 583, 588–89 (Sugerman, 1995). See also Community Counseling Ctr., Inc., 101 LA 1213, 1217 (Feldman, 1993) (arbitrator ordered his fee to be split between the parties despite loser-pay clause, where union prevailed on procedural issue and employer prevailed on merit issue).

[35]Mason & Hangar-Silas Mason Co. Inc., 103 LA 371, 378 (Cipolla, 1994) (arbitrator awarded back pay with no reinstatement).

[36]Abrams, Abrams, & Nolan, "Arbitral Therapy," with comments by McKendree & Schoeberlein, Proceedings of the 46th Annual Meeting of NAA, 269–89 (BNA Books, 1994).

Chapter 8

Evidence

Requiring the Production of Evidence

Use of Subpoenas

Where management failed to subpoena a witness, claiming that three days was insufficient to do so, the arbitrator ruled that sufficient time did exist and, if it had not, management could have asked for a continuance.[1]

Significance of Failure to Provide Evidence

Where a company built most of its case around oral and written reports by the key witness and then the company failed to call the key witness during arbitration, the arbitrator held that the omission of such testimony substantially weakened the credibility of critical pieces of evidence in the company's case.[2] The arbitrator stated that, by not calling the key witness, the company had deprived the union of the opportunity to cross-examine the witness and authenticate the written reports.[3]

In a situation involving a grievant's discharge for failing to timely submit to random alcohol testing, the grievant made a prearbitral allegation that he had repeatedly reminded his dispatcher of the pressing test obligation. The grievant further alleged that he received numerous additional pick up assignments from the dispatcher and that this contributed to his delay in reporting to the testing clinic. The employer, despite its knowledge of this allegation, failed to call this

---

[1]Indiana Gas. Co., 109 LA 116 (Imundo, 1997).
[2]Cal-Compack Foods, 105 LA 865 (Oestreich, 1995).
[3]Id.

particular dispatcher as a witness. The arbitrator held that the company's failure to call this witness created both a significant question as to whether the dispatcher would have confirmed the grievant's claims and an adverse inference against the company's overall position in the matter.[4]

Failure of Grievant to Testify

The right to assert the Fifth Amendment where there is a potential criminal issue is a constitutionally guaranteed right that an arbitrator must recognize in a public-sector case. In one case, the grievant, who was a police officer, refused to testify in the city's case on the grounds that the testimony might incriminate him.[5] After the city put on its case, the grievant took the stand, thereby waiving his Fifth Amendment right, and he was cross-examined.[6] The arbitrator held that it was irrelevant to the city's defense that the grievant had used the Fifth Amendment as a strategy to hear the city's case before testifying.[7]

Failure of a grievant to testify when discharged after his larceny conviction justified the arbitrator's drawing an adverse inference that the facts were credible to establish the misconduct.[8] In another case, the arbitrator held that although failure of a grievant to testify does not automatically set up a negative inference, the failure of the grievant to call any witnesses at all in his case allowed the arbitrator to determine that the company's case was unrebutted.[9]

The Lie Detector

Some arbitrators reject lie detector test results totally. They do so on the basis that it is the arbitrator's duty as the fact-finder to determine the credibility of the witnesses and because the reliability of lie detector test results is still in question by the scientific community. Other arbitrators draw a distinction between exculpatory findings and negative results. Even if the arbitrator allows exculpatory findings into evidence, the polygraph report is not allowed without voir dire or an opportunity to cross-examine the expert.[10] Where the polygraph test giver was not called as a witness, the report was not admitted into evidence.[11] The arbitrator rejected the report on the

---

[4]Advance Transportation Co., 105 LA 1089 (Briggs, 1995).
[5]City of Youngstown, 107 LA 588 (Skulina, 1996).
[6]Id. at 590.
[7]Id.
[8]City of Saginaw, 108 LA 188 (Daniel, 1997).
[9]Michigan Employment Sec. Agency, 109 LA 178 (Brodsky, 1997).
[10]City of Youngstown, 107 LA 588 (Skulina, 1996).
[11]Id.

grounds that the union had had no opportunity to cross-examine the expert and the arbitrator lacked sufficient testimony to qualify the witness's statement as expert testimony.[12]

Circumstantial Evidence

Arbitrators frequently decide cases on the basis of circumstantial evidence.[13] One arbitrator has explained:

> It is not unusual for an arbitrator to decide cases based on circumstantial evidence. To consider circumstantial evidence the arbitrator looks to see if the Grievant is affirmatively linked with the offense or omission, but this link need not be so strong that it excludes every other outstanding reasonable hypothesis. If the evidence presented by an employer makes out a *prima facie* case of guilt, it then places the burden of proof on the Grievant to offer rebuttal evidence.[14]

Consideration of Postdischarge Evidence

As a general rule, the determination of whether there was just cause for a discharge is judged on the facts known to the decision maker at the time the discharge determination was made. However, arbitrators frequently admit both postdischarge evidence and evidence of postdischarge conduct.[15] One arbitrator allowed after-acquired evidence of a second instance of the grievant's misconduct that resulted in his discharge because the grounds were no different from those upon which the discharge was predicated.[16] However, a second arbitrator rejected such after-acquired evidence, observing that the discharge "must rise or fall" based upon facts as they were known at the time of the termination.[17] While the postdischarge discovery of false statements on employment applications has been ruled an insufficient reason to dismiss grievances without reaching their merits, such information may be of value in the determination of an appropriate remedy.[18]

---

[12]Id.

[13]Kroger Co., 108 LA 229 (Frockt, 1997); American National Can Co., 105 LA 812 (Moore, 1995); Atlantic Southeast Airlines, 103 LA 1179 (Nolan, 1994): Exxon Co. U.S.A., 101 LA 777 (Baroni, 1993).

[14]American National Can Co., 105 LA 812, 816 (Moore, 1995).

[15]For a general analysis of this subject, see Nicolau, "The Arbitrator's Remedial Powers," Proceedings of the 43rd Annual Meeting of NAA, 73 (BNA Books, 1990).

[16]Bill Kay Chevrolet, 107 LA 302 (Wolff, 1996). See also AT&T, 102 LA 937, 940 (Kanner, 1994), where grievant was allowed to introduce evidence at the arbitration hearing that he did not disclose prior to his discharge.

[17]Safeway, Inc., 105 LA 718, 722 (Goldberg, 1995).

[18]Lenox Hill Hospital, 102 LA 1071 (Simons, 1994). See also McKennon v. Nashville Banner Publishing Co., 513 U.S. 352, 130 L.Ed. 2d 852, 115 S. Ct. 879, 66 FEP Cases 1192 (1995), for consideration of this issue in the context of a claim under the Age Discrimination in Employment Act of 1967.

A grievant's postdischarge misconduct was allowed as evidence that he was the aggressor in the assault leading to his discharge but was disallowed in considering the merits of his discharge or in determining an appropriate remedy.[19]

Evidence Obtained by Allegedly Improper Methods

As noted in the main volume, the views of arbitrators as to the use of evidence obtained in a reprehensible or distasteful manner may differ significantly. However, the inclination to accept and rely upon it appears to be fairly strong. One arbitrator allowed into evidence internal management documents, which the company contended were strictly confidential and the union failed to specifically explain its possession of, for the purpose of providing background information. The parties had a highly informal relationship, and it was not uncommon for documents prepared for internal consumption by one party to be obtained by the other.[20] Another arbitrator allowed into evidence videotapes of the grievant having sex with her supervisor in the hotel's banquet office. He found that the participants did not have a reasonable expectation of privacy under the circumstances.[21]

Testimony by Persons From Outside

Opinion Evidence by Expert Witnesses

A counselor's opinion that grievant, who was discharged for drug activity that occurred two years prior to his discharge, was likely to continue in drug-related activities once released from an alternative housing facility, was outweighed by grievant's 16-months' employment with the company without indication that he continued to engage in drug activity.[22]

Medical Evidence

Blood-alcohol test results have been admitted for the truth of the matter without testimony from the person administering the test where the laboratory that performed the test was independent from the employer and no issue was raised concerning chain-of-custody of the sample.[23]

---

[19]Pepsi-Cola Bottling Co., 107 LA 257 (Ross, 1996).
[20]National Steel Corp., 102 LA 1159, 1167–68 (Garrett, 1994).
[21]Wyndham Franklin Plaza Hotel, 105 LA 186 (Duff, 1995).
[22]Giant Eagle Markets Co., 101 LA 581 (Zobrak, 1993).
[23]United Parcel Service, 101 LA 589 (Briggs, 1993).

A doctor's statement that corroborated grievant's tendinitis in her arm and prohibited her from lifting heavy loads reinforced the arbitrator's conclusion that grievant did not intend to be insubordinate when she refused to do work directed by her supervisor.[24]

Protecting Witnesses

Where witnesses fear possible intimidation by the grievant or his supporters, an arbitrator does not violate the Federal Arbitration Act by keeping their identity secret until they testify.[25]

Employees will not be granted testimonial immunity in testifying about violations of their employer's attendance policy for which they were not cited.[26]

---

[24]Stockham Valve & Fittings, 102 LA 73 (Poole, 1993).
[25]Cemetery Workers & Greens Attendants Union Local 365 v. Woodlawn Cemetery, 152 LRRM 2360 (SDNY 1995).
[26]Paxar Systems Group, 102 LA 75 (La Manna, 1994).

Chapter 9

Standards for Interpreting Contract Language

Ambiguity

A "zipper" provision did not preclude consideration of extrinsic evidence in determining the intent of the word "works" under a contract clause which provided premium pay if the employee worked seven days within a workweek.[1]

Intent of the Parties

Arbitrators determine the intent of the parties from various sources, including the express language of the agreement, statements made at precontract negotiations, bargaining history, and past practice.[2]

---

[1]Spartan Stores Inc., 105 LA 549, 550 (Kanner 1995) (an issue concerning the ambiguity of contract language can always be resolved by consideration of extrinsic parol evidence).

[2]Hughes Aircraft Co., 105 LA 1187, 1192 (Concepcion, 1996) (the practice is clear, certain, consistent, repetitious, accepted, and, most important, was done by mutual agreement). But see Lockheed Aeronautical Sys. Co., 104 LA 840, 844 (Hewitt, 1995) (when the conditions that create and give rise to a past practice or working condition are modified or changed, there is no longer a basis for the practice and it fails; otherwise, any change in the benefit is subject to negotiations); Tecumseh Corrugated Box Co., 110 LA 458, 459 (Feldman, 1998) (elimination of prior practice upheld when company in contract negotiations announced it would no longer honor the practice, and company resisted the union's request to negotiate renunciation); and Crown Cork & Seal Co., 104 LA 1133, 1140 (Wolff, 1995) ("One must consider, too, the underlying circumstances which give a practice its true dimensions. A practice is no broader than the circumstances out of which it has arisen, although its scope can always be enlarged in the day-to-day administration of the agreement," quoting Arbitrator R. Mittenthal, "Past Practice and the Administration of Collective Bargaining Agreements," Proceedings of the 14th Annual Meeting of NAA, 30, 32, 33 (BNA Books, 1961).

Clear and Unambiguous Language

One arbitrator rejected the employer's argument that "while an arbitrator may grant relief for mutual mistakes, he may not do so in a case of unilateral mistake." The issue involved manning at the Kennedy Center, and the arbitrator found that both the employer and the union had made mistakes. While sustaining the grievance, he denied back pay since the union was partially responsible for the dispute.[3]

Avoidance of Harsh, Absurd, or Nonsensical Results

When one interpretation of an ambiguous contract would lead to harsh, absurd, or nonsensical results, while an alternative interpretation, equally consistent, would lead to just and reasonable results, the latter interpretation will be used.[4]

To Express One Thing Is to Exclude Another

Arbitrators frequently apply the principle that to expressly include one or more of a class in a written instrument must be taken as an exclusion of all others.[5]

Construction in Light of Context

Contract sections in dispute must be read in the context of the other sections in the agreement to establish the intent of the parties.[6]

---

[3]Kennedy Center, 101 LA 174, 178, 180 (Ables, 1993). ("Although not a mutual mistake as to the same idea, opinion or act, both parties made fundamental mistakes which produced a contract the union would never have accepted with reduced full-time positions—and the employer knew it. No such contract can stand—particularly a collective bargaining agreement.")

[4]General Elec. Co., 102 LA 261, 266 (Sugerman, 1993) (arbitrator cited general principle in *How Arbitration Works,* 354 (4th ed.) in adopting employee's interpretation of bumping provision in order to avoid a "harsh or nonsensical" result); Brown-Forman Beverage Co., 103 LA 292, 294 (Frockt, 1994) (applying "rule of reason" to ambiguous phrase "working the shift" in an attempt to bring consistency, rationality, and logic to the shift pay provision).

[5]Broughton Foods Co., 101 LA 286, 287 (Jones, 1993) (applying legal maxim in denying pay for time spent on pre-trip and post-trip inspections to hourly paid drivers); Macomb County, 96 LA 131, 133 (Glazer, 1990) (same). But see Jefferson Smurfit Corp., 102 LA 164, 166 (Duff, 1994) (recognizing the legal maxim but declining to apply it to union's contention that the naming of a specific company representative or his representative in step 3 of the grievance procedure was a limitation on the number of representatives the company could have at the grievance step meeting).

[6]WMATA, 108 LA 465, 470 (Feigenbaum, 1997) (finding that sentences should not be read in isolation but rather in concert with those surrounding them because they were part of the same thought); Spartan Stores Inc., 105 LA 549 (Kanner 1995); Giant Cement Co., 103 LA 146, 149 (Nolan, 1994); General Elec. Co., 102 LA 261, 265–266 (Sugerman, 1993).

Precontract Negotiations

Precontract negotiations frequently provide a valuable aid in the interpretation of ambiguous provisions. Where the meaning of a term is not clear, it will be deemed, if there is no evidence to the contrary, that the parties intended it to have the same meaning as that given it during the negotiations leading up to the agreement.[7] In such cases consideration will be given to all the circumstances leading up to the making of the contract.[8] In some cases, arbitrators will deny the grievance where it appears that the union was attempting to obtain through arbitration what it could not get through negotiations.[9] Sometimes the lack of discussion of a particular subject during negotiations may be indicative of intent.[10] Recording and minutes of bargaining meetings provide important evidence.[11] Not all evidence as to what occurred in negotiations is competent; however, there may be privileged communications not admissible into evidence.[12]

---

[7]Schnuck Markets, 107 LA 739, 743–44 (Cipolla, 1996); Copper & Brass Sales, Inc., 105 LA 730 (Nelson, 1995); Everfresh Beverages, Inc., 104 LA 577, 578 (Ellmann, 1994); Rhone Poulenc, 103 LA 1085, 1087 (Bernstein, 1994); National Steel Corp., 102 LA 1159, 1167–68 (Garrett, 1994); United Can Co., 102 LA 806, 808–10 (Hoh, 1993); Taylorville Community Sch. Dist., 102 LA 367, 373 (Nathan, 1993); Atascardero Unified Sch. Dist., 101 LA 673, 680–83 (Bickner, 1993). But see Giant Cement Co., 103 LA 146, 147 n. 1 (Nolan, 1994) refusing to consider union negotiator's statements to members before ratification vote, and refusing to consider evidence of informal discussions because contract contained clause which provided that the "parties' proposals and counterproposals shall not be referred to, in any way, in arbitration").

[8]See Kennedy Ctr., 101 LA 174, 179 (Ables, 1993) (stating that "[prior negotiations, discussions, meetings, complaints, grievances, unfair labor practice charges, disputes in arbitration or in court, leave foot-prints on what is troubling parties in a collective bargaining relationship"). Significantly, the types of bargaining history considered vary. See, e.g. Arbitrator Nelson in 105 LA 730, 734 (considering employer's statements and amended proposal); National Steel Corp., 102 LA 1159, 1167–68 (Garrett, 1994) (considering employer's internal memoranda); City of Columbus, 102 LA 477, 480 (Kindig, 1994) (considering employer's rejection of union proposal); Bickner in 101 LA 673, 680–83 (considering parties' bargaining notes).

[9]Josten Printing & Publ'g, 107 LA 505, 507 (Berger, 1996) (considering that employer dropped proposal during negotiations); Louis Dreyfus Corp., 106 LA 260, 262–64 (Berger, 1996) (considering that union's proposal was rejected by employer during negotiations); see infra note 13.

[10]Other arbitrators have found the lack of discussion concerning an issue at bargaining significant. See Broughton Foods Co., 101 LA 286, 287 (Jones Jr., 1993) (noting union's silence on contested issue during negotiations); see also Jefferson Smurfit Corp., 102 LA 164, 166–67 (Duff, 1994) (pointing out that union agreed to provisions at negotiations without objecting to employer's interpretation).

[11]See Schnuck Markets, 107 LA 739, 743–44 (Cipolla, 1996) (considering bargaining notes taken by officer to help interpret ambiguous provision of collective bargaining agreement addressing vendor stocking); Department of Defense Dependent Sch., 105 LA 211, 217 (Feigenbaum, 1995) (turning to bargaining notes to determine whether elimination of wage differential violated collective bargaining agreement but finding notes ambiguous); Daily Racing Form, Inc., 102 LA 23, 30–31 (Heinsz, 1993) (considering bargaining notes); Bickner in 101 LA 673, 680–83 (same).

[12]But see Arbitrator Garrett in 102 LA 1159, 1167–68 (finding that, where employer and union shared informal negotiating relationship, it was permissible for arbitrator to consider for limited purposes management's internal documents summarizing discussions with union).

If a party attempts but fails, in contract negotiations, to include a specific provision in the agreement, many arbitrators will hesitate to read such provision into the agreement through the process of interpretation.[13] The withdrawal or rejection during contract negotiations of a proposed clause spelling out a right has been held not to be an admission that the right did not exist without the clause, where the proponent stated at the time that it would stand firm on the position that the right existed even without the proposed clause.[14]

Industry Practice

Evidence of industry practice will not be given weight if too meager to furnish a reliable guide.[15]

Prior Settlements as Aid to Interpretation

If the parties themselves have previously arrived at a settlement that necessarily includes some form of contract interpretation, their settlement interpretation will be given significant weight by arbitrators who have been called upon to construe the same contract language.[16]

---

[13]See Arbitrator Berger in 107 LA 505, 507 (considering that, at negotiations, employer dropped proposal addressing issue); Berger in 106 LA 260, 262–64 (considering that union's proposal was rejected by employer during negotiations): Lockheed Aeronautical Sys. Co., 104 LA 803, 806 (Duff, 1995) (finding that employer's refusal during negotiations to accept proposals to limit its ability to subcontract supported employer's interpretation of subcontracting provision of agreement); Michigan State Univ., 104 LA 516, 520–21 (McDonald, 1995) (considering that union made and withdrew provision in last bargaining that went beyond clarification of existing language); Bethlehem Steel Corp., 104 LA 452, 455–56 (Das, 1995) (considering that union's proposal addressing issue was not agreed to by employer): Kindig in 102 LA 477, 480 (considering that employer had rejected union's proposal on same issue at negotiations).

[14]United Can Co., 102 LA 422, 424 (Randall, 1993) (declining to give interpretative value to company proposal, noting that "[a] change proposed for the purpose of clarification does not constitute an admission that the proponent does not, under the existing language, have the right set forth in the proposal").

[15]Kaiser Foundations Hosp., 102 LA 83, 84–85 (Knowlton, 1993) (considering industry practice and parallel provisions in other contracts, but finding them inconclusive on facts of case).

[16]See Campbell Group, 102 LA 1031, 1038–40 (Ferree, 1994) (finding that company's expansion of smoking ban to "all company property," including parking lot and "lean-to," is not reasonable when union and company earlier agreed to settlement of grievance to provide "lean-to" as smoking area. Notably, arbitrators also consider past arbitration awards that have addressed the same or related language in construing collective bargaining agreements. See, e.g., Gulf States Utils. Co., 102 LA 470, 475 (Massey, 1993) (noting that interpretation of transfer/promotion provision was consistent with arbitration 20 years earlier involving similar facts and contract language); Nevada Cement Co., 101 LA 725, 730 (Concepcion, 1993) (finding that prior arbitration award's interpretation of collective bargaining agreement to include past practice that Console Operators work eight-hour shifts gave practice contractual status).

Interpretation Against Party Selecting the Language

It is a standard rule of contract interpretation that ambiguous language will be construed against the party who proposed or drafted it.[17]

Company Manuals and Handbooks

Company-issued booklets, manuals, and handbooks that have not been negotiated or agreed to by the union are said to constitute a unilateral statement by the company and are not sufficient to be binding upon the union.[18] A handbook, however, may aid an arbitrator in interpreting inconclusive contractual language.[19]

Reason and Equity

It is widely recognized that if a contract is clear and unambiguous, it must be applied in accordance with its terms despite the equities that may be present on either side.[20] Arbitrators strive where possible, however, to give ambiguous language a construction that is reasonable and equitable to both parties rather than one that would give one party an unfair and unreasonable advantage.[21] Arbitrators

---

[17]Crown Cork & Seal Co., 104 LA 1133 (Wolff, 1995) (finding that ambiguity in work-schedule provision need not be construed against the employer because it was unclear which party drafted provision).

[18]See City of Miamisburg, Ohio, 104 LA 228, 232–234 (Fullmer, 1995) (finding that educational incentive provision in collective bargaining agreement controlled rather than provision concerning education reimbursement in employee handbook); Rhone Poulenc, 103 LA 1085, 1087–88 (Bernstein, 1994) (finding that statement in employee benefits handbook reserving right to employer to change benefits plan did not alter binding commitments made in collective bargaining agreement); Centel Bus. Sys., 95 LA 472, 478 (Allen, Jr., 1990) (stating that "[c]ompany-created handbook cannot take precedence over labor agreement language if there is conflict").

[19]Cf. Group Health Assocs., 102 LA 605, 608 (Feigenbaum, 1994) (concluding that physicians who were laid off less than five weeks after notice of employers' sale of business were entitled to five weeks' pay as guaranteed by closing agreement); Central Hudson Gas & Elec. Corp., 101 LA 894, 899–900 (Eischen, 1993) (finding that utility workers who worked in another utility company's territory during ice-storm emergency under mutual aid contract were entitled to wages based on special rate, which was established by company memorandum, rather than rate specified in mutual aid contract).

[20]See Excel Corp. v. United Food & Commercial Workers, 102 F.3d 1464, 1468 (8th Cir. 1996) (finding that arbitrator ignored plain meaning of agreement, and stating that "[a]lthough an arbitrator's award is given great deference by a reviewing court, the arbitrator is not free to ignore or abandon the plain language of [the agreement], which would in effect amend or alter the agreement without authority"); Arbitrator Imes in 97 LA 248, 251 (indicating that arbitrator must carry out intent of parties rather than interpret language according to arbitrator's sense of justice).

[21]Clen-A-Rama, 99 LA 70 (Concepcion, 1992) (finding that interpretation of party that is in conformity with logical and realistic reading of contracts should prevail); Arbitrator Allen in 95 LA 472 (reasoning that, where neither party's interpretation can be accommodated under contract language, arbitrator must fashion remedy as reason-

will also use "a rule of reason" to apply contract language in accordance with the parties' intent rather than in a literal fashion that is contrary to their intent.[22]

---

ably and logically as possible); Arbitrator Witney in 95 LA 1264, 1271 (finding that denying holiday pay for reporting to work two minutes late was unreasonable interpretation of contract provision requiring employee to work an eight-hour day immediately following holiday in order to qualify for holiday pay).

[22]Brown-Forman Beverage Co., 103 LA 292 (Frockt, 1994) (applying "rule of reason").

Chapter 10

Use of Substantive Rules of Law

General Considerations

As noted in the Main Edition, arbitration is a viable substitute for litigation with respect to many statutes as well as basic principles of law. Also included in the statutory arbitration arena are the Americans with Disabilities Act,[1] ("ADA") and the Family Medical Leave Act,[2] ("FMLA"). Since the implementation of these Acts in 1990 and 1993, respectively, arbitrators have been interpreting rights and applying the law under the Acts in their decisions.[3] Arbitrators con-

---

[1]42 U.S.C. §12101 et seq.

[2]29 U.S.C. §2601 et seq.

[3]For recent cases regarding ADA, see Johns Hopkins Bayview Med. Ctr., 105 LA 193, 197–98 (Bowers, 1995) (arbitrator found employer failed to provide a reasonable accommodation to employees who were injured on the job, thus finding employer violated the ADA); Alcoa Bldg. Prods., 104 LA 364, 368 (Cerone, 1995) (where the collective bargaining agreement is silent regarding the arbitrator's authority to address external legal issues, arbitrator found "both the potential conflict between federal law and the agreement, as well as parties' stipulations allow [arbitrator] to apply external law," such as the ADA); Meijer Inc., 103 LA 834, 840 (Daniel, 1994) (arbitrator ruled "under collective bargaining contract requiring just cause for disciplinary action against employee, rights established by law, such as ADA must be taken into consideration determining whether just cause exists"); Merrimack County Corrections Dep't, 102 LA 1096, 1098 (McCausland, 1994) (arbitrator ruled when employer imposed job qualifications employee could not meet, terminating employee who did not satisfy the requirements of a qualified individual with a disability did not violate ADA); Jefferson-Smurfit Corp., 103 LA 1041, 1048–49 (Canestraight, 1994) (arbitrator ruled that "absent any source of arbitral power to exercise jurisdiction in the area's external law by providing so in the collective bargaining agreement, it is not within arbitrator's jurisdiction to apply either the Rehabilitation Act of 1993 or the Americans with Disabilities Act of 1990"); Angus Chem. Co., 102 LA 388, 392–93 (Nicholas, 1994) (arbitrator analyzed the meaning of "qualified individual with a disability" under the ADA); Clark County Sheriff's Dep't, 102 LA 193, 197 (Kindig, 1994) (arbitrator relied on the ADA to rule that county improperly tried to make an accommodation under the ADA in violation of the collective bargaining contract); Thermo King Corp., 102 LA 612, 615–16 (Dworkin, 1993) (in determining whether employer's actions in discharging an alleged disabled employee were discriminatory, arbitrator, who was empowered to decide whether the discharge was just and fair in making this determination, looked to the ADA for guidance). But

tinue to hold that since the appointment and authority of the arbitrator are under the control of the parties, the parties can by the submission agreement expressly regulate (but do not often do so) the extent to which the arbitrator is to consider applicable law.[4] Courts continue to find that parties may expressly direct that the case be decided consistent with applicable law[5] and that they can provide in the submission agreement the extent to which the decision is to be final.[6]

Courts continue to hold that if the parties do not specifically limit the powers of the arbitrator in deciding various aspects of the issues submitted, it is presumed that they intend to make the arbitrator the final judge on any questions that arise in the disposition of the issue, including not only questions of fact but also questions of contract

---

see Altoona Hosp., 102 LA 650, 652 (Jones, 1993) (where union contends the employer violated the ADA, arbitrator ruled interpretation of the ADA is "a function of the appropriate agency or commission, and ultimately the court, not the arbitrator," where collective bargaining agreement does not permit arbitrator to consider ADA). For recent cases regarding FMLA, see General Mills, Inc., 107 LA 472, 475–76 (Feldman, 1996) (arbitrator interpreted the leave requirement under FMLA to determine whether employer had properly discharged employee who had already used all his leave under the Act); Apcoa, Inc., 107 LA 705, 711 (Daniel, 1996) (arbitrator has jurisdiction and authority over issues regarding FMLA where the parties, by agreement, incorporate into the contract the terms of the FMLA); Enesco Corp., 107 LA 513, 518 (Berman, 1996) (arbitrator ruled that the company's denial of leave to an employee under FMLA's one-year employment requirement, where employee had not been employed for over a year, was an error because the labor contract itself provided otherwise); Morgan Foods, Inc., 106 LA 833, 836 (Goldman, 1996) (arbitrator upheld employer's decision to dismiss employee, interpreting that FMLA "does not require that a leave of absence be granted simply because an employee wishes to be with an ill family member"); Grand Haven Stamped Prods. Co., 107 LA 131, 135–37 (Daniel, 1996) (arbitrator ruled that an employer could not require employees who needed FMLA leave to care for family members to exhaust their vacation benefits, even though FMLA provides an employer may require such, where collective bargaining agreement provided otherwise and the choice of such in the contract was rejected by both parties after FMLA's enactment).

[4][Updates footnote 2 in the Main Edition, on page 517.] See Alcoa Building Prods., 104 LA 364 (Cerone, 1995) (where the contract was silent regarding the arbitrator's authority to address external legal issues, arbitrator, based on potential conflict between federal law and the agreement as well as the parties' stipulation, applied external law); Multi-Clean, Inc., 102 LA 463 (Miller, 1993) (arbitrator lacked the authority to determine whether employer violated the ADA, where collective bargaining contract limits arbitrator jurisdiction to interpretation of contract terms only); Exxon Co. U.S.A., 101 LA 997 (Sergent, 1993) (arbitrator lacked jurisdiction to hear a dispute arising under "last chance agreement" insofar as it alleged the agreement violated the FLSA and the ADA, where asserted violations did not pose questions arising out of contract, where arbitrator's jurisdiction is limited to collective bargaining contract grievances).

[5][Updates footnote 3 in the Main Edition, on page 517.] See North Adams Regional Hosp. v. Massachusetts Nursing Ass'n, 889 F. Supp. 507, 513 (D. Mass. 1995) (court ruled that where the parties themselves empowered the arbitrator to determine whether the contract was violated, the arbitrator could reasonably resort to traditional rules of contract construction).

[6][Updates footnote 5 in the Main Edition, on page 517.] See Corporate Printing Co. Inc., v. New York Typographical Union No. 6, 147 LRRM 2918, 2921 (S.D.N.Y. 1994) (the parties, through the submission agreement, "determine the scope of the arbitrator's authority," and when part of the dispute is submitted with intent that the arbitrator's decision be final on the issue submitted, "arbitrator has authority and responsibility to issue a final . . . award").

interpretation, rules of interpretation, and questions, if any, with respect to substantive law.[7]

Courts continue to follow the principle set forth by the U.S. Supreme Court that in unrestricted submissions, "the interpretations of the law by the arbitrators in contrast to manifest disregard are not subject, in the federal courts, to judicial review for error in interpretation."[8] However, courts, under statute or under the common law, continue to be reluctant to honor any award that directs a party to commit an act that is clearly prohibited by law, or that is found to be contrary to a strong public policy.[9] Courts continue to construe narrowly the public policy exception to the rule that awards are not impeachable for errors of law,[10] and many have consistently refused to set arbitration awards aside on this basis.[11]

---

[7][Updates footnote 8 in the Main Edition, on page 518.] See Hirras v. National R.R. Passenger Corp., 10 F.3d 1142, 1145 LRRM 2137, 2140 (5th Cir. 1994) (court noted there is no statutory barrier to prevent submission of questions involving the interpretation of statute or case law).

[8][Updates footnote 10 in the Main Edition, on page 518.] See Willemijn Houdstermaatschappij v. Standard Micro, 103 F.3d 9, 12 (2d Cir. 1997) (the court, recognizing district courts may vacate arbitration awards when arbitrators are in manifest disregard of the law, defined manifest disregard as "something beyond and different from a mere error in the law or failure on part of the arbitrators to understand or apply the law. Manifest disregard is found if arbitrator understood the law but preceded to ignore it"); Matteson v. Ryder Sys., Inc., 153 LRRM 2745 (3d Cir. 1996) (court held "an arbitration award will, of course, be enforceable only to the extent it does not exceed the scope of the parties' submission); United Parcel Serv. v. Local 430, 55 F.3d 138, 149 LRRM 2395, 2397 (3d Cir. 1995) (court held where the parties' collective bargaining agreement provides for binding arbitration, courts are not authorized to reconsider the merits of an arbitrator's award. "A contrary rule would undermine the federal policy which favors settling labor disputes through arbitration"); Baltimore Teachers Union Local 340 v. Mayor of Baltimore, 671 A.2d 80, 151 LRRM 2706, 2714 (Md. Ct. App. 1996) (court held an arbitrator's refusal to grant a remedy where he was empowered to do so would seem to result in a mistake so gross as to "work a manifest injustice"); Prudential-Bache Sec., Inc. v. Tanner, 72 F.3d 234, 239–40 (1st Cir. 1995) (the court recognized "in order to demonstrate that an arbitrator recognized and ignored applicable law under manifest disregard of loss standard of review, there must be a showing in the record, that the arbitrator knew the law and expressly disregarded it").

[9][Updates footnote 12 in the Main Edition, at page 519.] See Exxon Corp. v. ESSO Workers' Union, Inc., 118 F.3d 841, 846, 155 LRRM 2782 (1st Cir. 1997) (in recognizing that courts must refrain from enforcing contracts that violate public policy, the court noted that "to determine whether a particular case fits within this classification, the court must first, review existing statutes, regulations, and judicial decisions, to ascertain whether they establish a well defined and dominant public policy, if so, the court must then determine whether the arbitral award clearly violates that public policy"); International Bhd. of Electric Workers v. Niagra Mohawk Power Corp., 950 F. Supp. 1227, 1234, 156 LRRM 2372 (N.D.N.Y. 1996) (court ruled because of "federal statutes, regulations and case law that support a finding of a well-defined and dominant public policy against employment of individuals who deliberately violate nuclear safety rules . . . and given the strong public policy issues involved, the court will review findings of arbitration panel de novo").

[10][Updates footnote 14 in the Main Edition, page 521.] See St. Mary Home v. Service Employees Int'l Union, 116 F.3d 41, 45, 155 LRRM 2456 (2d Cir. 1997) ("a court's authority to refuse to enforce an arbitrator's award on the public policy grounds is narrowly circumscribed to situations where the contract, as interpreted, would violate some explicit public policy that is well defined and dominant") quoting United Paperworkers Int'l v. Misco, Inc., 484 U.S. 29, 36 (1987).

[11][Updates footnote 15 in the Main Edition, on page 521.] See GB Goldman Paper Co. v. Local 286, 957 F. Supp. 607, 154 LRRM 2489, 2494 (E.D. Pa. 1997) (the court ruled

The cases continues to demonstrate that despite the lack of finality, arbitration remains a viable substitute for litigation even with respect to rights under statutes.[12]

Range of Views as to Application of "Law"

Views of Arbitrators

Arbitrators continue to hold that where contractual provisions being interpreted or applied have been formulated loosely, an arbitrator may consider all relevant factors, including relevant law.[13] They

---

that public policy concerning workplace safety was "not violated by arbitration award reinstating employee who was discharged for harassing fellow employees in violation of company rules," where arbitrator found employee's actions were not so extreme that reinstatement would violate public policy); UAW Local 771 v. Micro Mfg., Inc., 895 F. Supp. 170, 150 LRRM 2362, 2364 (E.D. Mich. 1995) (arbitrator's award reinstating employee who violated an explicit and well-defined public policy will not be vacated, because the arbitrator's decision itself does not violate any law or clear dictate of public policy; one seeking to vacate an arbitration award on public policy grounds must show that the award itself violates the law); UTU Local 1589 v. Suburban Transit Corp., 51 F.3d 376, 148 LRRM 2797, 2800 (3d Cir. 1995) (court upheld arbitrator's decision that employee discharge was too harsh when employer failed to demonstrate a company policy in favor of protecting coworkers and customers from violent conduct of employees was an explicit public policy that would undermine the arbitration award; public policy argument failed.); United Food & Commercial Workers Union, Local 588 v. Foster Food Prods., 146 LRRM 2793, 2801–04 (E.D. Cal. 1994) (upholding arbitrator's award for reinstatement of drivers who were discharged for failing or refusing to take a drug test, as not violating public policy).

[12][Updates footnote 21 in the Main Edition, on page 523.] See Patterson v. Tenet Healthcare, Inc., 113 F.3d 832, 837 (8th Cir. 1997) (court noted "the arbitrability of Title VII claims finds support in a Civil Rights Act of 1991, which states that 'the use of alternative means of dispute resolution, including . . . arbitration, is encouraged to resolve disputes arising under the acts or provisions of federal law amended by this title'"); Clallam County Public Hosp., 105 LA 609, 612 (Calhoun, 1995) (arbitrator applied the Civil Rights Act of 1964 in evaluating whether a company had made a sufficient effort to reasonably accommodate an employee's religious needs and practices); Minnegasco, Inc., 103 LA 43, 46 (Bognanno, 1994) (arbitrator considered Minnesota state law in evaluating public utility company's termination of pregnant employee with lifting restriction); City of Orange, 103 LA 1121, 1125 (Nicholas, 1994) (arbitrator used authority to consider city ordinances as well as collective bargaining agreement, since "it is well settled that the arbitrator has secondary jurisdiction to review and apply the relevant external law to any matter brought before him in an arbitration context"); Schuller Int'l, Inc., 103 LA 1127, 1131–32 (Allen, 1994) ("an arbitrator is not required to interpret all the federal and state laws, but he must follow the clear written interpretations and directives from recognized authority issuing a final decision as to the application of a particular law").

[13][Updates footnote 24 in the Main Edition, on page 526.] See Van Waters & Rogers, Inc. v. International Bhd. of Teamsters, 56 F.3d 1132, 1137, 149 LRRM 2525 (9th Cir. 1995) ("an arbitrator may look 'to (the law)' for guidance so long as the decision draws its essence from the [a]greement"); International Mill Serv., 104 LA 779, 781 (Marino, 1995) (declaring without analysis that arbitrator must examine "'external law,' specifically Title VII, definitions and standards and the concept of 'just cause'" to determine whether the company had just cause to discharge grievant, and whether grievant sexually harassed another employee); Johnson Controls World Servs., 104 LA 336, 342 (Goodstein, 1995) (interpreting the ADA to determine whether general equal opportunity clause in the contract required the company to accommodate); but see Union Camp Corp., 104 LA 295, 302 (Nolan, 1995) (observing that authorities on arbitral authority

also continue to find that where a contractual provision is susceptible to two interpretations, one compatible with and the other repugnant to an applicable statute, the statute is a relevant factor—
arbitrators should seek to avoid a construction that would make the
agreement invalid.[14] The cases further underscore the principle that
where the submission makes it clear that the parties want an advisory opinion as to the law, such opinion would be within the arbitrator's
role.[15] Arbitrators continue to find that even where a given statute
does not cover the parties, or does not apply directly to the case, or
permits variations through the collective agreement, the statute (or
cases construing it) may be a helpful guide if the agreement is ambiguous or contains no method of determining the issue.[16]

In American Sterilizer Co.,[17] the arbitrator relied on a prior
arbitrator's decision that the parties' collective bargaining agreement
specifically incorporated the ADA, and then interpreted the Act's application to the facts at hand).

---

to award tort damages for sexual harassment would have been more helpful than the
judicial authorities cited by the company); Clow Valve Co., 102 LA 286, 288 (Berger,
1994) (considering terms of the FLSA and the Iowa Workers' Compensation Law in
finding that company must compensate employee for time spent in a work-related medical visit).

[14][Updates footnote 24 in the Main Edition, on page 526.] See Dyno Nobel, Inc., 104
LA 376, 382–83 (Hilgert, 1995) (declining to uphold grievance at the risk of requiring
the company to violate OSHA); Seminole Fire Rescue, 104 LA 222, 227–28 (Sergent,
1994) (considering company's fear of violating ERISA of 1974 in interpreting collective
bargaining agreement).

[15][Updates footnote 24 in the Main Edition, on page 526.] See Grand Haven Stamped
Prods. Co., 107 LA 131, 135 (Daniel, 1996) (interpreting FMLA when the parties relied
on its interpretation in delineating their respective positions and referred to the statute in their contract); Johns Hopkins Bayview Medical Ctr., 105 LA 193, 197 (Bowers,
1995) (interpreting ADA when parties' agreement prohibited discrimination "to the
extent provided by law"); Alcoa Building Prods., 104 LA 364, 368 (Cerone, 1995) (parties consented to arbitrator interpretation of the ADA; Laidlaw Transit Inc., 104 LA
302, 305–06 (Concepcion, 1995) (sustaining grievance based on company's failure to
provide reasonable accommodation when union urged application of the ADA and company did not object); Consentino's Brywood Price Chopper, 104 LA 187, 189–90 (Thornell,
1995) (finding that company "failed to meet its contractual and statutory obligation of
reasonable accommodation" when union claimed company violated contract and the
ADA, each of which require reasonable accommodation for an employee with a physical
handicap).

[16][Updates footnote 24 in the Main Edition, on page 526.] See Henkel Corp., 104 LA
494, 499 (Hooper, 1995) (noting that Title VII was useful in deciding race discrimination issue, while observing that the outcome of the case "does not depend on the particular legal construct that the arbitrator chooses to employ"); Multi-Clean, Inc., 102
LA 463, 467 (Miller, 1993) (when parties failed to define "reasonable accommodation"
in the collective bargaining agreement provision addressing age and disability, the arbitrator turned to the ADA definition in interpreting the phrase's contractual meaning); Thermo King Corp., 102 LA 612, 615 (Dworkin, 1993) (recognizing that arbitrator
lacks authority to decide whether company violated the ADA but looking to the Act for
guidance in determining whether the company-imposed penalty on the grievant was
just and fair).

[17]104 LA 921, 924–25 (Dissen, 1995). See also Meiter, Inc., 103 LA 834, 840 (Daniel,
1994) ("Under a contract requiring just cause for disciplinary action against an employee, rights established by law, such as ADA, must be taken into consideration in
determining whether just cause exists"). But see Dinagraphics, Inc., 102 LA 947, 953

Arbitrators continue to find that external law should be disregarded where there is a clear conflict between the collective agreement and the law.[18]

Arbitrators continue to emphasize that they would not interpret or apply an agreement in a way that would require a party to commit an illegal act.[19] And, other arbitrators have indicated that they have no business interpreting or applying a public statute in a contractual grievance dispute.[20] Many arbitrators have indicated that they would feel free to comment on the relevant law if it appears to conflict with the collective bargaining agreement.[21] Others have held that in some instances to ignore external law would render an arbitrator's award a nullity.[22] In some instances, the parties have included federal and state laws in their agreement.[23]

Arbitrators continue to consider state statutes and regulations in deciding a grievance.[24]

(Paolucci, 1994) (when collective bargaining agreement did not prohibit discrimination based on disability, the ADA was inapplicable).

[18][Updates footnote 26 in the Main Edition, on page 527.] See, e.g., Olin Corp., 103 LA 481, 483 (Helburn, 1994) (company was not obligated to accommodate disabled employee in a way that violated contractually granted seniority rights).

[19][Updates footnote 31 in the Main Edition, on page 529.] See Champion Int'l Corp., 106 LA 1024, 1031 (Howell, 1996) (while the EEOC is responsible for enforcing the ADA, the arbitrator may consider the Act in interpreting the parties' collective bargaining agreement).

[20][Updates footnote 30 in the Main Edition, on page 528.] See, e.g., Textron Lycoming, 104 LA 1043, 1047 (Duff, 1995) (refusing to consider company's arguments based on statute- and policy-based safety considerations when the arbitrator's authority is limited to interpreting the terms of the collective bargaining agreement).

[21][Updates footnote 30 in the Main Edition, on page 528.] See Alcoa Building Prods., 104 LA 364, 368–69 (Cerone, 1995) (ADA compelled reasonable accommodation, but company went too far when it violated union member's contractual seniority rights to accommodate disabled employee); Rodeway Inn, 102 LA 1003, 1014–15 (Goldberg, 1994) (refusing to interpret contract in a manner that would be "repugnant" to the policies set forth in Title VII).

[22][Updates footnote 34 in the Main Edition, on page 530.] See, e.g., Raybestos Prods. Co., 102 LA 46, 54 (Kossoff, 1993) (company could override collective bargaining agreement provisions regarding smokers' rights if a statute, OSHA regulations, or binding court decision required an employer to subordinate smokers' right to nonsmokers' rights); Michigan Dep't of Corrections, 103 LA 37, 39 (Sugerman, 1994) ("Although plenary jurisdiction to interpret FOIA remains with the judiciary, I must examine the FOIA exemptions to the extent it is necessary to ascertain whether a contractual violation has occurred"). But see Rock Island County, 104 LA 1127, 1133 (Witney, 1995) (rejecting union's invitation to apply provisions of the FMLA when the union agreed to more limited leave terms in the parties' collective bargaining agreement).

[23][Updates footnote 35 in the Main Edition, on page 530.] See, e.g., City of Flint, 104 LA 125, 126–27 (House, 1995) (contract at issue in sexual harassment case incorporated the EEOC Guidelines on Discrimination Because of Sex and the Michigan state employment discrimination statute's definition of forbidden conduct); San Francisco Unified Sch. Dist., 104 LA 215, 217 (Bogue, 1995) (applying the federal and state disabilities laws to case arising out of contract that incorporated both by reference); Angus Chem. Co., 102 LA 388, 392 (Nicholas, 1994) (finding that employee was not "disabled" as defined in the ADA when the parties had explicitly incorporated the Act into the collective bargaining agreement).

[24][Updates footnote 39 in the Main Edition, on page 532.] See Michigan Dep't of Corrections, 104 LA 1192, 1194 (Sugerman, 1995) (assuming, without question, the authority to apply the FLSA and the Portal-to-Portal Act to the parties' wage dispute);

The question whether external law is expressly incorporated into the relevant provision of an agreement continues to determine the outcome of many cases.[25] In some situations matters external to a collective bargaining agreement may impinge upon it.[26]

U.S. Supreme Court Statements Regarding Arbitral Consideration of External Law

The holding in *Gilmer*[27] that Congress did not preclude the arbitration of statutory employment discrimination claims brought under ADEA remains valid. The Supreme Court has continued to issue rulings favoring arbitration, and lower federal courts have continued to rely on *Gilmer* to enforce employment-related arbitration agreements with respect to a broad range of statutory employment claims. However, the Court has yet to resolve the issue of whether the Federal Arbitration Act provides for enforcement of arbitration agreements in employment disputes; it is not yet settled whether arbitration agreements between employers and employees are enforceable with respect to federal statutory employment claims.[28]

Indiana Michigan Power Co., 103 LA 248, 252 (Alexander, 1994) (while the arbitrator's job is to determine whether just cause existed for the discharge, the statutory and decisional law under Title VII provides guidance in evaluating actionable conduct); Reed Mfg. Co., 102 LA 1, 6 (Dworkin, 1993) (declining to broadly construe management rights clause in the parties' collective bargaining agreement, noting "[s]ometimes the federal labor policy proscribes protections that not even the most broadly drawn Management Rights language in a contract can supersede"); APCOA, Inc., 107 LA 705, 711 (Daniel, 1996) (recognizing applicability of FMLA when parties incorporated the statute into their collective bargaining agreement, but commenting that contract may afford *greater* benefits than the statute); ENESCO Corp., 107 LA 513, 518 (Berman, 1996) (employer subject to statutory leave obligations is still bound by contractual leave promises that exceed the statutory requirement).

[25][Updates footnote 50 of the Main Edition, on page 534.] See, e.g., Rock Island County, 104 LA 1127, 1133 (Witney, 1995) (rejecting union's invitation to apply provisions of the FMLA when the union agreed to more limited leave terms in the parties' collective bargaining agreement); Jefferson-Smurfit Corp., 103 LA 1041, 1048 (Canestraight, 1994) (company's failure to accommodate disabled employee did not violate collective bargaining agreement when parties failed to expressly or implicitly incorporate federal disability laws into the agreement); Racine Unified Sch. Dist., 102 LA 327, 332 (Baron, 1993) (reasoning that the parties' agreement that designated the union as the exclusive bargaining unit "with all the rights and responsibilities under the Municipal Relations Act," which included protections related to conditions of employment, extended the arbitrator's jurisdiction to consider external law).

[26][Updates footnote 50 in the Main Edition, on page 534.] See, e.g., Michigan Dep't of Transp., 104 LA 1196, 1201 (Kelman, 1995) (analyzing Title VII's provisions in rejecting company's argument that lesser degree of discipline would have resulted in Title VII lawsuit against the company).

[27]Gilmer v. Interstate Johnson Lane Corp., 500 U.S. 20 (1991).

[28]Excellent discussions of ADR-related issues are found in Kaufmann & Chanin, *Directing the Flood: The Arbitration of Employment Claims,* 10 Lab. Law. 217 (1994), Bompey, Delikat & McClelland, *The Attack on Arbitration and Mediation of Employment Disputes,* 13 Lab. 21 (1997), and Siegel, *Changing Public Policy: Private Arbitration to Resolve Statutory Employment Disputes,* 13 Lab. Law. 87 (1997). Another good article is Eastman & Rothenstein, *The Fate of Mandatory Arbitration Amidst Growing Opposition: A Call for Common Ground,* 20 Empl. Rel. L. J. 595 (1995).

The arbitration of claims pursuant to an arbitration clause in a collective bargaining agreement must still be distinguished from the issue left open by *Gilmer,* thus, an arbitration decision arising out of a collective bargaining agreement will not preclude a subsequent suit in federal court based on statutory rights arising from the same underlying facts.

Statutory Law

The Family and Medical Leave Act (FMLA)[29] has become a factor in a significant number of labor arbitration cases. An FMLA issue frequently arises when an employer seeks to deal with an attendance-related issue, generally by discharge, and the union contends that a particular absence should not have been taken into account by reason of applicability of FMLA provisions.[30] Another example of a common FMLA issue is the employer's right to require employees to exhaust vacation pay as part of FMLA leave.[31]

Americans with Disabilities Act

As anticipated, ADA has been the frequent topic in the opinions of labor arbitrators. Issues of interest have included whether or not to consider issues of external law,[32] how to deal with conflicts between ADA and agreements,[33] and, of course, reasonable accommodation issues.[34]

Title VII of the Civil Rights Act

In the past several years, very little has changed regarding the way arbitrators deal with Title VII. However, in one notable development, collective bargaining agreements increasingly include nondis-

[29]29 USC §2601 et seq. with employment-related regulations at 29 CFR §825 et seq.

[30]Big River Zinc Corp., 108 LA 692 (Draznin, 1997) (discharge did not violate FMLA); General Mills Inc., 107 LA 472 (Feldman, 1996) (union raised FMLA as issue without any supporting evidence); Oxboro Clinic, 108 LA 11 (Jacobowski, 1997) (job placement).

[31]Grand Haven Stamped Prods. Co., 107 LA 131 (Daniel, 1996) (contract does not require employees to exhaust vacation pay).

[32]Stone Container Corp., 101 LA 943 (Feldman, 1993) (agreement did not permit examination of external law, but finding of contractual violation was consistent with ADA).

[33]Alcoa Bldg. Prods., 104 LA 364 (Cerone, 1995) ("Company went too far in attempting to comply with ADA"); Clark County Sheriff's Dep't, 102 LA 193 (Kindig, 1994) (employer violated contract in placing employee with no attempt to discuss with union).

[34]Multi-Clean Inc., 102 LA 463 (Miller, 1993) (arbitrator looked to ADA to define reasonable accommodation in termination of employee with medical restrictions); Johnson Controls World Serv., 104 LA 336 (Goodstein, 1995) (no violation of ADA reasonable accommodation obligation); Champion Int'l Corp., 106 LA 1024 (Howell, 1996), Rheem Mfg. Co., 108 LA 193 (Woolf, 1997).

crimination provisions.[35] Generally, these provisions, like Title VII, prohibit discrimination against employees based on race, color, sex, religion, and national origin.[36] Some agreements also prohibit discrimination based on age and disability[37] or on sexual orientation.[38]

These provisions appear to have resulted from the tension between discouraging discrimination in the workplace and adhering strictly to the terms of the collective bargaining agreement. Often arbitrators are asked to determine whether, pursuant to the terms of the collective bargaining agreement, a company has "just cause" to discipline an employee.[39] However, this task can become complicated when an employee engages in acts such as sexual harassment. Some collective bargaining agreements prohibit acts historically viewed as dischargeable offenses, such as refusal to obey an order, but do not prohibit acts, such as sex harassment, that violate Title VII.[40] Some arbitrators have hesitated to find fault with a company's actions when it attempts to discipline employees for discriminatory acts that are not specifically proscribed by the collective bargaining agreement but that violate Title VII.[41] This hesitation has brought the arbitrators dangerously close to altering the terms of the collective bargaining agreements. These arbitrators have rationalized that discriminatory behavior warrants discipline notwithstanding the absence of specific proscriptions in the contract[42] Arbitrators have utilized other provisions in the collective bargaining agreement, such as provisions allowing them to address extraneous law, as well as the public policies

---

[35]Goodyear Tire & Rubber, 107 LA 193 (Sergent, 1996) (provision in collective bargaining agreement states that the parties agree that there will be no discrimination based on race, color, religion, sex or national origin); Jefferson Smurfit Corp., 106 LA 673 (Imundo, 1996) (collective bargaining agreement states that the parties are subject to Title VII, the ADEA and the Rehabilitation Act, as amended).

[36]Firestone Synthetic Rubber & Latex Co., 107 LA 276 (Koenig, 1996); Goodyear Tire & Rubber, 107 LA 193 (Sergent, 1996).

[37]Southwest Airlines, 107 LA 270 (Jennings, 1996); Henkel Corp., 104 LA 494 (Hooper, 1995); Rodeway Inn, 102 LA 1003 (Goldberg, 1994).

[38]Beverly Enters., 109 LA 7 (Bard, 1997); Michigan State Univ., 104 LA 516 (McDonald, 1995).

[39]B.F. Goodrich Aerospace, 105 LA 1053 (Strasshofer, 1995); Moonlight Mushrooms, Inc., 101 LA 421, 425 (Dean, 1993).

[40]See City of Las Vegas, 107 LA 654 (Bergeson, 1996).

[41]In City of Las Vegas, the collective bargaining agreement did not specifically prohibit sexual harassment; instead, the agreement provided that "[j]ust cause exists when an employee commits an act of substance relating to the character or fitness of the employee to perform official duties that is contrary to sound public practices or acceptable work performance." Further, the agreement stated that examples of just cause include violations of city or departmental rules and regulations that "do not conflict with the terms of this agreement." Consequently, the arbitrator found that a city policy prohibiting "constant brushing against another's body" did not conflict with the terms of the collective bargaining agreement and therefore constituted just cause. 107 LA 654, 658 (Bergeson, 1996).

[42]Id.

inherent in Title VII, to find that discriminatory acts constitute just cause for the companies' prescribed discipline.[43]

In response to this dilemma of wanting to punish discrimination but finding the definition of "just cause" too narrow, unions and companies have increasingly negotiated nondiscrimination clauses in their collective bargaining agreements.[44] These provisions have the effect of authorizing arbitrators to follow federal law while in other respects adhering to the collective bargaining agreement.

The NLRA, the Arbitrator and the NLRB

Arbitrators continue to recognize and act on their authority to decide disputes involving both alleged unfair labor practices and violations of collective bargaining agreements.[45] Courts also recognize dual jurisdiction between the NLRB and arbitrators on disputes regarding matters historically within the Board's jurisdiction.[46] Both arbitrators and courts allow arbitration to proceed unless the dispute is "so primarily representational" that is falls within the Board's sole jurisdiction.[47]

Court Decisions

One arbitrator, relying upon case law, found that a grievance to secure a higher prevailing wage under Davis-Bacon was not arbitrable, the matter being exclusively under the jurisdiction of the Wage and Hour Administrator of the Department of Labor.[48]

---

[43]The arbitrator interpreted a provision of the collective bargaining agreement as giving him the authority to utilize external law, and in particular Title VII, when the provision stated that "[i]f any Article or Section of this Agreement . . . would be held invalid by operation of law . . . the remainder of this Agreement shall not be affected thereby, and the parties shall enter into immediate collective bargaining negotiations for the purpose of arriving at a mutually satisfactory replacement for such Article or Section." City of Dearborn Heights, 101 LA 809, 811 (Kanner, 1993).

[44]Boise Cascade Corp., 105 LA 223 (Michelstetter, 1995); Anderson Concrete Corp., 103 LA 433 (Kindig, 1994); Dinagraphics, Inc., 102 LA 947 (Paolucci, 1994); International Paper Co., 101 LA 1106 (Yancy, 1993).

[45]Swift Cleaning & Laundry, 106 LA 954, 960 (Nelson, 1995).

[46]International Union of Bricklayers & Allied Craftsmen Local 9 v. Carlton, Inc., 850 F. Supp. 498, 502 (S.D.W.Va. 1994).

[47]United Food & Commercial Workers Union Local 400 v. Shoppers Food Warehouse Corp., 35 F.3d 958, 961, 147 LRRM 2321, 2323 (4th Cir. 1994) (quoting Amalgamated Clothing & Textile Workers v. Facetglas, Inc., 845 F.2d 1250, 1252, 128 LRRM 2252, 2254 (4th Cir., 1988). See also Minn-Dak Farmers Co-op. Employees Org. V. Minn-Dak Farmers Co-op., 3 F.3d 1199, 1201, 144 LRRM 2214, 2216 (8th Cir.,1993); Textile Processors Local No. 1 v. D.O. Summers Cleaners & Shirt Laundry Co., 954 F. Supp. 153, 155, 154 LRRM 2574, 2576 (N.D. Ohio 1997); Road Sprinkler Filters Union Local 699 v. Grinnell Fire Protection System Co., 155 LRRM 2184, 2187 (E.D. Pa. 1997); Arbitrator Nelson in Swift Cleaning & Laundry, 106 LA at 960.

[48]Dyncorp, 101 LA 1193 (Richman, 1993).

In what is no longer an unusual area of dispute, an arbitrator, relying upon case law and statutes, decided against extending medical coverage to the same-sex partner of a covered employee.[49]

In one case, the arbitrator looked to the U.S. Supreme Court to decide not to credit National Guard training duty as "days worked" for vacation eligibility purposes.[50]

Reasonable accommodation issues under ADA and comparable state statutes arise frequently in arbitration. Arbitrators are looking to both case law and the extensive guidelines published by the EEOC.[51]

In a very unusual case, the arbitrator had to rely extensively upon the Supreme Court's and lesser court's admiralty decisions to determine the rights of Washington State Ferry food service employees to benefits when ill or injured while on duty.[52]

Arbitrators continue to be guided by court decisions.[53] They are especially cognizant of the decisions of the U.S. Supreme Court.[54] This is generally also true in cases involving sexual harassment[55] and other

---

[49]Kent State Univ., 103 LA 338 (Strasshofer, 1994).

[50]Concordia Foods, 102 LA 990 (Bernstein, 1994).

[51]San Francisco Unified School Dist., 104 LA 215 (Bogue, 1995).

[52]Marriott Int'l Inc., 106 LA 403 (Wilkinson, 1996).

[53][Updates footnote 147 in the Main Edition, on page 559.] See Hughes Aircraft Co., 107 LA 157 (Richman, 1996); Columbus Metro. Hous., 103 LA 104 (Fullmer, 1994) (citation to UPIU v. Misco, Inc., 108 S.Ct. 364, 126 LRRM 3113 (1987) for assistance in resolving after-acquired evidence issue); Curtis Sand & Gravel, 108 LA 64 (Richman, 1997) (arbitrability of postcontract discharge).

[54][Updates footnote 150 in the Main Edition, on page 559.] See Avnet, Inc., 107 LA 921 (Kadue, 1996) (nonunion arbitration—employment at will and emotional distress issues); Baltimore Sun Co., 107 LA 892 (Liebowitz, 1996) (current use of drug under ADA); Greene County Sheriff's Dep't, 107 LA 865 (Felice, 1996) (definition of "negligence"); Bethlehem Steel Corp., 105 LA 1175 (Das, 1996) (ERISA issues on pension eligibility); Lyondell Petrochemical Co., 104 LA 108 (Baroni, 1995) (use of court cases to decide breach of DFR grievance); Coca-Cola Bottling Co. of Michigan, 104 LA 97 (McDonald, 1994) (use of federal court decisions for guidance in resolving credibility); Michigan Dep't of Corrections, 103 LA 37 (Sugerman, 1994) (FOIA request), Martin-Brower Co., 102 LA 673 (Dilts, 1994) (FLSA decisions relied on to determine whether drug testing under DOT regulations is compensable); Taylorville Community School, 102 LA 367 (Nathan, 1993); Dyncorp Wallops Flight Facility, 101 LA 1033 (Jones, 1993) (extensive use of external law and agency decisions to determine validity of request to discharge nonjoining employee in right-to-work state where facility under U.S. Department of Defense); Young's Commercial Transfer, 101 LA 993 (McCurdy, 1993) (use of state arbitration law to determine that arbitrator had right to retain jurisdiction for application of remedy); Hendrickson Turner Co., 101 LA 919 (Dworkin, 1993) (Third Circuit decisions relied upon in interpreting last chance agreement grievance); Exxon Co., 101 LA 777 (Baroni, 1993) (case law to determine due process rights for searches); Helix Elec. Co., 101 LA 649, 651 (Kaufman, 1993) (federal law examined to determine availability of punitive damages); Kolar Buick, 101 LA 29 (Miller, 1993) (promissory estoppel criteria).

[55][Updates footnote 170 in the Main Edition, on page 562.] See Hughes Family Markets, Inc., 107 LA 331 (Prayzich 1996); T.J. Maxx, 107 LA 78 (Richman, 1996); International Mill Serv., 104 LA 779 (Marino, 1995); Rodeway Inn, 102 LA 1003 (Goldberg, 1994) (use of court decisions to determine protection to complainant of sexual harassment where complainant allegedly made slanderous remarks about owner); Renton School Dist., 102 LA 854 (Wilkinson, 1994); American Protective Servs., 102 LA 161 (Gentile, 1994) (used Supreme Court, Second Circuit and EEOC regulations in deciding case of discharge for sexual harassment by [not of] a female employee).

forms of discrimination.[56] And, official interpretations by executive departments are seriously considered when relevant.[57] This of course includes positions taken by the NLRB.[58] In contrast, administrative rulings may be relied upon but are not always controlling.[59]

Administrative Rulings

In a case where a witness for the union testified that the witness had violated the attendance policy but was not awarded points and was thereafter awarded discipline based on his testimony, the arbitrator relied upon *Public Service Electric Corp.,*[60] for authority to disallow the requested immunity.[61]

---

[56][Updates footnote 171 in the Main Edition, on page 562.] See Goodyear Tire & Rubber, 107 LA 193 (Sergent, 1996) (religious accommodation); Clellam County Pub. Hosp., 105 LA 609 (Calhoun, 1995) (religious accommodation); Boise Cascade Corp., 105 LA 223 (Michelstetter, 1995) (ADA issues); Minnegasco, 103 LA 43 (Bognanno, 1994) (pregnancy accommodation); MSI Services, 102 LA 727 (Madden, 1994) (placement in bargaining unit); Thermo King Corp., 102 LA 612 (Dworkin, 1993) (use ADA for guidance on claimed "handicap" drug problem); Multi-Clean, Inc., 102 LA 463 (Miller, 1993) (reasonable accommodation requirements under ADA); Angus Chem., 102 LA 388 (Nicholas, 1994) (ADA case determining whether employee "otherwise qualified"); Municipality of Anchorage, 101 LA 1127 (Carr, 1994) (ADA and arbitrability of statutory claim); City of Dearborn Heights, 101 LA 809 (Kanner, 1993) (attempt to reconcile ADA reasonable accommodation requirements with binding past practice of job assignments; scholarly opinion); Vicksburg Community Sch., 101 LA 771 (David, 1993) (religious belief accommodation); Michigan Dept. of P.H., 101 LA 713 (Kanner, 1993) (use of case law to find reverse discrimination).

[57][Updates footnote 176 in the Main Edition, on page 563.] See Eaglebudd Enters. Inc., 106 LA 659 (Franckiewicz, 1996) (Weingarten rights); Masolite Concrete Prods., 103 LA 10 (Keenan, 1994) (super-seniority for union steward issue); AT&T, 102 LA 931 (Kanner, 1994) (Fifth Amendment rights not included in Weingarten rights); Alcan-Toyo Am., 102 LA 566 (Draznin, 1993); Racine Unified Sch. Dist., 102 LA 327 (Baron, 1993) (grievance over bypassing union); Ralphs Grocery, 101 LA 634, 639 (Ross, 1993) (Weingarten rights cited to overturn discharge); Atlantic Southeast Airlines, 101 LA 515, 525 (Nolan, 1993) (awarding interest on back pay per NLRB formula); Granite Constr., 101 LA 297 (Richman, 1993) (NLRB law of agency decisions regarding drug testing); Jaite Packaging Co., 101 LA 105 (Strasshofer, 1993) (citing NLRB ruling re illegal strike and notice requirements).

[58][Updates footnote 177 in the Main Edition, on page 563.] See Hughes Aircraft Co., 105 LA 1019 (Richman, 1995) (excellent analysis of mid-term duty to bargain when adopting attendance rules); Anderson Wood Prods., 104 LA 1017 (Cocalis, 1995); Zebco Corp., 104 LA 613 (Cohen, 1995); National Maintenance & Repair Co., 101 LA 1115 (Fowler, 1993); Signature Flight Support, 101 LA 158 (Bognanno, 1993).

[59][Updates footnote 179 in the Main Edition, on page 563.] See Dunlop Tire Corp., 107 LA 483 (Heekin, 1996) (Social Security determination of nondisability not controlling for contract grievance); Georgia Pacific Corp., 106 LA 27 (Kahn, 1995) (finding by state OSHA agency that discharge of complaining employee was not violation of state nonretaliation statute not controlling on subsequent arbitration proceeding); World Jai-Alai, 104 LA 1157, 1164 (Haemmel, 1995); City of Los Angeles, 103 LA 1075 (Bergeson, 1994); Atlantic Southeast Airlines, 103 LA 1179 (Nolan, 1994) (use of NLRB principles applied to "duty to mitigate").

[60]115 LRRM 1006 (NLRB, 1983).

[61]Paxar Systems Group, 102 LA 75 (LaManna, 1994).

One arbitrator invoked the Code of Professional Responsibility governing attorney conduct to uphold the discharge of an attorney for a legal services plan because he practiced outside the plan.[62]

Arbitrators almost always look to the NLRB where a union official is disciplined. In one case where a union committeeman made improper and false statements about a supervisor/translator that caused great damage to labor management relations during negotiations, the arbitrator upheld the two-week suspension, relying upon NLRB precedent.[63]

In an unusual ruling, an arbitrator found that a company's unilaterally adopted drug testing program, to the extent it complied with DOT regulations, was valid; but those provisions that exceeded the regulations were not valid because they violated the Section 8(a)(5) (refusal to bargain in good faith) provision of Taft-Hartley.[64]

In aid of the continuing split among arbitrators regarding deductibility of unemployment compensation from back-pay awards, the arbitrator relied extensively upon court and NLRB decisions to find no deductibility.[65]

One arbitrator declined to rule on the applicability of a CBA to a separate facility of a dry cleaning establishment, relying upon more recent NLRB cases to determine that accretion issues should be decided by the Board.[66]

Agency Principles

Arbitrators continue to hold that parties are responsible for the acts of their authorized agents.[67] Even though the principal has not specifically authorized a particular act, a principal may be held responsible for the act of its agent that is within the scope of the agent's general authority.[68] However, the same rule does not apply to the act of a supervisor or other management representative if there is no basis to establish authority for the specific act.[69]

---

[62]UAW Legal Servs., 102 LA 449 (Cohen, 1993).

[63]Mid-West Chandelier Co., 102 LA 833 (Murphy, 1994); see also EWI Inc., 108 LA 50 (Brookins, 1997); Tennsco Corp., 107 LA 689 (Nicholas, 1996).

[64]Amerigas, 102 LA 1185 (Marino, 1994).

[65]Safeway, Inc., 104 LA 102 (Nelson, 1994).

[66]Swift Cleaning & Laundry, 106 LA 954 (Nelson, 1995).

[67][Updates footnote 189 in the Main Edition, on page 565.] See Avis Rent-a-Car System, 107 LA 197 (Shanker, 1996) (written extension of probationary period for less time than allowed by CBA held binding on company); Labrae Local Sch. Dist., 101 LA 246 (Sharpe, 1993) (school district bound by agent's agreement to pay employees' benefits).

[68][Updates footnote 193 in the Main Edition, on page 566.] See Roadway Express, Inc., 105 LA 114 (Eagle, 1995).

[69][Updates footnote 195 in the Main Edition, on page 566.] See City of Tarpon Springs, 107 LA 230 (Deem, 1996) (deputy chief didn't have authority to issue suspension; no double jeopardy where penalty subsequently increased); Container Corp. of America, 104 LA 263 (Baroni, 1995); City of Tacoma, 103 LA 950 (Bradburn, 1994).

Contract Principles

Promissory estoppel won the day for a union where the CEO of the company had promised in a letter to the bargaining unit 30 new jobs if the agreement being negotiated was ratified, where the company, after ratification, tried to transfer work that would have eliminated the jobs. The company was ordered to return sufficient work to keep 30 employees employed for the duration of the CBA.[70]

Where an employer, on the day prior to a ratification meeting, repudiated an agreement to pay for attendance at the meeting, the arbitrator found the repudiation to be effective and no obligation to pay was found to exist.[71] The fundamental principles of contract law continue to be recognized by arbitrators,[72] including the obligation to perform the contract despite the existence of hardships.[73]

The principle that there can be no binding contract without some objective indication that the parties intended to be bound continues to be applied by arbitrators.[74] Absence of a signed, written agreement or memorandum between the parties generally indicates that the parties had not concluded their discussions.[75] The oral modification of a side agreement, which is supported by consideration, would be enforceable.[76]

Remedies for Mistake

Parties who made different errors that together would lead to an unconscionable result were ordered to reform contract provisions

---

[70]Kuhlman Elec. Corp., 106 LA 429 (Duda, 1996).

[71]Litton Precision Gear, 107 LA 521 (Goldstein, 1996).

[72][Updates footnote 218 in the Main Edition, on page 570.] See Aurora City Sch., 108 LA 69 (Sharpe, 1997); Greenteam of San Jose, California, 103 LA 705 (McCurdy, 1994) (applied general contract principles to successors); City of Detroit, 102 LA 440 (Lipson, 1994) (parol evidence rule examined to determine validity of oral "side bar" agreement); International Paper Co., 101 LA 278 (Duff, 1993) (defining doctrine of "nunc pro tunc" to find provision of contract to be retroactive).

[73][Updates footnote 222 in the Main Edition, on page 570.] See St. Louis Symphony Soc'y, 106 LA 158 (Fowler, 1996); Sunnyside Coal Co., 104 LA 886 (Sharpe, 1995); City of Lake Worth, 101 LA 78 (Abrams, 1993).

[74][Updates footnote 223 in the Main Edition, on page 570.] See Q.C., Inc., 106 LA 987 (McGury, 1996) (settlement of prior discharge grievance was not a last chance agreement unless both parties agree that it is so); T. J. Maxx, 105 LA 470 (Richman, 1995); Globe Ticket & Label Co., 105 LA 62 (McCurdy, 1995); Kroger Grocery & Meats, 104 LA 422 (Duff, 1995); Mead Corp., 104 LA 161 (Krislov, 1995).

[75][Updates footnote 226 in the Main Edition, on page 571.] See Williams Furnace Co., 107 LA 215 (Monat, 1996) (no agreement found where proposed written settlement agreement of oral settlement of grievance is rejected; parties contemplated written settlement).

[76][Updates footnote 231 in the Main Edition, on page 571.] See Ccair Inc., 106 LA 56 (Nolan, 1995) (oral modification of agreement under RLA).

through bargaining,[77] but a mutual mistake was not grounds for reformation or rescission where the mistaken contract language improved description of the agreement.[78]

It has been held that a company's mistake in believing its proposal became part of the contract under the doctrine of acceptance by silence was unilateral and no agreement was concluded thereby.[79]

Arbitrators continue to grant reformation to correct a mutual mistake even where one of the parties did not realize the full ramifications of the provision signed.[80]

Unjust Enrichment

The principle of unjust enrichment has been used to deny back pay to a reinstated employee in a discharge case.[81] Pay for overtime hours not worked was denied on similar grounds, there being no evidence the employer had not acted in good faith in reducing hours of "overtime shifts."[82]

Waiver and Estoppel

It has been held that the doctrine of laches did not bar a claim by a retiring public employee for sick leave credit earned twenty years earlier while he was employed by other public entities.[83]

The scope of estoppel claims in arbitration cases continues to grow.[84]

---

[77]Kennedy Ctr., 101 LA 174 (Ables, 1993).

[78]Doss Aviation Inc., 107 LA 39 (Ferree, 1996).

[79]T. J. Maxx, 105 LA 470 (Richman, 1995).

[80]See, e.g., Guernsey County Dist. Public Library, 107 LA 435 (Sergent, 1996) (good-faith acceptance by the union of revised language proposed by the company did not change the mistake from unilateral to mutual), and Kansas City Power & Light Co., 105 LA 518 (Berger, 1995) (both parties misunderstood application of Fair Labor Standards Act to overtime hours covered by contract).

Later cases worthy of note are West Contra Costa Unified Sch.Dist. 107 LA 109 (Henner, 1996) (unilateral mistake was caused by a scrivener's error), and United Distillers Mfg., 104 LA 600 (Tharp, 1995) (employer unilaterally relied on erroneous cost information supplied by trustee bank in proposing conversion from profit sharing to multiple option plan for employees).

[81]Smurfit Recycling Co., 103 LA 243 (Richman, 1994).

[82]Ohio Edison Co., 102 LA 717 (Sergent, 1994).

[83]Union-Scioto Bd. of Educ., 106 LA 337 (1996).

[84]See, for example, the following Worldsource Coil Coating, 102 LA 17 (Florman, 1993) employer was not estopped from denying bumping qualifications of employees despite earlier instances where bumps were permitted and despite presumption of qualification. City of Novi, 101 LA 1028 (Brown, 1993) (union not estopped to challenge new leave policy when applied even though it had not done so when the policy was promulgated); Army and Air Force Exchange Service, 101 LA 1173 (Marlatt, 1993). (Federal agency estopped from claiming cost of preparing grievance on matter that was already moot); Odgen Fairmount Inc., 105 LA 492 (O'Grady, 1995) (union estopped from challenging hiring practice adopted at its behest and from which it had benefited for more than a year); Kansas City Fire Dept., 107 LA 519 (Berger, 1996) (employer estopped from contending condition of settlement agreement in discipline case had not been met);

The principle of equitable estoppel has appeared in two recent cases. In the first, *Goodman Beverage Co.*,[85] an employer was precluded from canceling the vacation of an employee who had paid for reservations in advance and there was no contractual provision authorizing the employer to alter vacation schedules. In the second, *International Paper Co.*,[86] estoppel against a company was denied, there being no proof of detrimental reliance by the employees. Meanwhile, on equitable grounds short of full estoppel, a union was prohibited from challenging layoff and work guarantee actions by the employer that the union had helped implement.[87]

The "acquiescence" of a first chief in paying annual clothing allowances in the past to firefighters retiring before the allowance due date was not a mistake but a continuation of a long, mutually accepted practice.[88]

One arbitrator decided evidence presented was not sufficient to prove the union had full knowledge of the facts and had "acquiesced" in a practice used by the employer to fill vacancies during layoff periods; hence, the union had not waived its right to grieve the matter.[89]

A company that apparently had acquiesced in a long-past practice of nonenforcement of an "early quit" rule advised the union of its intent to enforce the rule and posted notice accordingly, thus repudiating acquiescence and past practice. It was held the company had not waived its rule-making rights and did not have to reach mutual agreement with the union to enforce this rule.[90] A claim of waiver under a "zipper clause" was denied in City of Cleveland.[91]

Questions of timeliness in the use of grievance and arbitration procedures continue to be a major subject of arbitral decisions on waiver issues. The failure to act on a timely basis has been held to be

---

Triton College, 107 LA 796 (Greco, 1996) (employer estopped on theory of detrimental reliance to deny agreement granting employee time to reconsider and retract resignation); and City of Santa Cruz, 107 LA 1053 (Staudohar, 1996) (employer was not estopped from enforcing employee residency requirement).

[85]108 LA 37 (Morgan, 1997).

[86]101 LA 278 (Duff, 1993).

[87]Johnson Controls World Servs. Inc., 108 LA 191 (Specht, 1996).

For a later discussion of the distinction between "equitable" and "promissory" estoppel, see Central Hudson Gas and Elec. Corp., 101 LA 894 (Eischen, 1993). "Promissory" estoppel was applied to a contract violation in Kolar Buick. 101 LA 29 (Miller, 1993).

[88]City of Elyria, 106 LA 268 (Fullmer, 1996).

[89]General Telephone Co. of Calif., 106 LA 1043 (Grabuskie, 1996). For a "tacit acquiescence" case involving the absence of contract language despite the presence of a "zipper clause," see City of Frederick, 106 LA 298 (Neas, 1996).

[90]Michigan Hanger Co., 106 LA 377 (Smith, 1996).

[91]106 LA 195 (Cohen, 1995). For a discussion of the view of the National Labor Relations Board on zipper clause waivers, see Southern Bag Corp., 108 LA 348 (Overstreet, 1997).

a waiver.[92] However, there are a number of cases overruling claims of waiver.[93]

There are also cases in which a claim of waiver through untimeliness was rejected but the claiming party won on the merits.[94]

In many cases a claim of procedural waiver has been denied because the claim was first advanced at arbitration or at an advanced grievance step.[95]

In a similar vein, a number of decisions have addressed the issue of waiver caused by not objecting to or grieving action at an earlier opportunity. For example, a union was deemed not to have waived the right to grieve a new tipping policy for some employees even though a similar policy had been in effect for others without objection for several years.[96]And a union was held not to have waived its right to challenge (1) a new layoff point system by waiting until it was used by the employer[97]; (2) a random testing drug policy where twenty other employees had been tested earlier without protest[98]; or (3) a health care cost containment change made unilaterally by the employer where several earlier changes had not been grieved.[99]

In Clorox Co.,[100] it was held that the right to grieve a work standard was not waived by dropping earlier grievances where the purpose of dropping those grievances could not be determined.

The arbitrator decided in Gencorp Automative,[101] that a "last chance" agreement did not waive the contractual right to grieve and arbitrate discharge of the employee for "just cause." Nor did a verbal agreement between the company and the union to fill permanent jobs

---

[92]Summit Co. Ohio Engineer's Office, 101 LA 368 (Morgan, 1993) (filing of grievance); Schuykill Metals Corp., 102 LA 253 (O'Grady, 1994) (right to arbitrate); D.C. Public Sch., 105 LA 1037 (Johnson, 1995) (adding subject at arbitration step); and Monroe Mfg. Inc., 107 LA 877 (Stephens, 1996) (advancing grievance to next step in procedure).

[93]Jim Walter Resources Inc., 101 LA 385 (Feldman, 1993) (a joint waiver); VA Medical Ctr., 103 LA 74 (Gentile, 1994) (joint waiver by implied consent); and Michigan Capital Medical Ctr., 106 LA 893 (Mackraz, 1996) (lack of knowledge of work schedules of employees subject to bumping).

[94]City of Richmond, 102 LA 373 (Riker, 1994) (arbitrability of subject); Tinker Air Force Base, 102 LA 525 (Cipolla, 1994) (filing of grievance); and Stevens County, 105 LA 500 (Jacobowski, 1995) (step requirements).

[95]Sorg Paper Co., 102 LA 289 (Cohen, 1993) (late filing of grievances); City of Sterling Heights, 102 LA 1067 (Daniel, 1994) (arbitrability); Masolite Concrete Prods., 103 LA 10 (Keenan, 1994) (demand for arbitration); Defense Logistics Agency, 104 LA 439 (Gentile, 1995) (notification requirements); Stone Container Corp., 105 LA 385 (Berquist, 1995) (timeliness of grievance); Stevens County, 105 LA 500 (Jacobowski, 1995) (step requirements); Licking County, 105 LA 824 (Paolucci, 1995) (use of grievance forms); City of Fairbanks, 105 LA 903 (Landau, 1995) (existence of prior pending grievance on same subject without objection); and Lake Local Bd. of Educ., 108 LA 236 (Fullmer, 1997) (election of remedies).

[96]Sheraton Bal Harbour Resort, 102 LA 903 (Hoffman, 1994).

[97]Wilson Trophy Co., 104 LA 529 (Suardi, 1995).

[98]New Orleans Steamship Ass'n, 105 LA 79 (Nicholas, 1995).

[99]Excel Corp., 106 LA 1069 (Thornell, 1996).

[100]103 LA 932 (Franckiewicz, 1994).

[101]104 LA 113 (Malin, 1995).

without posting bids waive the right of an employee to a proper layoff notice.[102]

Acceptance by the union of modification of a discharge to a suspension during grievance proceedings did not waive the union's right to continue processing the grievance under the contract, particularly where the employer later offered further modification,[103] but acceptance of enhanced severance pay packages by employees on layoff waived their reinstatement rights even though they had been laid off in violation of the contract.[104]

Principles of Damages

In any discussion of damages and make-whole remedies it must be remembered that the terms "back pay" and "full back pay," used without modification, may be misleading. The reader is reminded that awards of "back pay" and "full back pay" are generally subject to mitigation and offsets. Accordingly, compensatory damages and make-whole terminology used here will not contain repeated references to such reductions.

As may be expected, decisions are mixed on the authority of an arbitrator to award monetary damages. Extra pay for grieving employees was denied in *Georgia-Pacific Corp.,*[105] despite a clear subcontracting violation where no employee was laid off or sent home early and there was no monetary injury. In *Union Camp Corp.,*[106] The arbitrator decided he had no authority to award monetary damages for mental distress. On the other hand, the arbitrator in *GTE North Inc.,*[107] awarded affected employees one-half of the $150,000 the company had saved by contracting out bargaining unit work while engaged in downsizing layoffs. One arbitrator applied the seamen's common law of "maintenance and cure" in awarding unearned wages and maintenance payments in *Marriott Int'l Inc.,*[108] and another arbitrator awarded lump-sum front pay and benefits instead of reinstatement and back pay to a wrongfully discharged employee.[109]

Meanwhile, one arbitrator enforced the Federal Employees Part-time Career Employment Act of 1978 in *Defense Commissary Agency,*[110] and another arbitrator used the Back Pay Act in *Federal Aviation Administration,*[111] to award back pay.

---

[102]Wisconsin Power & Light, 105 LA 22 (Imes, 1995).
[103]Greater Cleveland Transit Auth., 103 LA 270 (Feldman, 1994).
[104]United Cent. Telephone Co. of Texas, 104 LA 246 (Baroni, 1995).
[105]106 LA 980 (Moore, 1996).
[106]104 LA 295 (Nolan, 1995).
[107]106 LA 1115 (Coyne, 1996).
[108]106 LA 403 (Wilkinson, 1996).
[109]Piney Point Transp. Co., 103 LA 1117 (Crable, 1994).
[110]101 LA 850 (Wren, 1993).
[111]101 LA 886 (Bognanno, 1993).

Compensatory Damages

Relying on past practice and acquiescence of the fire chief, the arbitrator decided an annual uniform-purchase clothing allowance was payable to firefighters who had retired before the date of the payment.[112] The employer in *Roseville Community Schools* was ordered to pay at overtime rate school librarians required to work flexible schedules involving hours beyond the "school day" to meet state school library standards.[113]

In *Copley Newspapers*,[114] the arbitrator ordered the employer to pay a reporter $600 as a "make-whole" remedy for wrongful refusal of permission to write an article for a "non-competitive" magazine. Another arbitrator set aside a discharge and awarded full back pay but declined to reinstate the employee into a "volatile" situation. In lieu of reinstatement, the grievant was awarded six months' severance pay.[115]

In a more humorous vein, the arbitrator ordered *Oakland University* to reissue a parking permit to the union president and to reimburse him for costs of parking violations incurred while the permit was withheld,[116] and in *North Greene School District*,[117] the arbitrator ordered the employer to stop interfering with the issuance of passes by an athletic conference to teachers and to reimburse each teacher the price of admission to each event attended for which the teacher paid admission during a designated school year.

Recent awards have extended "make-whole" recovery beyond established out-of-pocket costs and money losses, often relying on an assumption that an employee would have done something or reached some status if the opportunity had been available. For example, in one case an employee was awarded an attendance bonus and pay for equalized overtime as part of back pay without loss of benefits, even though he resigned and did not return to work following his reinstatement from wrongful discharge.[118] In another case, the employer was ordered to review the grievant's performance appraisals to determine whether a suspension, set aside on procedural grounds in the nature of double jeopardy, had negatively affected the appraisals and, if so, to correct them.

---

[112]City of Elyria, 106 LA 268 (Fullmer, 1996).
[113]106 LA 1013 (Borland, 1996).
[114]107 LA 310 (Stallworth, 1996).
[115]Rodeway Inn, 102 LA 1003 (Goldberg, 1994).
[116]106 LA 872 (Daniel, 1996).
[117]107 LA 284 (Nathan, 1996).
[118]Vision-Ease, 102 LA 1106 (Mathews, 1994); USAF, 107 LA 1089 (Stephens, 1997). See also City of Omaha, 101 LA 476 (Bard, 1993), where the employer was ordered to grant a merit pay increase to an employee with no negative work history who had missed work for a considerable portion of the performance evaluation period because of injury. Evidence there indicated merit increases were essentially automatic for employees without negative work histories.

Arbitrators continue to condition make-whole awards on the occurrence of a future event.[119]

In some cases the nature of the alleged offense results in a back-pay award that is less than "make whole."[120] By the same token, an award may be lessened where the grievant was responsible for creating the problem.[121]

Arbitrators continue to grant interim back pay in disciplinary cases where procedural or technical errors occurred, even though the resulting discharge or suspension was sustained. In *Atlantic Southeast Airlines*,[122] a flight attendant who was wrongfully discharged for "refusing" to take a drug test later failed such a test after being returned to work. She was denied reinstatement but awarded back pay for the period between the wrongful discharge and the assumed date ten months later when she used the marijuana found in the failed test. A disciplinary demotion involving alleged sexual harassment was upheld in *Renton School District*,[123] but the demoted employee was awarded the difference in pay up to commencement of the arbitration hearing because the employer had refused to disclose to the employee the names of his accusers. In *Mason & Hangar—Silas Mason Co.*,[124] a discharge for failing a drug test was upheld, but back pay

---

[119]See, e.g., J.W. Costello Beverage Co., 106 LA 356 (Bickner, 1996) (60 days to prove ability); Mesa Distrib. Co., 106 LA 1166 (Rule, 1996) (pass physical examination and drug screen); APCOA, Inc., 107 LA 705 (Daniel, 1996) (12 weeks to provide medical certification of ability to return to work); and Darling Store Fixtures, 108 LA 183 (Allen, 1997) (90-day "last chance" to correct absence record).

[120]See, e.g., Maryvale Samaritan Medical Ctr., 103 LA 90 (White, 1994) (grievant who ignored orders was "her own worst enemy"); Greschlers' Inc., 103 LA 135 (Nadelbach, 1994) (clerk's improper conduct toward customer of a retail store); Smurfit Recycling Co., 103 LA 243 (Richman, 1994) (safety rule violation); Democratic Printing & Lithographing, 103 LA 327 (Weisbrod, 1994) ("atrocious" attendance record); Exxon Chem. Americas, 105 LA 1011 (Allen, 1996) (falsification of company document to conceal drunken driving conviction); Nabisco Brands Inc., 106 LA 422 (Wolff, 1996) (fighting); Tenneco Packaging Corp., 106 LA 606 (Franckiewicz, 1996) (insubordination); Avis Rent-A-Car System, 107 LA 197 (Shanker, 1996) (prior criminal conviction not disclosed on employment application); Weyerhaeuser Forest Prods., 108 LA 26 (Levak, 1997) (refusal to take drug test); and Smith Fiberglass Prods. 108 LA 225 (Allen, 1997) (unauthorized personal leave—hiding from threatening husband).

[121]See, e.g., Burlington N.R.R., 101 LA 144 (Massey, 1993) (employee responsible for much of delay in reaching arbitration); Grace Indus., 102 LA 119 (Knott, 1993) (failure to grieve demotion, which was a factor in ultimate discharge); Crown Divs. of the Allen Group, 103 LA 378 (Klein, 1994) (reduction in back pay by amount of property damage caused by grievant's carelessness for which she had been discharged); Ogden Support Servs., Inc., 104 LA 432 (Weisheit, 1995) (refusal to accept comparable job following reinstatement from gross negligence discharge); Buckeye Steel Castings Co., 104 LA 825 (Weatherspoon, 1995 (refusal of job assignment); Cone Mills Corp., 106 LA 23 (Nolan, 1995) (grievant unavailable for work because of illness and personal travel); Facility Management of Louisiana, 106 LA 879 (O'Grady, 1996) (grievant in jail for non-work-related offense) and Bruce Hardwood Floors, 108 LA 115 (Allen, 1997) (long-term employee with no history of drug use failed random drug test after mistakenly taking wife's medication).

[122]101 LA 515 (Nolan, 1993).

[123]102 LA 854 (Wilkinson, 1994).

[124]103 LA 371 (Cipolla, 1994).

was awarded because the employer's discharge procedure violated applicable federal regulations. In *United States Can Co.,*[125] partial back pay was awarded, but reinstatement was denied a chronically ill employee terminated after compiling an extensive record of absenteeism.

Failure to follow contract procedures frequently results in an award of full back pay.[126]

Awards may also involve more than strict monetary relief. In *City of Akron,*[127] the grievant was awarded one week's pay because the employer failed to notify the union that he would be relieved from duty. The employer was ordered to set grievant's discharge aside, treat that time off from work as unpaid medical leave, and reinstate him to his former position if he obtained proper medical clearance.

In *Gaylord Container Corp.,*[128] the arbitrator set aside a disciplinary demotion, replaced it with a minor suspension and awarded back pay for the difference in pay rates where the company had not followed progressive discipline principles.

Particular attention is called to *Rubbermaid Office Products,*[129] where the company, having closed its California plant and moved the work to Tennessee without offering its employees an opportunity to relocate there, was ordered to pay terminated employees the wages they would have earned from the date of termination through the duration of the labor agreement; and *Kuhlman Electric Corp.,*[130] where the arbitrator ordered the company to return sufficient equipment and assign available work to its Kentucky plant to permit employment of at least 30 employees during the remainder of the contract. In that case, the company had moved the equipment to a Mississippi installation.

Also of interest is *Border Patrol,*[131] where the agency was required to reinstate a Border Patrol Officer with full pay and benefits and to remove from his file a letter from the United States attorney that contained unsubstantiated allegations of dishonesty.

---

[125]104 LA 863 (Briggs, 1995).

[126]See S and J Ranch, 103 LA 350 (Bogue, 1994) (failure of notification); City of Newark, 107 LA 775 (Kindig, 1996) (lack of predisciplinary conference); Ken Meyer Meats, 107 LA 1017 (Sergent, 1996) (failure to investigate before imposing discipline); Southern Frozen Foods, 107 LA 1030 (Giblin, 1996) (lack of due process—no investigation); CR/PL Ltd. Partnership, 107 LA 1084 (Fullmer, 1996) (no investigation) Anheuser-Busch, Inc., 107 LA 1183 (Weckstein, 1996) (insufficient involvement of union and notice to employees in development of drug abuse policy); and Kroger Co., 108 LA 417 (Baroni, 1997) (absence of predischarge hearing and investigation). See also Kasle Steel Corp., 107 LA 1006 (Kerner, 1996) and Alaska Dep't of Transp., 108 LA 339 (Levak, 1997), (discipline reduced because of procedural and/or administrative errors); and Boeing Co., 101 LA 240 (Staudohar, 1993) (employer failed to give appropriate notice under Worker Adjustment and Retraining Notification Act).

[127]105 LA 787 (Kasper, 1995).

[128]107 LA 1138 (Allen, 1997).

[129]107 LA 161 (Alleyne, 1996).

[130]106 LA 429 (Duda, 1996).

[131]106 LA 1175 (Rezler, 1996).

In *Independent School District 309,*[132] the arbitrator awarded teachers an additional $500 for each sixth class period taught involuntarily during two school years.

In *Schnuck Markets, Inc.,*[133] an employer was given 60 days to correct a "contracting out" violation system. The union was ordered not to file grievances about the system during that period. In *Mount Sinai Hospital,*[134] the arbitrator ordered an employee reinstated with training "appropriate to polish her interpersonal skills."

Make-whole awards may include reimbursement for cost of lost benefits such as medical expenses,[135] health insurance premiums,[136] dental claims and tool claims,[137] protective eyewear,[138] and tuition reimbursement.[139] In one case an employer was required to reimburse travel expenses incurred by a firefighter to take paramedic training.[140]

Arbitrators have also restored contractual benefits,[141] and have ordered other positive action.[142] Make-whole award also extend to the recovery of lost premiums or other special pay,[143] and to pay for time worked for travel to the location of a special assignment.[144] Also, an

---

[132]101 LA 703 (Bognanno, 1993).

[133]107 LA 739 (Cipolla, 1996).

[134]105 LA 1047 (Duff, 1995).

[135]San Benito Health Found., 105 LA 263 (Levy, 1995).

[136]B.P. Oil Co., 106 LA 976 (Hewitt, 1996) and Klosterman Baking Co., 106 LA 257 (Beckjord, 1996).

[137]Kent Worldwide Mach. Works, 107 LA 455 (Duda, 1996).

[138]Stone Container Corp., 108 LA 249 (Hilgert, 1997).

[139]State of Oregon, 107 LA 138 (Downing, 1996).

[140]City of Cortland, 108 LA 406 (Skulina, 1997).

[141]City of Omaha, 101 LA 476 (Bard, 1993) (merit increase); City of Benton Harbor, 106 LA 847 (Ellmann, 1996) (various benefits denied temporarily disabled employee assigned to light duty while on workers' compensation); and Doss Aviation Inc., 107 LA 39 (Ferree, 1996) (accrued sick leave); Ohio Edison Co., 102 LA 717 (Sergent, 1994), and P.U.D. No 1 of Clark County, 107 LA 713 (Paull, 1996) (meal allowances); and Kent Worldwide Mach. Works, 107 LA 455 (Duda, 1996) (Christmas bonus).

[142]Internal Revenue Serv., 101 LA 341 (Donnelly, 1993), and D.C. Bd. of Educ., 101 LA 691 (Modjeska, 1993) (employees transferred to different sites offered opportunity to return to original post); Rodeway Inn, 102 LA 1003 (Goldberg, 1994) (formal apology to grievant, posting of notice to employees of award, and meeting on company time for union to discuss matter with employees); and City of Los Angeles, 103 LA 1075 (Bergeson, 1994) (employer ordered to change retroactively absence without approved leave to approved vacation time).

[143]Quantum Chemical Corp., 101 LA 26 (Caraway, 1993); Hughes Aircraft Co., 107 LA 157 (Richman, 1996), and McDowell Tire Co., 108 LA 196 (Berger, 1997) (severance pay); Naval Surface Warfare Ctr., 101 LA 640 (Shearer, 1993); George Koch Sons, 107 LA 153 (Murphy, 1996); P.U.D. No. 1 of Clark County, 107 LA 713 (Paull, 1996); and LTV Steel Mining Co., 108 LA 1 (Das, 1996) (overtime); Cambria County, Pa., 101 LA 330 (D'eletto, 1993), and U.S. Steel Mining Co., 105 LA 524 (Roberts, 1995) (weekend or holiday premium); San Benito Health Found., 105 LA 263 (Levy, 1995), and City of Frederick, 106 LA 298 (Neas, 1996) (vacations); American Drug Stores, 107 LA 985 (Richman, 1996) (shift premium); Chicago Bd. of Edu., 107 LA 999 (Kenis, 1996), and San Benito Health Found., 105 LA 263 (sick leave and pay); and Vicksburg Community Schools, 101 LA 771 (Daniel, 1993) ("business" leave).

[144]City of Beaverton, 107 LA 1205 (Calhoun, 1997) (employer ordered to pay employees for travel time between their homes and a training site 13 miles from their regular work location).

employer that refused to allow an employee to withdraw a resignation has been ordered to reinstate and make the employee whole.[145]

Make-whole awards have also been used where an employer unilaterally initiates changes in the terms and conditions of employment or in benefits provided for by contract,[146] and where an employer improperly "contracts out" or subcontracts bargaining unit work.[147]

But there must be a show of injury to justify such an award.[148] Thus, a subcontracting violation that did not adversely affect bargaining unit work did not call for a remedial order.[149] Also, no remedial order was granted where the arbitrator found too many "variables" in the evidence to justify such an order.[150]

---

[145]Atlantic Southeast Airlines, 102 LA 656 (Feigenbaum, 1994).

[146]Lightening Indus. Inc., 105 LA 417 (Mikrut, 1995); Excel Corp., 106 LA 1069 (Thornell, 1996); and Washington Mould Co., 106 LA 1139 (Imundo, 1996) (employer attempted unilateral change in health or medical insurance coverage, benefits or responsibility for payment of premiums in whole or part); Helix Elec. Inc., 101 LA 649 (Kaufman, 1993) (violation of manning ratio agreement); Burlington Medical Ctr., 101 LA 843 (Bailey, 1993) (violation of weekend work schedule agreement by requiring registered nurse to take off "low census" days to provide hours for part-time nurse); Dubovsky & Sons, 108 LA 19 (Marx, 1996) (layoff of permanent employees instead of temporary vacation replacements); Fina Oil and Chem. Co., 104 LA 343 (Nicholas, 1995) (employer delayed return to work of an employee injured on the job by requiring a third doctor's opinion in violation of contract language); Tucson Unified Sch. Dist., 106 LA 202 (Oberstein, 1996) (school district denied a contractual extra stipend to teacher acting as department chair); Copperweld Steel Co., 106 LA 918 (Duda, 1996) (company wrongfully broke continuous service of employee off work because of work-related injury); Enesco Corp., 107 LA 513 (Berman, 1996) (company denied pregnant employee's request for leave under contract's "good cause shown" clause); Phelps Dodge Magnet Wire Co., 108 LA 21 (Curry, 1996) (failure to provide light duty for employee injured off duty); and Goodman Beverage Co., 108 LA 37 (Morgan, 1997) (termination of an employee as a "quit" for not changing preapproved vacation for which he had paid in advance and could not get refund).
Of broader application are Sheraton Bal Harbour Resort, 102 LA 903 (Hoffman, 1994) (hotel instituted an automatic tipping policy applicable to some, but not all, employees in server and bartender job classifications); Albertson's Inc., 106 LA 897 (Kaufman, 1996) (employer denied negotiated annual pay raise to above-scale employees); Dayton's, 108 LA 113 (Jacobowski, 1997) (back pay instead of future makeup work is proper remedy for overtime violation); and Premier Private Sec., 108 LA 270 (Chumley, 1997) (company attempted unilaterally to change from cash allowances paid to employees to plans selected by company for health and pension benefit programs).

[147]Hexcel Corp., 101 LA 700 (Silver, 1993); Automatic Sprinkler Corp., 106 LA 19 (Wahl, 1995) (subcontract to nonunion contractor in violation of national agreement); and Montgomery Ward & Co., 106 LA 902 (Daly, 1996). See particularly Tennessee Valley Auth., 101 LA 218 (1993), where Arbitrator Bankston in a second supplemental award, following the employer's refusal to comply with earlier awards, ordered the employer to increase the size of the bargaining unit to the level that existed before subcontracting was instituted. In addition to a make-whole back pay award, Arbitrator Bankston issued a cease-and-desist order and ordered the employer to pay $25,000 to the union as partial reimbursement for costs, expenses and lost dues. In related topics, see Fingerhut, 105 LA 1146 (Lundberg, 1995) (use of temporary employees before recalling laid-off permanent employees), and City of Toledo, 106 LA 1005 (Sharpe, 1996) (use of non-bargaining-unit employees).

[148]Union Camp Corp., 104 LA 295 (1995). (Arbitrator Nolan declined to award monetary damages for "mental distress," assuming he had authority to do so, because there was no evidence of injury and any such award would be "purely speculative").

[149]Kroger Co., 105 LA 856 (Katz, 1996).

[150]Freeman Decorating Co., 102 LA 149 (Barow, 1994).

However, an employer was held to have violated the contract by refusing to return an injured employee to work where the employer failed to prove the employee was unable to perform the regular duties of the job, including lifting, within applicable medical restrictions.[151]

Damages Payable to Company or Union

The arbitral award will occasionally be made to the union on behalf of the grievants.[152] Also, an award based on past practice, in favor of the union, was made where the employer refused to pay the union representative for time spent.[153] Where the employer failed to comply with a prior award regarding the jurisdictional rights of the union, it was ordered to increase the size of the bargaining unit to pay $25,000 partial reimbursement for lost dues to the union, and to pay the union's costs and expenses.[154]

The "De Minimis" Rule

Where a grievance involves trifling or immaterial matters, in denying grievances arbitrators sometimes apply the rule of de minimis non curat lex.[155]

Interest on Award

Many arbitrators have refused to require that interest be paid on awards.[156]

---

[151]Borough of Frackville, 101 LA 480 (DiLauro, 1993). See also Rubbermaid Office Prods., 107 LA 161 (Alleyne, 1996) (company's evidence insufficient to prove it had subcontracted work to another location as the contract permitted; hence, a very substantial monetary award was issued in favor of its terminated employees); Kaiser Eng'g, 102 LA 1189 (Minni, 1994) (back pay remedy calculated only at straight time since the opportunity for overtime at this installation was "highly speculative").

[152]See Arbitrators Coyne in 106 LA 1115 ($75,000 ordered to be paid to the union to distribute to employees for subcontracting violations); Garrett in 105 LA 240, 247; Kaufman in 101 LA 649, 654; Richman in 101 LA 226, 232.

[153]See Arbitrator Fullmer in 104 LA 444; Gentile in 104 LA 439, 443.

[154]Tennessee Valley Authority Inter. Assoc. of Machinists and Aerospace Workers, 101 LA 218 (Blankston, 1993).

[155]See Arbitrator Grooms in 107 LA 412, 415; Sharpe in 106 LA 1005, 1012; Gentile in 106 LA 524, 528; Leibowitz in 105 LA 1041, 1043–5; Fullmer in 105 LA 173, 179.

[156]Arbitrator Kaufman in 107 LA 1213, 1216; Ferree in 107 LA 39, 52 (because the union was also somewhat at fault); Levy in 106 LA 1092, 1095; Allen in 105 LA 1011, 1019; Murphy in 103 LA 453 (because the delay of one year was not due to employer bad faith); Bailey in 101 LA 843, 849–50; Kaufman in 101 LA 649, 654; Bankston in 98 LA 1090 (because the delay was neither deliberate nor unreasonable); Mikrut in 98 LA 819, 827 (because the agreement was silent); Di Leone in 96 LA 657; Briggs in 95 LA 351 (because the violation of the agreement was neither malicious nor intentional); Wren in 95 LA 97, 104 (because the employer had acted in good faith); Stewart in 94 LA 975, 978 (because arbitration is restorative, not punitive); Prayzich in 94 LA 875 (because the agreement was silent, and the employer was not shown to have been dilatory); Nolan in 94 LA 669 (because the issue was not raised until the remedy hearing,

Arbitrators Hill and Sinicropi have noted that not awarding interest in arbitration may originally have been due to the "one-time and now-abandoned practice of the NLRB of not awarding interest on back-pay awards".[157] The NLRB abandoned the practice in 1962.[158] The arbitrator, after noting that interest was seldom requested and cautioning that interest should not be used as punishment, concluded that because of the time value of money, the awarding of interest was necessary to make a grievant whole.[159] It has been held that the awarding of interest is within the inherent power of an arbitrator.[160] It would appear from recent cases that a larger number of arbitrators are awarding interest where appropriate.[161]

---

and the employer was not shown to have been dilatory); Levak in 93 LA 132; Malin in 91 LA 1300, and in 91 LA 1293; Ross in 91 LA 1186; Kahn in 91 LA 831, 835 (because interest had not been a part of prior remedies); Nicholas in 87 LA 473; Yarowsky in 87 LA 283, 286–87 (because an award of interest would be a penalty in the circumstances); Bogue in 86 LA 1082 (because the employer's miscalculation of a wage increase had been in good faith); Boedecker in 85 LA 745, 753 (denied as to money due from prior award since no evidence demonstrated the employer's actions in the interim to be egregious enough to warrant interest being charged). But see Arbitrator Wren in 101 LA 850 (interest was awarded under the Back Pay Act).

[157]Remedies in Arbitration, 2nd ed. (BNA Books, 1991), p. 450.

[158]Isis Plumbing Co., 138 NLRB 716, 51 LRRM 1122, 1124 (1962), rev'd on other grounds NLRB v. Isis Plumbing Co., 322 F.2d 913, 54 LRRM 2235 (9th Cir. 1963). See also Florida Steel Corp., 231 NLRB 651, 96 LRRM 1070 (1977) (adaption by the NLRB of Internal Revenue Service's adjusted prime interest rate).

[159]Atlantic Southeast Airlines, 101 LA 515, 525–26 (Nolan, 1993).

[160]Falstaff Brewing Corp. v. Local No. 153, Teamsters, 479 F.Supp. 850, 103 LRRM 2008 (D.N.J. 1978).

[161]Sweeney in 108 LA 449, 453–54; Bickner in 106 LA 1033, 1042; Haemmel in 104 LA 1157, 1162–64 (because of the NLRB's practice and the employer's bad faith); Minni in 102 LA 1189, 1193; Feigenbaum in 102 LA 656, 660; Kessler in 99 LA 1223 (because the employer had benefited by withholding the grievant's severance pay); House in 99 LA 852, 858–59 (where vacation pay had been improperly withheld for five months to help ease an employer cash flow problem); Madden in 98 LA 1087; Strasshofer in 97 LA 1167; Mayer in 907 LA 275, 282; Bell in 95 LA 942 (on medical claims paid by the grievant); Simons in 95 LA 617, 631 (because the grievant was denied the timely use of the money, and because of the NLRB practice of invariably awarding interest); Fowler in 92 LA 876, 882 (to make whole where lump-sum pension payment had been delayed for three years); Corbett in 92 LA 281 (to make whole); Talarico in 91 LA 1097, 1101 (because outrageous, lewd, on-air remarks by disc jockeys had caused the grievant to resign); Huffcut in 91 LA 499, 505; Creo in 90 LA 281, 286; Talarico in 89 LA 1302 (money advanced to grievant is allowed as offset, with interest, against back pay award); Weisinger in 89 LA 1215, 1221 (awarded on delinquent contributions to benefits funds); McHugh in 89 LA 383, 384–85 (to make whole); Smith in 86 LA 866, 873 (to make whole, and to prevent employer from being unjustly enriched); Girolamo in 86 LA 683, 685–86 (on amount employer failed to roll over to retirement annuity); Howlett in 86 LA 305, 308; Stashower in 82 LA 1036, 1038 (to make whole). See Levy in 105 LA 263, 264 (who said interest would be awarded if there was delay); Levak in 93 LA 132 (who reserved the right to award interest in the event of undue delay by the employer in complying with the award); McDermott in 92 LA 1308, 1314; Williams in 73 LA 1292, 1300, 1302; Jones in 66 LA 354, 356.

Attorney Fees

Requests for attorney fees have generally been rejected by arbitrators.[162] But where circumstances dictate, arbitrators are willing to award them.[163] Also, under the Civil Service Reform Act of 1978, there is provision for awarding attorney fees.[164]

Mitigating Damages—Deduction of Outside Compensation

As with any breach of contract, the employee who has been suspended or discharged has an obligation to mitigate damages.[165] In a discharge or discipline case, where the issue is raised, arbitrators reduce the employer's liability by the amount of unemployment compensation and other compensation received by the employee during the period of his/her absence,[166] provided that such compensation was not a normal part of the employee's income prior to the suspension or discharge.[167] Many arbitrators will deny back pay where it is clear that the employee failed to take advantage of available reasonable employment opportunities.[168] When the issue is raised, the grievant

---

[162]Hockenberry in 108 LA 496, 502; Sweeney in 108 LA 449, 453 (where the evidence was insufficient to prove the employer's malice); Daniel in 107 LA 705, 713; Duff in 101 LA 890, 894 (holding that universal policy fails to authorize the arbitrator to grant attorney fees); Nolan in 101 LA 515, 526; Brisco in 100 LA 267, 278 (stating that even though the grievance was like a Fair Labor Standards Act case, the parties were still in arbitration); Weiss in 95 LA 1072, 1075–76 (because the employer had not acted in bad faith in violating a prior arbitration award); Wilkinson in 95 LA 107 (because a federal agency had reasonably relied upon instructions even though the instructions were contrary to unambiguous regulations).

[163]Arbitrator Daniel in 101 LA 1199 (where the employer continued to violate the agreement).

[164]See Arbitrator Wolff in 107 LA 621; Feldman in 106 LA 107 (where the grievant's blood type did not match the drug test sample). Seidman in 93 LA 920, 929–31 (where a federal agency had failed to conduct a proper investigation and had filed unnecessary motions and pleadings to harass the grievant).

[165]Arbitrator Nicholas in 101 LA 643, 646 (who noted the "arbitrator's inherent obligation to see that damages are mitigated").

[166]Arbitrator Nicholas in 108 LA 565, 572; Weston in 108 LA 284, 288; Morgan in 108 LA 37, 43; Giblin in 107 LA 1030, 1037; Sergent in 107 LA 1017, 1023; Pelofsky in 107 LA 645, 654; Ellmann in 107 LA 561, 566; Cerone in 107 LA 188, 192; Hodgson in 107 LA 27, 30; Bain in 106 LA 180, 185; Kaufman in 106 LA 132, 136; Poole in 105 LA 1194, 1201; Brookins in 105 LA 673, 681; Hayford in 105 LA 572, 576; Imes in 105 LA 391, 398; Shanker in 104 LA 933, 940–41; Feldman in 104 LA 486, 494; Nicholas in 104 LA 343, 348; Talarico in 104 LA 131, 136; Donnelly in 102 LA 1024, 1031; DiFalco in 102 LA 910, 917; Bethel in 102 LA 733, 736; Hilgert in 102 LA 545, 555; Van Auken-Haight in 102 LA 280, 285; Kenis in 102 LA 154, 160.

[167]Arbitrator Coyne in 105 LA 353, 356 (no offset of earnings from previously owned pizza business); McGury in 104 LA 191, 192; Silver in 98 LA 122, 125 (no offset for earnings from a doughnut shop); Allen in 92 LA 29. But see Cantor in 97 LA 573, 577–78 (who allowed the employer to reduce back pay by the amount earned from a part-time job that had been worked concurrently with his job with the employer).

[168]See Arbitrator Shanker in 107 LA 197, 202 (grievant did not seek employment diligently); Nolan in 106 LA 23; Weatherspoon in 104 LA 825, 828 (grievant refused a job assignment); Weisheit in 104 LA 432 (grievant refused comparable employment); Nolan in 103 LA 1179 (grievant had not applied for work as had been claimed); Wilkinson

or the union will be directed to provide proof of outside income.[169] When the arbitration process has been delayed by the employee or the union, the employer's back pay liability may be reduced.[170]

Judicial Notice and Presumptions

Arbitrators frequently take judicial notice of well-known facts and the ordinary meanings of words,[171] and, some arbitrators have taken "arbitral" notice.[172] Also, arbitrators use presumptions as aids in deciding issues,[173] and give effect to all the words in the agreement.[174]

Parol Evidence

Although the parol evidence rule continues to be applied in arbitration cases,[175] arbitrators are also cognizant of the exceptions to the

---

in 101 LA 496; Caraway in 100 LA 291, 295; Parent in 98 LA 531 (denied for the period when grievant refused training); Goodstein in 99 LA 879, 884 (grievant refused corrective surgery that could have hastened his return to work); Massey in 97 LA 1145, 1151 (grievant repeatedly refused tutoring); Prayzich in 97 LA 297 (grievant refused to return to work); Berger in 96 LA 585 (reduced because grievant refused reinstatement); Darrow in 96 LA 134 (reduced by amount that could have been earned in refused job); Prayzich in 94 LA 875 (reduced by amount that would have been earned had grievant not quit an interim job); but see contra, Nicholas in 94 LA 992 (where the back pay was not reduced since the employer offered no proof as to the reason the grievant quit); Richard in 93 LA 302, 310. But see Arbitrator Wahl in 103 LA 1015 (grievant did not need to register for work when no work was available); Arbitrator Bard in 95 LA 926 (reading of newspaper want ads was sufficient where employer did not show that filing an application with state unemployment office would have resulted in finding employment). Also see Arbitrator Sharpe in 93 LA 1155, 1159 (starting a new business satisfied the duty to mitigate damages).

[169]Arbitrator Berman in 107 LA 513, 519 (union directed to produce evidence); Kilroy in 107 LA 325, 328; Briggs in 105 LA 1089, 1094; Cohen in 105 LA 199, 204; Feldman in 104 LA 1006, 1012, and 102 LA 609, 612 (affidavits); McGury in 104 LA 191, 192; Briggs in 101 LA 589, 598; Bittel in 94 LA 1177 (approved an employer demand to see the tax returns of a reinstated employee and upheld the employee's discharge for refusing to comply with the request).

[170]Arbitrators Duff in 102 LA 317, 320; Bogue in 103 LA 350, 362; Dunham Massey in 101 LA 144, 153–54; DiLauro in 99 LA 353, 360; Hilgert in 96 LA 266, 273–74; Volz in 94 LA 448, 451.

[171]Arbitrators Richman in 104 LA 175, 177 (that smoking is unhealthy); Gentile in 103 LA 988, 991 (as to the greatness of the Aztec and Mayan cultures); Imundo in 103 LA 547, 557; Marino in 102 LA 1185, 1188; Brunner in 102 LA 737, 741–42; Jacobs in 102 LA 601, 605.

[172]Arbitrator McDowell in 94 LA 894, 899 (took "arbitral notice that there is an adverse relationship between smoking and health"); and Arbitrator Eisler in 93 LA 1677, 177 (took "notice that virtually any kind of message is being used . . . on home telephone answering devices").

[173]Arbitrator Howell in 107 LA 801, 805–6 (rejected the use of a presumption to discredit testimony due to the interest of the witness in the outcome of the case).

[174]Arbitrator Bittel in 101 LA 1122, 1125.

[175]Savannah Symphony Soc'y, 102 LA 575, 579 (Howell, 1994); Gangle in 94 LA 140, 144–45.

rule.[176] Precontract negotiations are admissible to aid in the interpretation of ambiguous language in the contract.[177] Also, a subsequent oral modification or a written agreement that modifies a written agreement can be enforced in arbitration.[178]

---

[176]Arbitrator Freedman in 97 LA 1016, 1018–19.

[177]Arbitrators Henner in 107 LA 109, 114; Kanner in 105 LA 549, 553; Duff in 102 LA 165, 166; Traynor in 101 LA 18, 20; McDonald in 101 LA 194, 198; Wren in 96 LA 570, 572 (explaining that "arbitral authority is quite liberal in allowing into evidence testimony with respect to contract negotiations, the parties' interpretation of terms in the agreement, and the like"); Freeman in 93 LA 199, 1202–3.

[178]See arbitrators Eagle in 105 LA 114, 116; Christopher in 103 LA 596; Dworkin in 102 LA 757.

Chapter 11

Precedent Value of Awards

Authoritative Prior Awards

Temporary Arbitrators

The continued binding force of a prior authoritative award on a contractual interpretation issue may be called into question by a material change in the conditions or circumstances under which the award was made. Arbitrators refuse to follow the prior precedent when the new conditions suggest that it is no longer reasonable to continue to apply the earlier decision.

Thus, twenty years after a 1973 arbitration award that required management "to continue to furnish nurses on all shifts and weekends," the company discontinued such staffing because the number of employees served had been reduced by more than one-half and it had instituted a program to train and equip employees to provide emergency medical response. Denying the union's grievance, the arbitrator found that "replacing old ways of doing things with new methods" . . . "[was] adequate to serve the safety needs of the Bargaining Unit personnel," and concluded that "[a]lthough the logic of . . . [the prior] award has survived, new methods and changing conditions require a different result."[1]

Persuasive Prior Awards

Changes in popular attitudes, often crystallized by federal legislation and regulation, may cause arbitrators to reexamine the premises and hence the continued vitality of earlier awards. For example,

---

[1]Packaging Corp. of Am., 102 LA 1099 (Odom, 1994).

95

in reviewing the discharge of an employee for the alleged sexual harassment of three female employees during a company-sponsored sales
conference held at a hotel, an arbitrator refused to follow several decisions reached a decade earlier in which similar and even more egregious episodes of sexual harassment were found not to constitute "just
cause" for discharge. He opined that the prior decisions were "not in
keeping with current arbitral thinking on the subject . . . [because]
both societal and judicial views on the seriousness of sexual harassment have undergone dramatic change between then and now."[2]

Precedent and Development of Substantive Principles

Arbitrators remain divided over the burden of proof applicable
in arbitration proceedings involving the discipline of an employee
charged with sexual harassment.

Despite a union's contention that "because the charge of sexual
harassment involves an accusation of moral turpitude and 'enormous
social stigma'" the employer must prove its case "beyond a reasonable doubt," a recent opinion sides with those who believe that the
standard should remain "preponderance of the evidence," as it is in
civil cases.[3]

Courts' Consideration of Precedential Value
of Prior Arbitration Awards

A subsequent interest arbitration award that overturns a prior
inconsistent grievance arbitration award is to be given prospective
effect only, according to the Ninth Circuit Court of Appeals.

Several months after a grievance arbitration award had held that
work given to production employees belonged to building trades employees who had been improperly laid off, the collective bargaining
agreement expired and an interest arbitration award allocated the
contested work to production workers in the new contract.

In denying the employer's contention that the earlier arbitration
award should be set aside as a result of the interest arbitration, the
court of appeals held that the later award resolved only the "parties'
dispute about the allocation of work between production and building trades workers for the purposes of a *new* contract" and "the reasonableness of [the] . . . interpretation of the old contract was not
affected by the [subsequent] decision."[4]

---

[2]Superior Coffee & Foods, 103 LA 609, 613 (Alleyne, 1994) (citing Equal Employment Opportunity Commission's Policy Guidance: Sexual Harassment; Newsday, Inc. v.
Long Island Typographical Union, 915 F.2d 840, 135 LRRM 2659 (2d Cir. 1990), cert.
denied, 111 S. Ct. 1314, 136 LRRM 2720 (1991)).

[3]Superior Coffee & Foods, 103 LA 609 (Alleyne, 1994).

[4]Sheet Metal Workers Int'l Ass'n, Local 359 v. Madison Indus., 84 F.3d 1186, 152
LRRM 2505 (9th Cir. 1996).

As noted in the main volume, several courts have held that a jury verdict may preclude arbitral review of the same issue and bar enforcement of any inconsistent arbitration award. However, in a decision significant for its analysis of the "meeting of the minds" doctrine,[5] the Seventh Circuit Court of Appeals upheld a district court judge's grant of a union's counterclaim to compel arbitration, but asserted that the judge's conclusion that "the disputed term unequivocally bears the meaning that she assigns to it . . . does not bind the arbitrator." The company had accepted a multiemployer collective bargaining agreement that contained an ambiguous minimum manning requirement. When the employer brought suit for rescission under Section 301 of the Taft-Hartley Act,[6] on the ground that there was "no meeting of the minds," the district court not only decided that a binding contract had been formed but also purported to resolve the ambiguity. Chief Judge Posner stated (with one judge on the panel disagreeing) that not only was the arbitrator free to interpret the contractual provision differently than the district court, but "[i]t will therefore be open to . . . [the employer] to argue to the arbitrator that, under a proper interpretation of the contract, there really was no meeting of the minds over the manning requirements and therefore that the contract should be rescinded after all."[7]

The traditional and less expansive view of an arbitrator's authority was applied by the Sixth Circuit Court of Appeals[8] in reviewing an arbitrator's conclusion, based upon the evidentiary record before him, that there was no enforceable agreement to arbitrate despite a district court's prior contrary determination. The district court had vacated the arbitration award on the grounds that the issue of arbitrability had not been submitted to the arbitrator and that his reexamination of the issue was barred by the doctrine of res judicata.

The court of appeals noted that resolution of a dispute over whether a valid agreement to arbitrate exists is traditionally reserved to the courts, and that the arbitrator had not indicated any reason why the district court's prior judgment was not a bar to his consideration of the issue:

> "Arbitrators are not free to ignore the preclusive effect of prior judgments under the doctrines of *res judicata* and *collateral estoppel,* although they generally are entitled to determine in the first instance whether to give the prior judicial determination preclusive effect."[9]

There are occasions, however, when it is a court, and not an arbitrator, that is guilty of exceeding its authority, and a subsequent arbi-

---

[5]Colfax Envelope v. Local No. 458-3M, Chicago Graphic Communication Int'l Union, 20 F.3d 750, 145 LRRM 2974 (7th Cir. 1994).

[6]29 U.S.C. §185.

[7]20 F.3d at 755, 145 LRRM at 2978.

[8]Aircraft Braking Sys. Corp. v. Local 856, United Automobile Workers, 97 F.3d 155, 153 LRRM 2402 (6th Cir. 1996), cert. denied, 117 S. Ct. 1311, 154 LRRM 2928 (1997).

[9]97 F.3d at 159, 153 LRRM at 2406.

tration award trumps a prior judicial judgment. In 1992 an employer was successful in vacating an arbitration award that had set aside the peremptory discharge of an employee for insubordination for failure to award the employee "institutional due process."[10] The contract provided that employees were subject to discharge for "just cause" but also included a section that listed reasons, including "insubordination" and "sleeping on duty," for which employees could be immediately discharged. The district court said that the arbitrator had exceeded her authority because once the employer had determined that an employee had been insubordinate, it could discharge that employee without observing any further procedural safeguards.

A year later the employer similarly discharged an employee for "sleeping on the job," and another arbitrator reduced the penalty to a suspension on the ground that the employer had failed to consider mitigating circumstances. The district court again vacated the award, but this time the court of appeals stepped in and reversed,[11] holding that the arbitrator could reasonably read both contractual provisions as requiring consideration of appropriate mitigating circumstances.

Since the arbitrator had arguably construed and applied the agreement, he fulfilled the precise task that the parties had bargained for him to do; the appellate court therefore held that both the district court's decision *sub judice* and its 1992 judgment were in error.

----

[10]Southern Council of Indus. Workers v. Bruce Hardwood Floors, 784 F. Supp. 1345, 139 LRRM 2775 (N.D. Tenn. 1992).
[11]Bruce Hardwood Floors v. Southern Council of Indus. Workers, 8 F.3d 1104, 144 LRRM 2622 (6th Cir. 1993).

Chapter 12

Custom and Past Practice

Custom and Practice as Part of the Contract

Arbitrators continue to recognize that workplace activity performed in a regular manner over time may give rise to formation of a past practice binding upon the parties as an implied term or condition of employment when the written agreement is silent on the subject.[1] One commonly used formulation of the elements constituting a past practice requires "clarity, consistency, and acceptability."[2] The term "clarity" embraces the element of uniformity.[3] The term "consistency" involves the element of repetition,[4] and "acceptability" speaks

---

[1]Mittenthal, "The Ever-Present Past," Proceedings of the 47th Annual Meeting of NAA (BNA Books, 1994). The paper was presented at the NAA's Continuing Education Conference in Pittsburgh, October 30, 1993. Also see Stanley, "Unambiguous Collective Bargaining Agreement Language Controls Unless Past Practice Is So Widely Acknowledged and Mutually Accepted That It Amends Contract," 74 U. Det. Mercy L. Rev. 389 (1997); Broida, A Guide to Federal Labor Relations Authority Law & Practice, Ch. 6 (1996).

[2]Crescent Metal Prods., 104 LA 724, 726 (Cohen, 1994); General Mills Inc., 101 LA 953, 958 (Wolff, 1993). See H. Meyer Dairy Co., 105 LA 583, 587 (Sugarman, 1995).

[3]See H. Meyer Dairy Co., 105 LA 583, 587 (Sugarman, 1995).

[4]Monroe County Intermediate School Dist., 105 LA 565, 567 (Brodsky, 1995) ("[A] practice can be established if, when one circumstance occurs, it is consistently treated in a certain way. The occurrence need not be daily or weekly, or even yearly, but when it happens, a given response to that occurrence always follows"); Weyerhauser Co., 105 LA 273, 276 (Nathan, 1995) ("A 'practice' as that concept is understood in labor relations refers to a pattern of conduct which appears with such frequency that the parties understand that it is the accepted way of doing something"); Brown-Forman Beverage Co., 103 LA 292, 294 (Frockt, 1994) ("[T]he general principle is that a practice exists when a certain result has been utilized in repetitive and identical circumstances") (citing General Refractories Co., 54 LA 1180 (1970)). A practice that is at best "checkered" does not exhibit the requisite repetitiveness to constitute a binding past practice. See Consolidation Coal Co., 104 LA 751, 756 (Franckiewicz, 1995). Mere habit or happenstance does not rise to the requisite level of frequency to create a binding practice. See Consolidation Coal Co., 106 LA 328, 332 (Franckiewicz, 1996). Moreover, one or two occurrences normally does not constitute a past practice. See Nature's Best, 107 LA 769, 772 (Darrow, 1996) (holding that one-time payment of wage differential does not

to "mutuality" in the custom or practice.[5] Arbitrator Jules J. Justin's classic definition[6] that the practice must be "unequivocal, clearly enunciated and acted upon,[7] and readily ascertainable over a reasonable period of time."[8] is also frequently cited. A number of arbitrators recognize that a past practice rises to the level of an agreement between management and labor if it is "clear, detailed, undisputed and binding."[9] This "substantive application" of past practice stands in contrast to the interpretive use of past practice in interpreting ambiguous contract language.[10] Arbitrators have characterized such binding practices as either extensions of the employment contract[11] or even a "separate, enforceable condition of employment."[12]

The party alleging the past practice must bear the burden of proving its existence.[13]

Though mutual acceptance is necessary in forming a binding past practice, the acceptance may be implied.[14] Arbitrators may infer such "mutual acceptance" from circumstantial evidence.[15] However, a few arbitrators require that the consent be specifically acknowledged orally or in writing.[16]

---

create past practice); Weyerhauser Co., 105 LA 273, 276 (Nathan, 1995) (holding that a past practice is not created by one prior experience); Globel Ticket & Label Co., 105 LA 62, 66 (McCurdy, 1995) (holding that one occurrence does not create a practice); Stevens County, 104 LA 928, 932 (Daly, 1995) (holding that two occurrences within four months does not establish a past practice).

[5]Michigan Hanger Co., 106 LA 377, 380 (Smith, 1996); Service Employees, 101 LA 483, 486 (Concepcion, 1993).

[6]Celanese Corp. of Am., 24 LA 168, 172 (Justin, 1954).

[7]See Gulf States Util. Co., 102 LA 470, 476 (Massey, 1993) ("The absence of an action . . . may not necessarily constitute a legitimate past practice. . .").

[8]See Lake Erie Screw Corp., 108 LA 15, 19 (Feldman, 1997); Grand Haven Stamped Products Co., 107 LA 131, 137 (Daniel, 1996); Kansas City Power & Light Co., 105 LA 518, 523 (Berger, 1995); Crescent Metal Prods., 104 LA 724, 726 (Cohen, 1994); City of York, 103 LA 1111, 1115 (DiLauro, 1994); Curved Glass Distribs., 102 LA 33, 36 (Eischen, 1993); Fry's Food & Drug, 101 LA 1179, 1181 (Oberstein, 1993).

[9]See Moco Thermal Indus., 106 LA 1182, 1187 (Hodgson, 1996); Schnuck Markets, 101 LA 401, 407 (Hilgert, 1993); Rexroth Corp., 101 LA 94, 98 (Bowers, 1993).

[10]See American Drug Stores, 107 LA 985, 988 (Richman, 1996).

[11]See Schnuck Markets, 101 LA 401, 407 (Hilgert, 1993) ("Practices themselves can become an extension of the Agreement where there is clear and convincing evidence that such practices have been well established and acted upon for an extended period of time").

[12]Albertson's, 106 LA 897, 900 (Kaufman, 1996).

[13]See Globe Ticket & Label Co., 105 LA 62, 66 (McCurdy, 1995).

[14]See T.J. Maxx, 105 LA 470, 474 (Richman, 1995), ("A proposal submitted in negotiations to change a past practice which is then withdrawn, may be evidence of the abandonment of an attempt to change the past practice"); Dixie Container Corp., 47 LA 1072, 1077 (Jaffee, 1966).) "Silence in the face of a statement of position during negotiations can give rise to a contractual obligation under the doctrine of acceptance by silence." Las Vegas Joint Executive Bd. v. Riverboat Casino, 817 F.2d 524, 125 LRRM 2942 (9th Cir. 1987)).

[15]See Michigan Hanger Co., 106 LA 377, 380–81 (Smith, 1996).

[16]See Fry's Food and Drug, 101 LA 1179, 1181 (Oberstein, 1993) ("For a past practice to be binding at some point, either management or the union must acknowledge it and approve of it. This acknowledgment and approval, by necessity, needs to be memorialized in such fashion for future generations so that they might recognize it as such"). At the very least, the party must be aware of the past practice. National Uniform Serv.,

Arbitrators continue to recognize that not all clearly established practices should be accorded binding effect. Some state as a general rule that to be binding, a practice must provide a major benefit to a substantial number of employees.[17] But, arbitrators are divided as to whether, if the benefit conferred by the practice originates in a non-contractual employer handbook, it must be followed by the employer.[18] Many hold that even if the benefit is not contractual in nature, the past practice may still supply a term of agreement.[19]

Arbitrators are less willing to find a practice binding where it significantly affects management rights.[20] But, one arbitrator noted that "[m]anagement's right to operate the workplace does not abrogate its duty to negotiate about major working condition changes. It cannot point to the former as an excuse to run roughshod over the latter."[21]

Regulation, Modification, or Termination of Practice as Implied Term of Contract

As a general rule, neither management nor labor can unilaterally alter a well-established and binding past practice.[22] However, because a custom or practice is the result of mutual responses to a given set of circumstances, arbitrators have held that a material change in circumstances underlying the practice will dissolve its binding effect.[23] A past practice may also lose its binding quality through

---

104 LA 901, 907 (Klein, 1995); Atlantic Southeast Airlines, 102 LA 656, 659 (Feigenbaum, 1994).

[17]See Consolidation Coal Co., 106 LA 328, 332 (Franckiewicz, 1996); Consolidation Coal Co., 105 LA 1110, 1115 (Talarico, 1995); Sheboygan County, 105 LA 605, 608 (Dichter, 1995); H. Meyer Dairy Co., 105 LA 583, 587 (Sugarman, 1995); Central Aluminum Co., 103 LA 190, 197 (Imundo, 1994).

[18]See City of Miamisburg, Ohio, 104 LA 228, 233 (Fullmer, 1995) ("[T]he arbitrator knows of no basis upon which the Employer can be held required [sic] to conform to a past practice in a non-contractual handbook benefit").

[19]Indiana Michigan Power Co., 107 LA 1037, 1041 (Render, 1997) ("[P]ast practice can serve the parties well even when operating under a non-contractual handbook").

[20]See Ottawa Truck Inc., 107 LA 844, 848 (Murphy, 1996); National Refractories & Minerals Corp., 107 LA 699, 702 (Feldman, 1996); American Red Cross, 106 LA 224, 228–29 (Grooms, 1996); St. Louis Coca-Cola Bottling Co., 105 LA 356, 360 (O'Grady, 1995); East Mfg. Corp., 105 LA 267, 269 (Strasshofer, 1995); Crescent Metal Prods., 104 LA 724, 726 (Cohen, 1994); Oberlin College, 103 LA 600, 601–02 (Chockley, 1994); Alcan-Toyo America, 102 LA 566, 571 (Draznin, 1993); City of Austin, 101 LA 947, 951 (Berquist, 1993).

[21]Alcan-Toyo America, 102 LA 566, 570–71 (Draznin, 1993).

[22]See Snap-On Tools, 105 LA 752, 755 (Fowler, 1995); Sheboygan County, 105 LA 605, 608 (Dichter, 1995); H. Meyer Dairy Co., 105 LA 583, 588 (Sugarman, 1995) (stating that the unilateral decision to alter a past practice was improper); Bayer, Inc., 105 LA 100, 102 (Duff, 1995) (stating that an alteration to a past practice "cannot be adopted by the unilateral decision of [m]anagement"); General Mills Inc., 101 LA 953, 958 (Wolff, 1993) ("Once [the binding practice is] established, however, such conditions 'may not be changed without the mutual consent of the parties'").

[23]See Goodyear Tire & Rubber Co., 107 LA 193, 196 (Sergent, 1996) (holding that circumstances surrounding the practice of being exempt from overtime draft for Sunday work have changed because Sunday work has become part of the regular work-

the manifestation of a party's lack of continuing assent, as by repudiation in negotiation,[24] a change in contract language,[25] or the filing of a grievance.[26]

On the other hand, if a well-established custom or practice is *not* repudiated during subsequent contract negotiation, the practice may by implication become an integral part of the contract.[27] Indeed, the process of negotiation is the proper forum for a party to negate or change a past practice or custom.[28] However, arbitrators continue to be unwilling to grant to any party by way of a past practice a benefit that they were unable to obtain at the bargaining table.[29] In some instances, arbitrators have gone so far as to say that they lack any authority to make such a grant.[30]

Contract Clauses Regarding Custom

A zipper clause in a collective bargaining agreement does not always constitute a clear and unmistakable waiver of the union's right to bargain over an employer's decision to change an existing condition.[31] In order to establish a waiver of the statutory right to bargain, even through a "zipper" clause, there must be a clear and unmistakable relinquishment of that right.[32] To meet this clear and unmistakable standard, the contract language must be specific, or it must be shown that the matter waived was fully discussed and explored, and that the waiving party consciously yielded its rights.[33]

week); Grand Haven Stamped Prods. Co., 107 LA 131, 137 (Daniel, 1996); United Refining Co., 105 LA 411, 415 (Harlan, 1995) (stating that the conditions underlying the practice of starting mediation sessions at 2:00 p.m. had changed significantly when the frequency of sessions increased dramatically); Reed Mfg. Co., 102 LA 1, 6 (Dworkin, 1993) ([O]nce the support disappears, so does the binding quality of the practice"); Lockheed Aeronautical Sys. Co., 104 LA 840, 844 (Hewitt, 1995) (stating that a change in attitudes regarding smoking was a change in underlying circumstances giving rise to the practice of permitting smoking). But see Cross Oil & Refining, 104 LA 757, 763 (Gordon, 1995) (citing Johns-Mansville Sales Corp. v. IAM Lodge 1609, 621 F.2d 756, 104 LRRM 2895 (5th Cir. 1980) and stating that individual health hazards to the smokers themselves are beyond the company's legitimate business interests, and limited smoking practices continue even in asbestos factories where medical reasons against smoking seem compelling).
[24]See Grand Haven Stamped Prods. Co., 107 LA 131, 137 (Daniel, 1996); Albertson's, 106 LA 897, 900 (Kaufman, 1996); Penn Emblem Co., 101 LA 884, 886 (Byars, 1993).
[25]See Bayer, Inc., 105 LA 100, 102 (Duff, 1995). See also Doss Aviation, Inc., 107 LA 39, 49 (Ferree, 1996) (stating that a past practice cannot be voided by language mistakenly inserted into a subsequent contract).
[26]Moco Thermal Indus., 106 LA 1182, 1187 (Hodgson, 1996).
[27]See Albertson's, 106 LA 897, 900 (Kaufman, 1996); Michigan Hanger, 106 LA 377, 381 (Smith, 1996); Panhandle Eastern Pipe Line Co., 103 LA 996, 1000 (Allen, Jr., 1994).
[28]See Daniels Co., 102 LA 1064, 1067 (Franckiewicz, 1994).
[29]See HS Automotive Inc., 105 LA 681, 686 (Klein, 1995); Lockheed Aeronautical Sys. Co., 104 LA 803, 805–06 (Duff, 1995).
[30]See Dean Foods Vegetable Co., 105 LA 377, 380 (Dichter, 1995).
[31]Miami Sys. Corp., 320 NLRB 71, 78, 153 LRRM 1077 (1995) (employer's decision to abolish a third shift may be the subject of bargaining).
[32]Exxon Research & Eng'g Co., 317 NLRB 675, 150 LRRM 1308 (1995).
[33]Bertram-Trojan, Inc., 319 NLRB 741, 150 LRRM 1321 (1995).

Question of Arbitrability

A union's request to conform the agreement to reflect past practice is arbitrable so long as the determination sought "merely seeks an interpretation of the existing Agreement as to whether it includes the implied term" and does not attempt to add a new term to the agreement. However, the union must follow grievance and arbitration procedures or risk losing the opportunity to reform the agreement.[34]

Custom and Practice Versus Clear Contract Language

If a past practice, although in existence for several years, arose from an obviously mistaken view of a contractual obligation, it need not be allowed to continue.[35] On the other hand, some decisions have supported the contrary view that the "parties' day-to-day actions, when they run counter to the plain meaning of the contract's words, evidence an intent to substitute that which they actually do for that which they said in writing they would do.' "[36]

Past practice dealing with employee discipline stands on a somewhat different footing and may be altered under the authority of a management rights clause, provided the employer gives prior notice of the change.[37]

Gap-Filling

Past practice has recently been upheld as a valid doctrine in a nonunion setting where the employer had a noncontractual handbook that pledged to treat employees fairly.[38] Thus, one award held that in order to treat employees fairly, an employer must take into

---

[34]United Parcel Serv. v. International Bhd. of Teamsters, 859 F. Supp. 590, 146 LRRM 2881 (D.D.C. 1994). (Past practice limited to the amount of package weight to 70 pounds and union threatened to strike if company unilaterally increased weight limit to 150 pounds. UPS, as a condition of a temporary restraining order, was ordered to arbitrate at the union's request. The union failed to request arbitration; therefore, the court granted summary judgment to UPS on this count.)

[35]City of Palo Alto, 107 LA 494, 498–99 (Riker, 1996). (Although for 25 years the city had paid employees on inactive military leave, the unambiguous language of the memorandum of agreement between the parties, based on state law, required only that employees be paid for active duty leave; therefore, the "unambiguous and clear language [of the agreement was] controlling.") See also "Discussion" of arbitrator John A. Hogan following Richard Mittenthal's "Past Practice and Administration of Bargaining Agreements," Proceedings of the 14th Annual Meeting of the NAA (BNA Books, 1961) (questioning "mutual acceptance" element if there had been no "meeting of the minds").

[36]City of Palo Alto, 107 LA 494, 498 (Riker, 1996) (quoting Wallen, "The Silent Contract v. Express Provisions," Proceedings of the 15th Annual Meeting of NAA (BNA Books, 1962)).

[37]Tecumseh Prods. Co., 107 LA 371, 378 (Keenan, 1996) (employer's notice that employees could be discharged for a first offense of fighting on company premises negated past practice of giving a two-week suspension for fighting).

[38]Indiana Michigan Power Co., 107 LA 1037 (Render, 1997).

account the way other employees have been treated in the past in similar circumstances. Where employees who completed a year-long training program had always been promoted, the arbitrator found that "the company made its initial commitment to these employees when it selected them for training,"[39] and if the company did not plan to promote them, it had a responsibility to inform the employees at the outset.[40]

---

[39]Id. at 1042.
[40]Id.

Chapter 13

Management Rights

Views Regarding Management Rights

Although some arbitrators insist that "management rights" are derived solely from explicit contractual provisions, most continue to recognize the concept that "residual rights" always reside in management.[1] Under this theory management retains all authority to conduct the enterprise that has not been specifically bargained away. Even where the agreement contains an express management rights clause, topics not expressly enumerated therein may be held to fall within the "residual rights" penumbra so long as their existence or exercise is not inconsistent with other provisions of the agreement[2] or binding past practice. The scope of such "implied" management rights remains the subject of frequent controversy.[3]

In a number of cases arbitrators have concluded that they have the power to identify "inherent rights" of the employer.[4] Still other

---

[1]Abtco, Inc., 104 LA 551 (Kanner, 1995); Akron Brass Co., 101 LA 289 (Shanker, 1993) (employer had right to prohibit smoking in lunchrooms because to do conformed to a widespread industrial pattern); see also Valmont Elec., Inc., 102 LA 439 (Hoffmeister, 1994) (employer had reason to discharge employees rather than just lay them off following closing of employer's business). Stone Container Corp., 101 LA 720 (Helburn, 1993), Phillips 66 Co., 101 LA 1146 (Sherman, 1993); Kelly Air Force Base, 98 LA 773 (O'Grady, 1992); Pearl Brewing Co., 98 LA 449 (Nicholas, 1992); Lockheed Aeronautical Sys., 98 LA 87 (Caraway, 1991); Oklahoma Pub. Serv. Co., 97 LA 951 (Overstreet, 1991); Detroit Edison Co., 96 LA 1033 (Lipson, 1991).

[2]City of Columbus, 105 LA 481 (Ferree, 1995), Leggett & Platt, Inc., 104 LA 1048 (Statham, 1995); Freeman Decorating Co., 102 LA 149 (Baroni, 1994); Johnson Controls, Inc., 101 LA 964 (Cohen, 1993); Montgomery Ward & Co., 98 LA 597 (Nicholas, 1992).

[3]Zebco Corp., 104 LA 613 (Cohen, 1995); Owens-Illinois, 102 LA 1196 (Feldman, 1994); Reed Mfg. Co., 102 LA 1 (Dworkin, 1993); A. E. Piston Prods. Co., 101 LA 98 (Fogelberg, 1993); American Crystal Sugar Co., 99 LA 699 (Jacobowski, 1992); see also Container Corp. of America, 91 LA 329 (Rains, 1988) (employer had inherent right to eliminate job classifications); Trap Rock Indus., Inc., 142 LRRM 2300 (3d Cir. 1992).

[4]Lenzing Fibers Corp., 103 LA 531 (Nicholas, 1994); Forms Mfrs., 103 LA 29 (Mikrut, 1994); Quaker Oats Co., 91 LA 271 (Schwartz, 1988).

arbitrators apply a "rule of reason" in determining the limits of management's implied authority.[5]

Management rights may be defined or limited in accordance with past practice or industry custom because they are considered to have been incorporated into the overall agreement.[6] However, a divergent past practice may be rejected in favor of an express management right.[7]

Inroads Made by Legislation

The 1990s has witnessed a decrease in congressional regulation affecting so-called management prerogatives. Most of the legislation that regulates the workplace environment has been detailed in the Main Edition. Employers should take note of the Uniformed Services Employment and Re-Employment Rights Act (1994)[8] and of amendments to the Fair Labor Standards Act, which adjusted the minimum wage to $5.15, effective September 1, 1997.

The Duty to Bargain: Right of Unilateral Action

It is well settled that unilateral decisions made by an employer during the course of a collective bargaining relationship concerning matters that are mandatory subjects of bargaining are regarded as per se refusals to bargain.[9] It is equally well established, with limited exceptions, that the decision to lay off employees is a mandatory subject of bargaining.[10]

Other topics found by the Board to be mandatory subjects of collective bargaining include implementation of a drug and alcohol testing policy,[11] production incentive bonuses,[12] on-call procedures,[13] and

---

[5]Kentucky Center for the Arts, 104 LA 971 (Ghiz, 1995); Hyatt Cherry Hill, 103 LA 99 (DiLauro, 1994); Potomac Edison Co., 96 LA 1012 (Talarico, 1991); East Ohio Gas Co., 91 LA 366 (Dworkin, 1988).

[6]Conoco, Inc., 104 LA 1057 (Neigh, 1995) (management rights clause did not dissolve past practice and customs that had existed for several years); Southern Calif. Edison Co., 104 LA 1072 (Concepcion, 1995); Crescent Metal Prods., Inc., 104 LA 724 (Cohen, 1994); see also Masterbilt Prods. Corp., 97 LA 1042 (Daniels, 1991) (practice of not converting temporary workers to full-time status after 60 days was an eight-year practice and therefore upheld).

[7]City of Marion, 91 LA 175 (Bittel, 1988) (prior assignment of inspectors exclusively to day shift did not create a binding past practice, and seniority clause was upheld).

[8]38 U.S.C. §§4301 et seq. (1994).

[9]Millwrights, Conveyors & Machinery Erectors Local Union No. 1031, 321 NLRB 30, 152 LRRM 1049 (1996).

[10]Id. This decision overrules the Board's earlier holding in Mike O'Connor Chevrolet, 209 NLRB 701, 85 LRRM 1419 (1974), cited in footnote no. 86, p. 665 of the Main Edition.

[11]Delta Tube & Fabricating Corp., 323 NLRB 153, 155 LRRM 1129 (1997).

[12]Sartorius, Inc., 323 NLRB 213 (1997).

[13]United Parcel Serv., 323 NLRB 98 (1997).

amendments to pension plans to comport with Internal Revenue Code requirements for tax-exempt status.[14]

Employers' claims that a union has "waived" its right to demand negotiations over changes in the terms and conditions of employment that are not specifically addressed in the collective bargaining agreement are subject to strict scrutiny. To establish a waiver of the statutory right to negotiate over mandatory subjects of collective bargaining, there must be a clear and unmistakable relinquishment of that right.[15] Management-rights language that merely reserves to the employer the authority to create and enforce reasonable rules does not rise to the level of a clear and unmistakable waiver.[16] Even a union's acquiescence in previous unilateral changes does not operate as a permanent waiver of its rights to bargain over the changes.[17]

Inroads Through Arbitration

"Protective" clauses continue to be a widely used method of preventing arbitrators from "interpreting away" management rights.[18] In addition to limiting an arbitrator's consideration to the literal text of the agreement, many clauses may expressly restrict the arbitrator's authority to the precise issues submitted for resolution.[19]

Management Rights Clauses

Although management rights clauses are common, there is no consensus as to their form or content.[20] Many management rights clauses contain a "saving clause," a clause indicating that management retains all rights not modified by the contract or that the enu-

---

[14]Trojan Yacht, Division of Bertram-Trojan, Inc., 319 NLRB 741, 150 LRRM 1321 (1995).

[15]Exxon Research & Eng'g Co., 317 NLRB 675 (1995); *Trojan Yacht*, 150 LRRM 1321.

[16]Southern Calif. Edison Co., 310 NLRB 1229 (1993).

[17]Owens-Brockway Plastic Prods., 311 NLRB 519 (1993); *Delta Tube*, 323 NLRB 153.

[18]Of 400 bargaining agreements analyzed in one survey, 82 percent placed some type of restriction on the arbitrator. Of those, 92 percent contained a general restriction prohibiting the arbitrator from adding to, subtracting from, or in any way altering contract language. BNA, Collective Bargaining Negotiations and Contracts (1996).

[19]For examples, see Oak Hills Local Schs., 108 LA 171, 173 (Oberdank, 1997); Shawnee Local Bd. of Educ., 104 LA 682, 684 (Weisheit, 1995) ("The arbitrator shall expressly confine himself/herself to the precise issue(s) submitted for arbitration and shall have no authority to determine any other issue(s) not so submitted.").

[20]Of 400 agreements analyzed in a BNA survey, 80 percent contained a management rights clause. BNA, Collective Bargaining Negotiations and Contracts (1996). For examples of detailed clauses, see Kiro, Inc., 151 LRRM 1268, 1269 (NLRB 1995) (television network); Reckitt & Colman, Inc., 108 LA 726, 727 (Thornell, 1997); Summit County Children Servs., 108 LA 517, 517–18 (Sharpe, 1997) (county agency); Summit County Children Servs., 108 LA 459, 461 (DuVal Smith, 1997) (same); American Drug Stores, Inc., 107 LA 985 (Richman, 1996); Phelps Dodge Magnet Wire Co., 108 LA 21 (Curry, 1996); Ottawa Truck, Inc., 107 LA 844, 845 (Murphy, 1996); American Red Cross, 106

merated rights in a detailed clause are not necessarily all-inclusive.[21] Such clauses may, in fact, strengthen the employer's position before the arbitrator.[22]

Control of Operation Methods

In the absence of restrictions in the agreement, arbitrators recognize management's broad authority to determine what is manufactured and how it is produced.[23] Additionally, in an effort to allow companies to operate on the most efficient basis, management has been allowed to eliminate job classifications and individual jobs for reasons of operational efficiency.[24] Barring restrictive contractual language, a job may be eliminated when most of the tasks previously fulfilled by this position "have been reduced to the point where the remaining tasks can be performed logically, efficiently and safely by other employees."[25] One arbitrator has held that such changes may be made even if they significantly and adversely affect the ability of the union to survive as a viable entity.[26]

LA 224, 225 (Grooms, 1996) (charitable organization); Central Mich. Univ., 102 LA 787, 789 (House, 1994) (university); I.T.T. Rayonier, Inc., 101 LA 865, 868 (Lane, 1993). For an example of statute detailing rights for public employers, see Butte Sch. Dist. No. 1, 108 LA 265, 266 (Prayzich, 1997) (considering effect of Mont. Code Ann. §39-31-303 (1995)).

[21]Of 400 contracts in BNA survey, 44 percent contained a savings clause. BNA, Collective Bargaining Negotiations and Contracts (1996). For examples, see Integrated Distrib. Sys., 108 LA 737 (Neas, 1997) (all decisions on matters or subjects not defined by agreement are reserved to employer); Arcata Graphics Distrib. Corp., 102 LA 961 (Hart, 1994) (nothing in agreement shall be construed or interpreted as denying or limiting rights of company to exercise all customary and usual rights of management); Gulf States Util. Co., 102 LA 470, 471 (Massey, 1993) (rights are not all-inclusive but indicate types of matters where rights shall belong to or are inherent to management); I.T.T. Royonier, Inc., 101 LA 865, 868 (Lane, 1993) (enumerated rights not exclusive).

[22]St. Louis Coca-Cola Bottling Co., 105 LA 356, 360 (O'Grady, 1995) (finding savings clause "controlling" when it authorized company "to exercise rights not specifically set forth in the Agreement upon which the parties negotiated or had the opportunity to negotiate whether or not such rights have been exercised by the Company in the past.").

[23]Georgia-Pacific Corp., 107 LA 872, 876 (Neigh, 1996); Arizona Chem. Co., 107 LA 836, 842–43 (Grooms, 1996); Houston Lighting & Power Co., 106 LA 1188, 1194 (Johnson, 1996); International Paper Co., 108 LA 1207, 1210 (Hart, 1997); See infra note 6 and accompanying text.

[24]I.T.T. Rayonier, Inc., 101 LA 865 (Lane, 1993) (15 of 20 positions were eliminated in the company's attempt to become more competitive by way of a profit improvement program); Hyatt Cherry Hill, 103 LA 99 (DiLauro, 1994) (the company, following a management rights clause, eliminated a cashier's classification and position and then required the food servers to complete these duties without a pay raise); Illinois Cement Co., 108 LA 667 (Kossoff, 1997) (cement manufacturer facility eliminated former Console Helper A, B, and C classifications when each of these positions was renamed and given additional duties, making them new classifications).

[25]International Paper Co., 108 LA 1207, 1211 (Hart, 1997).

[26]Zebco Corp., 104 LA 613 (Cohen, 1995) (a company in need of additional space moved its packaging operation and most of the union employees to a new location but required the employees to be nonunionized).

Under general management rights clauses the authority to determine the types of machinery and equipment to be utilized has been inferred[27] in the absence of specific restrictions in the agreements.[28] Even if the changes in methods of operation cause loss of seniority and jobs for some employees, they will be allowed so long as they are made in good faith and are not otherwise wrongful.[29]

However, though in many situations management's unilateral determination of the methods of operations will prevail, bargaining is usually required before changes in working conditions are allowed.[30]

Wage Adjustments Following Changes in Operation Methods

Though many disputes over management's authority to institute new or changed operating methods reach arbitration,[31] such claims have occasionally been held nonarbitrable.[32]

---

[27]City of North Olmsted, 106 LA 865 (Miller, 1996) (because of the general management rights clause, the city was not required to invest in new computer equipment to continue direct deposits when the bank unilaterally discontinued its manual direct deposit system). See also Schnuck Markets, Inc., 101 LA 401, 407 (Hilgert, 1993).

[28]French Paper Co., 106 LA 737, 739 (House, 1996) ("The Management's Rights clause of the Agreement gives to management the right to promulgate rules and regulations so long as they are not inconsistent or in conflict with the provisions of this Agreement."). See St. Louis Coca-Cola Bottling Co., 105 LA 356, 360 (O'Grady, 1995).

[29]International Paper Co., 108 LA 1207 (Hart, 1997) (company was allowed to eliminate a job classification and demote the workers); Hyatt Cherry Hill, 103 LA 99 (DiLauro, 1994) (company was allowed to eliminate a cashier's position).

[30]Macy's, 108 LA 489 (Gregory, 1997) (company was allowed to determine method of operations regarding the implementation of two separate shifts but was not allowed to unilaterally change the working conditions by issuing and requiring workers to wear certain clothing); Regional Transp. Dist., 107 LA 813 (Finston, 1996) (company was properly determining methods of operation when it implemented mechanic work teams); Georgia-Pacific Corp., 108 LA 90 (Frost, 1996) (company was not allowed to unilaterally change working conditions regarding its absenteeism program); Klamath Falls Fire Dist. No. 1, 106 LA 789 (Buchanan, 1996) (company was not allowed to unilaterally adopt working conditions, requiring firefighters to take physical fitness test); Alcan-Toyo Am., 102 LA 566 (Draznin, 1993) (company was not allowed to unilaterally make changes in working conditions regarding policy of absenteeism and tardiness). But see Conoco, Inc., 104 LA 1057 (Neigh, 1995) (company was not allowed to determine method of operation in regard to scheduling replacement workers when an agreement with the union predetermined this process); Sheboygan County, 105 LA 605 (Dichter, 1995) (company was not allowed to unilaterally change past practice of using compensatory time for sick leave); Arch of Illinois, 104 LA 1102 (Cohen, 1995) (company was not allowed to unilaterally change its starting times on work shifts); Consolidation Coal Co., 105 LA 1110 (Talarico, 1995) (company was not allowed to unilaterally change its past practice of paying workers for a minimum of four hours' overtime when they called employees in to work for times other than those in their regular schedule).

[31]Lawrence Paper Co., 107 LA 730 (Murphy, 1996) (grievance was denied and the company was allowed to keep the incentive rate on a machine at its established rate).

[32]See, e.g., Dyncorp., 101 LA 1193, 1196 (Richman, 1993).

Hourly Rated Employees

While the rule continues to be that a substantial increase in workload as should be accompanied by an increase in hourly rate,[33] an increase in productivity is not necessarily viewed as an increase in workload. Thus, arbitrators may require a grievant to show "how much of the increased productivity . . . may be attributed to the machine itself and how much to the crew" before determining whether increased compensation is merited.[34] Often these decisions reflect an arbitrator's interpretation of what constitutes "substantial changes" or "significant changes."[35]

Production Standards, Time Studies, and Job Evaluation

Arbitrators generally allow management broad leeway in unilaterally setting reasonable production standards and using discipline to enforce them.[36] However, it is essential that workers be given adequate notice of the production standard before disciplinary action is taken.[37]

Although it is still common to use time studies for establishing production standards, companies may be restricted by contract from unilaterally conducting these studies and implementing changes to incentive programs without permitting the union to participate in the process.[38] Some contracts prohibit an arbitrator from establishing or modifying incentive rates. Nonetheless, arbitrators have held

---

[33]Arizona Chem. Co., 107 LA 836, 844 (Grooms, 1996); Interated Health Servs., 107 LA 384, 392 (Dean, 1996); North Pittsburgh Telephone Co., 101 LA 931, 942–43 (Garret, 1993).

[34]Menasha Corp., 108 LA 308, 311 (Ellman, 1997); see also Mead Prods., 104 LA 730 (Borland, 1994) (arbitrator found there was no significant change; thus employees were not entitled to an increase in wages when a warehouse computer information system was installed).

[35]Cooper Indus., Inc., 104 LA 383 (Imundo, 1995) (arbitrator determined that installing a new computer system in the shipping department was a substantial change and should be accompanied by a wage increase); Mead Prods., 104 LA 730 (Borland, 1994) (arbitrator held that the installation of a warehouse computer information system was not a significant change; thus employees were not entitled to an increase in wages).

[36]Ingalls Shipbuilding, Inc., 101 LA 583 (Koenig, 1993) (employee discharged where company required to meet rigorous standards); see also Cardinal Health, Inc., 108 LA 1039 (Larocco, 1997) (company was allowed to continue using a one-in-a-thousand error production rate and to discipline those with notice of the standard who continually failed to meet it); Hertz Corp., 103 LA 65 (Poole, 1994) (company was allowed to implement a new production standard system and to discipline those who failed to perform acceptably).

[37]Cummins Cumberland, Inc., 106 LA 993 (Heekin, 1996) (arbitrator did not allow the company to discipline an employee for failing to meet the production standard when it did not provide proof that notice was posted or transmitted to the employees after a new policy was implemented).

[38]Permold, Corp., 101 LA 390 (DiLeone, 1993) (after acquiring a better saw, the company was not allowed to unilaterally implement a new production standard since the operation was considered to have been changed). But see Lawrence Paper Co., 107

that they may still determine whether the process for establishing the rates is equitable.[39]

Control of Quality Standards

Arbitrators continue to recognize that management has a right to control the standards of quality of its products. Management in appropriate circumstances may discharge or discipline employees whose production fails to meet quality standards. In upholding the decision of a shipyard company to discharge an employee for unsatisfactory work, one arbitrator declared: "Producing an acceptable Naval or Commercial vessel is what the shipyard business is all about. The quality of the welding must pass rigorous testing, or the shipyard cannot remain in business."[40]

Job and Classification Control

Establishing, Eliminating, and Combining Jobs and Classifications

Controversies over the establishment, elimination, and combination of jobs and classifications are resolved according to well-established principles of arbitral jurisprudence.[41]

Interjob and Interclassification Transfer of Duties

Absent limitations in the agreement, management retains the right, under recent decisions as in past awards, to transfer work from one classification to another.[42]

LA 730 (Murphy, 1996) (company reserved the right to contractually modify, amend or adjust previously established standards upon significant changes but was obligated to notify the union, which could then pursue a grievance).

[39]Lawrence Paper Co., 107 LA 730, 735 (Murphy, 1996).

[40]Cardinal Health, Inc., 108 LA 1039 (LaRocco, 1997) (production standard of one error per thousand lines filled was reasonable); Champion Dairypak, 105 LA 462 (Allen, Jr., 1995) (employee discharged for neglect of duties); S & J Ranch, 103 LA 350 (Bogue, 1994) (employee discharged for poor quality of work); Southwestern Bell Tel. Co., 102 LA 531 (Nolen, 1994) (employee discharged for tone and manner complaints).

[41]Illinois Cement Co., 108 LA 667 (Kossoff, 1997) (employer did not violate contract when it combined operator classification with helper classifications); Lake Erie Screw Corp., 108 LA 15 (Feldman, 1997) (employer did not have right to unilaterally create training position); Houston Lighting & Power Co., 106 LA 1188 (Johnson, 1996) (employer did not violate contract where agreement contains no "work peculiar" clause basing job assignment on classifications); Marmon/Keystone Corp., 106 LA 519 (Franckiewicz, 1996) (combined job treated as newly created position); Port Everglades Auth., 104 LA 65 (Wahl, 1995) (elimination of job not improper where employer may determine the size and composition of its working force); Hyatt Cherry Hill, 103 LA 99 (DiLauro, 1994) (elimination of job not improper where employer may determine the size and composition of its working force).

[42]Washington Teachers Union, 108 LA 821 (Bernhardt, 1997) (employer violated contract when it reclassified secretary where job duties did not change); I.T.T. Rayonier,

Assignment of Duties and Tasks

In the absence of contract limitations, management has broad discretion in assigning individual duties and tasks to workers.[43]

As noted in the Main Edition, employees may challenge the fairness of the rate paid for a job after management changes its content.[44]

Hiring of Employees

Under the Americans with Disabilities Act (ADA),[45] employers are prohibited from discriminating against employees on the basis of handicap. Therefore, preemployment inquiries into an applicant's medical history are prohibited—such inquiries being permitted only

---

101 LA 865 (Lane, 1993) (transfer of work not improper where positions were hybrid classification).

[43]Rheem Mfg. Co., 108 LA 193 (Woolf, 1997) (reassignment to lower-grade job upheld); ITT Higbie Baylok, 108 LA 178 (Duda, Jr., 1997) (employer did not violate contract where it required operators rather than setup employees to set up line where there were no written job descriptions); Butte School Dist. No. 1, 108 LA 265 (Prayzich, 1997) (contract not violated by reassignment to less favorable job); Farmland Indus., 108 LA 363 (Pelofsky, 1997) (contract did not limit employer's right to assign trained personnel outside the department); Kokomo Gas & Fuel Co., 108 LA 1056 (Imundo, Jr., 1997) (employer did not violate contract when supervisor performed work where work did not displace employee regularly assigned to do the job); Midamerican Energy Co., 108 LA 1003 (Jacobowski, 1997) (employer did not violate contract when it assigned work to mechanics even though technicians had traditionally done that work where contract obligates both parties to efficiency); Quanex Corp., 108 LA 841 (House, 1997) (employer violated contract where it left job vacant in three-person operation); Grief Bros. Corp., 108 LA 818 (Harland, 1997) (employer violated contract when it allowed supervisor to perform bargaining unit work); Northwest Ind. Symphony Soc'y, 106 LA 185 (Nathan, 1996) (management has right to determine job content where it has right to determine nature of activities); City of Orange, Texas, 103 LA 1121 (Nicholas, Jr., 1994) (duties improperly assigned where the contract states working conditions to remain unchanged); Albertson's, Inc., 103 LA 793 (Peck, 1994) (arbitrator not to determine classification where contract provides that employer will judge qualifications); Servicemaster Co., 103 LA 411 (McGury, 1994) (restructuring proper where contract has no limitation on work performed); White-New Idea Farm Equip. Co., 101 LA 461 (High, 1993) (unit work properly assigned to management employees as result of technological change); North Pittsburgh Tel. Co., 101 LA 931 (Garrett, 1993) (substantial technological change); North Pittsburgh Tel. Co., 101 LA 931 (Garrett, 1993) (substantial change of duties improper); Caterpillar, Inc., 101 LA 372 (Daniel, 1993) (duty improperly assigned to nonunit employee).

[44]Cleveland Elec. Illuminating Co., 108 LA 120 (Franckiewicz, 1997) (meter readers entitled to higher pay for reading commercial and industrial meters); Menasha Corp., 108 LA 308 (Ellman, 1997) (no right to wage increase where no substantial change in workload or job content); Integrated Health Servs., 107 LA 384 (Dean, Jr., 1997) (addition of similar duties and unrelated duties entitle employee to pay increase); Arizona Chem. Co., 107 LA 836 (Grooms, Jr., 1997) (operators given supervisors' duties entitled to wage increase); Cooper Indus., Inc., 104 LA 383 (Imundo, Jr., 1995) (substantial change in job requires new rate); Mead Prods., 104 LA 730 (Borland, 1994) (employees were not entitled to a wage increase where employer did not change duties and functions within the job classifications but only method of completion); Schnadig Corp., 101 LA 1166 (Duff, 1993) (employees entitled to higher rate under temporary transfer).

[45]42 U.S.C.§§12101 et seq.

following an offer of employment and pursuant to a postoffer medical examination.[46]

Moreover, to strengthen the prohibitions against considering an applicant's union activity in hiring decisions, the Supreme Court has held that employers cannot refuse to hire applicants who are seeking employment for the sole purpose of organizing the work force (a practice generally known as "salting").[47]

Determination of Size of Crews

In the past, labor arbitration decisions were seemingly equally divided as to whether management had the right unilaterally to determine crew size. However, in the absence of a contract provision restricting management's authority to determine the number of employees assigned to a crew,[48] the more recent arbitration decisions appear to recognize the setting of crew size to be a managerial prerogative[49] in the absence of a threat to employee safety.[50]

Even if a contract provision mandates a minimum number of employees to man a crew, if the employer in good faith after making a reasonable effort cannot find enough qualified employees to fill the positions, the employer is not required to hire or promote underqualified individuals to fill out the complement.[51]

Technological and Process Changes

Arbitrators have recognized management rights to reduce the size of work crews upon the introduction of technological advances enabling greater efficiency.[52]

---

[46]42 U.S.C. §12112(d).

[47]NLRB v. Town & County Elec., Inc., 116 S.Ct. 4580 (1995).

[48]Quanex Corp., 108 LA 841 (House, 1997) (employer violated collective bargaining agreement when it unilaterally decreased crew size from three to two people by not filling a vacancy. The contract and past practice mandated union negotiation over job duties, rates of pay, and job combinations).

[49]WCI Steel, 103 LA 115 (Duda, 1994) (employer did not violate collective bargaining agreement when it decreased the number of boiler operator positions from two to one); American Red Cross, 103 LA 580, 585 (Garret, 1994) (employer did not violate collective bargaining agreement when it evaluated manpower needs and decreased number of employees at blood donor sites).

[50]Pennsylvania Steel Techs., 105 LA 189 (Kahn, 1995) (decreasing the number of strand operators from two to one did not create a substantial risk to health and safety because other workers, although not in the immediate vicinity, were near to help if there was an accident. The arbitrator found that risks present were not created as a result of or attributable to reduction in crew size.).

[51]Savannah Symphony Soc'y, 102 LA 575 (Howell, 1994) (employer did not violate the collective bargaining agreement when only 26 of 35 slots were filled, because employer made reasonable effort to find qualified individuals; it was in the middle of the performing season, and employer was not required to fill all of the 35 positions).

[52]WCI Steel Inc., 103 LA 114 (Duda, 1994) (employer did not violate collective bargaining agreement with the introduction of caster slabs to strip mill, to increase efficiency; employer thus required only one operator rather than two for occasional fine tuning on some of the coils); James River Corp., 102 LA 893, 896 (Jones, 1994) (arbitra-

Change in Types of Operations, Methods, or Procedures

The elimination of positions, previously required by a 40-year-old arbitration decision, was upheld as a management right when the fundamental operations of the company changed to obviate the need for the now redundant positions.[53]

The creation of new jobs outside the bargaining unit as a result of new functions undertaken by an employer has also been upheld as a management prerogative.[54]

The elimination and reclassification of jobs as a result of the complete restructuring and reorganization of work processes have also been recognized as falling within the scope of residual managerial rights.[55]

Workload and Idle Time

Management may, when confronted with a lack of work, reclassify jobs and combine duties of various jobs to achieve greater efficiency.[56]

Safety or Health Hazard

Management has the right to direct crew to work under conditions of extreme heat and humidity if there is a compelling public necessity for the work to be performed.[57]

Vacancies

One decision has ruled that when the union and the company have a past practice of negotiating job classifications, work duties,

---

tor upheld the elimination of jobs, as result of new computer technology; management has right to improve productivity of operations to enable company to compete effectively in global economy).

[53]Packaging Corp. of Am., 102 LA 1099 (Odom, 1994) (employer did not violate the contract when it eliminated plant nurses for the second and third weekend shifts, because the nature of the operation had become less dangerous, and the company trained employees on different shifts in emergency medical care to substitute for these nurses; employer entitled to seek new and more efficient methods to serve the same needs).

[54]Appalachian Reg'l Healthcare, 103 LA 297 (Duff, 1994) (employer did not violate the collective bargaining agreement when it created an in-house bill collector group, rather than hiring an outsider, because the members of the billing clerks bargaining unit had separate and distinct duties from those of the new collectors unit).

[55]Cleveland Elec. Illuminating Co., 105 LA 817 (Franckiewicz, 1995) (employer did not violate collective bargaining agreement when it eliminated jobs, following redesign of internal mail delivery system to achieve greater efficiency).

[56]Hyatt Cherry Hill, 103 LA 99 (DiLauro, 1994) (employer, in financial difficulty, did not violate the contract when it eliminated cashier classification and added those duties to food servers without increasing salary, to maintain efficiency of the employees and reallocate their responsibilities in accordance with their abilities).

[57]Virginia Elec. & Power Co., 102 LA 445 (McCluskey, 1993) (employer did not violate collective bargaining agreement by requiring workers to work in extreme heat and

pay rates, and job combinations, management may not unilaterally refuse to fill a vacancy.[58]

Scheduling Work

Though management generally has the right to change work schedules, contract provisions limiting this right may prohibit the employer from unilaterally doing so.[59] Thus, when a contract sets a maximum and minimum number of workdays in a week, management's scheduling discretion is limited to that range and cannot extend beyond the contract's parameters.[60]

Emergency Changes in Work Schedule

An employer may temporarily reassign employees to work in a different department, classification, or shift or on overtime if required by an unanticipated business necessity.[61]

Emergencies, Acts of God, and Conditions Beyond the Control of Management

Management has broad discretion to determine the membership of a work crew when faced with a bona fide emergency. However, this discretion must be exercised reasonably, nondiscriminatorily, and in good faith.[62]

Similarly, management may select employees junior in service for overtime opportunities occasioned by an emergency if the more senior employees are not capable of handling the situation.[63]

---

humidity when the work was necessary at that specific time and employer had taken all necessary precautionary steps to prevent damage to workers' health).

[58]Quanex Corp., 108 LA 841 (House, 1997) employer violated the contract when it did not fill vacancy on crew; parties had negotiated every job classification and rate of pay in past and for the current contract).

[59]H. Meyer Dairy Co., Inc., 108 LA 765 (West, 1997) (employer violated collective bargaining agreement when it reduced the number of days in a workweek from four to three when the contract allowed for discretion between four and five days).

[60]Willamette Indus., 107 LA 897 (Howell, 1996) (employer violated collective bargaining agreement when it unilaterally changed the workweek from a four-day/10-hours-per-day week to a five-day/8-hours-per-day week without consulting the union as required by the contract).

[61]Wagner Castings Co., 103 LA 157 (Talent, 1994) (employer did not violate collective bargaining agreement when workers from another classification were required to complete a last-minute order made by the company's largest client).

[62]Central Pa. Water Supply Co., 101 LA 873 (Talarico, 1993) (when a large water main broke, employer had the right to choose employees able to fix the problem most capably; however, employer must have a reason for choosing one employee over another and cannot make arbitary decisions).

[63]Central Pa. Water Supply Co., 101 LA 873 (Talarico, 1993) (employer did not violate seniority overtime provisions when faced with an emergency and a senior-employee who did not perform well in high pressure situations).

On the other hand, though management can require employees either to report during severe weather conditions or incur absence points, its policy must be applied equitably. In one case an employer was held to have violated the contract when it provided transportation during a snowstorm for some employees but penalized for their absences those who were not offered a ride.[64]

One arbitrator has held that when a holiday work schedule has been established, management cannot change its collective mind and cancel the shift without paying employees at the overtime rate for the holiday that they would have otherwise worked.[65]

In general, however, the assignment and scheduling of overtime and holiday work lie within management's discretion.[66]

Overtime

Right to Require Overtime

Management has the right to make reasonable demands for overtime upon employees when the agreement is silent on the subject.[67] Although management is able to discipline employees for refusing to work overtime, employees' refusal to work overtime in protest against an employer's unilateral schedule changes was held to be protected concerted activity under the National Labor Relations Act.[68]

Right to Subcontract

Standards for Evaluating Propriety of Subcontracting

Arbitrators continue to look at the particular circumstances of each case to determine whether management can subcontract under the terms of the agreement. Where the agreement is silent on the subject, some arbitrators have held that a management rights provi-

---

[64]Schuller Int'l, 107 LA 1109 (Hockenberry, 1996).

[65]Fairbanks North Star Borough, 103 LA 615 (Landau, 1994) (employer violated contract when it unilaterally canceled holiday work and did not pay shift workers overtime for the holiday or straight pay for the day that it was closed. The cancellation was unprecedented and not attributable to an emergency, an act of God, or circumstances beyond the company's control.).

[66]American Greetings Corp., 107 LA 1209 (West, 1996) (employer did not violate the contract when it did not grant overtime work to maintenance employees who had no training on equipment, despite practice of granting overtime when equipment is being installed, serviced, or modified).

[67]Ironton Iron Inc., 105 LA 257 (High, 1995) (company had scheduled mandatory overtime to compensate for production delays under a management rights clause allowing this authority; the right to schedule overtime was limited only by the reasonableness of the amount); Ohio Edison Co., 102 LA 717 (Sergent, 1994) (company change in scheduling overtime shift from 8 to 7.5 hours to avoid having to provide a break for a second meal was unreasonable).

[68]NLRB v. Mike Yurosek & Sons, 149 LRRM 2094 (9th Cir. 1995).

sion supplies the authority.[69] The more prevalent view, however, is that the employer's business interest must be balanced against the impact on the bargaining unit.[70]

An employer's decision to subcontract may violate not only the contract but also federal labor law. The National Labor Relations Board reviews an employer's decision to subcontract to determine whether it is "inherently destructive" of the employees' "Section 7" rights.

In *International Paper*,[71] the employer, during negotiations, permanently subcontracted bargaining unit work during a lawful lockout of employees. Applying the "inherently destructive" doctrine, the Board held that the decision to permanently subcontract the work violated Section 8(a)(3) of the Act. The Board noted that not only did employees lose their jobs, but also those employees returning from the strike to perform nonsubcontracting work would have to work side by side with the "independent contractor" employees. Under these circumstances the employer's decision seemed to render impotent the employees' right to resist the employer's bargaining proposals.

In rendering this decision the Board issued the following guiding principles for future application of the "inherently destructive" doctrine:

1. The severity of harm to employee rights caused by the employer's conduct must be determined, and such determination should include the severity of harm suffered by the employees for exercising their rights as well as the severity of the impact on the statutory right being exercised.
2. Conduct of temporary duration that seeks to put pressure on union members to accept particular management proposals must be distinguished from conduct that has "far reaching effects which would hinder future bargaining" or "creates visible and continuing obstacles to the future exercise of employee rights."
3. A distinction also must be drawn between an employer's "hostility to the process of collective bargaining" and its simple intention to support its bargaining position as to employee compensation and other matters.
4. Conduct may be inherently destructive of employee rights if it discourages collective bargaining "in the sense of making it seem a futile exercise in the eyes of employees."

---

[69]GES Exposition Servs., 108 LA 385 (Levy, 1997).

[70]Gaylord Container Corp., 106 LA 461 (Baroni, 1996). (Subcontracting rights depend upon the balancing of an employer's legitimate interest in efficiency and the union's legitimate interest in job security).

[71]International Paper, 318 NLRB 1253 (1997).

Notice of Intent to Subcontract; Duty to Bargain

In *Dubuque Packing Co., Inc.*,[72] the National Labor Relations Board set forth a new standard by which to judge whether an employer has an obligation to bargain over its decision to relocate work to a new plant. The Board borrowed a portion of the test required to meet this new standard in developing criteria to determine whether an employer must bargain over its decision to subcontract. In *Mid State Ready Mix*[73] and *Power Inc.*,[74] the Board focused on whether the decision includes a change in the scope and direction of the business. If it does, then a bargaining obligation does not attach. However, if the employer is simply replacing one group of employees with another group, to perform the same work, then the employer must bargain with the union over its decision to subcontract.[75]

Assigning Work Out of Bargaining Unit

Arbitrators continue to examine a number of factors in determining whether, absent express contractual language, an employer can transfer job functions of employees in the bargaining unit to employees outside the bargaining unit. In *Cleveland Electric Illuminating Co.*,[76] for example, the panel identified the following relevant factors: whether in the past work had been performed exclusively by bargaining unit employees; whether layoffs, displacement from jobs, or loss of pay to employees resulted from transfer of work; the effect on the bargaining unit; the amount of work involved; the legitimacy of the company's reasons for the change; whether a change had occurred in the type of work being performed; whether the change was

---

[72]303 NLRB 386 (1991).

Under the test formulated in *Dubuque,* the general counsel has the initial burden of establishing a prima facie case that the decision is a mandatory subject of bargaining by meeting a two-part test. First, the general counsel must establish that the decision involved a relocation of unit work. Second, the general counsel must establish that this relocation of unit work was unaccompanied by a basic change in the nature of the employer's operation. If the general counsel satisfies this two-part test, the burden then shifts to the employer to rebut the general counsel's prima facie case by establishing any one of the following: (1) the work performed at the new location varies significantly from the work performed at the former plant; or (2) the work performed at the former plant is to be discontinued entirely and not moved to the new location; or (3) the employer's decision involves a change in the scope and direction of the enterprise.

Even if the employer is unable to rebut the general counsel's prima facie case, it may still show that the decision to relocate was a nonmandatory subject of bargaining by proffering one of two affirmative defenses. The employer can establish an affirmative defense by showing either of the following by a preponderance of the evidence: (1) that labor costs (direct and/or indirect) were not a factor in the decision or (2) that even if labor costs were a factor in the decision, the union could not have offered labor cost concessions that could have changed the employer's decision to relocate.

[73]307 NLRB 809 (1992).

[74]311 NLRB 599 (1993).

[75]Under this test, unlike the one set forth in *Dubuque,* the Board will not consider labor costs as an affirmative defense that can be utilized by an employer.

[76]105 LA 817 (Franckiewicz, Stevers, Boyle, 1995).

in response to changes in the economic climate; and whether the transfer of work was caused by a reorganization or change in work methodology or processes. The panel concluded that the determination of whether a transfer of work was permissible should be made on a case-by-case basis. Because the work at issue had been primarily a nonunit function in the past, and because the transfer of work occurred during a company reorganization, the panel concluded that there was no violation of the agreement.

Where the unambiguous language of a contract provided only that a company could subcontract maintenance work, the company was found entitled to subcontract other types of work, including production work.[77] Conversely, where a collective bargaining agreement did not restrict the company from having outside vendors stock soda but was ambiguous regarding whether the company could use these vendors to stock private-label soda from the company's own warehouse, the arbitrator looked to extrinsic evidence to aid in interpreting the contract.[78] Because products from the company's warehouse had not previously been stocked by outside vendors, and because evidence from both the company negotiator and the company president supported the contention that the provision was intended to include only outside products, the arbitrator found that the company had violated the contract.

Does a listing of job classifications in a collective bargaining agreement freeze the classification structure during the life of the contract, thereby precluding the company from reassigning work? One arbitrator, following what he believed was the more modern view, concluded that "the rights of the management clause prevailed over the classification clause, particularly in the light of economic necessity which demands increased efficiency in job assignments and in operations generally."[79]

In cognate decisions adopting this line of reasoning, other arbitrators have held that where a contract does not expressly prohibit the elimination of jobs or reassignment of work, a company generally can eliminate jobs, combine positions, and reassign work.[80]

Plant Rules

Arbitrators continue to be called upon to assess the validity of plant rules that restrict or ban smoking on company property and

---

[77]In re Lockheed Aeronautical Sys. Co., 104 LA 803 (Duff 1995). Similarly, where the contract gave a company the right to abolish or create new jobs, the company did not violate the agreement when it eliminated a janitorial position and hired an outside contractor to perform the work. James River Corp., 104 LA 475 (Bittel, 1995).

[78]In re Schnuck Markets, Inc., 107 LA 739 (Cipolla, 1996).

[79]James River Corp., 102 LA 893 (Jones, 1994).

[80]International Paper Co. Natchez, Miss. Facility, 108 LA 1207 (Hart, 1997) (employer properly eliminated technician position where certain job duties were transferred to employees at different location and computerized information system reduced

the discipline imposed on employees who flout the rules. In several recent arbitral decisions, arbitrators have upheld grievances over the application of "no smoking" policies.[81] In one, an employee admittedly walked off his shift without permission to smoke a cigarette in a non-restricted area. The employee was discharged under the company's conduct rules, which authorized the discharge penalty for the first offense of smoking in an unauthorized place or at an unauthorized time. The arbitrator concluded that violation of the rule did not per se establish "good cause" for termination. Instead, the arbitrator considered that although the break was taken at an unauthorized time, the grievant did not smoke in a restricted area and hence did not threaten either the health or the safety of coworkers, such threats being the stated reasons behind the rule. Moreover, he noted that the penalty for leaving one's job without permission was only a corrective interview for the first offense, and that the grievant had 14 years of service with a good performance record. Finding that the discharge was without just cause, the arbitrator instead imposed a six-month disciplinary suspension without pay.[82]

Arbitrators also frequently have been called upon to assess the extent to which companies can establish and enforce drug and alcohol policies. In several recent decisions, arbitrators have declined to uphold disciplinary measures for violations of these policies.[83]

In *Bayer Corporation*,[84] for example, the agreement provided that any drug and alcohol program would attempt to achieve an "optimum level of rehabilitation consistent with overall safety and efficient operation." An employee whose job performance was otherwise deemed satisfactory was discharged after he had failed his second drug test. Following his first positive test, the employee was required to undergo only one hour of counseling. After his second positive test, he was required to undergo an additional two hours of counseling. Although recognizing that an employee's failure of two drugs tests would ordinarily call for the discharge penalty, the arbitrator concluded that a total of three hours of counseling did not constitute the

---

some of technician's former duties); Illinois Cement Co., 108 LA 667 (Kossoff, 1997) (employer within its rights to combine job classifications as part of effort to cross-train employees and increase efficiency).

[81]Barnstead-Thermolyne Corp., 107 LA 645 (Pelofsky, 1996); Hobart Corp., 103 LA 547 (Imundo, 1994); Lincoln Brass Works, Inc., 102 LA 872 (Haskew, 1994).

[82]Barnstead-Thermolyne Corp., 107 LA 645 (Pelofsky, 1996).

[83]Bayer Corp., 108 LA 316 (Zobrak, 1997); Kelly-Springfield, 108 LA 984 (Nicholas, 1997) (discharge for failing drug test held too severe where employee sought rehabilitation for second offense but employer had unilaterally changed policy to permit only a single use of employee assistance program); Bruce Hardwood Floors, Center, Texas, 108 LA 115 (Allen, 1997) (discharge for testing positive on one drug test held to be without just cause where grievant had no history of drug use during 26 years of employment, explanation of positive test was credible, and grievant tested negative week before and week after positive test). See also Industrial Powder Coatings, Inc., 103 LA 519 (Statham, 1995); J.A. Jones Co., 103 LA 161 (Talarico, 1994); Schnuck Markets, Inc., 102 LA 1016 (Suardi, 1994).

[84]108 LA 316 (Zobrak, 1997).

required optimum level of rehabilitation. Accordingly, he ruled that upon successful completion of a comprehensive rehabilitation program, the grievant was to be returned to his former job, but without back pay or benefits.

Recent challenges to employer-promulgated absenteeism policies,[85] safety rules,[86] sexual harassment policies,[87] policies regarding confidential information,[88] and employee dress codes[89] have met with mixed results. The rulings in these cases tend to be highly fact-specific.

Layoff of Employees

Bumping

Arbitrators continue to construe the term "layoff" broadly to include any reduction in the normal workweek that results in loss of

---

[85]Mead Containerboard, 105 LA 1068 (Goodman, 1995) (upholding absenteeism policy as reasonable where it adequately defined terms "habitual tardiness or chronic absenteeism"); Simpson Indus., 104 LA 568 (Bressler, 1995) (upholding right of company to unilaterally institute new absenteeism policy under agreement that only required company to submit new rules to union beforehand, which the company did); Chanute Mfg. Co., 101 LA 765 (Berger, 1993) (rejecting company's elimination of rolling period for removing stale absences as unreasonable, but upholding new limits on personal day-off policy to entire day units as reasonable); Darling Store Fixtures, Paragould, Ark., 108 LA 183 (Allen, 1997) (discharge for excessive absenteeism violated contract where most of employee's absences normally would have been excused, employee did not receive last-chance letter, grievant's disciplinary record had been cleared, and management appeared to make questionable disciplinary assessments in attempt to set employee up for discharge).

[86]Packaging Corp., 106 LA 122 (Nicholas, 1996) (upholding grievance by employee violating weapons policy where company failed to consult union first, as required under agreement; arbitrator nonetheless stated that he believed company policy was proper); Golden State Foods Corp., 108 LA 705 (Gentile, 1997) (upholding discharge for workplace violence based on grabbing of coworker where six weeks prior to the incident, employer had distributed and implemented zero tolerance policy for actual or threatened violence).

[87]American Mail-Well Envelope, 105 LA 1209 (Paull, 1995) (upholding sexual harassment policy but sustaining grievant's claim that three-day suspension was not justified); Abtco, Inc., 104 LA 551 (Kanner, 1995) (male employee properly discharged, under last-chance agreement, for sexually offensive conduct against female employee).

[88]US West Communications, Inc., 107 LA 791 (Yehle, 1996) (discharge of 25-year employee by telephone company for first violation of code of conduct that prohibited personal use of company information upheld where policy was unambiguous and communicated to employees); Southwestern Bell Tel. Co., 107 LA 928 (Nolan, 1996) (upholding discharge of two telephone company salesclerks for personal use of confidential information in violation of known rule prohibiting such use).

[89]Macy's, 108 LA 489 (Gregory, 1997) (company violated agreement when it unilaterally instituted mandatory dress code where clothing requirement was mandatory subject of bargaining between parties); Fairmont-Zarda Dairy, 106 LA 583 (Rohlik, 1995) (sustaining grievance based on no-beard policy where no uniform industry ban existed, no government regulations supported ban, no intracompany problem existed, no showing was made that beard cover was unavailable as alternative, and long hair and mustaches were permitted); Motion Picture & Television Fund, 103 LA 988 (Gentile, 1994) (upholding company's right to prohibit operator/receptionist from wearing nose jewelry); Albertson's, Inc., 102 LA 641 (Darrow, 1994) (upholding policy requiring conservative hairstyles, given discretion afforded to company, company's desire to protect public

work. For example, in *Yaffe Printing Co.,*[90] where the contract provided that the last employee hired would be the first laid off, the company reduced the workweek for all employees when sales declined by closing the plant on Fridays and staggering work assignments pro rata. The arbitrator concluded that the contract did not guarantee work for all employees but required that the available hours be distributed on the basis of seniority. Accordingly, the company was directed to make whole the senior employees who were improperly laid off.

If the contract provides that seniority governs only "where ability, skill and qualifications are equal," an employer can consider factors such as absenteeism and disciplinary status in determining whether to lay off an employee out of seniority.[91] However, a company was held to have violated the contract by laying off a senior employee who had received only one point less on evaluations than a retained junior employee and, accordingly, was judged to be "substantially" equally qualified in experience, skill, and efficiency.[92] Where there was work to be done in a classification whose members were on layoff status, an employer was prohibited from bringing in employees from another classification instead of recalling the in-classification employees from layoff.[93]

In *Johnson Controls World Service, Inc.,*[94] the arbitrator considered whether a union could successfully challenge the furloughing of government employees during a federal government shutdown. The union had been consulted by the company prior to the furlough and had even assisted the company in implementing it. Since the union had not reserved any contractual claims relating to the furlough, the arbitrator held that it was equitably estopped from later pursuing grievances based on an alleged loss of work.

Arbitrators continue to recognize a company's prerogative to deny bumping rights to senior employees who fail to meet contractually specified fitness and ability qualifications[95] or who fail to demonstrate

image, fact that employees not covered by policy had no public contact, and existence of long-standing practice).

[90]1010 LA 1019 (Pelofsky, 1993).

[91]Houston Power & Lighting Co., 102 LA 582 (Nicholas, 1994); see also H & K Dallas, Inc., 108 LA 600 (Moore, 1997) (company properly laid off two senior employees where one of junior employees retained had demonstrably greater skills and abilities and the other employee was in different classification); Lawrence Berkeley Nat'l Lab., 108 LA 376 (Silver, 1996) (employer did not violate contract or discriminate against black employee by laying him off where at least 30 percent of his job duties were eliminated, many of remaining duties were assigned to a number of employees other than the white employee who allegedly received favorable treatment, and the remaining evidence, including statistical evidence, did not support grievant's position).

[92]Matanuska Elec. Ass'n, Inc., 107 LA 402 (Landau, 1996).

[93]Associated Univs., Inc., 105 LA 1041 (Liebowitz, 1995); see also Dubovsky & Sons, Inc., 108 LA 19 (Marx, 1996) (employer violated contract by laying off three employees while temporary vacation employees continued to work).

[94]108 LA 191 (Specht, 1996).

[95]Northrop Grumman Corp., 107 LA 850 (Nicholas, 1996) (company properly denied senior employee bumping rights where contract provided that senior employee

that they can become qualified to perform the work within a contractually specified period of time.[96] Arbitrators also have upheld the denial of bumping rights where the position sought is outside the bargaining unit.[97] Conversely, where the language of the agreement did not permit bumping during layoffs of less than five consecutive workdays, but the past practice had allowed bumping during layoffs of any length, the company was found to have improperly laid off senior employees during a short-term layoff without allowing them to exercise bumping rights.[98]

Promotion and/or Transfer of Employees

A number of recent arbitral decisions have reaffirmed the general rule that, consistent with the terms of the agreement, management can consider skill, ability, and experience along with seniority in making promotions.[99] In *International Paper Co., Veratec Division,*[100] for example, the arbitrator upheld the employer's decision to adopt a "team concept" for one of its production lines instead of the traditional organization. The arbitrator concluded that the broad language of the agreement, which gave management the right to "reduce, alter, combine, transfer, assign, or cease any job, department, or service"[101] allowed the company to implement the team concept without consulting or bargaining with the union.

---

had to possess substantially equal ability, skill, and efficiency, and company determined that he did not meet these criteria); Anderson Concrete Corp., 103 LA 433 (Kindig, 1994) (company properly denied bumping rights where senior employee never held sought-after position, he was at best minimally qualified for position, there was no contractual requirement that he be given tryout period, and company had consistently conditioned bumping rights on fitness and ability qualifications).

[96]Phillips Pipeline Co., 105 LA 1132 (Goodman, 1996) (employee properly disqualified after bumping where he could not learn new job skills within required one-month period); Coca-Cola Bottling Co. of Mich., 104 LA 97 (McDonald, 1994) (employer again laid off two employees properly when they could not demonstrate ability to perform necessary tasks within 20 working days, as required under the contract).

[97]Worldsource Coil Coating, Inc., 102 LA 17 (Florman, 1993); see also Grey Eagle Distribs., Inc., 107 LA 673 (Pratte, 1996) (company properly laid off senior employee and allowed junior employee to do light-duty work, which was not always performed by classified employees and was not, therefore, deemed to be bargaining unit work); Alsco, Div. of Amerimark Bldg. Prods., Inc., 106 LA 1146 (Rybolt, 1996) (employer properly brought junior employee back from layoff where return was not to specific job opening but in downsizing situation where junior employee was being brought back to do whatever work was necessary).

[98]Central Aluminum Co., 103 LA 190 (Imundo, 1994); but see Hewitt Soap Co., Inc., 107 LA 761 (Fullmer, 1996) (company properly declined to lay off three probationary employees in addition to 21 employees with seniority where contract did not require that probationary employees be laid off along with employees with seniority and none of senior employees attempted to exercise bumping rights to bump probationary employees).

[99]Ardco, Inc., 108 LA 326 (Wolff, 1997); Lehigh Portland Cement Co., 105 LA 860 (Baroni, 1995); Spontex, Inc., 105 LA 254 (Modjeska, 1995); Nordson Corp., 104 LA 1206 (Franckiewicz, 1995); Lafarge Corp., 104 LA 592 (Hoffmeister, 1995); Bowater, Inc., 103 LA 1000 (Nolan, 1994).

[100]107 LA 1042 (Hooper, 1996).

[101]Id.

In *Conoco, Inc.*,[102] an employer was held to have properly denied an otherwise qualified employee promotion to a crane operator position where, after a psychological evaluation called into question his fitness for this stressful position, the employee declined to undergo further examination.[103] However, where an employer relied on a test that did not accurately reflect relative qualifications for promotion, and the employer did not take into account the grievant's successful performance history, the arbitrator ruled that the unsuccessful senior bidder was entitled to the promotion.[104] Similarly, where the tests administered by an employer in making promotions decisions were not directly related to the qualifications required for the job in question, the arbitrator ruled that the company could not deny promotions to employees based on the test results.[105]

Is an employee entitled to be "promoted" to a lower-rated job? Citing the dictionary definition of this term, and agreeing with earlier decisions, an arbitrator ruled that a grievant could not insist upon the requested demotion.[106]

In a case involving an alleged breach of duty of fair representation, it was held that a union was blameless when it refused to pursue a grievance on behalf of an employee who attempted to decline a promotion.[107] The arbitrator ruled that since the contract allowed only the two most senior employees to "freeze" in their present positions rather than be promoted, the grievant, a less senior employee, was properly required to accept the promotion notwithstanding his reluctance to do so.

Another recurrent problem is whether an employee with a disability that prevents him or her from performing his in-classification job may or must be transferred to another classification the duties of which the employee is able to perform. In *Minnegasco, Inc.*,[108] the arbitrator considered whether a company that had placed a disabled employee on a leave of absence because it determined it could not reasonably accommodate her in her present position should have instead temporarily transferred her to another classification out of contract-mandated seniority order. Although the union agreed to waive the contractual transfer restriction, the company declined to do so.

---

[102]102 LA 417 (Goodstein, 1994).

[103]See also Hughes Aircraft Co., 107 LA 596 (Richman, 1996) (employer reasonably declined to permit employee to take promotion test where she had weight-lifting restrictions that precluded her from performing all normal job duties of that classification and vocational rehabilitation plan was based on permanent inability to perform lifting tasks of type required); Lion, Inc., 109 LA 19 (Kaplan, 1997) (company did not violate agreement when it required each applicant for warehouse position to have commercial driver's license even though this arguably discriminated against older employees, where contract did not contain nondiscrimination clause and union failed to make out claim of discrimination).

[104]Kansas City Power & Light Co., 104 LA 857 (Berger, 1995).

[105]GTE Telephone Operators, South, 103 LA 1205 (Duff, 1994).

[106]Forms Mfrs., Inc., 103 LA 29 (Mikrut, 1994).

[107]Lyondell Petrochem. Co., 104 LA 108 (Baroni, 1995).

[108]103 LA 43 (Bognanno, 1994).

The arbitrator ruled that the company had properly excluded the grievant from her present position on the basis of her disability, and that it had no obligation under external law to waive the bargained-for contract provisions governing temporary transfers.

In *Alcoa Building Products*,[109] the employer did attempt to accommodate a disabled employee who was certified as able to return to work with limitations on lifting, by displacing a successful bidder from a job that did not require heavy lifting. Relying upon pertinent Equal Employment Opportunity Commission guidelines, the arbitrator ruled that the company had no duty under the Americans with Disabilities Act, and no right under the collective bargaining agreement, to rescind the promotion awarded to the successful bidder.

The issue in *Dinagraphics, Inc.*,[110] was whether an employer could disqualify an employee from his electrician position and permanently transfer him to an inspector position because he suffered from arthritic gout, which prevented him from performing his electrician duties satisfactorily. The arbitrator concluded that since the contract was silent on the issue, the employer, as a matter of inherent prerogative, had the right to transfer an employee who could not perform the job for which he was being paid, and the employee was not entitled to retain his former position under the Americans with Disabilities Act.

Sometimes a transfer is made for the purpose of training an employee to operate another type of equipment. In *Arcata Graphics Distributing Corp.*,[111] the arbitrator considered whether, in the absence of a contractual provision, an employer can temporarily transfer a senior employee from his preferred shift in order to train him on a different machine. The contract provided that the employer was required to cross-train employees but was silent on whether seniority affected training assignments. Since the machine in question was not being operated on the grievant's regular shift, and the grievant was promptly returned to his preferred shift following the training, the arbitrator concluded that the company's action was reasonable and taken in good faith, and so denied the grievance.

Seniority, moreover, does not control transfers to fill newly created positions where the contract requires only that seniority be followed when a vacancy occurs in an existing job.[112]

Sometimes employees who have been temporarily transferred to another, more highly rated position do not perform all the duties of the new position. In cases where the temporary transferee does not perform the "core functions" of the new position, the transferee has

---

[109]104 LA 364 (Cerone, 1994); see also Ralph's Grocery Co., 109 LA 33 (Kaufman, 1997) (company violated contract by permitting employees at one facility to bid on interim jobs at another facility where agreement permitted multifacility bidding only on annual basis).
[110]102 LA 947 (Paolucci, 1994).
[111]102 LA 961 (Hart, 1994).
[112]Flat River Glass Co., 102 LA 842 (Maniscalco, 1994).

been held not to be entitled to the higher rate.[113] However, where the employee is transferred to a new position (e.g., a setup man), but assigned responsibilities consistent with those of a higher-rated job (e.g., a "leadman"), the company is required to pay the wage rate of the higher classification.[114]

Demotion of Employees

Nondisciplinary demotions continue to be upheld where an employee is found to lack the qualifications for the job,[115] or whose performance on a new job fails to meet management's standards.[116] Disciplinary demotions for poor performance may be reviewed under general standards of "reasonableness," rather than the traditional "just cause" criteria. Accordingly, any disciplinary demotion must be supported with proof that the employee was performing poorly and had been warned of the poor performance.[117]

Some arbitrators have held that demotion is not a permissible form of discipline for misconduct unless this sanction is expressly provided for in the contract.[118] Contracts that authorize a demotion penalty may provide that it may be imposed only consistently with "just cause" principles.[119]

The role of seniority in determining whether employees can voluntarily demote themselves into a lower job classification is unclear. Some arbitrators hold that seniority may be used by employees to voluntarily demote themselves into a lower job.[120] Others have held that the right to voluntarily demote oneself into a lower job is not an inherent incident of seniority but must be expressly provided for in the contract.[121]

Merit Increases

Management may grant individual employees a merit increase without bargaining with the union where the contract specifical-

---

[113]Escalade Sports, Inc., 108 LA 781 (Witney, 1997); Ottawa Truck, Inc., 107 LA 844 (Murphy, 1996).

[114]Capitol Mfg. Co., 102 LA 865 (Duda, 1994).

[115]Cabell Huntington Hosp., 105 LA 980 (Bethel, 1995) (demotion upheld where employee failed to achieve national certification program even though the certification was only an employer-mandated, not a state-mandated, requirement).

[116]Natco Ltd. Partnership, 102 LA 771 (Marcus, 1994) (inability to get along with other supervisors and inability to manage valid reasons to demote newly appointed supervisor).

[117]GES Exposition Servs., 108 LA 311 (Levy, 1997); Regional Transp. Dist., 104 LA 1201 (Yehle, 1995); Stein Printing Co., 101 LA 553 (Byars, 1993).

[118]Gaylord Container Corp., 104 LA 1139 (Allen, 1997).

[119]Avis Rent A Car Shuttlers, 105 LA 1057 (Wahl, 1995) (employee who engaged in sexually offensive behavior allowed the company to demote the employee under principles of just cause, but arbitrator ruled that permanent demotion is excessive and should be converted to temporary demotion.

[120]Tetra Pak Inc., 108 LA 471 (Fowler, 1997).

[121]Alltel Florida, 101 LA 799 (Thronell, 1993).

ly allows management to make discretionary "overscale pay-ments."[122]

Bonuses

The right to a quality-based bonus does not follow employees who transfer to a new department even though these employees are pro-ducing a product similar to the type produced in the old department.[123] Furthermore, where a contract provides that bonuses are paid to those employees "actively at work," employees receiving sickness/accident benefits or workers' compensation benefits are not entitled to the bonuses.[124]

Compulsory Retirement

As discussed in the Main Edition, forced retirement of older work-ers is illegal under the Age Discrimination in Employment Act (ADEA).[125] Accordingly, arbitration decisions discussing compulsory retirement have become virtually extinct. One noteworthy change to the ADEA's prohibition on compulsory retirement occurred on De-cember 31, 1993, with the repeal of 29 U.S.C. §631(d). This section, prior to its repeal, permitted institutions of higher learning to force professors over the age of 70 serving under a contract of unlimited tenure to retire.[126]

Disqualifying Employees for Physical or Mental Reasons

Arbitral resolution of disability cases has undergone a sea change as a result of the Americans with Disabilities Act. Increasingly, arbi-tral decisions are informed by ADA case law, the statute's implement-ing regulations, EEOC guidelines, and parallel state laws.[127]

---

[122]Anderson Wood Prods. Co., 104 LA 1017 (Cocalis, 1995).

[123]Pretty Prods., Inc., 103 LA 1107 (Kindig, 1994).

[124]USS, A Division of USX Corp., 106 LA 193 (Leyland, 1995).

[125]See Weaver v. Amoco Prod. Co., 70 FEP Cases 931 (5th Cir. 1995). See also Kalvinskas v. California Inst. of Tech., 71 FEP Cases 1647 (9th Cir. 1996) (offsetting long-term disability benefits by amount employee could have collected under pension if he retired reduced employee's income stream to zero and constituted illegal forced re-tirement).

[126]29 U.S.C. §631(d) (repealed by P.L. 99-592, 6(b)).

[127]Flamingo Hilton-Laughlin, 108 LA 545, 554–57 (Weckstein, 1997) (in determin-ing whether employee was "disabled" and whether employer was required to restruc-ture job as a reasonable accommodation, arbitrator looked to ADA's statutory language, regulations, and case law); Boise Cascade Corp., 105 LA at 229–32 (in determining employee's obligation to disclose physical impairment during medical examination, ar-bitrator interpreted ADA, regulations, case law, and Minnesota Human Rights Act and interpretive case law).

Arbitrators have repeatedly held that employers must reasonably accommodate employees who have physical or mental impairments, and have looked to the ADA for guidance.[128] The right to a reasonable accommodation has been found not only where the collective bargaining agreement expressly incorporates the ADA, or includes a nondiscrimination clause covering disability,[129] but also under a general "just cause" provision.[130]

Under contracts that specifically incorporate the protections provided by the ADA, arbitrators have held, in accord with the ADA, that the employer is required to offer a reasonable accommodation to qualified employees who would otherwise be unfit to perform their currently assigned duties.[131] Consistent with ADA precedent, however, arbitrators have also held that employers are not precluded from terminating a physically or mentally disabled employee where a proposed accommodation is refused.[132] Moreover, an employee's status as an alcoholic has not been found to excuse the employee's poor attendance or failure to satisfactorily meet performance standards.[133] At least one arbitrator has ruled, however, that under the ADA, a mentally impaired employee who obtained posttermination treatment rendering the chance of relapse or reoccurrence low was entitled to reinstatement.[134]

Arbitrators have also addressed physical and mental qualifications under collective bargaining agreements that neither expressly prohibit discrimination against disabled employees nor incorporate the ADA. For example, just-cause discharges have been upheld where despite the employer's provision of the requested reasonable accommodation, the employees could not perform the essential functions of

---

[128]Courts have also had to consider the impact of collective bargaining agreement arbitration provisions on disability discrimination claims. E.g., Maher v. New Jersey Transit Rail Operations, Inc., 125 N.J. 455 (1991) (plaintiff's failure to arbitrate his state law disability discrimination claim warranted dismissal).

[129]Flamingo Hilton-Laughlin, 108 LA 545 (Weckstein, 1997) (reasonable accommodation required by nondiscrimination clause that explicitly incorporated Americans with Disabilities Act). Accord, AAFES Distrib., 107 LA 291 (Marcus, 1996) (Continental Cement Co., 107 LA 829 (Hilgert, 1996); Boise Cascade Corp., 105 LA 223 (Michelstetter, 1995); Multi-Clean, Inc., 102 LA 463 (Miller, 1993).

[130]National Linen Supply, 107 LA 4 (Ross, 1996) (employer's ability to reasonably accommodate employee's condition incorporated into just-cause standard); Beckett Paper Co., 106 LA 1135 (Goggin, 1996) (same).

[131]Multi-Clean, Inc., 102 LA 463 (Miller, 1993) (employer must ascertain whether a reasonable accommodation could be made to provide grievant with employment).

[132]Flamingo Hilton-Laughlin, 108 LA 545 (Weckstein, 1997) (employer did not violate collective bargaining agreement by discharging employee, after employee refused to accept a new position offered as a reasonable accommodation, in light of the fact that such refusal rendered the employee ineligible as a "qualified individual with a disability" under the EEOC guidelines).

[133]Continental Cement Co., 107 LA 829 (Hilgert, 1996) (although alcoholism is a statutory disability under the ADA, employees must meet attendance and other work-performance obligations).

[134]AAFES Distrib., 107 LA 291 (Marcus, 1996) (employee who suffered from schizophrenic disorder was discharged without just cause despite obscene and abusive language, bizarre behavior, and unexcused absences, where her postdischarge treatment greatly reduced the chance of a relapse).

their jobs.[135] This requirement (i.e., that disabled employees be able to perform, with or without a reasonable accommodation, the essential functions of their positions) is included in the express language of the ADA.

The ADA provides that where an employee poses a direct threat to the health or safety of others that cannot be eliminated with reasonable accommodation, that employee is not qualified to perform his essential job functions. In one case the summary discharge of an employee with a psychiatric disorder that triggered outbursts against coworkers was upheld because the misconduct was so egregious that it rendered the employee unfit to work.[136]

Discharges of employees addicted to alcohol or illegal drugs have been upheld where the employees were deemed medically unfit because of their failure to comply with a rehabilitation program.[137]

On March 25, 1997, the EEOC Guidance on Psychiatric Disabilities and the Americans with Disabilities Act, ADA Manual 70:1281 et seq. (Guidelines) was issued. The Guidelines take an expansive view of mental disabilities, which are defined largely in terms of the disorders set forth in the Diagnostic Statistical Manual, and discuss some of the unique accommodation issues raised in the context of such disabilities. It is anticipated that the Guidelines will become a reference point for arbitrators in cases where a mental condition is raised as a defense to discipline or discharge.

As this supplement goes to press, the United States Supreme Court has heard argument in several cases involving the interpretation and application of the ADA.[138]

When interpreting collective bargaining agreements, arbitrators have also applied the provisions of the Family and Medical Leave Act of 1993 (FMLA).[139] The FMLA has been applied even when the labor contract does not expressly incorporate the statute.[140]

---

[135]National Linen Supply, 107 LA 4 (Ross, 1996) (employer is not obligated to retain an employee who is so disabled that he cannot consistently perform his job); Beckett Paper Co., 106 LA 1135 (Goggin, 1996) (employee could not be accommodated, nor did postdischarge treatment warrant reinstatement, where doctor found employee so disabled as to be unable to perform the essential functions of his job).

[136]Rohm & Haas, 104 LA 974 (Koenig, Jr., 1995) (a discharged employee who suffered from bipolar disorder was not disparately treated where other employees had been discharged for directly threatening coworkers, even though future outbursts could be controlled by medication).

[137]Westinghouse Hanford Co., 101 LA 46 (Nelson, 1993) (employer's conclusion that an employee was medically unfit because of the employee's failure to follow an alcohol rehabilitation program was not unreasonable).

[138]E.g., No. 98-536-Olmstead v. L.C., 138 F.3d 893 (11th Cir. 1998); No. 97-1992-Murphy v. United Parcel Service Inc., unpublished-(10th Cir. 1998); No. 97-1943-Sutton v. United Airlines, Inc., 130 F.3d 893 (10th Cir. 1998); No. 98-591-Albertsons Inc., v. Kirkingburg, 143 F.3d 1228 (9th Cir., 1998).

[139]29 U.S.C.§§2611 et seq. See Apcoa, Inc., 107 LA 705 (Daniel, 1996) (employer impermissibly discharged employee where employer failed to notify employee that leave was designated as FMLA leave).

[140]See Big River Zinc Corp., 108 LA 693 (Draznin, 1997) (employer properly discharged employee who did not return from FMLA leave at time he was supposed to

The FMLA requires covered employers to provide eligible employees with 12 weeks' unpaid leave during a 12-month period for their serious health conditions. Upon conclusion of the FMLA leave, the employer must reinstate the employee to his or her original job or, if that is unavailable, to an equivalent position. An employer's duty to provide eligible employees with FMLA leave is in addition to, not a substitution for, the employer's obligation to reasonably accommodate the employee pursuant to the ADA. Thus, an employee who becomes "disabled" (as defined by the ADA) may be entitled to 12 weeks of FMLA leave as well as additional leave to reasonably accommodate his or her ailment.

Significance of Workers' Compensation Disabilities and Costs

An employer may require an employee to return to work after a physician determines, in connection with the employee's application for workers' compensation benefits, that the employee is not disabled.[141] Typically state laws include antiretaliation provisions in their workers' compensation statutes that may be implicated where an employer's treatment of an employee receiving such benefits differs from its handling of employees on other types of leave.[142]

Right to Require Physical Examination

Under contracts containing a disability nondiscrimination clause, it has been held that an employer may conduct a physical examination to ascertain an employee's functional fitness to return to work.[143] Although arbitrators have generally deemed the ADA and the FMLA incorporated into contractual nondiscrimination clauses, there is no such consensus about incorporating statutory or regulatory standards for requiring physical examinations.[144] The ADA's interpretive regulations permit employers to "require a medical examination (and/or inquiry) of an employee that is job-related and consistent with busi-

---

report to work and who did not provide timely response to request for information regarding his medical status).

[141]City of Santa Cruz, 104 LA 660 (Pool, 1995) (although employee produced a statement of a physician in support of her contention that she was disabled, city had just cause to discharge firefighter for willful failure to return to work after psychiatric examination conducted to determine eligibility for workers' compensation benefits concluded that employee was not disabled).

[142]See Jefferson-Smurfit Corp., 103 LA 1041 (Canestraight, 1994) (employer did not terminate employee in violation of Missouri law in retaliation for her filing a workers' compensation claim, where the employee was not discharged until seven months after company officials and employee last discussed claim).

[143]Cessna Aircraft Co., 104 LA 985 (Thornell, 1995) (employer had the right to require an employee who had been on a leave of absence because of a workplace injury to take a physical examination in order to ascertain the employee's ability to perform the job, but employer is nevertheless required to accommodate any existing disability).

[144]See Cessna Aircraft Co., 104 LA 985 (Thornell, 1995).

ness necessity."[145] Moreover, under the FMLA an employer may have a uniformly applied policy or practice that requires all similarly situated employees who take leave for a serious health condition to obtain and present certification from the employee's health care provider that the employee is able to resume work.[146]

Further, under contracts that do not expressly prohibit disability discrimination, arbitrators have held that an employee has the right to be paid for time spent taking a physical examination,[147] and that employers may not indiscriminately or inconsistently require physical or psychological examinations.[148]

Drug and Alcohol Testing

Though drug tests are not considered medical examinations under the ADA, tests to determine how much, if any, alcohol an individual has consumed are considered medical examinations and are not statutorily exempt.[149] Although not governed by the ADA, the implementation of drug tests is a mandatory subject of bargaining under the National Labor Relations Act, and arbitrators continue to invalidate drug testing programs that are unreasonable in their implementation or administration.[150] Conversely, employers' disciplinary actions based on a drug-testing policy will be upheld where the policy is reasonable in both design and implementation.[151]

Where the testing policy has not been consistently applied, employees who have been terminated for refusing to take a drug test have been reinstated with back pay.[152]

---

[145]29 C.F.R. 1630.14(c).

[146]29 C.F.R. 825.310(a).

[147]City of Washington, 108 LA 892 (Wren, 1997) (requiring an employee to submit to a physical examination is tantamount to ordering him to perform work, and therefore the employee is entitled to a premium for time spent in taking physical examination).

[148]City of Monmouth, 105 LA 725 (Wolff, 1995) (city was not permitted to require employee on leave for shoulder injury to submit to psychological examination or drug test prior to employee's return to work).

[149]EEOC Guidance on Pre-Employment Disability-Related Inquiries and Medical Examinations Under the ADA, ADA Manual §§70:1103 et seq.

[150]Pioneer Flour Mills, 101 LA 816 (Bankston, 1993) (where employer's requirement that employee submit to drug test was not based on reasonable suspicion, employee's right to privacy prevails).

[151]Integrated Distrib. Sys., 108 LA 737 (Neas, 1997) (policy permitting employer to test an employee "any time an employee is involved in an accident" is reasonable and employer is not obligated to give the employee the right to talk to the union representative where the policy does not extend such a right); Atlas Processing Co., 106 LA 172 (Baroni, 1996) (employer reasonably unilaterally implemented random drug testing program after just-cause program failed); Jefferson Smurfit Corp., 106 LA 306 (Goldstein, 1996) (drug testing policy's differentiation between major and minor injuries with regard to mandatory testing was reasonable); Wooster City Bd. of Educ., 102 LA 535 (High, 1993) (employer reasonably scheduled off-duty testing of employees to accommodate individuals with scheduling problems where collective bargaining agreement did not restrict time of testing).

[152]Munster Steel Co., Inc., 108 LA 597 (Cerone, 1997) (employer unlawfully discriminated against employee by requiring employee to submit to drug test on the day of

Selection and Control of Supervisors

Arbitrators do not have the authority to require an employer to discipline a supervisor or to force a supervisor to rectify wrong-doing.[153]

---

an in-plant injury where on other occasions employees where permitted to be tested at a later date).

[153]Union Camp Corp., 104 LA 295 (Nolan, 1995) (arbitrator did not have authority to require the employer to discipline a supervisor who sexually harassed subordinates or to require supervisor to apologize, although arbitrator was empowered to require the employer to take necessary measure to ensure that supervisor did not commit such harassment in the future).

Chapter 14

Seniority

Source of Seniority "Rights"

Contractual Seniority Rights, the Civil Rights Act, Other Legislation, and Arbitration

The exemption in §703(h) of the Civil Rights Act of 1964[1] immunizing the noninvidiously discriminatory, "routine application" of a bona fide seniority system has been extended beyond Title VII to both the Age Discrimination in Employment Act[2] (ADEA) and the Americans with Disabilities Act (ADA).[3]

Thus, a school district's refusal to hire an older teacher because her salary position, based on a collectively bargained, experience-driven wage schedule, would have been "too high" did not violate the ADEA.[4] The salary schedule was viewed as a seniority system and was established for a nondiscriminatory purpose. Consequently, it was not violative of the ADEA despite the disparate affect on older teachers seeking employment with the district.

In determining whether a seniority system is discriminatory, courts have applied the burden-shifting analysis used for disparate

---

[1]42 U.S.C. §703(h).

[2]29 U.S.C. §623(f)(2); Hiatt v. Union Pac. R.R. Co., 65 F.3d 839, 150 LRRM 2265 (10th Cir. 1995), cert. denied, 116 S. Ct. 917 (1996) (no violation of ADEA where railroad had long-standing policy of not carrying over brakemen's seniority upon promotion to conductor; fact that older brakemen were disadvantaged by mandatory promotions to conductor irrelevant so long as seniority policy is applied uniformly).

[3]42 U.S.C. §12112(b)(5)(A); Eckles v. Consolidated Rail Corp., 94 F.3d 1041, 155 LRRM 2653 (7th Cir. 1996), cert. denied, 117 S. Ct. 1318 (1997) (the ADA does not require an employer to offer an employee an accommodation that would require the "otherwise valid seniority rights of other employees to be trumped"). This case will be discussed further in the next section titled "Americans with Disabilities Act."

[4]EEOC v. Newport Mesa Unified Sch. Dist., 893 F.Supp. 927, 68 FEP Cases 657 (C.D. Cal. 1995).

treatment claims under Title VII.[5] In an arbitration case in which a union claimed that a discharge was racially motivated and violative of the antidiscrimination provision of the collective bargaining agreement, the arbitrator was faced with the "burden of proof" question in determining whether the evidence should be considered until a Title VII standard or the traditional "just cause" requirement.[6] The arbitrator concluded that under either line of analysis the employer must establish that it had a valid and genuine reason for taking the challenged employment action.

Americans with Disabilities Act

Arbitrators continue to be called upon to resolve the conflicts between the "reasonable accommodations" that must be afforded employees under a disability and the terms of the collective bargaining agreement.[7]

The conflict most often emerges when the employer grants a request for a shift change, transfer, or reassignment of duties for an employee who does not otherwise possess the requisite seniority.[8]

But it is generally agreed that the ADA is not an "affirmative action" statute requiring employers to put in place measures before an employee with a disability makes known to the employer the need for an accommodation.[9] Once an employee makes the need for accommodation known, however, the employer must determine what accommodations it can make without "undue burden" that will enable it to place the employee in an available appropriate position for which the employee is qualified.[10]

Arbitrators who have considered the ADA in reaching "reasonable accommodation" decisions under collective bargaining contracts rely on contract provisions that call for the supremacy of any laws or governmental regulations[11] or antidiscrimination

---

[5]Dodd v. Runyon, 114 F.3d 726, 74 FEP Cases 738 (8th Cir. 1997) (employee's motion for summary judgment denied where factual issue existed as to whether seniority system was administered in a discriminatory fashion).

[6]Henkel Corp., 104 LA 494 (Hooper, 1995).

[7]City of Dearborn Heights, 101 LA 809 (Kanner, 1993) (employer properly transferred police lieutenant from the night shift because of his diabetic condition, even though he did not have such a contractual right, where no other reasonable accommodation could be made).

[8]Daly-Rooney, "Reconciling Conflicts Between the Americans with Disabilities Act and the National Labor Relations Act to Accommodate People with Disabilities," 6 DePaul Bus. L.J. 387, 392 (1994).

[9]O'Melvery, "The Americans with Disabilities Act and Collective Bargaining Agreements: Reasonable Accommodation or Irreconcilabe Conflicts?," 82 Ky. L.J. 219 (1994) (setting aside certain jobs for persons with disabilities not required).

[10]San Francisco United School Dist., 104 LA 215 (Bogue, 1995).

[11]Champion Int'l Corp., 106 LA 1025 (Howell, 1996) (contract provided that its terms are superseded by applicable laws or regulations); City of Dearborn Heights, 101 LA 809 (Kanner, 1993) (agreement stated that contract language could be declared invalid by operation of law).

clauses,[12] or express agreements between the parties[13] to justify recourse to external law.

In *Eckles v. Consolidated Rail Corp.*,[14] the Seventh Circuit held that the ADA did not require an employer to provide an accommodation to a disabled employee that would violate the collectively bargained seniority rights of other employees. Moreover, unless the employee demonstrates that he or she is qualified to perform the essential functions of the job offered, accommodation is not required.[15]

However, one district court has held that the existence of a seniority system does not automatically take precedence over an employee's conflicting request for accommodation,[16] but rather is a factor to be considered in determining whether the requested accommodation is reasonable.

Arbitrators have followed the *Eckles* approach, concluding that the ADA does not require the bumping of more senior employees or the creation of a job in order to provide a reasonable accommodation.[17] It is unclear, however, whether the *Eckles* holding would be extended to a situation where a nonunion employer refused to provide an accommodation that would violate the employer's unilaterally promulgated seniority system.[18]

Seniority Units

Arbitrators continue to recognize that seniority units may be multiplant,[19] departmental,[20] or based upon an occupational group or

---

[12]San Francisco Unified School Dist., 104 LA 215 (Bogue, 1995) (ADA standards utilized in case of teacher with multiple sclerosis where agreement prohibited discrimination on the basis of "handicapped condition").

[13]Alcoa Bldg. Prods., 104 LA 364 (Cerone, 1995) (stipulation of parties).

[14]94 F.3d 1041, 155 LRRM 2653 (7th Cir. 1996), cert. denied, 117 S. Ct. 1318 (1997).

[15]Schmidt v. Genessee County Road Comm., 1996 U.S. Dist. LEXIS 17727 (E.D. Mich. 1996); Massey v. Scrivner, Inc., 901 F.Supp. 1546, 150 LRRM 2629 (W.D. Okla. 1994).

[16]Emrick v. Libbey-Owens-Ford Co., 875 F.Supp. 393, 4 Am. Disabilities Cas. (BNA) 1 (E.D. Tex. 1995).

[17]Alcoa Bldg. Prods., 104 LA 364 (Cerone, 1995) (company violated agreement when it removed a more senior employee in favor of a disabled employee); Olin Corp., 103 LA 481 (Helburn, 1994) (employer not obligated to accommodate the needs of a disabled worker in a manner that interferes with the rights of a more senior employee); but see City of Dearborn Heights, 101 LA 809 (Kanner, 1993) (reassignment of a disabled employee to a shift occupied by a more senior employee viewed as job restructuring and not bumping).

[18]McGlothlen & Savine, "Individual Rights and Reasonable Accommodations under the Americans with Disabilities Act: Eckles v. Consolidated Rail Corp.: Reconciling the ADA with Collective Bargaining Agreements: Is This the Correct Approach?," 46 DePaul L. Rev. 1043 (1997).

[19]Cone Mills Corp., 103 LA 745 (Byars, 1994) (employee who has completed three-month probationary period at one of employer's plants and is subsequently transferred to another plan may not be discharged as probationary employee).

[20]Safeway Stores Inc., 107 LA 448 (Snider, 1996) (defining departments for shift preference); Stone Container Corp., 101 LA 720 (Helbum, 1993) (employer did not violate contract when it assigned less senior employees to nonbargaining unit work); Norwalk Furniture Corp., 100 LA 1051 (Dworkin, 1993) (contract limited exercise of employees' bargaining rights to their own department).

classification,[21] but the seniority dates of employees who transfer from one plant or unit to another may be calculated differently for different purposes. In one case the original hire date of a transferred employee was used to calculate his benefits, but the date he began to work in the bargaining unit in the new plant was the date for calculating his seniority for other purposes.[22]

Seniority Standing and Determining Length of Service

In the absence of a contrary provision in a collective bargaining agreement, employees who transfer to a new plant may retain their seniority status and may not be required to complete a new probationary period.[23]

Agreements often award "superseniority" for union officers and stewards[24] so that they may be retained in employment while employees with longer service are subject to layoff. The rationale for superseniority is that, for the overall good of the entire bargaining unit, it may be advantageous to retain a union officer in a layoff situation so that if a grievance or other problem arises, there is a responsible union official present to deal with it.[25] Superseniority provisions, however, "are presumptively unlawful" if used to grant preferences for purposes other than layoff and recall.[26] Ordinarily, before a union official may exercise superseniority, the official must be qualified to perform the work available.[27]

Arbitrators have held that employees retain[28] and even accrue[29] seniority during absences due to injury or illness. On the other hand,

---

[21]Lear Corp., 108 LA 592 (Goldberg, 1997) (separate seniority system for restricted duty employees upheld); Duraloy, 100 LA 1166 (Franckiwicz, 1993) (employees may have seniority in multiple departments).

[22]ARCO Chem., 102 LA 1051 (Massey, 1994).

[23]Cone Mills Corp., 103 LA 745 (Byars, 1994).

[24]USS-Fairless Works, 102 LA 810 (Petersen, 1993) (a grievance committeeman whose job was eliminated was properly recalled pursuant to a superseniority provision).

[25]Duraloy, 100 LA 1166 (Franckiewicz, 1993) (employer improperly failed to afford superseniority to recording secretary in addition to grievance committeeman, where each employee had different authoritative responsibilities).

[26]NLRB v. Joy Tech. Inc., 990 F.2d 104, 142 LRRM 2865 (3d Cir. 1993) (a labor contract's superseniority clause that permits union committeepersons and stewards to invoke superseniority for purposes beyond layoff and recall is "presumptively invalid"); AmeriMark Bldg. Prods., Inc., 104 LA 1066 (Klein, 1995) (superseniority exercisable only with respect to order of layoff and not order of recall).

[27]General Dynamics, 101 LA 187 (Richman, 1993) (steward not entitled to superseniority where not qualified to perform work available, but company violated contract by failing to notify union of impending layoff of steward).

[28]Bethlehem Steel Corp., 100 LA 466 (Kahn, 1992) (employee did not lose seniority during absence for work-related injury); Waterous Co., 100 LA 278 (Reynolds, 1993) (contract provision stating specifically that seniority shall not be lost because of injury or illness).

[29]Public Serv. Co. of Oklahoma, 107 LA 1080 (Allen, Jr., 1997) (where contract language ambiguous, past practice used to determine that seniority continued to accumulate during leave of absence).

one arbitrator determined that seniority may not accumulate during a layoff.[30]

Seniority Standing

In general, seniority may be accumulated during the probationary period but not for time served as a "temporary" employee.[31] Some contracts expressly provide that part-time employees do not accrue seniority.[32]

Seniority Lists

Where a collective bargaining agreement specifically provides a window for challenging a seniority list, the failure to timely protest may preclude the union's challenge.[33]

Service Outside the Seniority Unit

A contract may provide that an employee may work in a second position for a certain period of time without losing his or her seniority in the first position.[34] In one case, where the employee worked outside the bargaining unit one day beyond the time permitted under the contract to retain seniority, the arbitrator nevertheless refused to allow the forfeiture of the accrued seniority. Despite the expiration of the period, the arbitrator reasoned that the employee should not be penalized because he had timely made a good faith effort to inquire about returning to his original position.[35]

A contract may also provide that an employee's accrued seniority is not retained when the employee is transferred to an exempt position.[36] Moreover, absent contractual language to the contrary, employees may not be credited with seniority for services rendered before their entry into the bargaining unit.[37]

---

[30]Klein Mfg., 104 LA 18 (Traynor, 1993).

[31]Id.; Cone Mills Corp., 103 LA 745 (Byars, 1994) (employee accrued seniority during probationary period); see also Alltel Pennsylvania Inc., 108 LA 872 (Oberdank, 1997) (where contract denies contractual rights to temporary employees, regular employees not entitled to seniority credit for time served as temporary employees).

[32]Pace Fox Valley Div., 101 LA 912 (Kohn, 1993).

[33]Burns Sec. Servs., 101 LA 441 (McCausland, 1993).

[34]Gaylord Container Corp., 102 LA 1206 (Hooper, 1994).

[35]Champion Int'l Corp., 108 LA 104 (Statham, 1997).

[36]Kansas City, Kan., 100 LA 534 (Berger, 1993) (former unit members who are now nonunit supervisors have no right to use their previously accumulated unit seniority to bid into bargaining-unit positions).

[37]ARCO Chem., 102 LA 1051 (Massey, 1994) (date employee began to work in new plant and bargaining unit, rather than total time with company, is used for determining seniority rights but not for determining continuous service-related benefits such as pension and vacation entitlements and salary rate that accrued pursuant to commitments made by employer to employee prior to his joining bargaining unit).

Extension of Seniority Rights to Different Plant or Successor Employer

A "successor employer" is required to bargain with the union that had represented its predecessor's employees[38] but is not bound by the predecessor's union contract.[39]

Merger or Sale of Company

Whether the surviving corporation is obligated to honor the entire collective bargaining agreement of the merged entity, or one of its provisions or a past practice under the agreement relating to seniority or other terms, remains a factual issue for the arbitrator to determine according to whether there was an express or implied assumption agreement.[40]

Merger of Seniority Lists

When facilities are merged, an agreement may limit job bidding at the surviving facility to employees working in the facility, and an employer that permitted employees from the closed facility to bid into openings in the surviving facility was found to have violated a letter agreement.[41]

As the Main Edition pointed out, of the five methods used in merging seniority lists pursuant to a consolidation of plants or departments, the "length of service" method continues to be the most widely used.[42]

---

[38]Canteen Corp. v. NLRB, 103 F.3d 1355, 154 LRRM 2065 (7th Cir. 1997) (discussing elements of "successor employer" concept—i.e., substantial continuity of operations and of workforce); B.F. Goodrich v. Betkoski, 99 F.3d 505 (2d Cir. 1996) (adopting the "substantial continuity" test); see also NLRB v. Staten Island Hotel Ltd. Partnership, 101 F.3d 858, 153 LRRM 3067 (2d Cir. 1996) (successor employer's refusal to hire a significant number of the predecessor's bargaining unit employees was based on anti-union animus. NLRB properly ordered successor employer to pay former employees at rates earned under predecessor's collective bargaining agreement).

[39]Southward v. South Cent. Ready Mix Supply Corp., 7 F.3d 487, 144 LRRM 2464 (6th Cir. 1993) (successor employer cannot be bound by substantive terms of predecessor's labor contract, even if its business is "substantial continuation" of predecessor's operations, when it neither is predecessor's "alter ego" nor has voluntarily assumed contractual obligations).

[40]St. Louis Symphony Soc'y, 106 LA 158 (Fowler, 1996) (after music school merged with symphony orchestra, union that had represented orchestra had jurisdiction over dispute at music school).

[41]Ralph's Grocery Co., 109 LA 33 (Kaufman, 1997) (arbitrator did not award a remedy because union had "selectively enforced" the agreement).

[42]Amax Coal Co., 104 LA 790 (Stoltenberg, 1995) (where two unions who represented employees at one mine were combined, length of service, rather than dovetailing, was proper method); Larocqul v. R.W.F. Inc., 8 F.3d 95, 144 LRRM 2649 (1st Cir. 1993) (arbitrator did not exceed his authority when he upheld company's decision to dovetail seniority lists, where the arbitrator had to reconcile the labor contracts of two separate corporate divisions that were being merged).

Loss of Seniority

Arbitrators continue to uphold contractual provisions that call for the loss of seniority in the event an employee experiences a lengthy absence from work due to illness or injury.[43]

Seniority Provisions

Many collective bargaining agreements provide that the order of recall from layoff is to be based solely on length of seniority-qualifying service,[44] but modified seniority clauses that consider the "training, skill, experience, fitness or ability" of unit members are common.[45]

Under emergency or other exigent circumstances the need for special qualifications may allow the employer to disregard seniority and recall a junior employee out of seniority order.[46] Thus in one case the recall of junior employees was found appropriate because they possessed the necessary skills and competence that the company needed during an emergency condition created by a flood, and more senior employees did not.[47]

Modified Seniority Clauses

A contract provision requiring vacant leadman positions to be filled by the *"most senior* qualified employee" seeking the position was interpreted as a "sufficient ability" clause that did not allow the employer to select a junior employee whom it viewed as the "senior *most qualified* employee."[48]

---

[43]Food & Commercial Workers Local 88 v. Shop 'N Save Warehouse Foods Inc., 113 F.3d 893, 155 LRRM 2278 (8th Cir. 1997) (employer did not violate labor contract when it rehired, as new employee, former employee who was discharged for failing to obtain full return-to-work release); Davies Can Co., 103 LA 877 (Strasshofer, 1994) (employer had just cause to terminate seniority of employee injured on job where collective agreement unambiguously called for loss of seniority after four-year absence).

[44]Sunnyside Coal Co., 104 LA 886 (Sharpe, 1995); Hughes Aircraft Co., 101 LA 415 (Prayzich, 1993).

[45]Waco Tribune Herald, 108 LA 370 (Jennings, 1997) (senior employee properly denied preference to work day shifts in favor of junior employee with specialized training); Conagra Inc., 106 LA 784 (Suardi, 1996) (leeway given to employer in determining recall in order to recognize and consider specialized skill, experience, and ability); Houston Lighting & Power Co., 103 LA 179 (Fox, 1993) (reduction-in-force procedure that took into account qualifications and seniority did not violate contract where contract provided that seniority governed reductions in force when ability, skill, and qualifications were equal); Type House + Duragraph, 102 LA 225 (Miller, 1993) (layoff and failure to recall were valid under contract provision giving employer the right to have "sufficient qualified employees").

[46]Alsco, 106 LA 1146 (Rybolt, 1996).

[47]Conagra Inc., 106 LA 784 (Swardi, 1996); Eagle Iron Works, 103 LA 903 (Murphy, 1994).

[48]DynAir Fueling of Nevada, 102 LA 230 (Mikrut, Jr., 1993) (the most senior, not most qualified, employee entitled to the position).

Under a "relative ability" clause requiring the employer to select the least senior employees in the event of a layoff where "ability, skill and qualification are equal,"[49] the arbitrator denied the grievance of a more senior employee who had been selected for layoff because he scored lower on an employer-developed rating system than the retained junior employees.

Pursuant to a "hybrid" seniority clause that required promotions to be based on "length of service and ability," an arbitrator upheld the right of the employer to select a junior employee to fill the position.[50] The arbitrator rejected the union's contention that the more senior, but less qualified, employee should have been selected and trained during the 30-day trial period afforded by the contract to all promoted employees. The arbitrator noted that though the difference in length of service between the two employees was relatively insignificant, the difference in their ability was substantial, and the position in dispute was one of the most critical and highest-skilled jobs in the bargaining unit.

Review of Management's Determination: Evidence and Burden of Proof

In the majority of reported decisions involving the interpretation of a "relative ability" seniority clause, the union must prove bad faith, arbitrariness, capriciousness, or discrimination on the part of the employer, or prove that the employer's evaluation of abilities was clearly wrong.[51]

However, in a recent case involving the interpretation of a "relative ability" seniority clause, an arbitrator concluded that both the union and the employer were required to present whatever evidence they could in support of their respective positions, and that each party had the "burden of the affirmative" on particular aspects within the development of the case. The burden of proof was upon the employer to disclose a legitimate reason for bypassing the senior employee, and the union had to produce sufficient evidence that the evaluation process was unreasonable or discriminatory.[52]

Factors Considered in Determining Fitness and Ability

Use of Tests

When a contract provides that any employee who possesses "sufficient qualifications" to perform a particular job is entitled to a pro-

---

[49]Houston Lighting & Power Co., 103 LA 179 (Fox, Jr., 1993).
[50]Trident NGL, Inc., 101 LA 353 (Allen, Jr., 1993).
[51]Lehigh Portland Cement Co., 105 LA 860 (Baroni, 1995).
[52]Houston Lighting & Power Co., 103 LA 179 (Fox, Jr., 1993).

motion based on seniority, test results used by the employer to evaluate qualifications must relate specifically to the requirements of that job.[53]

Trial or Break-in Period on the Job Versus Training

A "trial period" is sometimes viewed as the best test of whether an employee can do the job. Thus it has been held that an employee who had the right to bump into other jobs upon his return from a work-related injury was to be afforded a trial period to demonstrate his ability to perform the requested work.[54]

Attendance Records

Poor attendance has been held to be a valid reason to deny a more senior employee a promotion where the contract permitted the employer to give consideration to ability.[55]

Sex as a Factor

When friction between employees makes it impossible for them to work together, companies may transfer the junior employee from his or her classification or shift. However, when an employer that had followed this procedure in the past removed a female employee from her classification and shift because she had complained of sexual harassment by a male coworker, an arbitrator ruled that the action violated the contract.[56]

Age as a Factor

Youth can be a proper consideration and an advantage in competition for promotions when it is perceived as associated with the knowledge of the latest techniques or the job. Where a collective bargaining agreement did not provide for promotion by seniority, an arbitrator found that the employer did not act in an arbitrary, capricious, or discriminatory manner when it selected the least senior bidder, in part because the arbitrator believed the junior employee was more knowledgeable about the latest needs and techniques of the position.[57]

---

[53]GTE Tel. Operations, South, 103 LA 1205 (Duff, 1994) (failure to pass a general aptitude test administered by employer did not indicate that bidder lacked sufficient qualifications to perform the job); Lehigh Portland Cement Co., 105 LA 860 (Baroni, 1995) (employer properly used test in deciding to promote two junior employees where test was job-related).

[54]Zinc Corp. of Am., 101 LA 643 (Nicholas, 1993).

[55]United Can Co., 102 LA 422 (Randall, 1993).

[56]Champion Int'l Corp., 105 LA 429 (Fullmer, 1995).

[57]Johnston Controls Inc., 101 LA 964 (Cohen, 1993).

Chapter 15

Discharge and Discipline

Employer Action Pending Court Hearing on Conduct of Employee

In several cases arbitrators have set aside the suspension of an employee pending the disposition of criminal charges arising from off-duty conduct because the misconduct was found not to be directly tied to the workplace,[1] or otherwise to have adversely affected the employer.[2] But arbitrators continue to uphold suspensions and subsequent discharges of employees who are ultimately found guilty of criminal charges when the illegal conduct relates to, or adversely affects, the employer's business.[3]

Types of Penalties

Arbitrators continue to review the propriety of using demotions as a form of discipline. One arbitrator upheld a disciplinary demotion because it was not specifically prohibited by the labor agreement.[4] However, another arbitrator sustained the grievance of an employee demoted for failure to satisfactorily perform the duties of a position to which she had been promoted as a disciplinary action taken with-

---

[1]Babcock & Wilcox Co., 102 LA 104 (Nicholas, 1994).

[2]Startran, Inc., 104 LA 641 (Baroni, 1995); Southern Nuclear Operating Co., 102 LA 97 (Abrams, 1993).

[3]Dunlop Tire Corp., 104 LA 653 (Teple, 1995) (employer had just cause to discharge employee who pled guilty to drug possession on company property); Ernst Enters., 103 LA 782 (Doering, 1994) (employer had just cause to discharge driver whose guilty plea to driving under the influence of alcohol resulted in the suspension of his driver's license and resulting inability to perform assigned duties); Leestown Co., 102 LA 979 (Sergent, 1994) (discharge not too severe for employee determined by an unemployment appeals referee to have fraudulently obtained unemployment benefits from the employer).

[4]Northwest Publication, Inc., 104 LA 91, 96 (Bognanno, 1994).

142

out "just cause" because the employer did not make a serious effort to train the employee in her new position.[5]

Burden and Quantum of Proof

In a number of recent awards where employees have been discharged for alleged conduct that is especially stigmatizing or seriously criminal, arbitrators have required the employers to prove their cases by "clear and convincing evidence" or "evidence beyond a reasonable doubt."[6]

Proof in Group Discipline Cases

Employers may discipline all employees who participate in a prohibited work stoppage,[7] but it has been held that the discipline should be commensurate with an employee's degree of participation or culpability.[8]

---

[5]Klauser Corp., 102 LA 381, 383 (McCurdy, 1994).

[6]Vista Chem. Co., 104 LA 818 (Nicholas, 1995) (employer must prove by clear and convincing evidence that employee was justly discharged for sexual harassment and arbitrator should impose strict scrutiny approach to charges of sexual harassment because of the stigmatizing effect of such charges); Indianapolis Plant of Carrier Corp., 103 LA 891 (Lipson, 1994) (employer's burden of proof in defending its discharge of employee for selling drugs is clear and convincing evidence whether or not the grievant is charged with committing a crime); J. R. Simplot Co., 103 LA 865 (Tilbury, 1994) (standard of proof for discharge for acts of industrial sabotage should be clear and convincing evidence, which is something more than mere preponderance and means that trier of fact must find more than a slight tilt on the scale of justice); Yellow Freight Sys., Inc., 103 LA 731 (Stix, 1994) (employer that discharges employee for theft must provide evidence to sustain charge beyond a reasonable doubt); Hy-Vee Food Stores, 102 LA 555 (Berquist, 1994) (just cause did not exist for three-day suspension where employer failed to prove by clear and convincing evidence that grievant was dishonest when he failed to perform assignment); GTE North, 102 LA 154 (Kenis, 1993) (just cause did not exist to discharge employee for dishonesty for falsification of company records where employer failed to prove by clear and convincing evidence grievant was responsible for alleged false entry); Exxon Co. U.S.A., 101 LA 777 (Baroni, 1993) (just cause existed to discharge grievant for theft where it was clearly and convincingly shown that he improperly removed company property for several years); Atlantic Southeast Airlines, 101 LA 515 (Nolan, 1993) (clear and convincing standard of proof required for company to prove employee should be discharged for refusal to take drug test). Contra, Superior Coffee & Foods, 103 LA 609 (Alleyne, 1994) (preponderance of the evidence test used by arbitrator to evaluate serious charges of sexual harassment despite claim that employer should prove its charge beyond a reasonable doubt because charge of sexual harassment involves accusation of moral turpitude and social stigma); Wholesale Produce Supply Co., 101 LA 1101 (Bognanno, 1993) (company need only prove by a preponderance of evidence that it properly discharged employee for dishonesty since labor arbitration is not a criminal court of law and reliance on standard of beyond a reasonable doubt is inappropriate).

[7]Plainville Concrete Servs., 104 LA 811 (High, 1995) (drivers who called in sick in a concerted effort to avoid scheduled overtime work violated no strike agreement where they provided no evidence that they were really sick); Domino Sugar Corp., 101 LA 41 (Allen, 1993) (employer properly disciplined employees who engaged in concerted sickout but reduced their suspensions because the work stoppage was restricted to only one shift and employees gave management time to prepare for the absences).

[8]Public Utility Dist., No. 1 of Clark County, 103 LA 1066 (Paull, 1994) (warning letters properly given to employees who affirmatively participated in illegal work stop-

Review of Penalties Imposed by Management

Authority of Arbitrator to Modify Penalties

Absent a "just cause" requirement for discipline in the contract, some arbitrators may be hesitant to modify penalties imposed by management. In a case where an arbitrator found that the "just cause" standard was neither expressed nor implied in the labor agreement, the arbitrator declined to review management's decision to discharge an employee.[9] The infraction committed was identified in the agreement as punishable by discharge, and since the "harsh" penalty imposed complied with the agreement negotiated by the parties, the arbitrator concluded he had no authority to inquire further.

Factors in Evaluating Penalties

Nature of the Offense: Summary Discharge Versus Corrective Discipline

As previously noted, summary discharge in lieu of corrective discipline of the employee is reserved for the most serious offenses. The definition of a disqualifying "serious offense" remains elastic. Sleeping on duty, at least where the act is intentional and the employee attempts to avoid detection usually warrants termination even though it is the employee's first offense.[10] (See Table of Offenses at the end of this chapter.)

In one case, summary discharge was deemed appropriate for a single act of negligent work performance. A service technician did not perform a crucial pressure test required by the employer's protocol and thus failed to find a gas leak in the customer's heater connector.[11] Because of the risk of explosion and fire to which the customer was exposed by the oversight, the arbitrator found the violation of the employment responsibilities justified the employee's immediate discharge.

In another case, the arbitrator determined just cause existed for summary discharge of an employee for making racial slurs where several employees had complained of the racial comments and the employee had ignored previous warnings regarding his offensive language.[12]

---

page but penalty reduced to oral warning for other grievants who participated only passively).

[9]Preferred Transp., Inc., 108 LA 636, 640 (Gentile, 1997). See also Mercury Consol., Inc., 101 LA 309 (Schubert, 1993) (arbitrator had no authority to review disciplinary action taken by employer where labor agreement lacked "just cause" requirement).

[10]Voca Corp., 105 LA 368 (Rybolt, 1995).

[11]BHP Petroleum/Gasco Inc., 102 LA 321 (Najita, 1994).

[12]Eagle Snacks, Inc., 103 LA 741 (Baroni, 1994). See also Fry's Food Stores of Arizona, Inc., 99 LA 1161 (Hogler, 1992) (summary discharge of employee who made disparaging comment to homosexual coworker upheld because of serious nature of offense).

For misconduct deemed less serious, arbitrators are likely to follow progressive discipline procedures.[13] Arbitrators are especially likely to set aside or reduce penalties where the employee had not previously been reprimanded and warned that his conduct would trigger the discipline. Thus, demotion of an employee for absenteeism was found to be inappropriate where, although the employer had warned the employee that his absenteeism was a problem, the employer had failed to inform him that he could be demoted if his attendance did not improve.[14] Even when the misconduct is of a serious nature, the employee must not be lulled into believing that he will not be subject to sanction. Thus, the discharge of an employee for insubordination was set aside because the employee had been insubordinate in the past without being subject to any discipline.[15]

Due Process and Procedural Requirements

Borrowing from the constitutional imperative of due process operative in the governmental employment context, arbitrators have fashioned an "industrial due process doctrine." To satisfy industrial due process, an employee must be given an adequate opportunity to present his side of the case before being discharged by the employer. If the employee has not been given such an opportunity, arbitrators will often refuse to sustain the discharge or discipline assessed against the employee.

In one case, an employee's discharge for pulling a knife on a coworker was set aside where the subject employee had never been interviewed. Fairness dictated that the employee be given the opportunity to tell his side of the story.[16]

Industrial due process also requires management to conduct a reasonable inquiry or investigation before assessing punishment.[17] Where neither the grievant nor his union was allowed to confront those accusing the grievant of wrongdoing at any time prior to the arbitration, the arbitrator determined that the grievant was prevented from preparing to fairly meet the charges, and was denied industrial due process:

> Procedural fairness requires an employer to conduct a full and fair investigation of the circumstances surrounding an employee's conduct and to provide an opportunity for him to offer denials, explanations, or justifications that are relevant before the employer makes its final decision, before its position becomes polarized.[18]

---

[13]See Webster Indus., 107 LA 147 (Statham, 1996); PQ Corp., 101 LA 694 (Pratte, 1993).

[14]Gaylord Container Corp., 107 LA 1138 (Allen, 1997).

[15]Tenneco Packaging Corp., 106 LA 606 (Franckiewicz, 1996).

[16]CR/PL Limited Partnership, 107 LA 1084 (Fullmer, 1996).

[17]Southern Frozen Foods, 107 LA 1030 (Giblin, 1996); see also Westvaco Corp., 105 LA 180 (Nolan, 1995) (recognizing that minimal investigation satisfies due process requirements).

[18]Shaefer's Ambulance Serv., 104 LA 481, 486 (Calhoun, 1995).

In contrast, due process requirements were found to have been met in a case in which the employer had failed to post a rule warning that dishonesty might lead to discharge. The arbitrator recognized:

> While fair warning is essential to any disciplinary code, some rules of the workplace are so obvious that no employee can claim ignorance of them or of their consequences. The clearest example is theft. Every employee knows that stealing from an employer is completely unacceptable even if the employer had not posted a rule to that effect.[19]

Last Chance Agreements

The use of last chance agreements under which an employee, otherwise subject to discharge, is permitted to retain his employment provided he agrees to observe special conditions and limitations not imposed upon other employees has been the subject of recent arbitral criticism. In *Hendrickson Turner Co.*,[20] the arbitrator spoke out against agreements wherein the subject employee gives up his right to resort to the grievance procedure should he again be disciplined by the employer:

> Last-chance agreements are troublesome for arbitrators. They violate fundamental precepts associated with labor-management contracts and confirmed by a half-century of published arbitral opinions. Perhaps the most venerated of all principles is that the written agreement is supreme. Its provisions control absolutely.
>
> . . . . .
>
> There are also intrinsic rules for collective bargaining relationships that are universally observed with or without definitive language to support them. No employee can be denied contractual rights; no employee can be singled out for disparate treatment; all employees must be dealt with fairly and equitably. Most important of all (though never expressed in a contract): an employer is prohibited from exercising its reserved powers arbitrarily, capriciously, or discriminatorily.
>
> Last-chance agreements go against contractual principles. They license disparate treatment in that they single out an employee and deny him/her a grievance right. They deprive the affected individual of just-cause protections guaranteed to every other member of the bargaining unit. It is illogical to believe that last-chance and collective bargaining agreements can coexist.

In Lenzing Fibers Corp.,[21] the arbitrator observed that last chance agreements cannot waive certain fundamental contractual rights:

---

[19]Westvaco Corp., 105 LA 180, 185 (Nolan, 1995). (See "Knowledge of Rules, Warnings," *infra* this chapter).
[20]101 LA 919, 922 (Dworkin, 1993).
[21]105 LA 423 (Sergent, 1995).

Notwithstanding the deference which should be afforded such agreements, it is necessary to observe that they do have some basic limitations. Foremost among these is that such an agreement should not cause an employee to relinquish basic contractual rights, particularly the right to grieve and be confronted in the arbitration procedure with the evidence against him and the opportunity to challenge that evidence and to present a defense. Therefore, an arbitrator should reject any condition which forfeits any right of the grievance procedure. Even in cases such as this the grievant is entitled to his "day in court" and the Employer is obliged to present at that time such evidence as will prove that the last chance agreement has been violated.[22]

Nonetheless, arbitrators have held that a union[23] can enter into last chance agreements that relinquish an employee's right to have the employer establish just cause for any subsequent disciplinary action.[24] But these rights must be expressly waived, according to one arbitrator, who held that last chance agreements, which are silent as to, and do not expressly waive, just-cause standards, do not relieve the employer from having to prove just cause for the discharge.[25]

The majority of arbitrators uphold discharges under last chance agreements that clearly and unambiguously define the conditions of employment and the grounds for immediate termination.[26] But some arbitrators have overturned discharges pursuant to last chance agreements if they are persuaded that the application of the agreement would be unfair under the circumstances.[27]

Weingarten *Violations*

As noted in the Main Volume, the National Labor Relations Board remedies a *Weingarten* violation (where union representation is denied an employee required to participate in a meeting or investigatory interview with management which might lead to discipline being taken against him) by issuing a cease and desist order if the em-

---

[22]Id. at 428. See also Gencorp Automotive, 104 LA 113 (Malin, 1994) (the collective bargaining agreement, not the last chance agreement, controls the jurisdiction of the arbitrator); City of Stillwater, 103 LA 684 (Neas, 1994).

[23]"It is the Union, not the employee, which enters into 'Last Chance Agreements' with the employer that modify the terms of the Collective Bargaining Agreement. Employees covered by a collective bargaining contract are powerless to enter into such agreements without the consent of the Union." Merchant's Fast Motor Lines, 99 LA 180, 183 (Marlatt, 1992).

[24]Merchant's Fast Motor Lines, 99 LA 180 (Marlatt, 1992); Butler Mfg. Co., 93 LA 445 (Dworkin, 1989).

[25]GTE of Florida, Inc., 108 LA 1115, 1119 (Cohen, 1997).

[26]See A. Schulman, Inc., 105 LA 1076 (Duda, 1996); Bethlehem Structural Prods. Corp., 105 LA 205 (Witt, 1995); FDL Foods, Inc., 104 LA 1079 (Flaten, 1995); Philip Morris U.S.A., 104 LA 948 (Florman, 1995); Borg-Warner Diversified Prods., 101 LA 1014 (Malin, 1993); compare Packaging Corp. of America, 105 LA 898 (Weisheit, 1995) (last chance agreement that was too broad in scope was unenforceable).

[27]USS, 108 LA 897 (Petersen, 1997) (arbitrator reinstated employee who was terminated for violation of a last chance agreement for attendance because there was no evidence that the employee, who accidentally sustained an injury to his hand at home and thereby failed to report to work, "intentionally made himself unavailable for work" in violation of the last chance agreement); Drummond Co., Inc., 106 LA 250 (Sergent, 1996).

ployee was suspended or discharged, but not by requiring reinstatement unless the discipline was imposed because of the employee's involvement in concerted activities.

In *Williams Pipeline Co.*,[28] an employee who had reasonable cause to believe that his participation in an investigatory meeting with management would lead to disciplinary action's being taken against him requested that the bargaining unit's sole union steward attend the meeting. Because the union steward was not at work and could not be contacted, at the employee's request another union member, a former union steward, attended the meeting. The meeting resulted in the employee's discharge. The Board adopted the opinion of the administrative law judge, which found that the employer had violated the employee's *Weingarten* rights because the employer, upon discovering that the union steward was unavailable, failed to advise the employee that the employer would not proceed with the interview unless the employee was willing to proceed without a union representative. Furthermore, the judge found that the employee's consent to the nonsteward's presence in the interview neither transformed the nonsteward into a union representative nor waived the employee's right to union representation at the interview.

In *Henry Ford Health System*,[29] the employer had an unconventional practice. In disciplinary cases, the employer initially determining the discipline for the alleged misconduct and then later referred the matter to an investigatory council to determine whether there were facts sufficient to support the discipline measures. The employer denied employees' requests for union representation at the hearings before this investigatory council. The Board determined that the denial of representation violated the employees' *Weingarten* rights because the employer's disciplinary actions were not final and binding until they were reviewed by the council.

Unlike the Board, arbitrators may order reinstatement or other appropriate relief if an employee's *Weingarten* rights have been violated. In making that determination, arbitrators have continued to hold that the employer has the initial burden of advising an employee of the nature and purpose of the meeting so that the employee is sufficiently informed as to whether he can or should exercise his right to union representation.[30] Once this burden has been fulfilled, the burden shifts to the employee to request union representation. Accordingly, arbitrators have consistently found that an employee's *Weingarten* rights were not violated if he failed to request union representation in an investigatory meeting that he had reasonable cause to believe would lead to disciplinary action against him.[31]

---

[28]315 NLRB 1, 147 LRRM 1168 (1994).
[29]320 NLRB 1153, 152 LRRM 1033 (1996).
[30]County of Cook, 105 LA 974 (Wolff, 1995); Anchorage Hilton Hotel, 102 LA 55 (Landau, 1993).
[31]D.C. Dep't of Corrections, 105 LA 843 (Rogers, 1996); Benjamin Logan Bd. of Educ., 105 LA 1168 (Fullmer, 1995).

Not all meetings with management entitle employees to have union representation. In *Jefferson Smurfit Corp.*,[32] a suspension for insubordination was upheld where an employee, who reasonably should not have had any fear of discipline resulting from a meeting with supervisors who were investigating a sexual harassment claim of which she was not the subject, wrongfully refused her supervisor's repeated requests to engage in the fact-finding meeting unless she had union representation.[33]

The role of the union representative during investigatory meetings was explored in *Corpus Christi Army Depot.*[34] There, the arbitrator, relying on 5 U.S.C. Section 7114(a)(2)(B),[35] which embodies the *Weingarten* principles, held that a union's representational rights may not interfere with an employer's legitimate examination or compromise its integrity. The arbitrator upheld disciplinary measures levied against a union representative for interfering with an employer's legitimate endeavors to determine whether another employee was under the influence of alcohol. The representative had provided gum to the suspected drunk employee to mask the odor of alcohol and had physically restrained the employee from participating in the examination. In *AT&T*,[36] it was emphasized that *Weingarten* did not grant an employee the right to rely on a union steward's advice not to answer questions during an interview. The employee had no Fifth Amendment right to refuse to answer questions propounded by his employer that pertained to the subject matter of a pending criminal trial because the Fifth Amendment protects citizens against being compelled to answer incriminating questions propounded by the government, not by a private employer.

Finally, it has been held that disciplinary measures should not automatically be overturned if an employee has not been prejudiced by a violation of his *Weingarten* rights.[37] However, such a violation may be a factor in reducing a discharge to a lesser form of discipline.[38]

Postdischarge Conduct or Charges

The reported arbitral decisions continue to reflect the view that evidence of an employee's postdischarge conduct is admissible not only for the purpose of supporting or refuting the original grounds for

---

[32]106 LA 673 (Imundo, 1996).

[33]See also Health Care & Retirement Corp., 105 LA 449 (Duff, 1995); Eaglebudd Enters., Inc., 106 LA 659 (Franckiewicz, 1996).

[34]108 LA 1006 (Halter, 1997).

[35]5 U.S.C. §7114 is a part of the Labor-Management and Employee Relations provisions within the Government Organization and Employees Act, 5 U.S.C. §§101–8913.

[36]102 LA 931 (Kanner, 1994).

[37]Bi-State Dev. Agency, 105 LA 319 (Bailey, 1991) (the violation must prejudice the employee before the disciplinary actions should be overturned).

[38]Anchorage Hilton Hotel, 102 LA 55 (Landau, 1993).

termination, but also for testing the employee's availability and determining whether reinstatement is an appropriate remedy.[39]

In *AT&T*,[40] the arbitrator suggested several contexts in which postdischarge conduct should be considered:

> In my view, post discharge evidence garned by either party can be admitted during arbitral hearing. An extreme example serves to make the point. In the event a post-discharge witness confesses to a theft charged against the grievant; or witness recants a prior statement given to the employer thereby denoting the grievant's innocence, it flies in the face of fairness and justice to simply ignore such evidence. Conversely, where, for example, the grievant was discharged for being under the influence of alcohol on the job and subsequent to the discharge the employer discovered empty liquor bottles in his locker; or an employee is discharged for the theft of an item valued at $5.00 and subsequent to discharge it is discovered that he stole items valued at $500.00, again such evidence should be admitted at arbitral hearing.

> In my opinion, it is not consequently discovered evidence but rather subsequently discovered grounds for discharge that is precluded at arbitral hearing. An employer is limited to the grounds set forth at the time of discharge. But neither the employer nor the union is precluded from offering at arbitration, evidence that is discovered post discharge.[41]

Whether evidence of postdischarge rehabilitation should be considered when determining the appropriate remedy for employees who have been discharged for violating the employer's alcohol use policy remains unsettled. *Ocean Spray Cranberries, Inc.*,[42] provides an extensive review of the decisions on this topic. Several arbitral decisions have allowed evidence of employees' successful participation in postdischarge treatment to mitigate the discharge penalties.[43]

Double Jeopardy

Employees who have been initially suspended while the employer conducted an investigation that led to discharge sometimes claim they have been impermissibly subject to double jeopardy. As one arbitrator noted, "While an employee cannot be twice punished for the same offense, it is permissible for an employee to be suspended pending investigation for possible termination."[44]

Even when a suspension preceding final disciplinary action is with pay, the same result has been reached. When an employee had been suspended with pay and then later demoted, the arbitrator de-

---

[39]Shaefer's Ambulance Serv., 104 LA 481 (Calhoun, 1995). See also Pepsi-Cola Bottling Co., 107 LA 257 (Ross, 1996) (evidence of postdischarge misconduct by grievant admitted to determine the method of operation used by grievant).

[40]102 LA 931 (Kanner, 1994).

[41]Id. at 940. See also Bill Kay Chevrolet, 107 LA 302 (Wolff, 1996).

[42]105 LA 148 (Dichter, 1995).

[43]USS, 104 LA 82 (Dybeck, 1994); Meijer, Inc., 103 LA 834 (Daniel, 1994); AAFES Distrib., 107 LA 290 (Marcus, 1996).

[44]City of Virginia, 108 LA 59, 63 (Daly, 1997); see also Government of the Virgin Islands, 103 LA 1055 (Kessler, 1994).

termined that the suspension was designed to allow the employer to consider its options and to allow the employee to reconsider her rigid position. The arbitrator concluded: "Employers should do exactly what occurred in this case—provide a cooling off period."[45]

Grievant's Past Record

Employees who have a past record of discipline may be given a harsher disciplinary penalty than first-time offenders. Thus, an employer's imposition of severer discipline on employees with prior disciplinary records than employees without a disciplinary history, although both groups were active participants in an improper work stoppage, was upheld:

> Certainly, the past disciplinary history of any particular grievant is a factor in determining or evaluating the appropriateness of a penalty. Any offense may be ameliorated by the lack of previous discipline, just as any offense may be exacerbated by a poor record.[46]

In determining whether a discharge will withstand review, arbitrators appear to consider the nature of the prior penalties assessed as well as the seriousness of the employee's earlier offenses. Where an employee had been given a one-day suspension for an earlier offense and had never received a long-term disciplinary suspension, the arbitrator held: "The lack of any long disciplinary layoff in . . . [the employee's] record indicates that this discharge was premature.[47] It has also been held that if a long-term employee has not been disciplined in some time, and any deficiencies in the employee's early years of employment appear to have been corrected, an employer may not consider prior instances of discipline in order to justify a decision to discharge the employee.[48]

Length of Service With Company

Arbitrators continue to consider long-term service with an employer as a mitigating factor when reviewing employee discharges.[49] In a case in which the employee had been discharged for sleeping on the job, the arbitrator wrote:

> The company must give some credence to seniority. It is not my intent to . . . lay out the rule that seniority should govern. However, seniority is an extremely important facet of the makeup of an employee. It shows loyalty, it shows recognized ability, it shows efficiency and it is even recognized in the contract in the determining of . . . [bid] classifications.[50]

---

[45]Northwest Publications, Inc., 104 LA 91 (Bognanno, 1994).
[46]Public Util. Dist. No. 1 of Clark County, 103 LA 1066 (Paull, 1994).
[47]Tri-County Beverage Co., 107 LA 577, 581 (House, 1996).
[48]Webcraft Games, 107 LA 560 (Ellman, 1996).
[49]Smurfit Recycling Co., 103 LA 243 (Richman, 1994); cf. Motor Transp., 103 LA 303 (Johnson, 1994).
[50]Arch of Illinois, 107 LA 178, 181 (Feldman, 1995).

In contrast, another arbitrator rejected the union's argument that consideration should be given to an employee's 23 years of service when the employee had been discharged for harassing female employees. He reasoned:

> Although it is difficult to articulate a precise rule, long service is properly taken into account as a mitigating factor for minor misconduct. Seniority is not a mitigating factor when determining discipline appropriate for intentional major misconduct that directly and repeatedly violates a written prohibition, particularly when the miscreant has been instructed to cease and desist.[51]

Knowledge of Rules; Warnings

An employee must receive clear notice of both what the employer expects and what the exact penalty will be for failing to meet the employer's expectations.[52] An employer did not have just cause to issue a warning to an employee who did not meet production standards where the employee was not properly put on notice that not meeting standards could lead to discipline.[53]

The "prior notice" requirement also applies to a company's drug policy. The discharge of an employee in whose car marijuana was found was set aside where the union was notified of the company's drug policy banning possession of drugs in automobiles on company property on the same day the employee's car was searched, and the policy was mailed to employees.[54] Similarly, the termination of an employee who failed a drug test was overturned because he had not been informed that the drug policy under which such failure would have resulted in suspension pending rehabilitation[55] had been changed to allow immediate discharge.

Lax Enforcement of Rules

An employee discharged for smoking marijuana was reinstated because his behavior had been condoned by the employee's supervisor, who had smoked marijuana in the presence of the employee. The opinion stated:

> Employees was entitled to clear notice that rules will be enforced. Where, however, rules are not enforced but violations thereof are accepted by management, employees are lulled into believing that such rules are not serious. In effect, employees are "sand bagged" into violating rules and then are unfairly punished for a violation.[56]

---

[51]International Extrusion Corp., 106 LA 371, 374 (Brisco, 1996).
[52]Customized Transp., 102 LA 1179 (Stallworth, 1994).
[53]Cummins Cumberland, Inc., 106 LA 993 (Heeking, 1996). See also Consolidated Drum Reconditioning, 108 LA 523 (Richman, 1997) (employee's poor productivity did not justify discharge where he did not receive warning notices for poor productivity).
[54]Anheuser-Busch Inc., 107 LA 1183 (Weckstein, 1996).
[55]Pacific Offshore Pipeline Co., 106 LA 690 (Kaufman, 1996).
[56]Chivas Prods. Ltd., 101 LA 546, 550 (Kanner, 1993).

But when an employer gives notice that it intends to enforce rules violations that had previously gone unpunished, the employee must obey them. As an example, despite the fact that similarly situated employees had been treated more leniently in the past, an employer was held to have had just cause to discharge an employee who grabbed another employee offensively. The discharge was justified because the employer had distributed a "zero tolerance"-for-violence policy prohibiting this kind of behavior six weeks before the incident.[57]

Unequal or Discriminatory Treatment

If rules and regulations are not consistently applied and enforced in a nondiscriminatory manner, arbitrators will refuse to sustain a discharge or will reduce a disciplinary penalty.[58] Applying this general rule, one decision recognized:

> [T]here must be reasonable rules and standards of conduct which are consistently applied and enforced in a non-discriminatory fashion. It is also generally accepted that enforcement of rules and assessment of discipline must be exercised in a consistent manner; thus all employees who engage in the same type of misconduct must be treated essentially the same.[59]

However, arbitrators will uphold variations in punishments among employees if a reasonable basis exists that justifies such differences. In one case, the employer was held to have had just cause to discharge an employee who had coordinated and served as leader in a "sickout" that violated the labor contract.[60] The arbitrator reasoned that the instigator could be punished more harshly with discharge, even though other employees only received warnings.

Charges of Antiunion Discrimination

The imposition of discipline upon an employee who is a union officer or active in union matters, without a showing of animosity or open hostility, is held to be insufficient to sustain a defense that the penalty was discriminatorily[61] imposed in retaliation for the employee's representative status or conduct. But when the behavior of a union official exceeds the limits of workplace propriety, even when the charged action itself appears to have been in furtherance of legitimate union leadership interest or action, some discipline—includ-

---

[57]Golden States Food Corp., 108 LA 705 (Gentile, 1997).
[58]Schuller Int'l, 107 LA 1109 (Hockenberry, 1996); Gemala Trailer Corp., 108 LA 565 (Nicholas, 1997); Mead Chilpaco Mill, 106 LA 1066 (Feldman, 1996); Geauga County, 106 LA 280 (DiLeone, 1996).
[59]Munster Steel Co., 108 LA 597, 600 (Cerone, 1997).
[60]Lockheed Martin, 108 LA 482 (Gentile, 1997).
[61]Preferred Transp., Inc., 108 LA 636, 639 (Gentile, 1997); Folsom Return to Custody, Inc., 101 LA 837 (Staudohar, 1993). NLRB v. Town & Country Elec., Inc., 116 S. Ct. 450 (1995).

ing discharge—has been sustained.[62] However, one arbitrator has held that a union officer's belligerent behavior that caused damage to company property is not sanctionable absent a showing of "wrongful intent."[63]

Management Also at Fault

Where an employee had been disciplined for assaulting a supervisor, the supervisor's behavior could be considered in mitigation of the offense. Thus, when a young employee with no history of violence, who had just returned to work after having been hospitalized for a mental condition, assaulted his supervisor, he was reinstated without back pay, in part because the abusive supervisor had taunted the employee.[64] Similarly, where an employee was found to be "constructively insubordinate" in leaving work without permission because she feared that she might lose her temper and assault her supervisor because of his hostile tone and manner of direction, her discharge was held to be without just cause.[65]

Consideration of management's procedural error caused an arbitrator to reinstate with "half back pay" a probationary employee for failure to report a criminal conviction to his employer.[66]

The defense in disciplinary cases that management was at fault may also involve issues of "toleration" or "disparate treatment." The discharges of two male employees who cornered another male employee in a dark room, forcibly lowered his pants, restrained him, and threatened sexual assault were set aside because company supervisors had been involved in or had observed similar but less aggressive acts of male-on-male sexual harassment without taking disciplinary action.[67]

If an employee's errant behavior is the result of a mental or physical problem that the employer knew or should have known about, arbitrators also tend to consider the condition a mitigating factor.[68]

The discharge of an employee who sat down on a conveyer and cursed when suspended for the safety offense was set aside because the employee had earlier complained to the employer about back pain. The arbitrator explained that it is "common medical knowledge that physical pain causes tempers to become short and people to lose some control."[69] Similarly, a technician who signed certain laboratory forms without completing the necessary tests was reinstated by an arbitrator who attributed the technician's "mental lapse" to a "stressful emotional condition" caused by his employer's denying him leave to be with his seriously ill wife.[70]

---

[62]Converters Paperboard Co., 108 LA 149 (Brodsky, 1997), Stone Container Corp., 106 LA 475, 478–80 (Gentile, 1996). On safety matters, see Rebar Eng'g, Inc., 105 LA 662, 666 (Riker, 1995); Dye Golf Servs., Inc., 104 LA 449, 451 (Darrow, 1995).
[63]PQ Corp., 106 LA 381, 383–84 (Cipolla, 1996).
[64]Bethlehem Structural Prods. Corp., 106 LA 452, 455–56 (Witt, 1995).
[65]HDS Servs., 107 LA 27, 29–30 (Hodgson, 1996).
[66]Avis Rent-A-Car Sys., 107 LA 197, 200–202 (Shankr, 1996).
[67]Coca-Cola Bottling Co., 106 LA 776, 777, 782 (Borland, 1996). See also the discussion of "Law Enforcement of Rules" and "Unequal or Discriminatory Treatment," supra).
[68]Bethlehem Structural Prods. Corp., 106 LA 452, 455–56 (Witt, 1995).
[69]Gaylord Container Corp., 107 LA 431, 434–35 (Henner, 1996).
[70]Dial Corp., 107 LA 879 (Robinson, 1997).

Arbitral Remedies in Discharge and Discipline Cases

Where managerial disciplinary actions are modified, arbitrators occasionally apply some uncommon remedies such as loss of seniority, loss of other benefits under the agreement,[71] probation or final warning,[72] reinstatement conditioned upon some special act or promise by employee,[73] reinstatement conditioned upon proof of mental or physical fitness,[74] reinstatement conditioned upon the employee's not holding union office,[75] reinstatement to a different job,[76] and various other sanctions.[77]

[71]Moss Supermarket, 99 LA 408 (Grupp, 1992) (employee who was constructively discharged, reinstated with only half pay due to her refusal to accept different job).

[72]County of Hennepin, 105 LA 391 (Imes, 1995) (probationary reinstatement with back pay while employer trains employee); Anchorage School Dist., 105 LA 281 (Tilbury, 1995) (probationary reinstatement without back pay while employee completes anger management sessions); Town of Cromwell, 101 LA 388 (Stewart, 1993) (suspension of police officer reduced to written warning and probation while employee undergoes training for drawing firearms); San Francisco Newspaper Agency, 93 LA 323 (Koven, 1989) (discharge for filing spurious overtime claim reduced to final warning subject to suspension or discharge for any future rule violation).

[73]East Liverpool Bd. of Educ., 105 LA 161 (Duda, 1995) (discharge for $1.00 theft reduced to suspension if employee admits responsibility and promises no further misconduct); Laidlaw Transit, Inc., 104 LA 302 (Conception, 1995) (reinstatement of employee suffering from depression upon agreement to take medicine as prescribed); Chardon Rubber Co., 97 LA 750 (Hewitt, 1991) (discharge for insubordination and reporting to work under influence of alcohol reduced to suspension if employee posts apology on bulletin board); Ohio State Highway Patrol, 96 LA 614 (Bittel, 1991) (discharge for DUI reduced to 90-day suspension if employee furnishes psychologist's statement he is capable of assuming duties); Ohio Lime Co., 96 LA 38 (Bressler, 1990) (reinstatement conditioned on employee's agreeing similar unauthorized absence may result in termination and on submitting medical fitness certificate); Metropolitan Transit Auth., 94 LA 857 (Nicholas, 1990) (discharge for positive drug test reduced to conditional reinstatement including drug screening and rehabilitation).

[74]City of Akron, 105 LA 787 (Kasper, 1995) (employee who requested demotion due to health to be reinstated upon submission of evidence of mental and physical ability to perform); General Mills, 99 LA 143 (Stallworth, 1992) (employee suffering from seasonal depression disorder conditionally reinstated. Mutually selected physician to determine fitness for duty. Parties to agree on plan to reasonably accommodate employee without undue hardship on employer); James River Corp., 96 LA 1174 (McDonald, 1991) (employee suffering anxiety and depression reinstated upon clearance from treating psychologist and employer's medical expert).

[75]Freeman Decorating Co., 108 LA 887 (Baroni, 1997) (employee who had disrupted construction work while acting as shop steward prohibited from serving as steward in the future).

[76]Summitt City Bd. of Mental Retardation, 100 LA 4 (Dworkin, 1992) (reassignment of teacher accused of sexual misconduct conditioned upon psychological finding of fitness); Eastwood Printing Co., 99 LA 957 (Winograd, 1992) (employee placed on medical leave after sustaining temporary disability reinstated to a prior position he had held in the past so as not to displace employee who replaced him); Kaiser Permanente & Serv. Employees, Local 49, 99 LA 490 (Henner, 1992) (discharge reduced to suspension and transfer to more suitable position where absenteeism due to seizures); Colonial School Dist., 96 LA 1122 (DiLauro, 1991) (suspension and transfer to different bus route for driver accused of making improper advances toward female passengers); International Paper Co., 94 LA 409 (Matthews, 1990) (transfer in lieu of termination for employee suffering permanent partial disability).

[77]Public Util. Dist. #1, 103 LA 1066 (Paull, 1994) (written warning for active participants in improper work stoppage, oral warning for passive participants); Hendrickson Turner Co., 101 LA 919 (Dworkin, 1993) (discharge changed to voluntary quit under last chance agreement); V.A. Medical Center, 99 LA 951 (Fowler, 1992) (union ordered to publish correction in its newsletter following derogatory article about supervisor); Astabula County, 94 LA 303 (Sharpe, 1990) (employer ordered to provide more informa-

Remedies in sexual harassment cases have included ordering a supervisory employee to keep away from females "to the maximum extent," although the arbitrator lacked authority to require the employer to discipline the supervisor, order him to apologize, or award damages for pain and suffering;[78] reinstating a teacher under a "no touching" agreement regarding female students;[79] ordering an employer to investigate harassment and discrimination charges and report its findings;[80] demoting the employee, but with back pay from the date of demotion to the date of arbitration because the employer failed to disclose the accusers' names until the hearing;[81] ordering the employer to post the terms of an arbitration award and to discuss sexual harassment with its employees.[82]

In a number of awards arbitrators have upheld the imposition of discipline upon an employee where the employer failed to comply with a procedural or due process requirement, but nevertheless have found the employee entitled to a back pay remedy because of the employer's lapse. When such management errors do not require the overturning of a discharge, the options utilized by arbitrators have included back pay from the date of the grievance to the date of the arbitral award because the employer violated its discharge procedure;[83] one week's back pay for failing to give notice;[84] back pay from the date of discharge to the date of the Step 2 grievance meeting, which was first time the employee was afforded union representation;[85] back pay and benefits from the date of discharge to the day after the arbitration hearing because of failure to advise the employee of the specific charges prior to the discharge,[86] and one month's back pay for the employer's failure to obtain union representation before administering a drug test.[87]

In one case a discharge for misuse of a government computer was reduced to a suspension, but the union was awarded attorney fees because the federal employer had failed to conduct a proper investigation, and the union had to respond to the unfounded charges.[88]

---

tion showing basis for supervisor's conclusions regarding employee's performance); Union-Tribune Publishing Co., 93 LA 617 (McBrearty, 1989) (discharge upheld for possession of drugs but employee entitled to severance pay, which may be withheld only for "gross misconduct or willful neglect of duty," and employee's addiction rendered conduct not "willful").

[78]Union Camp Corp., 104 LA 295 (Nolan, 1995).
[79]Independent School Dist. No. 255, 102 LA 993 (Daly, 1994).
[80]Great Lakes Naval Training Ctr., 102 LA 827 (Yaney, 1994).
[81]Renton School Dist., 102 LA 854 (Wilkinson, 1994).
[82]Rodeway Inn, 102 LA 1003 (Goldberg, 1994).
[83]Mason & Hanger-Silas Mason Co., 103 LA 371 (Cipolla, 1994).
[84]City of Akron, 105 LA 787 (Kasper, 1995).
[85]Bi-State Dev. Agency, 96 LA 1090 (Cipolla, 1991).
[86]Chromalloy American Corp., 93 LA 828 (Woolf, 1989).
[87]Bi-State Dev. Agency, 105 LA 319 (Bailey, 1995).
[88]U. S. Dep't of Agriculture, 93 LA 921 (Seidman, 1989).

The inclusion of attorney fees[89] and interest on back pay[90] awards has appeared more frequently in the reported cases as part of a "make whole" remedy.

---

[89]Vandenberg Air Force Base, 106 LA 107 (Feldman, 1996) (attorney's fees awarded to union where employer discharged employee although blood type in drug sample did not match); Port of Tacoma, 99 LA 1151 (Smith, 1992) (employer to pay employee's attorney's fees incurred in gender discrimination lawsuit against her supervisor); U.S. Dep't of Agriculture, 93 LA 920 (Seidman, 1989).

[90]Champlain Cable Corp., 108 LA 449 (Sweeney, 1997) (no proof union steward encouraged walkout); City of Cleveland, 103 LA 534 (Miller, 1994); Atlantic Southeast Airlines, 101 LA 515 (Nolan, 1993) (from date of discharge to date employee failed new drug test); Central State Univ., 97 LA 1167 (Strasshofer, 1991) (back pay with statutory interest).

Table of Offenses

Offense	Discharge Upheld	Lesser Penalty Upheld (as assessed by employer)	Penalty Reduced by Arbitrator	No Penalty Permitted
Absenteeism	108 LA 136 Krislov	106 LA 284 Heekin	108 LA 831 Ellmann	109 LA 65 Franckiewicz
	106 LA 833 Goldman	106 LA 250 Sergent	106 LA 915 Feldman	108 LA 225 Allen
	106 LA 807 Duda	97 LA 1161 Berquist	99 LA 490 Henner	108 LA 183 Allen
	105 LA 970 Duda	96 LA 1074 Goldstein	99 LA 143 Stallworth	100 LA 638 Draznin
	99 LA 393 Lipson	94 LA 365 Kindig	908 LA 57 Dohen	99 LA 724 Dworkin
	99 LA 239 Kahn	93 LA 1079 Knowlton	96 LA 1174 McDonald	96 LA 951 Concepcion
	98 LA 1203 Hilgert		96 LA 429 Aronin	96 LA 560 Cohen
	98 LA 201 Nicholas			96 LA 143 Statham
	98 LA 105 Baroni			94 LA 361 Stoltenberg
	97 LA 777 Byars			93 LA 423 Bankston
	97 LA 653 Nolan			
	93 LA 1186 Rivera			
Tardiness	106 LA 753 Kaufman	108 LA 1098 Modjeska	105 LA 913 Kaufman	106 LA 369 Flaten
	106 LA 117 Richard		104 LA 777 Johnson	105 LA 440 Pelofsky
	104 LA 358 Borland		98 LA 387 Talarico	
	93 LA 1186 Rivera			
	93 LA 441 Dworkin			

Offense	Discharge Upheld	Lesser Penalty Upheld (as assessed by employer)	Penalty Reduced by Arbitrator	No Penalty Permitted
Loafing		106 LA 1125 Draznin		99 LA 929 Corbett
		97 LA 597 Oestreich		
		95 LA 1119 Cohen		
Absence from work (Leaving work early)	108 LA 692 Draznin	108 LA 533 Kessler	108 LA 929 DiLauro	108 LA 758 Nicholas
	108 LA 545 Weckstein	106 LA 84 Teple	102 LA 545 Hilgert	106 LA 879 O'Grady
	104 LA 949 Florman	104 LA 1069 O'Grady	102 LA 545 Allen	
	104 LA 660 Pool		98 LA 777 Ellmann	
	104 LA 281 Lundberg		97 LA 734 Bittel	
	102 LA 274 Henner		94 LA 1026 Gordon	105 LA 946 Katz
	98 LA 898 Wolff		94 LA 340 Duda	105 LA 524 Roberts
	97 LA 489 Killingsworth			98 LA 688 Weiss
	94 LA 325 Borland			98 LA 205 Goodman
				97 LA 572 Cantor
				96 LA 1223 Avins
				96 LA 803 Talarico
				93 LA 687 Feigenbaum
				93 LA 239 Schwartz

Offense	Discharge Upheld	Lesser Penalty Upheld (as assessed by employer)	Penalty Reduced by Arbitrator	No Penalty Permitted
Leaving Post (Includes early quitting)	105 LA 581 Barron	108 LA 218 Hockenberry	98 LA 675 Hockenberry	106 LA 823 Katz
	108 LA 628 Feldman	96 LA 758 Morgan	106 LA 464 Odom	105 LA 353 Coyne
	108 LA 974 Frankiewicz	95 LA 1119 Cohen	105 LA 572 Hayford	
	93 LA 1241 Johnson	94 LA 1069 O'Grady	98 LA 611 Bittel	
			98 LA 23 Sartain	
			96 LA 480 Wray	
			96 LA 395 Dworkin	
			96 LA 149 Weiss	
			96 LA 109 Roberts	
			93 LA 947 Jones	
Sleeping on Job	106 LA 442 Cohen		99 LA 945 Dissen	
	105 LA 368 Rybolt		97 LA 1206 Rivera	
	98 LA 710 Kubie		93 LA 530 Cipolla	
	98 LA 183 Kanner			
	98 LA 171 Statham			
	93 LA 505 Dworkin			

Offense	Discharge Upheld	Lesser Penalty Upheld (as assessed by employer)	Penalty Reduced by Arbitrator	No Penalty Permitted
Assault and Fighting Among Employees	108 LA 705 Gentile	105 LA 812 Moore	106 LA 12 Duff	108 LA 417 Baroni
	106 LA 1135 Goggin		105 LA 648 Wren	106 LA 289 Giblin
	105 LA 205 Witt		94 LA 1047 Fowler	105 LA 1063 Rogers
	97 LA 739 Nolan		93 LA 189 Gentile	105 LA 907 Herring
	97 LA 356 Bickner			100 LA 900 Sass
	94 LA 920 Zirkel			
Horseplay	93 LA 580 Chandler	96 LA 477 Millious	106 LA 422 Wolff	105 LA 865 Oestreich
			106 LA 11 Duff	
			105 LA 529 Hockenberry	
			96 LA 828 Conley	
Insubordination	109 LA 60 Cantor	106 LA 1121 Kaufman		
	108 LA 166 Bailey	106 LA 659 Franckiewicz		
	108 LA 158 Cohen	98 LA 512 Neigh		
	108 LA 305 Richman	96 LA 984 Allen	108 LA 149 Brodsky	106 LA 1033 Bickner
	108 LA 804 Staudohar	94 LA 117 Hogler	106 LA 875 Shieber	106 LA 381 Cipolla
	106 LA 103 Coyne	94 LA 492 Talarico	105 LA 606 Franckiewicz	106 LA 62 Nathan

Offense	Discharge Upheld	Lesser Penalty Upheld (as assessed by employer)	Penalty Reduced by Arbitrator	No Penalty Permitted
Insub-ordination, *continued*	106 LA 88 Brunner		106 LA 27 Kahn	106 LA 8 Rogers
	105 LA 662 Rikor		105 LA 942 Gentile	98 LA 1145 Murphy
	97 LA 356 Bickner		105 LA 468 Rogers	98 LA 976 Cohen
	96 LA 792 Ricker		97 LA 750 Hewitt	98 LA 126 Nicholas
	94 LA 1087 Ross		97 LA 477 Avins	97 LA 774 Kilroy
	94 LA 773 Harkins		93 LA 520 Randall	97 LA 403 Wright
	94 LA 585 Woolf		93 LA 91 Rocha	97 LA 393 Concepcion
	94 LA 225 Nielson			96 LA 55 Caraway
	94 LA 751 Bognanno			94 LA 233 Winograd
	94 LA 457 Richard			
Racial slur	99 LA 1169 Rivera	106 LA 624 Alexander	106 LA 670 Strasshofer	105 LA 737 Kindig
	97 LA 367 Cox	94 LA 1023 Feldman	100 LA 27 Cerone	
		93 LA 311 Statham		
Threat or Assault of Management Repre-sentative	108 LA 100 Thornell		108 LA 59 Dalky	108 LA 50 Brookins
	108 LA 715 Krislov		106 LA 907 Kanzer	98 LA 1 Volz
	106 LA 353 Daly		106 LA 452 Witt	97 LA 473 Doepken
	105 LA 372 Cohen		105 LA 1053 Strasshofer	96 LA 56 Feldman
	98 LA 713 Wolff		98 LA 644 Hodgson	95 LA 895 Goggin
	97 LA 121 Richard		97 LA 705 Halperin	

Offense	Discharge Upheld	Lesser Penalty Upheld (as assessed by employer)	Penalty Reduced by Arbitrator	No Penalty Permitted
Abusive Language to Supervision		98 LA 218 Thornell	98 LA 952 Richman	99 LA 1038 Allen
		96 LA 1109 Talarico	93 LA 277 Dobry	
		94 LA 253 Knott		
Profane or Abusive Language (Not toward supervision)	109 LA 52 Strasshofer	106 LA 481 McGury	108 LA 648 Staudohar	108 LA 582 Daly
	109 LA 86 Oberstein	106 LA 841 Lurie	106 LA 275 Caraway	
	94 LA 610 Cantor		94 LA 600 Duda	94 LA 1217 Knowlton
	94 LA 497 Briggs			
	93 LA 24 Canestraight			
Falsifying Employment Application	105 LA 876 Beckjord		106 LA 1209 Howell	108 LA 1016 Heekin
	105 LA 223 Michelstetter		106 LA 564 Bard	95 LA 425 Seidman
	104 LA 255 Feigenbaum		102 LA 65 Jones	
	102 LA 692 Duda		93 LA 381 Cohen	
	99 LA 134 McDonald			
	94 LA 690 Pratte			
	94 LA 249 Nicholas			
	93 LA 739 Eisele			
	93 LA 124 Gentile			

Offense	Discharge Upheld	Lesser Penalty Upheld (as assessed by employer)	Penalty Reduced by Arbitrator	No Penalty Permitted
Falsifying Company Records (Including time records, production)				102 LA 316 Duff
	108 LA 1163 Caffera		106 LA 801 Nathan	
	104 LA 579 Rivera		106 LA 680 Grabuskie	
	97 LA 293 Canetraight		105 LA 1011 Allen	
	96 LA 1090 Cipolla		102 LA 55 Landau	
	96 LA 823 Concepcion		100 LA 67 Halprin	
	96 LA 644 Hilgert		96 LA 904 Marino	
	95 LA 401 Cipolla		94 LA 725 Kaufman	
Disloyalty to Government (Security risk)		97 LA 1038 Caraway	97 LA 1065 Borland	
		93 LA 977 Block	93 LA 920 Seidman	
			93 LA 393 Kravit	
			93 LA 339 Knott	
Theft	105 LA 923 O'Grady	106 LA 836 Frost	108 LA 1111 Feldman	106 LA 364 Pool
	105 LA 398 Robinson	102 LA 520 Stiteville	106 LA 1066 Feldman	
	104 LA 699 Fullmer		105 LA 161 Duda	
	102 LA 979 Sergent		100 LA 1066 Imes	
	99 LA 1137 McKay		98 LA 664 Miller	
	99 LA 609 Goldberg		98 LA 301 House	

Offense	Discharge Upheld	Lesser Penalty Upheld (as assessed by employer)	Penalty Reduced by Arbitrator	No Penalty Permitted
	97 LA 1007 Verploeg		97 LA 377 Duff	
	96 LA 541 Allen		97 LA 166 Daly	
	94 LA 745 Seidman		98 LA 176 Murphy	
	94 LA 621 Berquist		97 LA 166 Daly	
	93 LA 1113 Yarowsky		96 LA 176 Murphy	
	93 LA 1038 Zobrak		94 LA 667 Shearer	
	93 LA 604 Flannagan		94 LA 575 Smith	
			94 LA 334 Hewitt	
Dishonesty	108 LA 631 Daniels	96 LA 1074 Goldstein	106 LA 577 White	102 LA 555 Berquist
	106 LA 997 Bowers		104 LA 933 Shanker	102 LA 154 Kenis
	106 LA 945 Klein		102 LA 910 Difalco	93 LA 377 Goldstein
	97 LA 912 Prayzich		99 LA 353 DiLauro	
	96 LA 644 Hilgert		96 LA 692 Feldman	
	94 LA 1083 Goodstein		96 LA 172 Hockenberry	
			94 LA 1246 Lubow	
			93 LA 114 Wilmoth	

Offense	Discharge Upheld	Lesser Penalty Upheld (as assessed by employer)	Penalty Reduced by Arbitrator	No Penalty Permitted
Disloyalty to Employer (Includes competing with employer, conflict of interests)	105 LA 970 Hart	106 LA 528 Nelson	99 LA 649 Allen	102 LA 733 Bethel
	98 LA 109 Riker	104 LA 634 House	98 LA 1178 Allen	98 LA 361 Wolff
	98 LA 16 Darrow	104 LA 312 Imundo	98 LA 982 Seinsheimer	96 LA 897 Nolan
	94 LA 1065 Das		98 LA 597 Nichols	96 LA 1 Kanner
	94 LA 841 Ables		98 LA 122 Silver	
			96 LA 46 Grinstead	
Moonlighting (Excluding competing with employer)	98 LA 786 Gallagher	98 LA 944 Wilkinson	102 LA 508 Cluster	95 LA 465 Sass
			99 LA 1072 Roumell	
Unsatisfactory Performance (Includes incompetence, low productivity and poor or improper job performance)	108 LA 1125 Bickner	108 LA 216 Thornell	108 LA 1115 Cohen	108 LA 311 Levy
	106 LA 927 White	98 LA 886 Stewart	106 LA 492 Braverman	106 LA 1175 Rezler
	105 LA 988 Nathan	95 LA 201 Cohen	105 LA 391 Imes	106 LA 1110 Marx
	105 LA 462 Allen	94 LA 389 Braverman	105 LA 37 Murphy	106 LA 993 Heekin
	98 LA 188 Daniel	94 LA 199 O'Grady	99 LA 401 Volz	106 LA 726 Marcus
	97 LA 542 Dworkin	93 LA 808 Duda	98 LA 406 Riker	98 LA 504 Jacobs
	96 LA 609 Curry		98 LA 112 Madden	98 LA 286 Daniel
	96 LA 556 Hart		97 LA 1145 Massey	97 LA 1210 Lang
	94 LA 1080 Hewitt		97 LA 1045 Nicholas	97 LA 12 Halperin
			97 LA 675 Ellmann	96 LA 957 Neigh

Offense	Discharge Upheld	Lesser Penalty Upheld (as assessed by employer)	Penalty Reduced by Arbitrator	No Penalty Permitted
			97 LA 387 Kilroy	94 LA 11 Cohen
			96 LA 294 Dworkin	
			94 LA 1053 Kahn	
			93 LA 526 Miller	
Refusal to Accept Job Assignment	104 LA 113 Malin	106 LA 148 Kohn	106 LA 510 Nolan	101 LA 73 Poole
	94 LA 1303 Baroni	96 LA 212 Abrams	97 LA 603 Cohen	98 LA 131 Modjeska
			97 LA 592 Silver	
			94 LA 178 Cipolla	
Refusal to Work Overtime	96 LA 633 Nolan	106 LA 813 Imundo	94 LA 423 Goldstein	99 LA 776 Giblin
		96 LA 855 Gibson	93 LA 707 Goodstein	97 LA 1020 Byars
		96 LA 32 Mancini		94 LA 647 Crane
				93 LA 836 Morgan
Negligence	98 LA 357 Ipavac	99 LA 837 Valentine	108 LA 484 Dissen	108 LA 833 Smith
	97 LA 542 Dworkin	99 LA 88 Hewitt	105 LA 325 Henner	98 LA 263 Meredith
	94 LA 21 Baroni	98 LA 500 Kanner	105 LA 33 Fowler	98 LA 251 Dybeck
		97 LA 1029 Thornell	98 LA 789 Hooper	96 LA 297 Berger
		97 LA 162 Kerner	96 LA 995 Roumell	94 LA 217 Koven
		97 LA 1150 Anthony	96 LA 931 Roberts	

Offense	Discharge Upheld	Lesser Penalty Upheld (as assessed by employer)	Penalty Reduced by Arbitrator	No Penalty Permitted
Negligence, continued			96 LA 798 Mackraz	
			96 LA 585 Berger	
			96 LA 1085 Duff	
			93 LA 575 Morris	
Damage to or Loss of Machine or Materials	106 LA 132 Kaufman	109 LA 116 Imundo	98 LA 434 Staudohar	108 LA 565 Nicholas
	105 LA 591 Hewitt	98 LA 1082 Cipolla	96 LA 585 Berger	106 LA 708 Neyland
	604 LA 260 Feldman			
	102 LA 685 D'Spain			
	98 LA 197 VanPelt	97 LA 55 Jones	95 LA 195 Nicholas	94 LA 217 Koven
	94 LA 979 Dybeck			94 LA 17 Kessler
Prohibited Strike	104 LA 203 Prayzich	105 LA 774 Lalka		94 LA 1033 Witney
		104 LA 811 High		
Misconduct During Strike	108 LA 1153 Baroni	94 LA 929 Levask	93 LA 1097 Cohen	98 LA 8 Feldman
	106 LA 466 Silver			94 LA 211 Dworkin
				93 LA 777 Aronin
Refusal to Cross Picket Line		98 LA 41 O'Grady	94 LA 595 Goldsmith	

Offense	Discharge Upheld	Lesser Penalty Upheld (as assessed by employer)	Penalty Reduced by Arbitrator	No Penalty Permitted
Union Activities	106 LA 103 Coyne	108 LA 618 Baroni	108 LA 920 Nadelbach	106 LA 1103 Allen
	105 LA 1126 Wyman	102 LA 833 Murphy	105 LA 332 Shieber	106 LA 988 McGury
	105 LA 662 Riker	97 LA 252 McHugh	104 LA 30 Baroni	105 LA 595 Daniel
	94 LA 559 Bogue	96 LA 972 Richman	94 LA 1229 Kaufman	104 LA 682 Weisheit
	93 LA 721 Chandler	94 LA 1075 Volz	94 LA 1097 Gentile	98 LA 805 Duff
		94 LA 67 Kaplan		96 LA 713 Bowers
		93 LA 450 Wilcox		96 LA 60 Murphy
				94 LA 1257 Prayzich
				94 LA 283 Madden
Slowdown	97 LA 1006 Madden		108 LA 482 Gentile	108 LA 449 Sweeney
	93 LA 203 Bressler		99 LA 297 Massey	106 LA 988 McGury
				96 LA 294 Conaway
Possession or Use of Intoxicants	108 LA 649 O'Grady	97 LA 850 Strasshofer	106 LA 215 Borland	106 LA 1100 Felice
	108 LA 641 Howell		97 LA 802 Oberdank	106 LA 1072 Cohen
	106 LA 131 Brown		97 LA 564 Wolff	106 LA 740 Darrow
	106 LA 839 Thornell		96 LA 1185 Volz	105 LA 740 Briggs
	105 LA 1081 Thornell		96 LA 419 Marcus	102 LA 492 Bogue
	105 LA 626 Frocht		106 LA 215 Borland	100 LA 649 Williams

Offense	Discharge Upheld	Lesser Penalty Upheld (as assessed by employer)	Penalty Reduced by Arbitrator	No Penalty Permitted
Possession or Use of Intoxicants, *continued*	105 LA 148 Dichter		97 LA 802 Oberdank	99 LA 1017 Volz
	99 LA 812 Dee		97 LA 564 Wolff	99 LA 770 Briggs
	99 LA 664 Murphy		96 LA 1185 Volz	
	96 LA 1193 Odom		96 LA 419 Marcus	
	96 LA 71 Dworkin		96 LA 319 Brisco	
	94 LA 543 Sharpe		94 LA 862 Rule	
	93 LA 415 Hill		94 LA 581 Talarico	
	93 LA 41 Allen		93 LA 1075 Gallagher	
Possession or Use of Drugs	108 LA 1134 Skulina	108 LA 355 Suntrup	1108 LA 339 Levak	108 LA 936 Briggs
	108 LA 737 Neas	102 LA 85 Cohen	108 LA 316 Zobrak	108 LA 115 Allen
	106 LA 387 Kaufman	99 LA 677 Hoffman	108 LA 26 Levak	106 LA 936 Singer
	104 LA 653 Teple		106 LA 690 Kaufman	
	102 LA 513 Duff		106 LA 38 Frost	
	106 LA 97 Baroni		102 LA 817 Grabuskie	106 LA 470 Hooper
	105 LA 939 Nolan		98 LA 1097 Harr	102 LA 813 Grooms
	105 LA 54 Imundo		97 LA 327 Freedman	102 LA 97 Abrams
	98 LA 1065 Baroni		96 LA 365 Cohn	97 LA 1113 Downing
	97 LA 343 Weckstein		96 LA 126 Hendrix	97 LA 271 D'Spain

Offense	Discharge Upheld	Lesser Penalty Upheld (as assessed by employer)	Penalty Reduced by Arbitrator	No Penalty Permitted
	96 LA 1208 Sergent		94 LA 783 Madden	997 LA 30 Nicholas
	96 LA 1165 Goldstein		94 LA 489 Fullmer	96 LA 862 Harr
	96 LA 808 Duda		93 LA 20 Christopher	95 LA 1037 Roberts
	96 LA 20 Gentile		93 LA 20 Christopher	
	94 LA 1172 Garrett			
	94 LA 971 Eisele			
	94 LA 721 Sisk			
	93 LA 435 Allen			
	93 LA 273 Allen			
Distribution of Drugs	108 LA 229 Frockt		102 LA 104 Nicholas	96 LA 657 DiLeone
	96 LA 1208 Sergent		96 LA 325 Statham	93 LA 145 Goulet
	96 LA 435 Reynolds			
	94 LA 721 Sisk			
Obscene or Immoral Conduct	108 LA 1201 Brand	105 LA 133 DiLauro	108 LA 282 Duff	109 LA 11 Cohen
	108 LA 411 Bankston	99 LA 756 Goldstein	93 LA 969 McKay	108 LA 857 Sergent
	100 LA 795 Allen	98 LA 271 Stanton	93 LA 167 Eisler	106 LA 1092 Levy
	96 LA 1113 Gentile			105 LA 110 Feldman
				94 LA 297 Nicholas

Offense	Discharge Upheld	Lesser Penalty Upheld (as assessed by employer)	Penalty Reduced by Arbitrator	No Penalty Permitted
Gambling			98 LA 1015 Halperin	106 LA 126 Gentile
				95 LA 148 Goldstein
Attachment or Garnishment of Wages		.		
Abusing Customers (Includes abuse of public agency clientele)	97 LA 367 Cox	98 LA 102 Byars	106 LA 1153 Richard	108 LA 793 Franckiewicz
	96 LA 465 Grinstead	94 LA 983 Knowlton	97 LA 221 Flaten	94 LA 147 McKee
Abusing Students, Patients or Inmates	109 LA 79 Brookins	108 LA 994 Soll	102 LA 1057 Duff	98 LA 306 Riker
	106 LA 344 Oberdank	106 LA 887 Goodman	99 LA 821 Staley	
	106 LA 210 Hewitt	104 LA 369 Franckiewicz	96 LA 916 Dworkin	
	102 LA 79 Millious	98 LA 545 Levak		
	99 LA 551 McCurdy	98 LA 219 Frost		
	99 LA 406 Seidman			

Offense	Discharge Upheld	Lesser Penalty Upheld (as assessed by employer)	Penalty Reduced by Arbitrator	No Penalty Permitted
Sexual Harassment	108 LA 993 Thornell	106 LA 776 Borland	108 LA 787 Staudohar	108 LA 791 Kindig
	108 LA 924 Moore	100 LA 866 Levak	106 LA 652 Wolfson	105 LA 429 Fullmer
	106 LA 550 Fullmer	100 LA 48 Strasshofer	106 LA 360 Imes	100 LA 105 Berquist
	106 LA 371 Brisco	96 LA 1122 DiLauro	106 LA 68 Daly	93 LA 1205 Clarke
	106 LA 322 Donnelly	94 LA 289 Boyer	105 LA 1057 Wahl	93 LA 365 Cantor
	105 LA 718 Goldberg		105 LA 1037 Johnson	
	105 LA 304 Heekin		104 LA 991 Bernhardt	
	104 LA 551 Kanner		100 LA 444 Daniel	
	104 LA 125 House		100 LA 105 Berquist	
	102 LA 737 Brunner		100 LA 63 Kaufman	
	102 LA 701 McHugh		98 LA 440 Griffin	
	103 LA 353 Bickner		97 LA 617 Bard	
	102 LA 161 Gentile			
	99 LA 969 Fullmer			
	99 LA 134 McDonald			
	99 LA 337 LaManna			
	97 LA 957 Baroni			

Chapter 16

Safety and Health

Safety and health matters continue to be critical issues that must be resolved in the labor-management relationship. Under the federal Occupational Safety and Health Act, management has the general duty to provide a safe and healthy workplace.[1] Management also has the statutory duty under the National Labor Relations Act to bargain with employees' collective bargaining representatives concerning workplace issues, which include safety and health.[2] These issues encompass not only traditional safety and health concerns but also such problems as employee exposure to cigarette smoke, toxic substances, and even violence from coworkers and the public. Moreover, employee refusals to work in the presence of perceived unsafe or unhealthy workplace conditions raise disciplinary questions under protective statutes and contractual provisions. Safety and health also must be taken into consideration under the Americans with Disabilities Act[3] when an employer provides reasonable accommodation to an employee with a disability or when such employee presents a danger to himself or others. Arbitration continues to provide an expedient and economical forum in which such safety and health issues are resolved.

Management Rights and Obligations in Safety and Health Matters

Management has the right to transfer an employee to a light-duty job over the employee's objections, if the medical documentation so recommends, because the employer has the legal duty to protect the health and safety of employees and retains the right to direct its working forces and transfer employees.[4] Management may also sub-

---

[1]29 U.S.C. §6110.
[2]29 U.S.C. §158(a)(5).
[3]42 U.S.C. §12101 et seq.
[4]ITT Automotive, 105 LA 11 (Shanker, 1995).

contract work that would be unsafe for its workers to perform with
the equipment the employer has, despite language in the contract
limiting subcontracting.[5]

However, management's obligation to provide employees with a
safe work environment does not require it to provide ideal conditions.
"Less safe" was not considered "unsafe" where the employer laid off
39 resident-care workers in a mental health facility but took other
measures to ensure employee safety.[6] Similarly, management was not
required to provide a two-way communications system for teachers
who felt endangered by increased gang activity, where adult hall
monitors and off-duty police were hired and a telephone was installed
to give teachers access to administrative offices and outside help.[7]

The presence of asbestos in the workplace has given rise to a
number of decisions concerning employer's obligations. In one case
an employer attempted to shield itself from liability by claiming that
the union had failed to prove the level of exposure to asbestos. However, because the employer blocked access to the information by controlling the testing,[8] the arbitrator refused to allow the employer to
benefit from its own inaction or regulatory or contractual violation.
In another case, the employer was required to pay employees envi-
ronmental differential pay even though the level of exposure to asbestos at work was one-half of the average set by the Occupational
Safety and Health Administration, because the exposure was greater
than is commonly encountered in the environment at large and there
is no known safe level of exposure.[9] However, where the city removed
loose asbestos pipe insulation and there was no evidence of how long
the condition had existed or whether firefighters were actually exposed to asbestos, the city was not required to maintain the firefighters'
names in a special medical file or notify them that they might have
been exposed to asbestos.[10]

Employee Obligations in Safety Matters

Employer rules requiring prompt reporting of on-the-job injuries
are reasonably related to the orderly and safe operation of the business. They are designed to facilitate immediate aid to an injured
worker, to establish a record of the injury in order to investigate, de-
tect, and remedy any hazardous condition, and to furnish notice to

[5]Basin Coop. Serv., 105 LA 1070 (Cohen, 1996).
[6]Michigan Dep't of Mental Health, 101 LA 325 (McDonald, 1993); see also Packaging Corp. of Am., 102 LA 1099 (Odom, 1994) (company may eliminate use of nurses on
second and third shifts and on weekends despite 20-year-old award requiring nurses on
all shifts because number of employees per shift was reduced by more than half and
other means of emergency care were provided).
[7]Racine Unified School Dist., 108 LA 391 (Imes, 1996).
[8]Department of the Navy, Glenview Naval Airbase, 102 LA 294 (Draznin, 1993).
[9]Veterans Admin., 99 LA 229 (Duff, 1992).
[10]City of Chicago, 99 LA 343 (Cox, 1992).

appropriate officials charged with responsibility for determination of whether the injuries are compensable.

One arbitrator sustained the discharge of an employee who failed to report his injury promptly although he was aware of his duty to do so.[11]

Safety Rules

Cases involving an employer's right to implement no-smoking policies continue to arise with regularity. Arbitrators generally have held that management has the right to implement rules restricting smoking under the employer's rule-making authority or its duty to provide a safe and healthy work environment, so long as the limitation or outright ban is not unreasonable, arbitrary, or capricious[12] and as long as it advances legitimate business objectives.[13] One arbitrator held that the company may ban smoking both inside and outside the plant based on its right to control its property.[14] Furthermore, management is under no contractual obligation to expend money to modify its plant or equipment to accommodate smokers.[15]

However, where the parties' collective bargaining agreement provides that smoking is permitted in restricted areas, management may not unilaterally ban smoking in all areas.[16] Thus, a company's unilateral implementation of a no-smoking policy was held to have violated its collective bargaining agreement because it ended a practice of allowing employees to use outside smoking areas.[17] The parties' agreement contained a "preservation of privilege provision," which stated that any privilege not mentioned in the agreement and enjoyed by employees would be incorporated into the agreement. The arbitrator

---

[11]Pioneer Flour Mills, 107 LA 379 (Bankston, 1996) (employee also had dismal employment record and had notice that further rule violations could subject him to discharge).

[12]Timkin Co., 108 LA 422 (Kindig, 1996); Akron Brass Co., 101 LA 289 (Shanker, 1993); Koch Ref. Co., 99 LA 733 (Cohen, 1992).

[13]Newlex Plant, ITT Higbie Baylock, 105 LA 1084 (Florman, 1996) (no-smoking policy is reasonable because it conforms to overall corporate policy, provides a healthy, safe, comfortable environment, reduces absenteeism, combats low productivity and high health care costs, promotes negotiated wellness program, and addresses scientific concerns with hazards of smoking in workplace).

[14]Norris Plumbing Fixtures, 104 LA 174 (Richman, 1995).

[15]Cummins Engine Co., 104 LA 522 (Goldman, 1995) (management has no obligation to preserve opportunity to engage in unhealthy behavior on company premises); see also Akron Brass Co., 101 LA 289 (Shanker, 1993) (management need not incur costs to accommodate smokers).

[16]Hobart Corp., 103 LA 1089 (Millious, 1994); Hobart Corp., 103 LA 547 (Imundo, 1994) (discusses difference between a policy and a rule where contract states that new rules are subject to negotiation); Campbell Group, Div. of Scott Fetzer Co., 102 LA 1031 (Ferree, 1994) (settlement of grievance providing for outside lean-to for smoking became part of contract after it survived contract negotiations); Raybestos Prods. Co., 102 LA 46 (Kossoff, 1993) (specific language on permitted smoking areas given more weight than general language regarding employer's agreement to protect health and safety).

[17]Cross Oil & Ref. of Ark., 104 LA 757 (Gordon, 1995) (arbitrator found that provision incorporating "any privilege or benefit" embraces more than "past practice").

concluded that the parties' bargaining history reflected that smoking was a privilege afforded employees. In contrast, another arbitrator held that even if the right to smoke is a recognized past practice, the practice cannot prevail where the conditions that gave rise to it no longer obtain. The arbitrator noted that as information about the health risks associated with smoking has become widely disseminated, public attitudes and employer liability have changed correspondingly.[18] See further discussion in "Employee Complaints of Specific Hazards," later in this chapter.

Increased violence in the workplace has prompted employers to implement specific policies against workplace violence to protect workers from physical harm and threats of physical harm. A company may promulgate "Anti-Violence Policies" that express a "zero tolerance" for actual or threatened violence in the workplace. In adopting such a policy, one company cited guidelines from the California Department of Industrial Relations' Division of Occupational Safety and Health).[19] The guidelines state that "[s]ome mental health professionals believe the belligerent, intimidating or threatening behavior by an employee or supervisor is an early warning sign of an individual's propensity to commit a physical assault in the future."[20]

Pursuant to such a policy the discharge of an employee who threatened a coworker was sustained.[21] Arbitrators are increasingly requiring employers to take seriously an employee's threats of physical harm. In one case, the arbitrator held that the company had an obligation to remove an angry employee who made provocative remarks about the murder of employees at the post office and about getting a shotgun from home.[22] The arbitrator held that such remarks when made in anger could not be construed as having been made in jest. In yet another case, the employer was found to have violated its safe work environment obligation under its collective bargaining agreement when supervisors failed to stop or take action against an employee who threatened another employee with physical harm and emotional, social, and psychological distress.[23]

Where an act is inherently dangerous, however, an employer does not have to specifically prohibit employees from engaging in it before taking disciplinary measures. For example, employees do not have to be told at a safety meeting that rolling under a railroad car on the track is unsafe. An employee may be disciplined for doing so without having been given prior warning.[24]

---

[18]Lockheed Aeronautical Sys. Co., A Division of Lockheed Corp., 104 LA 840 (Hewitt, 1995).

[19]California Department of Industrial Relations, Division of Occupational Safety and Health Guidelines for Workplace Security (1995).

[20]Golden States Foods Corp., 108 LA 705, 707 (Gentile, 1997).

[21]Ibid.

[22]Trane Co., 106 LA 1018 (Kindig, 1996) (grievant's angry remarks, together with two other serious charges, were considered just cause to discharge).

[23]Department of the Air Force, Randolph Air Force Base, 102 LA 358 (Wolff, 1993).

[24]Snap-On Tools Corp., 104 LA 180 (Cipolla, 1995).

Refusal to Obey Orders—The Safety Exception

The recognized "safety exception" to the "obey now—grieve later" doctrine has also been held applicable where the hazard arises from the employee's own medical condition rather than from the working conditions.[25]

Of course, an employee's right to refuse to do work in abnormally hazardous conditions may be made the subject of specific contract language.[26]

In all such cases the employee who refuses an assignment must show that the asserted safety or health hazard is the real reason for the employee's refusal.[27]

The Range of Arbitral Reasoning

Diversity continues to characterize arbitration decisions as to the appropriate standard under which an employee's refusal to perform work on account of health or safety hazards may be reviewed.[28]

The "Reasonable Person" Approach

The "reasonable person" criterion in one form or another remains the approach favored by the greatest number of arbitrators.[29]

Must Employees Explain Their Refusal?

Where the reason for an employee's fear is not readily apparent, an employee must be prepared to explain to an employer the basis for the safety concerns,[30] unless the employer has refused to listen.[31] Once

---

[25]Pittsburg v. Midway, 106 LA 624 (Alexander, 1996).

[26]CF Motor Transport, 103 LA 303 (Johnson, 1994) (contract required that a reasonable person would have believed the equipment was unsafe under the circumstances confronting the employee).

[27]Cyclops Corp., 107 LA 631 (Stanton, 1996); Colletti Trucking, 105 LA 507 (White, 1995); Dye Golf Servs., Inc., 104 LA 449 (Darrow, 1995); National Maintenance & Repair, 101 LA 1115 (Fowler, 1993).

[28]Peoples Natural Gas Co., 107 LA 882 (Zobrak, 1996) (employer "bears the burden of proving that the grievant's concerns were not reasonable"); Pittsburg & Midway, 106 LA 624 (Alexander, 1996) (employee must prove "reasonable grounds" for believing a job will be abnormally and immediately dangerous); Georgia-Pacific Corp., 106 LA 27 (Kahn, 1995) (employee must act in "good faith" in refusing a direct order); CF Motor Transport, 103 LA 303 (Johnson, 1994) (applying a "reasonable person" standard); National Maintenance & Repair, 101 LA 1115 (Fowler, 1993) (noting the lack of any objective criteria to substantiate the alleged safety concerns); Knauf Fiber Glass GmbH, 101 LA 823 (Ipavec, 1993) (employee failed to establish there was an actual risk of personal injury).

[29]Peoples Natural Gas Co., 107 LA 882 (Zobrak, 1996); Pittsburg & Midway, 106 LA 624 (Alexander, 1996); CF Motor Transport, 103 LA 303 (Johnson, 1994).

[30]Georgia-Pacific Corp., 106 LA 27 (Kahn, 1995).

[31]Peoples Natural Gas Co., 107 LA 882 (Zobrak, 1996).

a concern has been articulated, the employee may be required to provide some evidence to substantiate the concern.[32]

The Statutory Picture: OSHA, NLRA §7, LMRA §502

A number of cases have arisen under the Surface Transportation Assistance Act of 1982 (STAA) regarding when a driver may refuse to operate a motor vehicle. In one case, a driver refused to operate an oil truck because he would sometimes have to stand in the street to unwind the delivery hose and pass it beneath the truck. Because the driver could offer nothing more than a subjective fear of imminent physical danger, his refusal to operate the truck was held not to be protected by the STAA.[33]

Another driver's refusal to drive a tractor-trailer hauling a 20-ton load was found to be protected because objective evidence supported the driver's belief that the tractor lacked power to haul the load at a safe speed on an interstate highway. Two drivers had noticed the same problem, even though a later inspection failed to disclose anything wrong, and a mechanic drove the tractor over the same highway at an acceptable speed. The Second Circuit Court of Appeals rejected the employer's claim that there must be objective proof that a truck is actually unsafe, and concluded the STAA protects a driver whose fears are objectively reasonable at the time of the refusal.[34] A driver who stopped for a nap after having been awake 19.5 hours was similarly protected. His claim of fatigue was supported by other drivers, who told him he was "weaving."[35]

The National Labor Relations Board (NLRB) has continued to uphold the right of employees to act in concert by striking over safety issues.[36] It also has upheld an employee's right to raise safety-related questions during employee meetings, either on his or her own behalf,[37] or as a designated spokesperson for other employees.[38]

However, questions have been raised regarding the NLRB's interpretation of Section 502 of the Labor Management Relations Act (LMRA), which provides that employees are not deemed to have engaged in a "strike" when they cease work "in good faith because of abnormally dangerous conditions for work." The NLRB's decision in *TNS, Inc.*[39] was remanded by the District of Columbia Court of

---

[32]Georgia-Pacific Corp., 106 LA 27 (Kahn, 1995); Colletti Trucking, 105 LA 507 (White, 1995); CF Motor Transport, 103 LA 303 (Johnson, 1994); Knauf Fiber Glass GmbH, 101 LA 823 (Ipavec, 1993).
[33]Castle Coal & Oil Co., Inc. v. Reich, 55 F.3d 41 (2d Cir. 1995).
[34]Yellow Freight Sys., Inc. v. Reich, 38 F.3d 76 (2d Cir. 1994).
[35]Yellow Freight Sys., Inc. v. Reich, 8 F.3d 980 (4th Cir. 1993).
[36]Magic Finishing Co., 323 NLRB 28, 154 LRRM 1230 (1997); California Oilfield Maintenance, Inc., 311 NLRB 1079, 145 LRRM 1239 (1993).
[37]Talsol Corp., 317 NLRB 290, 151 LRRM 1097 (1995).
[38]Grimmway Enters., Inc., 315 NLRB 1276, 148 LRRM 1247 (1995).
[39]309 NLRB 1348, 142 LRRM 1045 (1992) (see the Main Volume, Chapter 16, "Compatibility of Award With Employee Rights Under Statute," at 985).

Appeals for further proceedings to clarify its interpretation of Section 502.[40] Two of the four Board members had held that the employees had to show either a significant change for the worse in their working conditions or that the cumulative effect of their exposure to depleted uranium had reached the point where further exposure would pose an unacceptable risk. A third Board member criticized that standard but concurred in the result because working conditions were not the "sole cause" of the walkout. The court of appeals found the concurring opinion to be "patently meritless." Because the NLRB's standard lacked majority support, the court refused to defer to the ruling. It remanded the case to the Board for the articulation of a majority-supported standard applying Section 502 to employees exposed to low-level radiation.

Compatibility of Award With Employee Rights Under Statute

Because an employee's reliance upon statutory rights depends upon the existence of objective evidence to substantiate the employee's fears, the use of a subjective test by arbitrators interpreting contractual language is likely to result in divergent outcomes. This is demonstrated by conflicting results in cases where an employee's physical condition was the basis for a refusal to work.

At least one arbitrator held that an employee's physical condition cannot provide a basis for refusing to work, because it does not make the working conditions abnormally and immediately dangerous.[41] A gash on the employee's thumb, which reportedly was just beginning to heal, did not justify his refusal to clean grease from equipment. By contrast, the STAA protected an employee whose refusal to continue driving was based upon his physical condition. Termination of a driver who stopped for a nap when unduly fatigued was held to violate the STAA.[42] An Administrative Law Judge (ALJ) and the Secretary of Labor (Secretary) both refused to defer in that case to a five-word arbitration award that reduced the employee's three-day suspension to a one-day suspension.

In another case, an arbitrator upheld termination of an employee who refused to make deliveries based upon a subjective fear of serious injury. An ALJ found the refusal to make deliveries was not protected by the STAA. The Secretary disagreed, concluding that the employee had been unlawfully terminated. However, the Secretary's order was set aside on appeal.[43]

---

[40]Oil, Chem. & Atomic Workers Int'l Union v. NLRB, 46 F.3d 82, 148 LRRM 2461 (D.C. Cir. 1995).
[41]Pittsburg & Midway, 106 LA 624 (Alexander, 1996).
[42]Yellow Freight Sys., Inc. v. Reich, 8 F.3d 980 (4th Cir. 1993).
[43]Castle Coal & Oil Co., Inc. v. Reich, 55 F.3d 41 (2d Cir. 1995).

Employee Complaints of Specific Hazards

As noted, arbitral decisions on the banning of cigarette smoking lack consistency.[44] Many view cigarette smoking as just another term or condition of employment that the parties may allow through collective bargaining or past practice.[45] However, a growing body of arbitration decisions upholds policies that totally ban cigarette smoking on the basis of the health hazards and the increased health care costs associated with smoking, as well as the potential employer liability arising from "secondhand smoke."[46] See also, "Safety Rules," *supra*, this chapter.

Physical or Mental Condition as a Safety Hazard

Under the ADA and analogous antidiscrimination provisions of collective bargaining agreements, an employee's physical or mental condition may be considered a safety hazard either to himself or to others. Employers are under an obligation to reasonably accommodate an employee with a disability, but not if such accommodation would create a safety hazard.[47] The employer has a countervailing obligation to provide a safe and healthy workplace for all employees, including an employee with a disability. Physical and mental conditions that pose a safety hazard are determined on an individual basis. Arbitrators rely on medical evidence and on evidence concerning workplace conditions and job requirements in determining whether the employee's physical or mental condition is a safety hazard. Employers are not permitted to generalize in assuming that certain physical or mental conditions automatically constitute safety hazards.

[44]See the Main Volume, Chapter 16, "Employee Complaints of Specific Hazards" at 988–89.
[45]See, for example, Cross Oil & Refining, 104 LA 757 (Gordon, 1995) (smoking ban adopted under health and safety clause did not override broad contract clause promising no changes in employee privileges); PMI Food Equipment Group, 103 LA 547 (Imundo, 1994) (company could not unilaterally adopt indoor smoking ban despite undisputed evidence that ban was adopted out of desire to protect nonsmokers, and evidence of harmful effects of smoking); Raybestos Prods. Co., 102 LA 46 (Kossof, 1993) (company could not unilaterally adopt no-smoking policy where it knew of dangers of passive smoke and still agree to long-standing smoking provision in contract negotiations); Campbell Group, 102 LA 1031 (Ferree, 1994) (despite obligations under health and safety clause, company cannot ban outdoor smoking because tobacco is not illegal, and company can do little to protect employees from themselves).
[46]See, for example, Norris Plumbing Fixtures, 104 LA 174 (Richman, 1995) (upholding adoption of policy that totally banned smoking because of risk to employees themselves and increased health risks); Lockheed Aeronautical Sys. Co., 104 LA 840 (Hewitt, 1995) (conditions underlying past practice have changed sufficiently to justify no-smoking policy because of concerns over liability for secondhand smoke, the obligation to provide safe and healthy workplace, and the public perception that having a smoke-free environment raises a "public policy" inference); Lincoln Brass Works, 102 LA 872 (Haskew, 1994) (management rights clause allows rule making to protect safety of employees subsequent to EPA's designation of dangers of secondhand smoke).
[47]Rheem Mfg. Co., 108 LA 193 (Wolff, 1997); Champion Int'l Corp., 106 LA 1024 (Howell, 1996); Cessna Aircraft Co., 104 LA 985 (Thornell, 1995).

Management Action: Transfer, Demotion, Layoff, Leave of Absence, or Termination

The increasing prevalence of workplace violence has spawned a growing number of arbitration awards holding that an employer's obligation to provide a safe working environment requires "zero tolerance for violence" policies and the discipline or removal of employees who threaten or engage in violence.[48]

---

[48]Trane Co., 106 LA 1018 (Kindig, 1996); Hackett Brass Foundry, 107 LA 1199 (Allen, 1996); Advance Circuits, Inc., 106 LA 353 (Daly, 1996); Johnston Coca-Cola Bottling Group, Inc., 106 LA 88 (Brunner, 1995); Central Illinois Public Serv., Co., 105 LA 372 (Cohen, 1995); Department of the Air Force, Randolph Air Force Base, 102 LA 358 (Wolff, 1993).

Chapter 17

Employee Rights and Benefits

Vacations

Vacation issues continue to be productive sources of grievance arbitrations.

An employee's contractual rights to vacation benefits[1] are of two types: time off from work and pay.[2] The significance of the "time off" aspect of vacations was illustrated in an unusual context. An employee who was discharged while on vacation received an arbitral award of reinstatement with backpay. When the employer sought to reduce the backpay by the amount earned by the employee at another company during the vacation, the arbitrator disallowed the offset, reasoning that "[a]n individual's vacation belongs to that individual and if one chooses to work at a different job during that time, rather than relaxing, that is the prerogative of the individual."[3]

Disputes over entitlement to vacation pay are more common. In one decision, employees were held to be entitled to vacation pay when the employer ceased its operations prior to the employees' anniversary dates of employment, despite the fact that the contract provided that vacation pay was to be issued on an employee's anniversary date. Because the agreement contained other language that permitted the taking of earned vacation prior to an employee's anniversary date, the arbitrator ruled that employees who met the work requirements for vacation were entitled to their full vacation pay.[4]

In determining whether or not time served on National Guard duty should count toward vesting of vacation benefits, the contract, and not federal law, will be dispositive. A disappointed reservist who had met all other contract requirements for vacation except the num-

---

[1]See "The Common Law of the Labor Agreement: Vacations," 5 Indus. Rel. J.J. 603 (1983).

[2]See E.K. Wood Prods., 105 LA 1153, 1155 (Dobry, 1995).

[3]Park 'N Fly, 108 LA 611, 612 (Marino, 1997).

[4]Canteen Corp., 101 LA 925 (Borland, 1993).

ber of days worked the previous year contended that he would have satisfied the minimum requirement but for the compulsory guard duty.

The union argued that the Veterans' Benefits Act[5] required that he be given vacation credit for the guard duty time. The Act provides that National Guard personnel with military training obligations lasting less than three months must be granted a leave of absence for the period required to carry out their training and that they must be returned to work with the seniority status and pay that they would have had if not absent for duty.

The arbitrator found the Supreme Court's decision in *Monroe v. Standard Oil Co.*[6] controlling. There the Court explicitly found that the Act "does not entitle a reservist to benefits that are conditioned upon work requirements demanding actual performance on the job." Because in the present case vacations were based upon work requirements and not remaining-in-continuous-service status, the company was justified in denying vacation to the guardsman-employee because he had not been at work the requisite number of days.[7]

The extent of vacation entitlements typically varies with length of service. Part-time or temporary service prior to an employee's becoming a full-time or "regular" employee may not be credited toward vacation entitlements unless the contract so provides.[8]

When an employee transfers to another of the company's plants, a question may arise as to whether seniority for vacation entitlements is based on the total length of employer service or only service at the plant. For example, a contract provided that vacation could be taken after one year of continuous service, but the agreement defined "company seniority" as the length of an employee's continuous service beginning with the date on which the employee began to work for a particular plant. When an employee with five years' seniority was transferred to another plant, the question arose as to whether she was properly permitted to schedule her vacation within her first year at the new plant. Citing the employee's ambiguous status under the collective bargaining agreement and the absence of any language specifically denying the employee her accrued benefits, the arbitrator determined that the employee was eligible for vacation because at no time was there a break in service.[9]

―――――――

[5]Vietnam Era Veterans' Readjustment Assistance Act of 1974, as amended, 38 U.S.C. §4301(b)(3).
[6]452 U.S. 549, 107 LRRM 2633 (1981).
[7]Concordia Foods, 102 LA 990 (Bernstein, 1994).
[8]Fremont Hotel & Casino, 102 LA 220 (Randall, 1993) (service prior to becoming a regular employee was not counted where ambiguous contract language was defined by past practice to that effect); E.K. Wood Prods. Co., 105 LA 1153 (Dobry, 1995) (employees' service on a part-time basis was not counted toward vacation pay where the contract granted vacation to "regular employees" and part-timers had not been considered regular employees).
[9]ARCO Chem., 102 LA 1051 (Massey, 1994).

Scheduling Vacations

Many labor agreements do not unambiguously resolve the potential conflicts between employer and employee preferences for vacation scheduling.[10] One arbitrator has noted: "[I]t is well settled that the rights of employees to take their vacations at personally convenient times is a valuable benefit afforded by an appropriately worded . . . [collective bargaining agreement."[11]

As set forth in the Main Volume, labor agreements frequently provide that when two or more employees compete for the same vacation time off, seniority prevails.

In one case, a rule requiring that employees submit vacation requests 48 hours in advance was invalidated because the labor agreement provided only that "[v]acations will be taken at such times of the year as not to interfere with the efficient scheduling of operations in the plant."[12]

But where a contract gave the company the right to "determine when each employee may take his vacation," this "clear language" governed notwithstanding the existence of an inconsistent past practice, and an employer's refusal to allow one-day vacations unless notice was received in advance of the day was upheld.[13]

"Clear contract language" may also inure to the benefit of the employee. When an employer claimed that "past practice" supported its position that it could limit its drivers' vacations to the summer, when milk was not delivered to schools,[14] an arbitrator ruled that the contract clearly provided for nonsummer vacation periods, and this unambiguous language controlled.

Operational Needs—Arbitrators continue to place the burden of persuasion upon employers who deny employees' vacation requests that are facially in compliance with the contract or past practice to provide that the denial is reasonable on the basis of the employer's operational needs. Thus, under a contract providing that "[p]reference of vacation shall be granted to employees according to seniority on dates requested when in the judgment of the employer such date will not impair operations," the company implemented a policy of not scheduling vacations during holiday weeks. An arbitrator noted that "[i]f the company wanted sole discretion, without being required to provide justification, to determine whether vacations would be

---

[10]See Lewis County, 107 LA 321, 323–24 (Stuteville, 1996) (agreement not violated when employee's vacation scheduling request was denied even though no other employee was scheduled for same vacation period. Contract providing that not more than one employee be on vacation at the same time set only a maximum limitation, not a minimum guarantee).

[11]National Linen Service, 110 LA 476, 479 (Frockt, 1998).

[12]Stone Container Corp., 108 LA 917, 920 (Bain, 1997).

[13]Sanderson Plumbing Prods., 106 LA 535 (Howell, 1996).

[14]Meyer Bros. Dairy, 107 LA 481 (Scoville, 1996).

permitted during holiday weeks, then it should have negotiated unambiguous language to that effect."[15]

A similar result was reached when an employer attempted to use shift seniority for vacation picks under a contract providing that seniority was measured by the length of service with the employer, and that an employee's preference for vacation time off, considered in order of seniority, was to be accommodated "whenever possible." The arbitrator reasoned that "whenever possible" was to be understood in the context of "operational needs," and the company's general right to designate each employee's vacation period did not override the specific contractual seniority provisions.[16]

A contract provided that "[v]acation and personal leave schedules must be arranged so as not to interfere with the regular and efficient conduct of the business of the company" and that "[v]acation selection will be granted on a seniority [length of continuous on-the-job service] basis by departments, so far as possible preference as to dates being given in the order of length of such service."[17] In the past, if after an employee's vacation selection had been approved, the employee was transferred to another department, the company would hire a part-timer to fill in. The company issued a statement, challenged by the union, that henceforth transferred employees would only be permitted to take vacation time still open in the new department. The arbitrator found the question was not resolved by the contract but relief on the prior practice in deciding that already selected vacations would transfer with the employees.

What happens when "operational needs" require the recall of an employee who has already started his vacation? Finding itself unexpectedly short of drivers, a beverage distributor ordered the grievant to cut short his preapproved vacation by one week. The employee had in the past rescheduled vacations when requested by the company. However, in this case the driver had prepaid for an out-of-state vacation and could return early only upon payment of substantial additional airfare. He informed the company that he would return to work as originally scheduled after his two-week vacation. The company considered the failure to return a voluntary resignation and terminated his employment. The arbitrator disagreed, holding that the company was equitably estopped since it had unilaterally changed the scheduled vacation that it had previously approved and upon which the employee had relied in booking his travel. The prior episodes of employee acquiescence were not precedential because in those instances the driver had not planned out-of-state trips.[18]

Vacation Shutdown—An employer's decision to require employees to use their accrued vacation during a temporary closure of the

[15]National Linen Serv., 110 LA 476, 479 (Frockt, 1998).
[16]Baltimore Sun Co., 103 LA 363, 370 (Cushman, 1994).
[17]Schmidt Baking Co., 104 LA 574, 575 (Wahl, 1995).
[18]Goodman Beverage Co., 108 LA 37, 42 (Morgan, 1997).

business is subject to the labor agreement and past practice that does not conflict with the agreement. Although for more than 20 years a plant had never experienced a vacation shutdown, the employer was entitled to impose one since the agreement unambiguously gave the employer the right to "designate any periods of time during the year for the shutting down of plant operations, for the taking of vacation."[19] The arbitrator explained, "Even twenty years of a consistently applied past practice cannot serve to nullify the clear and unambiguous language of the Agreement."[20]

Vacation Period Fixed by Contract—Where a labor agreement referred to two six-month vacation scheduling periods, summer and winter, an arbitrator held that the employer in a seasonal business could not, when challenged, limit employee vacations to the summer off-season, as it had done in the past.[21]

Remedy for Forced Vacations—Fashioning a remedy when vacation scheduling grievances prove meritorious can sometimes be a daunting task. In one case, though the arbitrator found that the employer had improperly restricted the taking of vacations to a minimum of one week at a time, the arbitrator declined to permit the employee to unilaterally select his remaining vacation days, the remedy sought by the union. Instead, only prospective relief was granted, and the employer was directed to abide by the contract in the future.[22] In other grievances, however, that may be the very relief the union requests.[23]

Calculation of Vacation Pay [New Topic]

Questions often arise regarding the proper calculation of vacation pay, such as whether vacation pay includes an overtime compensation component. One arbitrator held that it did not on the basis of the bargaining history for the current contract. The employer's past practice had been not to include overtime in vacation pay, and although the issue had arisen during negotiations, no change was made in the contract language.[24]

Vacation Benefits: Deferred Wages or "Refresher"?

Whether the parties intended vacation benefits to serve as "deferred wages" or to refresh the employee can arise in grievances regarding carryover or forfeiture of unused vacation from one year to the next. While acknowledging that accumulated vacation pay is a

---

[19]Willamette Indus., 106 LA 1113 (Stoltenberg, 1996).
[20]Id. at 1115.
[21]Meyers Bros. Dairy, 107 LA 481 (Scoville, 1996).
[22]Borough of Doylestown, Pa., 109 LA 1080 (DiLauro, 1997).
[23]See National Linen Serv., 110 LA 476 (Frockt, 1998).
[24]Hydro Conduit Corp., 105 LA 964 (Kaufman, 1995).

form of deferred earnings and that in some jurisdictions employees are entitled by statute to compensation for accumulated but unused vacation time upon termination of employment, an arbitrator noted that the parties may provide for a maximum vacation pay accumulation and require employees to "use it or lose it." The precise issue before him was whether accrued vacation benefits were capped at 520 hours or at 520 hours plus the number of hours accumulated in the previous year, under a contract that provided, "[v]acation may be carried forward with a maximum of five hundred twenty (520) hours . . . throughout the year." The arbitrator held that the 520-hour limit was a "rolling" maximum.[25]

Retirement as Affecting Vacation Benefits

As noted in the Main Volume, vacation vesting issues commonly arise when an employee retires. One of the most frequent sources of dispute is the maximum amount of unused vacation that can be cashed out upon retirement. When a labor agreement provided that an employee was entitled to accumulate up to 320 hours of vacation but could not carry over vacation time "for more than two (2) years,"[26] the employer argued that this provision was subject to its past practice of limiting vacation carryovers to 240 hours. The arbitrator determined that the former 240-hour carryover limit was actually a function of the maximum vacation allowance in prior contracts and concluded that the specific language of the present contract controlled the issue. The grievant was awarded a full vacation cash-out upon his retirement.[27]

Layoff as Affecting Vacation Benefits

Is the time an employee spends on layoff status to be included in the calculation of his vacation entitlements?

Where a contract provided for a vacation accrual rate based upon time worked by an employee following the employee's anniversary date, an employer was held not to be entitled to adjust the employee's anniversary date by excluding the months during which the employee was on layoff status. The arbitrator held that an employee not in pay status in any given month did not earn vacation pay in that month, but that nothing in the contract suggested that layoffs could affect an employee's anniversary date. To the contrary, the contract expressly recognized that an employee's anniversary date could occur while an employee was on a leave of absence and hence not in pay status.[28]

In another case, although a contract provision allowed for the proration of vacation benefits for employees who voluntarily or invol-

---

[25]City of Duncan, 106 LA 398 (Cipolla, 1996).
[26]Cuyahoga Community College, 109 LA 268, 269 (Klein, 1997).
[27]Id. at 273.
[28]McDonnell Douglas Aerospace West, 104 LA 252 (Rothstein, 1995).

untarily terminated their service with the employer, an arbitrator held that an employer was not entitled to prorate the vacation benefits of employees who had been laid off for more than one year. The arbitrator found that a layoff with a right of recall was not the equivalent of a termination, and the past practice of the employer had been to pay full vacation benefits to employees who had been laid off.[29]

Industrial Injury Leave as Affecting Vacation Benefits [New Topic]

Are employees placed on contractually compensable, "full pay" industrial injury leave entitled to credit toward sick leave and vacation entitlements as well as to the receipt of holiday pay? The answer depends upon the contract provisions. Thus under a sheriff department's contract stating that "all employees shall" receive these benefits but specifically denying benefits to employees on uncompensated leave of absence, an arbitrator held that entitlement to the benefits required nothing more than status as an employee. His interpretation was supported by the perceived purpose of the injury leave—to provide employees full protection against loss—and the fact that contracts between the union and other sheriff departments expressly conditioned the benefit entitlements upon being in active work status.[30]

Family and Medical Leave Act Eligibility as Affecting Vacation Benefits [New Topic]

The Family and Medical Leave Act of 1993 ("FMLA")[31] provides that either the employer or the employee may elect to use vested vacation time to cover an otherwise unpaid FMLA leave of absence.[32] A U.S. Department of Labor regulation, however, specifically states that if the collective bargaining agreement so provides, the choice belongs solely to the employee.[33]

Thus an employer's insistence that an employee use his vacation entitlements to cover absences for which an FMLA leave would have been available was found to violate a contract that gave employees the right to choose their vacations subject to the employer's "staffing needs."[34] The evidence failed to establish that staffing needs were adversely affected by this employee's choosing to save his vacation entitlement.[35]

---

[29]Fabrick Mach. Co., 104 LA 555 (Saardi, 1995).
[30]Trumbull County Sheriff's Dep't, 105 LA 545 (Nelson, 1995).
[31]29 U.S.C. §§2611 et seq.
[32]Id. at §2612(d)(2)(A).
[33]29 C.F.R. §825.700(a). See also Union Hosp., 108 LA 966, 971 (Chattman, 1997) ("So long as the FMLA provisions in question do not preempt or invalidate the portion of the collective bargaining agreement at issue, an arbitrator must always adhere to the clear and unambiguous language of the CBA").
[34]Id. at 973.
[35]Id. Accord, Grand Haven Stamped Prods. Co., 107 LA 131 (Daniel, 1996).

Holidays

A contract provision stated that an employer was required to allow "time off for all legal holidays with pay" including, in addition to the holidays enumerated in the agreement, "any other holiday which may hereafter be declared a general holiday by the President of the United Sates or by an act of Congress." An arbitrator held that the employer was obliged to recognize as a "legal holiday" the "National Day of Mourning" for former President Nixon, which had been declared by presidential proclamation. In the absence of any evidence of relevant bargaining history, the arbitrator relied upon the dictionary definition of the term "legal holiday," the practice of other employees who had similar contract language in their agreements, and the fact that this employer had followed the leave practices of the federal government in the past, all of which supported the treatment of the National Day of Mourning as a holiday.[36]

Work Requirements

Many employers discourage the "stretching" of holidays by requiring employees to work their shifts that immediately precede and follow a holiday as a precondition to receiving holiday pay.

In cases where an employee's absence on a required workday before or after the holiday is "excused," arbitrators are divided as to whether the employee qualifies for holiday pay. In one such case, where the employee had actually worked on the holiday, an arbitrator held that taking sick leave on a required pre- or post-holiday workday did not deprive the employee of holiday pay because his absence was not offensive to the purpose of such provisions—namely, to prevent employees from "extending" holidays—and the contract excused compliance if the absence was for a bona fide reason.[37] Similarly, another arbitrator held that taking sick leave on a required workday did not defeat eligibility for holiday pay even though the absent employee did not produce a doctor's note to support his claim of illness where neither the contract nor past practice required such verification.[38] In several other cases, however, arbitrators have held that even excused absences on a required workday do not entitle the employee to holiday pay.[39]

---

[36]Sheet Metal Workers' Nat'l Pension Fund, 103 LA 764 (Kaplan, 1994).
[37]Willamette Indus., 107 LA 1213 (Kaufman, 1997).
[38]Bureau of Engraving, 106 LA 315 (Bard, 1996).
[39]LTV Steel Mining Co., 107 LA 1094 (Doepkin, 1996) (employee out of work because of surgery on day after holiday, but was on medical leave and had failed to work any other day during pay period; contract required employee to have worked or have been on vacation during holiday pay period); CWC Kalamazoo Inc., 105 LA 555 (Roumell, 1995) (employee took vacation day on day after holiday and then called in sick on next regularly scheduled work day, but did not provide medical documentation); Curved Glass Distribs., 102 LA 33 (Eischen, 1993).

In interpreting a contract requirement that an employee must work "his next workday" in order to be eligible for holiday pay,[40] an arbitrator held that the reference was to the individual's work schedule, not the plant's operating schedule.[41]

Part-Day Absence or Tardiness on Surrounding Day

Tardiness on a required workday has been held not to deprive the employee of entitlement to holiday pay[42] unless the tardiness constitutes a substantial portion of the scheduled workday.[43]

Holidays Falling During Layoff

After an employer became bankrupt and its employees were placed on layoff status, another company bought the bankrupt's assets and called back the laid-off employees.

The employees subsequently grieved the new employer's refusal to provide holiday pay. The arbitrator concluded that since the holiday had occurred prior to the call-back, the employees were not entitled to the compensation.[44]

Vacation or Leave as Affecting Holiday Pay

Under a contract providing for holiday pay for holidays falling during a vacation period, an arbitrator ruled that employees who took one approved vacation day on the day after the holiday and were sick on the next day were not entitled to holiday pay. The "vacation period" was interpreted to mean more than an isolated vacation day.[45]

An employer who, in order to cut costs, sought to preclude employees from taking their vacation during any week in which a holiday fell on a weekday was held to have violated the labor agreement. The employer could restrict the scheduling of vacation only in those limited situations where operations would otherwise be impaired.[46]

---

[40]CWC Kalamazoo Inc., 105 LA 555, 559 (1995).

[41]Id. at 560.

[42]Josten's Printing & Publishing Div., 107 LA 505 (Berger, 1996); (one hour and one-half late); National Uniform Serv., 104 LA 901 (Klein, 1995) (employees reported between 30 and 42 minutes late); Greenburg Presbyterian Home, 102 LA 506 (Jones, 1993).

[43]National Uniform Serv., 104 LA 901 (Klein, 1995) (employee 6 hours and 55 minutes late on day before holiday); but see Monarch Tile, 101 LA 585 (Hooper, 1993) (employee who worked only 3 hours on the day after a holiday held entitled to holiday pay where the contract merely provided that the employee "report" for work on the employee's next regularly scheduled workday).

[44]Clark Bar America, Inc., 106 LA 856 (Paolucci, 1996).

[45]CWC Kalamazoo, Inc., 105 LA 555 (Roumell, Jr., 1995).

[46]National Linen Serv., 110 LA 476 (Frockt, 1998).

Holidays Falling on Nonworkdays

A contract stated that employees would be paid for holidays that did not fall on a Saturday. At the time, the plant operated on the traditional Monday-through-Friday, five-day workweek. Subsequently, the employer changed to a nontraditional workweek. An arbitrator directed the company to consider the Good Friday holiday as a day worked for purposes of computing weekly overtime for employees who were not scheduled to work on Fridays.[47]

Other Holiday Issues

Absent contract language specifically excluding or defining benefits for probationary employees, they are entitled to holiday pay to the same extent as nonprobationary employees.[48]

Under a bargaining agreement stating that benefits would not exceed 100 percent of daily pay, an employee receiving workers' compensation was held to have been entitled only to so much of holiday pay as would, together with workers' compensation, equal 100 percent of his daily pay.[49]

Leaves of Absence

Despite an attendance policy stating that "[e]mployees who are absent for any reason in excess of six months" would be terminated, an arbitrator set aside the discharge of warehouse employee who had been absent for more than six months on workers' compensation. The arbitrator noted that the policy had not always been strictly enforced and inferred that the company considered "fairness" as an element in its enforcement decisions. Fairness here required granting the grievant a leave of absence because there was no proof that the employee, after he had been released by his physician for return to work, was unable to perform his duties.[50]

Sick Leave

A labor organization employer refused a field staff member's request for sick leave to undergo nonemergency surgery because his services were then needed for the conduct of a membership drive. Although the contract did not expressly require management approval before accrued sick leave could be utilized, an arbitrator denied the ensuing grievance, reasoning that management had retained the right to control the use of sick leave so long as it did not act "arbitrarily,

---

[47]Friskies Petcare Prods., 110 LA 20 (Thornell, 1998).
[48]Seven-Up Bottling Co., 108 LA 587 (Staudohar, 1997).
[49]Stone Container Corp., 105 LA 537 (Allen, Jr., 1995).
[50]Magnolia Marketing Co., 107 LA 102 (Chumley, 1996).

discriminatorily or capriciously." An employee, the arbitrator continued, is not free to set his own schedule, and where the surgery could be rescheduled to a time when the employee could be better spared from the performance of his duties, the employer acted reasonably in refusing the request.[51]

The calculation of sick leave entitlements in terms of either hours or days usually presents no problem so long as the workday is standardized. However, when some employees regularly worked four 10-hour shifts, and the contract provided for a maximum accrual of 22 days of sick leave, the employees grieved the company's allowance of a maximum accrual of 176 hours instead of 220 hours. The arbitrator found that the contract contemplated 8-hour work days, and the prior practice was consistent with the company's calculation of sick leave.[52]

Can an employee be involuntarily placed on unpaid medical leave of absence by his employer? One arbitrator answered "yes" in a case where the company temporarily placed an employee on medical leave because, according to his physician, his medication made him sensitive to heat above 75 degrees, and the plant temperature was in the 90- to 95-degree range. The contract gave the company the right to relieve employees from duty for legitimate reasons. The arbitrator concluded that the company had acted reasonably, in light of the danger to the employee, in not permitting the grievant to continue working.[53]

Maternity or Maternity-Related Leave

Relying on the collective bargaining agreement and the Family and Medical Leave Act (FMLA), an arbitrator concluded that discharging an employee at or about the time she requested a pregnancy leave violated both the FMLA and the agreement.[54] The employee had some ten days prior to her discharge verbally advised her supervisor and the payroll clerk of her desire for a pregnancy leave. The arbitrator ruled that the request triggered a duty on the part of the company to conduct an investigation to determine whether such a leave was appropriate under the FMLA. However, the company conducted no investigation but instead discharged the employee for violation of its three-day "no-report" rule, an event occurring after her request for leave.[55]

---

[51]Indiana State Teachers Ass'n, 104 LA 737 (Paolucci, 1995); see also Land-O-Sun Dairies, Inc., 105 LA 740 (Draznin, 1995) (employee who refused mandatory overtime on ground of illness properly discharged under company policy which treated such refusal as a "voluntary quit" since employee's claim of illness was not timely communicated to employer or supported with sufficient information to allow employer to determine whether to grant grievant an exception).
[52]Huntleigh Transp. Servs., 101 LA 784 (Marino, 1993).
[53]Siemens Energy & Automation, Inc., 108 LA 537 (Neas, 1997).
[54]Pace Indus., Inc., 109 LA 1 (Gordinier, 1997).
[55]Id. at 3.

The same result was reached by another arbitrator, who also re-instated a female employee after she had been similarly terminated for failing to meet a three-day call-in requirement.[56] The employer had refused to grant the employee the FMLA leave she sought, claiming that the worker was not eligible for the maternity leave because she had not been on the payroll one year. The arbitrator found no one-year requirement in the labor contract[57] and concluded that the employee was entitled to the leave, which, if granted, would not have required the employee to call in every three days.

Can an employee be placed on maternity leave against her wishes? An arbitrator found a public utility employer could place a pregnant employee on leave when her job as a mechanic required her regularly to lift objects heavier than the 30-pound limit recommended by her physician. The company rejected two alternatives proposed by the union. The first, requiring coworkers to lift heavier items, was found to be unreasonably disruptive. The second, allowing the pregnant employee to transfer to an available cafeteria position, was held to violate a contractual provision that forbade discrimination in trans-fers based on disability or sex. Although the union agreed to waive this provision, the company did not, since it was planning to subcon-tract the operation. The arbitrator held that "a bilateral agreement requires bilateral waiver."[58]

Leave for Union Business

Although requests for union leave can be made only by a small fraction of the workforce, they produce a disproportionate percentage of the grievances filed over employers' leave restrictions or denials. In one case, significant for its requirement that the employer prove a leave denial to be reasonable, an employer's reasons for denying un-paid leave to a local union president so that he could participate in the union's "Lobby [Congress] Week" was held to be insufficient.[59] The focus of Lobby Week was the potential reorganization of two dis-tricts of the U.S. Army Corps of Engineers, a subject that qualified as "of mutual concern" to the parties. The Corps asserted that it had denied the request because an "emergency weather situation" had developed, requiring the union president's services. The president did not possess any essential skill necessary to meet the emergency that management described.[60] In fact, hundreds of other employees were granted leave during the emergency. The arbitrator found that the request had actually been denied because management did not

---

[56]Enesco Corp., 107 LA 513 (Berman, 1996).
[57]Id. at 518–19.
[58]Minnegasco, 103 LA 54 (Bognanno, 1994).
[59]U.S. Army Corps. of Engineers, 104 LA 30 (Baroni, 1995).
[60]Id. at 34.

like the views on the issue that the president would express before Congress.[61]

When a contract limited leaves of absence to two years but did not so restrict leaves for union business, an arbitrator refused to imply a similar limitation and allowed a union officer to maintain his seniority and employment relationship indefinitely.[62]

Not all requests for union leave or released time have been so successful in arbitration. Thus, a union was held to have violated the collective bargaining agreement when a local president used official time to attend a district caucus where she was unexpected seated as a voting delegate.[63] The contract allowed the use of official time only for joint labor/management committee activities, not for internal union business.[64] The arbitrator, however, found that there was no "willful abuse of official time" because the local president did not originally intend to get involved in internal union business, and did not think she would be seated as a delegate and be eligible to vote.[65]

A union's request that its president be given one-half day released time for union business was denied despite the union's especially large membership.[66] The union failed to present sufficient evidence that its business could not be administered unless the union president were granted free time during the workday.[67]

Under a consistently observed master labor agreement provision requiring an employee to obtain supervisory approval to discuss union matters during duty hours, an arbitrator found that an unsanctioned meeting between a national union representative and a bargaining unit member during work time to discuss a grievance violated the agreement.[68] Even in the absence of such a provision, the arbitrator continued, management could reasonably prohibit employees on duty from coming and going at will to meet one another.[69] The union was ordered to seek approval in the future for the release of employees during their shifts.[70]

Turning to public sector labor relations, a county did not violate a collective bargaining agreement by denying a request for a 35-day union leave so that an employee could attend union training sessions. Such a leave, the arbitrator decided, need not be granted in the absence of an express contractual mandate or a binding past practice.[71] The contract provided that union leave "may," rather than "shall," be granted. The county had at one time granted such leave to two em-

[61]Id.
[62]Panhandle Eastern Pipe Line Co., 103 LA 996 (Allen, 1994).
[63]Army & Air Force Exchange Serv., 108 LA 618 (Baroni, 1997).
[64]Id. at 621.
[65]Id. at 622.
[66]Wooster City Bd. of Educ., 108 LA 502 (Feldman, 1997).
[67]Id. at 505.
[68]Army & Air Force Exchange Serv., 107 LA 758 (Allen, 1996).
[69]Id. at 762.
[70]Id. at 763.
[71]Auglaize County, 110 LA 916 (Sugerman, 1998).

ployees, but this was insufficient to establish the requisite past practice.[72]

When a steward leaves his work station to attend to a union function without supervisory authorization, he may be subject to discipline. Under a collective bargaining agreement that allowed stewards a reasonable time to handle employee problems after first notifying a supervisor, an employer was found to have had good cause to discharge a shop steward who left his work area to report on an alleged altercation without giving such notice.[73] The steward, the arbitrator noted, had had disciplinary problems in the past.

Whether a union officer must be paid for time spent on union business is determined by the contract. Thus, on the basis of the collective bargaining agreement, an arbitrator decided that a local union president was entitled to pay for time spent at a Step III grievance meeting but not entitled to pay for time spent at a predischarge meeting.[74] Since the company had for many years made payment to successive local union presidents for their attendance at Step III meetings, this "practice" informed the otherwise silent text. However, because the agreement specified pay only for settling "grievances," meetings concerned only with a potential discharge were not within the scope of the provision.[75]

Contrarily, under an agreement that authorized pay for attendance of union representatives only at scheduled grievance meetings, an employer was found to have improperly withheld pay for time spent in performing other union duties. There, however, union officials had regularly been compensated while engaged in union business, and the employer had never denied prior requests for such time off except during actual production constraints. These circumstances led the arbitrator to conclude that a binding past practice had been established.[76]

Where a union's proposal to appoint stewards in certain work areas was rejected by a federal agency, the actual time spent by local officers and stewards from other departments in representing the employees in the unrepresented work areas was held to be compensable.[77] However, the arbitration costs were not included in the reimbursement.[78]

Conversely, a number of decisions have denied requests to be paid for time spent on at least some aspects of union business.

Thus, an employer did not have to pay its union members for time spent at a ratification meeting despite the fact that a manager had initially offered to pay employees for attending.[79] The labor con-

---

[72]Id. at 919.
[73]Nature's Best, 110 LA 365 (Gentile, 1998).
[74]Morton Salt, 104 LA 444 (Fullmer, 1995).
[75]Id. at 448.
[76]Motor Wheel Corp., 102 LA 922 (Chattman, 1994).
[77]Defense Logistics Agency, 104 LA 439 (Gentile, 1995).
[78]Id. at 443.
[79]Litton Precision Gear, 107 LA 52 (Goldstein, 1996).

tract stated that employees must be paid for "authorized work," but no evidence of relevant bargaining history or past practice was available as an interpretive aid. An arbitrator held that because the employer had no "right to control" the union meeting, the employees' attendance could not be considered "authorized work."[80] The arbitrator considered he lacked the authority to enforce the manager's oral offer to pay because it arose outside the labor contract.[81]

A union representative is not entitled to pay for the time spent in preparing his own grievance. So ruled an arbitrator for the reason that in pursuing his "pro se" grievance, the officer was not acting in a "representative capacity."[82]

The shoe was on the other foot (even though it was found not to fit) when an employer filed a grievance seeking reimbursement from a union for payments made to a union representative in negotiating a union contract covering another bargaining unit. Believing that the service would conflict with his scheduled day shift work hours, the representative had performed his regular work at night and negotiated during the day. The arbitrator held that since the federal agency employer had allowed other employees to work flexible hours for other purposes, the union representative was also entitled to have flexible work hours in order to engage in union activities,[83] and the agency could not restrict the working hours of the representative to the day shift.[84]

Does a union member continue to accumulate seniority while on leave to hold union office? The question arose in the context of a contractual provision stating that seniority of full-time union officers "shall be held as it existed" at the time they take office.[85] Although the arbitrator recognized that the contractual text tended to support the company's position that seniority did not accumulate during the leave, he noted that previous officers who had returned to their jobs continued to accrue seniority during the time they were on leave, and used this "past practice" to interpret the "ambiguous contract language" favorably to the union.[86]

When union leave is unavailable to cover an absence, compensable sick leave may not be resorted to as a subterfuge. An employee who sought to take sick leave to picket on behalf of an affiliated union then on strike was discharged under a contractual "no-strike" clause that prohibited union members from participating in "strikes" and "picketing" or from assisting, encouraging, or participating in any of these actions.[87] Concluding that this provision applied to the

---

[80]Id. at 57.
[81]Id. at 58.
[82]Id. at 145.
[83]Department of Air Force, 107 LA 890 (Harr, 1996).
[84]Id. at 891.
[85]Public Serv. Co. of Oklahoma, 107 LA 1080 (Allen, 1997).
[86]Id. at 1083.
[87]Merck-Medco Rx Servs., 110 LA 782 (Baroni, 1998).

employee's activities, the arbitrator found that the company had just cause for terminating the services of the employee. Although the union president had previously been permitted to utilize union leave for the same purpose, she had not misrepresented her actions or abused sick leave. Her case therefore afforded no exculpatory precedent.[88]

In a case of collateral interest, an arbitrator struck down a state employer's requirement that union staff representatives must give one week's written notice before visiting work areas.[89] The collective bargaining agreement allowed union representatives to visit work areas to the extent the visits did not disrupt work activities. Since the contract did not contain any requirement for giving written advance, the state could not unilaterally impose such a restriction.[90]

Leave for Jury Duty

An employer may require its employees who are called for jury duty to report to work before reporting to court. A labor contract provided that employees assigned to the 6:00 a.m.–2:00 p.m. shift must work the difference between their regular eight hours and the time spent in jury duty.[91] A letter written by a management representative to a union official stated that employees whose shift began prior to the jury reporting time could be required to report for work first.[92] However, an employee selected for jury service had been excused from coming into work prior to reporting to court and had not had her shift changed. When she clocked in after being released by the court, an arbitrator decided that she was entitled to overtime compensation for all work performed after 2:00 p.m. on that day.[93]

In a related scenario an arbitrator held that a collective bargaining agreement that allowed grievances to be filed regarding any "condition of employment" authorized a union to pursue a grievance for the denial of pay to a school employee who took a day off to testify in a trial.[94]

Funeral Leave

One troubling and recurring problem is whether in-laws are covered within the "family" funeral leave provision of a contract. Thus where a collective bargaining agreement provided for leave in the event of a death in the employee's "immediate family" and included within the definition grandparents and in-laws of the "immediate family," such as mothers-in-law, an arbitrator held that the death of a

---

[88]Id. at 789.
[89]State of New Hampshire, 108 LA 209 (McCausland, 1997).
[90]Id. at 211.
[91]Sacramento Transit Dep't, 110 LA 855 (Bogue, 1998).
[92]Id. at 857.
[93]Id. at 858.
[94]Cochraine-Fountain Sch. Dist., 110 LA 324 (Dichter, 1998).

grandparent-in-law had not entitled an employee to the paid funeral leave she had received from her county employer.[95] Nevertheless, the employer's attempt to recover the payments some seven months later was held to be untimely.[96] Fairness required that there be some time limit imposed on the county's right to dock its employees' paycheck to recoup such improvident payments, and seven months was too long.

The definition of "immediate family" in another funeral leave provision included "father, mother, spouse, sister, brother, father-in-law, mother-in-law or child," but did not include a "wife's stepfather."[97] The omission was held to be dispositive of an employee's claim based upon this relationship. Although the employer had previously granted such leave, it did so because the employee had misrepresented the relationship of the deceased, and the prior case could not serve to enlarge the scope of the contractual provision.[98]

When asked to determine whether summer-school bus drivers working pursuant to 9-month contracts were entitled to the same bereavement leave as 12-month employees, an arbitrator held that bereavement leave was available for all employees in the bargaining unit.[99] The contract provision failed to make any distinction between the two groups while other sections of the agreement expressly stated whether or not they were available to 9-month employees. The fact that secretaries, who were also on 9-month contracts, had been denied certain benefits during the summer was not deemed relevant, since secretaries were not included within the same agreement.[100]

Employees who falsely claim bereavement leave and take the time off to attend to other matters are subject to discipline up to and including discharge.

In an analogous case, an employee who had requested personal leave on short notice to attend a funeral but drove a tour bus instead was held to have been appropriately discharged after lying to his employer about his whereabouts.[101] The arbitrator rejected the employee's contention that personal days are a "private matter," such that an employer has no right to inquire into an employee's whereabouts on such days.[102] The employer had an "absolute right" to expect honesty from its employees even in the absence of a specific policy, and the employee's past misconduct obviated progressive discipline.[103]

The assignments of college faculty members typically vary during the week. On days on which there are no scheduled class hours, they are usually not required to report to work. A question arose as to

---

[95]National Uniform Serv., 104 LA 982 (Fullmer, 1995).
[96]Id. at 985.
[97]Northville Public Schs., 104 LA 801 (Daniel, 1995).
[98]Id. at 802.
[99]Cahokia School Dist. #187, 106 LA 667 (Marino, 1996).
[100]Id. at 670.
[101]Meijer Inc., 108 LA 631 (Daniel, 1997).
[102]Id. at 636.
[103]Id. at 635.

whether a teacher who had been absent from work for an entire week
was properly charged for a day of funeral leave when she attended
the funeral of her father, which fell on a day on which she had no
scheduled hours.[104] An arbitrator took cognizance of an established
policy that deemed an employee to be "absent," even if she was not
scheduled to teach, if that day fell between two or more days when
she was unable to meet her scheduled classes. Relying on the parties'
understanding of the definition of a "day" and a "week," as those terms
appeared in the labor contract, the arbitrator found that the employer's
assessment of the leave was appropriate.[105]

Leave for "Personal Business"

Does an employee qualify for personal leave if he is incarcer-
ated? Under a contract provision allowing personal leave for "unusual
and compelling reasons" arbitrators came to opposite conclusions. An
earlier decision had ordered the company to grant leave to an employee who had been sentenced to jail for second-degree sexual assault. There the arbitrator found the absence had not caused the company any great inconvenience, the offense seemed to be wholly unrelated to the employee's work in the plant, and the employee had a
14-year record of unblemished service. But, in the later case, the arbitrator held that the company had discretion to deny personal leave
for an employee to serve a 14-month federal prison term for possession and intent to distribute marijuana.[106] The contract stated that
an employee using an unauthorized drug "on or off the company premises" would be subject to immediate discharge.[107] Further, this employee had less than three years' seniority, and a record of unexcused
absences and was working in a plant with a history of drug-related
offenses.

Where a collective bargaining agreement provided that personal
leave is not to be "unreasonably withheld," an arbitrator upheld a
city's denial of the request of an officer to use one day during his
vacation period as a "personal day" instead of a "vacation day" in
order to chaperone his child's class trip.[108] Although the arbitrator
found that chaperoning a class trip would ordinarily be an appropriate reason for the grant of a personal day, the agreement also deferred the use of personal leave to the use of the "most appropriate"
leave.[109] Because the request for a personal day came during the time
the officer was on vacation, the day was more properly characterized
as a vacation day.[110]

[104]Jefferson Community College, 107 LA 1166 (Franckiewicz, 1997).
[105]Id. at 1171.
[106]Dunlop Tire Corp., 106 LA 84 (Teple, 1995).
[107]Id. at 88.
[108]City of Sandusky, 104 LA 897 (Keenan, 1995).
[109]Id. at 900.
[110]Id. at 901.

When requests for personal leave were not usually granted, the union grieved and requested that a total of 10 percent of the workforce be allowed at any one time to use personal leave.[111] Agreeing with the union that time off was not readily available when requested, the arbitrator fashioned a remedy that set the number of employees per shift who could take personal leave but correspondingly limited the number from each classification who could be absent at the same time.[112]

A contract provided that employees with "perfect attendance" during a three-month period were to be awarded an extra "personal day" off. An employee who had been on leave of absence for three weeks but who otherwise had worked all of his scheduled shifts was denied the award. Despite a contract provision stating that days-off work while on approved leaves of absence would not be counted against an employee for attendance control purposes, an arbitrator refused to extend this treatment to the provision for an extra personal day.[113] He concluded that allowing the personal day would undermine the purpose of the perfect attendance provision.[114]

There may be occasions when an employer may not sanction an employee for absences even when an employee has not applied for leave. Thus, a 17-year employee with a good work record who had been discharged because she was absent from work for eight consecutive workdays without reporting off was awarded reinstatement because she was hiding from her husband, who had threatened her.[115] The employer had sent a warning letter to her home but did not require that she sign for it; thus, the employee never knew her employer was attempting to contact her or that her job was in jeopardy. Because the spousal abuse claimed by the employee was a compelling personal reason for granting a leave of absence at the time the employee left work, her failure to notify the company did not justify the discharge.[116]

An employer violated a collective bargaining agreement by forcing leave without pay on employees who were temporarily unable to work because of a non-work-related injury and who, although they had exhausted sick leave entitlements, did have unused annual leave.[117] The company was required to notify the employees that they could use their then accrued and available annual leave.[118]

One arbitrator has held that if an employee's job performance is adversely affected by his employer's refusal to grant a leave of absence, the performance lapses will not justify the employee's discharge.

---

[111]Wooster City Bd. of Educ., 108 LA 501 (Feldman, 1997).
[112]Id. at 505.
[113]Manor West Retirement Ctr., 106 LA 764 (Cohen, 1996).
[114]Id. at 766.
[115]Smith Fiberglass Prods., 108 LA 225 (Allen, 1997).
[116]Id. at 229.
[117]Johnson Controls World Servs., 104 LA 336 (Goodstein, 1995).
[118]Id. at 343.

Thus, a quality-control technician, discharged for failure to properly inspect carton seals, was reinstated where the employer's denial of a leave of absence created anxiety in the employee and contributed, in part, to his mistakes.[119] The employee had requested a leave of absence to be with his wife, who required surgery after a miscarriage. However, the employee had been previously disciplined for failure to report quality-control problems, and the arbitrator concluded that the employee was also at fault. Consequently, his reinstatement was without backpay.[120]

What happens when an employee whose request for a leave of absence has been granted changes her mind and wants to continue to work? In a case where the labor agreement was silent as to a professional musician employee's right to seek rescission of an administrative leave after it had been granted, an arbitrator held that the employer had discretion to grant or refuse an employee's request to cancel the leave.[121] The arbitrator also ruled that in the absence of any specific contractual entitlement, the employee was not entitled to be placed on the orchestra's substitute list for recall to work during the term of her administrative leave.[122]

Family and Medical Leave Act (FMLA) [New Topic]

The Family and Medical Leave Act[123] provides that collective bargaining agreements that allow greater benefits to employees than those available under the FMLA are to be given effect. Thus, where a contract permitted leaves for good cause without length-of-service requirements, the FMLA's one-year minimum was not controlling.[124]

FMLA leave is not available for an employee to care for a live-in companion, since the Act does not treat such a "significant other" as a spousal equivalent. Specific mutual obligations arise from the marital relationship that are notably absent from mere cohabitation.[125]

Furthermore, the FMLA does not preclude termination of an employee for failure to comply with contractual medical leave requirements. When an employee on FMLA leave does not return to work when scheduled and does not provide timely responses to requests for further information, the employee may be discharged.[126]

On the other hand, an employer violated the FMLA by discharging an employee who did not return to work upon expiration of the

---

[119]Dial Corp., 107 LA 879 (Robinson, 1997).
[120]Id. at 882.
[121]Pacific Symphony Ass'n, 108 LA 85 (Gentile, 1997).
[122]Id. at 89.
[123]29 U.S.C. §§2611 et seq.
[124]Enesco Corp., 107 LA 513 (Berman, 1996).
[125]Morgan Foods, Inc., 106 LA 833, 836 (Goldman, 1996).
[126]Big River Zinc Corp., 108 LA 692, 698 (Draznin, 1997).

leave, because it failed to properly notify her that her leave time was being charged as FMLA.[127]

The accurate calculation of FMLA leave utilization becomes particularly important in cases where an employee who has apparently exhausted FMLA leave entitlements faces termination under an employer's "no-fault" attendance policy. In one decision where the union belatedly questioned the company's accounting of FMLA time, an arbitrator held that the union had the burden of proving error and the company was not required to prove that the termination was proper.[128]

"Moonlighting" and Outside Business Interest

Many collective bargaining agreements contain provisions prohibiting employees from engaging in outside employment with business "in competition" with their primary employers. Arbitrators consistently have held that such competition must be "more than minimal." One arbitrator observed that "per se rules are to be avoided" in favor of a "rule of reason" that examines the particularized facts of the case.[129] Applying that reasoning, where a reporter for a newspaper wrote articles for a monthly magazine, the arbitrator held that the two employers were not "in competition" because they had different markets, different topical coverage areas, and different advertisers.[130] Conversely, a data systems analyst was held to have been properly discharged where he was also working for his wife's computer company, which was involved in the same areas of business as his primary employer, and the primary employer's investigation revealed that the employee had been performing services for his wife's company during his work hours for the primary employer.[131]

Incompatibility of dual employment may arise from circumstances other than the existence of economic competition between a primary and a secondary employer. Discharges of lawyers[132] and paralegals[133] employed by legal aid organizations have been upheld where their secondary employment violated their organization's charter and jeopardized the status of the legal services program. Of course, an ownership interest as well as an employment status can give rise to a prohibited conflict of interest. Thus, bank examiners may be prohibited from purchasing stock in banks over which their employer agency had regulatory authority.[134]

---

[127]Apcoa, Inc., 107 LA 705 (Daniel, 1996).
[128]General Mills, Inc., 107 LA 472 (Feldman, 1996).
[129]Copley Newspapers, 107 LA 310, 313–14 (Stallworth, 1996).
[130]Id. at 314–16.
[131]Michigan Employment Sec. Agency, 109 LA 178, 183–84 (Brodsky, 1997).
[132]UAW Legal Servs. Plan, 104 LA 312, 321–22 (Imundo, 1995).
[133]Texas Rural Legal Aid, 108 LA 411, 415 (Bankston, 1997).
[134]FDIC, Chicago Region, 104 LA 277, 281 (McGury, 1995).

Arbitrators are divided as to whether an actionable conflict of interest exists where an employee's spouse or other close relative is employed in a competing or potentially competitive business. One arbitrator upheld a telecommunications company's requirement that an employee's wife discontinue her affiliation with Amway or face discharge because Amway also sold telephone equipment.[135] The arbitrator noted that the employee himself occasionally sold telephone equipment, and although his wife did not herself sell telecommunication supplies for Amway, the distributors, for whose sales the wife was accountable, might do so.[136] However, in another case, an arbitrator refused to sustain the discharge of an employee whose father worked for the company's prime competitor even though the company was concerned that the employee might disclose a newly developed secret process to his father.[137] The employee did not work directly with the secret process, had not done anything that would indicate a lack of loyalty to the company, and saw his father infrequently, and the company had not attempted to implement a less severe option than discharge, such as requiring the employee to execute a nondisclosure agreement.[138]

Arbitrators continue to uphold discipline up to and including discharge for employees who take time off from work for the purpose of working a second job, but who misrepresent the reason for the leave to their primary employer. An arbitrator found that the company had just cause to discharge an employee who requested personal leave to attend a funeral but who instead drove a tour bus for his second employer and then lied about his whereabouts when questioned later about the matter.[139] Further, an employee who had been granted extended sick leave for a supposed parasitic intestinal infection was found to have been properly discharged where he gained weight during the leave and was regularly seen at the site of a family business.[140] On the other hand, another arbitrator refused to uphold the discharge of an employee who was on leave to attend college courses where the employee worked in an unpaid capacity for the family business while attending the courses.[141]

Personal Appearance: Hair and Clothes

Although arbitrators continue to find that employers are entitled to implement reasonable grooming rules, the application of those rules

---

[135]Southwestern Bell Tel. Co., 107 LA 662, 667–68 (Heinsz, 1996).
[136]Id. at 668.
[137]Chrome Deposit Corp., 102 LA 733, 736 (Bethel, 1994).
[138]Id. at 735–36.
[139]Meijer, Inc., 108 LA 631, 635–36 (Daniel, 1997). See also topic "Funeral Leave," *supra* this chapter.
[140]Cincinnati Mine Mach. Co., 106 LA 284, 287–88 (Heekin, 1996).
[141]Flamingo Hilton Hotel/Casino, 104 LA 673, 674 (Draznin, 1995).

to ban the wearing of certain articles of clothing[142] may be successfully contested, particularly if the rules are not consistently enforced.
In a case involving an employee who wore a shirt at work from the
"Hooters" restaurant chain, the arbitrator found that the shirt was
"indecent" within the common meaning of the word and the wearing
of it violated the prohibition contained in the company's dress code.[143]
Nevertheless, the arbitrator set aside the discipline because the employee had worn the shirt on prior occasions without incident, and other
employees had worn, or brought, vulgar and sexually explicit clothes
and items into the workplace without having been disciplined.[144]

Employees often attempt to justify their failure to observe their
employer's grooming rules on the ground of religious requirement or
cultural expression.[145] One arbitrator found discharge of an employee
inappropriate where the employee had refused an order to tuck in his
shirt on the ground that his Muslim faith prohibited obedience with
this requirement of his employer's dress code. The arbitrator concluded that the employee should have first been allowed an opportunity to prove his contention.[146] On the other hand, a Hispanic employee who had contact with the public and who wore a nose ring
contrary to the employer's regulations was found to have been appropriately disciplined despite her contention that the wearing of the
nose ring was part of her "cultural heritage."[147] The arbitrator, following a Ninth Circuit Court of Appeals decision[148] observed that it is
axiomatic that an employee must often sacrifice individual self-ex-
pression during working hours. There is nothing in Title VII that
requires a private employer to allow employees to express their cultural identity.[149]

An employer has the right to order an employee to discontinue
wearing attire that might give offense not only to its customers but
also to coworkers and might cause disruption of the work environment. For example, where a Hispanic employee wore a West African
head scarf to work, and numerous African-American employees complained that the employee's attire was disrespectful, the arbitrator
ruled that the company had "not only a right but an obligation" to
instruct the employee to remove the scarf.[150]

---

[142]Bethlehem-Center School Dist., 105 LA 285, 288 (Talarico, 1995) (both the banning of specific apparel and the application of a subjective standard such as "professional attire" raise grievable issues).
[143]Clarion Sintered Metals, Inc., 110 LA 770, 773–74 (Cohen, 1998).
[144]Id. at 776.
[145]As noted in the Main Volume, an in-depth treatment of federal and state constitutional and statutory protection against discrimination in employment is beyond the
scope of this volume. See, however, topic "Accommodation of Employee Religious Beliefs," *infra* this chapter.
[146]Liberty Med. Ctr., Inc., 109 LA 609, 614 (Harkless, 1997).
[147]Motion Picture & Television Fund, 103 LA 988, 992 (Gentile, 1994).
[148]Garcia v. Spun Steak Co., 998 F.2d 1480, 62 FEP Cases 525 (9th Cir. 1993).
[149]Id. at 992.
[150]USCP-WESCO, Inc., 109 LA 225, 229 (Grabuski, 1997) (however, discharge for
refusing to remove the scarf was held to be too severe, and the employee was reinstated
without backpay).

Although dress codes may not interfere with employees' §7 rights under the National Labor Relations Act to wear clothing proclaiming support of a union, one arbitrator decided that the employer "can restrict 'T' shirts, buttons, and other 'solidarity' messages that genuinely disrupt its business and its authority to manage."[151] In such cases, the needs of the company and the employee must be balanced. Complete prohibitions on pro-union attire cannot be enforced when options providing reasonable accommodation of the employees' §7 rights are available. Thus, where a company demonstrates special needs, such as when customers are inspecting the facility and might be hesitant to do business with a company whose employees appear disaffected, a reasonable accommodation could include having employees bring in clothes to cover up pro-union attire when customers tour the workplace.[152]

Regardless of whether a work rule banning pro-union attire is ultimately deemed arbitrary or in conflict with labor legislation, employees who engage in self-help rather than complying with work orders and then grieving are not likely to be rewarded.[153]

Divergent male and female grooming standards continue to be challenged. For example, a male airline steward with long hair grieved his employer's short-hair requirement, claiming sex discrimination since females were not subject to the same restrictions. The arbitrator denied the grievance, concluding that the airline was not arbitrary, capricious, or inconsistent in establishing different grooming standards for the two sexes.[154]

The Employer's "Image"

An employer's requirement that employees who interact with the public conform to reasonable, albeit special, grooming rules is typically upheld by arbitrators. As noted in the Main Volume, the decisive issue is whether the employee has contact with the public. An arbitrator upheld a company's work rule requiring short hair for its truck drivers who had client contact, despite the fact that there was no such rule for warehouse employees who did not have such interaction.[155] Similarly, a male airline steward who came into contact with the public could be required to keep his long hair tucked under his cap so as to maintain the employer's image.[156]

---

[151]Reed Mfg. Co., 102 LA 1, 6 (Dworkin, 1993).
[152]Id. at 7–8.
[153]Park Mansions, Inc., 105 LA 849, 852 (Duff, 1995); USCP-WESCO, 109 LA 225, 230 (Grabuski, 1997).
[154]Southwest Airlines, 107 LA 270, 275 (Jennings, 1996) (see also topic "The Employer's Image," infra this chapter).
[155]Albertsons, Inc., 102 LA 641, 644–45 (Darrow, 1994).
[156]Southwest Airlines, 107 LA 270, 274–75 (Jennings, 1996) (quoting Elkouri & Elkouri, How Arbitration Works 765–66 (1985)).

Safety and Health Considerations

Health and safety concerns with respect to personal appearance standards have been raised infrequently since publication of the Main Volume.

Two decisions came to different conclusions about employer "no-beards" policies. In one case, employees who were engaged in the production of chemicals were sometimes required to use respirators. The employer adopted a no-beards policy in order to ensure improved respiratory protection based on its belief that the applicable OSHA regulations required such a policy. After concluding that he was capable of interpreting statutory law to the extent that it was relevant to the issues presented in the arbitration, the arbitrator found that the company was correct and denied the grievance.[157]

A second decision dealt with a company's prohibition against the wearing of beards in its dairy plant. The no-beards policy had been adopted after an outbreak of food poisoning associated with the consumption of pasteurized milk products processed by another dairy. An arbitrator found the rule unreasonable since beards had not been prohibited by any governmental regulation, the industry had not adopted or sponsored a uniform beard ban practice, and there was no problem within the plant creating the need for such a policy. Further, the company allowed mustaches of any length and had failed to show that alternatives, such as beard covers, were unworkable. The arbitrator stressed that the policy invaded the private life of employees by regulating their off-duty appearance.[158]

Accommodation of Employee Religious Beliefs

Arbitrators generally require proof that an employee's request for special accommodation is based upon an obligation imposed by the employee's religion. Thus, the grievance of an employee who had been discharged for living in her husband's residence outside the city limits in violation of a city college's stated policy was denied because the employee had presented no evidence that her religion required her to cohabit with her husband.[159]

Assuming the validity of the claimed religious requirement, employers are not bound to accept the employee's choice of accommodation.[160]

---

[157]Dyno Nobel, Inc., 104 LA 376 (Hilgert, 1995).
[158]Fairmont-Zarda Dairy, 106 LA 583 (Rohlik, 1995).
[159]City Colleges, 104 LA 86 (Eagle, 1995).
[160]Rodriguez v. City of Chicago, 156 F.3d 771 (7th Cir. 1998) (police department's offer to allow officer to transfer to precinct that did not contain an abortion clinic was a reasonable accommodation despite the fact that the officer preferred to stay in the same precinct and be permanently exempted from guarding an abortion clinic).

The opinions issued by the United States Supreme Court in *Trans World Airlines, Inc. v. Hardison*[161] and *Ansonia Board of Education v. Philbrook*[162] continue to provide definitive guidance as to whether an employer has made a reasonable accommodation. In applying the standards announced by the Supreme Court, the federal courts focus on whether the employment practice at issue is "neutral"[163] and whether an accommodation would require a breach of a collective bargaining agreement or otherwise impose an undue hardship on the employer.[164]

Arbitration decisions have, to a large extent, followed the lead of the federal decisions. In one case, a Seventh Day Adventist, who was discharged for refusing to work a Saturday schedule, sought to have her termination set aside on the ground that her religion precluded her from working on Saturdays. Citing *Hardison* in support of a decision that Title VII does not require the company to violate its collective bargaining agreement in order to accommodate the religious beliefs of its employees,[165] an arbitrator upheld the discharge.

In another decision, an arbitrator found that Title VII does not require an employer to permit an employee to use paid leave in order to observe religious holidays. However, the arbitrator went on to find that the grievant was entitled to two days' paid leave under the collective bargaining agreement.[166]

If an employer does offer a religious accommodation that discriminates against other employees, it will be invalidated. Thus, after noting that the Supreme Court had indicated in *Hardison* that a neutral seniority system could not constitute an unlawful employment practice even if the system produced discriminatory effects, one arbitrator held that an employer had violated the collective bargaining agreement by excusing an employee from a Sunday work requirement.[167]

The reasonableness of an offered accommodation is often at issue. By way of illustration, an employer's proposal to allow a worker to become a part-time employee and work a split shift was reasonable under *Hardison* despite the fact that the worker did not wish to be classified as a part-time employee.[168]

---

[161]97 S. Ct. 2263, 14 FEP Cases 1697 (1977).

[162]107 S. Ct. 367, 42 FEP Cases 359 (1986).

[163]Beadle v. Hillsborough County Sheriff's Dep't, 29 F.3d 589, 65 FEP Cases 1069 (11th Cir., 1994) (employer offered reasonable accommodation for employee disadvantaged by neutral shift rotation system when it offered to allow him to swap shifts with other employees and to provide him with an employee roster).

[164]Lee v. ABF Freight Sys., Inc., 22 F.3d 1019, 64 FEP Cases 896 (10th Cir., 1994) (adjustment in call-in procedure would violate collective bargaining agreement and thus constituted an undue hardship); Brown v. Polk County, Iowa, 101 F.3d 1012 (8th Cir. 1995) (employer not required to allow employee to print Bible notes on employer's word processor on ground of undue hardship).

[165]Moonlight Mushrooms, Inc., 101 LA 421 (Dean, 1993).

[166]Vicksburg Community Schs., 101 LA 771 (Daniel, 1993).

[167]Cleveland Pub. Library, 105 LA 781 (Smith, 1995).

[168]United Parcel Serv., 103 LA 1143 (Winograd, 1994).

A special problem arises when an employee is asked to perform work offensive to his religion beliefs. An employer was deemed to have failed to reasonably accommodate an employee's religious beliefs under Title VII by requiring the objecting employee to erect a Christmas tree despite the fact that other employees could have been used to complete the task at the same cost.[169]

Where no accommodation is available that would prevent undue hardship on an employer's business, the employer is not required to compromise its ability to get work done. Thus, an employer may not be compelled to obtain replacements at premium rates in order to accommodate an employee who wanted Sundays off for religious reasons.[170]

One emerging issue is whether the employer is subject to liability for failure to prevent supervisors or coworkers from harassing an employee because of his religious beliefs. In one arbitration, the grievant, a born-again Christian, had been exposed to scatological language regularly uttered by a coworker. Although he was especially sensitive to this foul language, he had not been singled out because of his religion, since the entire work force had been similarly targeted.[171]

Protection Against Sexual Harassment

In the context of a suit alleging male-upon-male sexual harassment, *Oncale v. Sundowner Offshore Services Inc.*,[172] a unanimous Supreme Court defined the elements that, under an objective "reasonable person" standard,[173] make up a hostile work environment. The Court also made clear that Title VII is not a general civility code that seeks to regulate genuine, but innocuous, differences in the ways men and women routinely interact with members of the same sex and of the opposite sex. It forbids only behavior so objectively offensive as to alter the conditions of the victim's employment. "Conduct that is not severe or pervasive enough to create an objectively hostile or abusive work environment—an environment that a reasonable person would find hostile or abusive—is beyond Title VII's purview."[174]

The opinion proceeded to caution that courts and juries should not mistake ordinary socializing in the workplace, such as male-on-male horseplay or intersexual flirtation, for discriminatory "conditions of employment." The court cited the following example: "A

---

[169]Clallam County Pub. Hosp., 105 LA 609 (Calhoun, 1995).

[170]Goodyear Tire & Rubber Co., 107 LA 193 (Sergent, 1996). Also see United Parcel Serv., 103 LA 1143 (Winograd, 1994).

[171]Champion Int'l Corp., 105 LA 429 (Fullmer, 1995).

[172]118 S. Ct. 998 (1998). Preceding the *Oncale* decision, Arbitrator David T. Borland held that male-on-male horseplay with sexual undertones violated the company's sexual harassment program; Coca Cola Bottling Co., 106 LA 776 (Borland, 1996). See topic "Same-Sex Harassment."

[173]118 S. Ct. at 1003 (the behavior is to be "judged from the perspective of a reasonable person in the plaintiff's position, considering all the circumstances").

[174]Id. at 1002–03.

professional football player's working environment is not severely or pervasively abusive, for example, if the coach smacks him on the buttocks as he heads onto the field—even if the same behavior would reasonably be experienced as abusive by the coach's secretary (male or female) back at the office."[175] "The conduct," the Court continued, must be viewed not in a vacuum, but within "a constellation of surrounding circumstances, expectations, and relationships which are not fully captured by a simple recitation of the words used or the physical acts performed."

Further, as one arbitrator has trenchantly observed, it should be borne in mind that "sexual jokes, posters, propositions and the like that were loosely tolerated as the workplace norm twenty years ago are unacceptable and illegal today."[176]

The line between acceptable conduct and unacceptable sexual harassment can be a very fine one. Employees spend a great deal of their daily time in the company of other employees. It is inevitable that propinquity between employees can lead to the development of various types of social relationships. How one manifests inappropriate conduct, considering such a relationship, is not subject to easy definition.

One arbitrator attempted the line-drawing task by establishing some specific rules: "It is friendly to tell a co-worker that she looks particularly pretty this morning. It is unacceptable to tell a co-worker who is not a personal friend that you are attracted to her. It is unavoidable and healthy that one's eyes should be drawn to a sexually attractive person. It is unacceptable to deliberately stare to the point which the other persons feels uncomfortable."[177]

When one party to a relationship ends that relationship, sexually oriented conduct that had been consensual in the past is no longer consensual, and, if continued over objection, may constitute sexual harassment.[178]

But not all harassment of an employee of the opposite sex constitutes "sexual harassment." In one case following the break-up of a consensual social relationship, the rejected employee made a series of "hang-up" phone calls to the rejecting employee. The arbitrator refused to uphold a charge of sexual harassment.[179]

After another such break-up, a female employee became uncomfortable working with her former boyfriend, and the company determined that they could no longer work together. Both were said to have been at fault for the deterioration of requisite workplace civility and cooperation. The female employee was removed from her classification and shift with adverse financial consequences. The union complained that even if the company was correct, it acted improperly,

---

[175]Id.
[176]International Mill Serv., 104 LA 779, 782 (Marino, 1995).
[177]Norfolk Naval Shipyard, 104 LA 991, 992 (Bernhardt, 1995).
[178]Hughes Family Markets, 107 LA 331 (Prayzich, 1996).
[179]City of Austin, Minn., 95-1 ARB para. 5082 (Fogelberg, 1994).

since, if there was equal fault, there should have been equal treatment. The company replied that, as a matter of past practice, it had handled shift and classification removals based on seniority and pointed out that the female worker was the junior of the two employees.

The arbitrator found the agreement could not be interpreted to allow removal of the complainant and that the past practice was inapplicable since the prior transfers were not occasioned by charges of sexual harassment. Accordingly, the grievant was ordered reinstated to her former shift and classification.[180] The arbitrator observed: "Whether sexual harassment complaints have merit or not, it is important that the complainant be protected from retaliation. Otherwise legitimate complaints will remain buried because the complainants will be afraid to come forward. Also, rightly or wrongly, there is a perception in some circles that women are frequently penalized for making complaints of sexual harassment."

Prior to the reasonable-person standard announced by the Supreme Court in *Oncale* to measure whether workplace behavior created a hostile work environment, a diversity of standards had been fashioned by arbitrators and the courts to determine whether contested conduct amounted to sexual harassment. Many arbitrators endorsed the Ninth Circuit's "reasonable woman" test set forth in *Ellison v. Brady*.[181] Others adopted a subjective criterion such as the "most sensitive woman." These decisions should now be reassessed in light of the *Oncale* opinion.

Those arbitrators who have endorsed the *Ellison* rationale have emphasized that the test "what is offensive to the reasonable woman" is appropriate because men and women perceive shop talk differently.[182] In one such case, after investigating a noninvolved employee's tip, a company discharged a male Spanish-speaking, newly hired employee for making lewd remarks about female coworkers' body parts and inquiring about their sexual activities. However, he had gone out of his way to be helpful to these employees by carrying heavy boxes for them, and several of the women claimed not to be offended by his behavior.

Adopting the reasonable-woman standard because the sex-blind reasonable-person standard tends to be male-biased, the arbitrator selected one of the female witnesses who he concluded was a "reasonable target" of such conduct as the most credible.[183] The arbitrator

---

[180]Champion International Corp., 105 LA 429, 434 (Fullmer, 1995).

[181]974 F.2d 812, 55 FEP Cases 111 (9th Cir., 1991).

[182]"Sexual harassment issues often turn on the context of words and conduct. The same words and conduct that can be perceived as innocent and friendly in one context, can be perceived as predatory and threatening in another, and of course, this often occurs in 'shop talk' cases and in cases of insubordination. It must be understood that men and women are socialized differently. They use language differently, interpret verbal and physical symbols differently, and use and respond to humor differently." International Mill Serv., 104 LA 779, 781–82 (Marino, 1995).

[183]TJ Maxx, 107 LA 78 (Richman, 1996) (summarizing workplace conduct and appropriate discipline).

opined that the allegations of sexual harassment were to be judged from the perspective of this asserted victim. Since this reasonable target had failed to report the employee and testified that she did not feel the grievant "had crossed the line," and considering the grievant's overall helpful behavior to female employees, the arbitrator ordered the grievant to be reinstated, but without backpay.[184]

Some arbitrators look to the other end of the spectrum and base their determination whether an employee had engaged in sexual harassment upon the reactions of the most sensitive of the affected employees. Thus, in one situation a male employee told "dirty" sexual jokes, showed sexually suggestive cartoons, and simulated a penis with a broom handle to other male employees. Most employees, including female employees, did not find this conduct offensive, but two young women found his actions shocking. Applying a "sexual harassment is in the eyes of the beholder standard," the arbitrator condemned the conduct.[185]

However, often the conduct that was found to have constituted sexual harassment under one standard would be condemned under any standard.[186] Thus, one arbitrator rejected the defense of a disciplined employee that he did not know that his behavior was actionable, ruling that the grievant should have known.[187] Sexually offensive conduct can be so egregious that arbitrators uphold the sanction without specifying either the standard of review or the burden of proof.[188]

In reviewing whether the degree of discipline imposed under the "just cause" standard is excessive, some arbitrators compare sexual harassment with criminal offenses, noting that such behavior should be considered in the nature of a misdemeanor rather than a felony.[189]

---

[184]Id. at 83.

[185]Safeway Stores, 108 LA 787 (Witney, 1997). It is of interest that, following grievant's discharge, 23 employees wrote letters of protest to the employer, 17 of those employees being female. It was conceded that grievant had not solicited the letters.

[186]In International Mill Serv., 104 LA 779 (Marino, 1995), the arbitrator upheld the discipline of a male employee who had repeatedly asked the female victim to go to bed with him, promised her a good time if she slept with him, asked her to take off her clothes and roll around on the floor with him, and touched her legs and buttocks with his hands, books, and pieces of construction material. Although this conduct was judged under the "reasonable woman" standard, the conduct would likely be found sanctionable under the "reasonable person" test).

[187]Potlatch Corp., 104 LA 691 (Moore, 1995).

[188]AMG Indus. Inc., 106 LA 322 (Donnelly, 1996) (after an argument between two employees, a male employee turned on the plant intercom system and directed a message to the victim—"suck me!"; International Extrusion Corp., 106 LA 371 (Brisco, 1996) (grievant told a female coworker that she had such a nice buttocks she should give some to other female employees who did not have enough, and he found her so exciting that he had to go to the bathroom to masturbate); Simkins Indus., Inc., 106 LA 551 (Fullmer, 1996) (grievant's conduct included patting female employee on the buttocks while saying "I need a good dirty woman for Saturday night—I'd pay ten dollars for it," making tongue displays, thrusting hips, looking down her shirt, rubbing his fingers up her back, and words and actions of similar nature).

[189]Safeway Inc., 109 LA 769 (DiFalco, 1997) (sexual harassment is not as serious misconduct as workplace violence or theft and a "zero tolerance program" does not

Should employers be held to a higher burden of proof when an employee is discharged on charges of sexual harassment because of the moral turpitude connotations and social stigma likely to attach to the offense? One decision concluded that the standard "preponderance of the evidence" test should apply.[190]

The scope of an anti-sexual harassment policy may go beyond protection of employees and reach inappropriate sexual conduct by an employee to a customer.[191]

Harassment in Schools: Teachers and Students [New Topic]

Because teachers are in an authority position with respect to their students, charges of sexual harassment of juveniles typically result in high-profile publicity. However, even if the evidence confirms that the complained-of conduct actually occurred, it may not constitute "sexual harassment."[192] For example, a student, citing four incidents, reported that she was being sexually harassed by her teacher. First, in a conversation with the student, the teacher indicated he would assist her if she did something for him. The student asked him what he meant, and he answered, "I don't know, but I'll think of something."[193] Although the teacher stated it was an innocent remark, the student inferred that his comment contained a sexual innuendo. The second episode took place in front of 30 other students and involved the teacher's embracing the student and rubbing her arm. The teacher asserted he did so only to stop the student from braiding another's hair, behavior that the teacher considered inappropriate in the classroom. The third incident consisted of the teacher's grabbing the student's bag after she boarded a city bus. The teacher averred he did so only to get her attention so that he could greet her. In the fourth encounter, the teacher stopped by the student's father's car, in which she was a passenger, and stared inside as they drove away. The teacher maintained that he thought he recognized the passenger as a student and simply wanted to see who it was.

Noting that the incidents in the bus and automobile were devoid of sexual connotations, the arbitrator concluded that sexual harassment requires more than feeling "uncomfortable" in encounters with a male teacher.[194] Nevertheless, the arbitrator found that the teacher's

---

mandate discharge. "It is generally considered that sexual harassment is a learned behavior of varying degrees of seriousness, and it can be unlearned through the appropriate imposition of sanctions to correct that behavior, at least in most instances." Hence a discharge was reduced to a suspension without pay. For a similar comparison to "major and minor crimes," see Firestone Rubber & Latex Co., 107 LA 276 (Koenig, Jr., 1996).

[190]Superior Coffee & Foods, 103 LA 609 (1994).

[191]United Parcel Serv., Inc., 104 LA 417 (Byars, 1995), employee told dirty jokes and made lewd remarks to customers); Pepsi Cola Bottling Co. of St. Louis, 108 LA 993 (Thornell, 1997) (a customer's employee was sexually harassed by the grievant).

[192]D.C. Public Schools, 105 LA 1037 (Johnson, 1995).

[193]Id. at 1038–39.

[194]Id. at 1040.

initial verbal offer of assistance amounted to an inappropriate double-entendre. Consequently, his discharge was reduced to a suspension.

Under similarly ambiguous circumstances, a teacher who asked a student to get up on her desk and perform in her cheerleading outfit to gain the attention of the class to a subject may have engaged in "advertising through sex appeal," but his conduct, according to an arbitrator, was not necessarily improper. However, he went too far in making comments admittedly containing "sexual innuendos." Nonetheless, citing the absence of an applicable school district policy concerning such behavior, the arbitrator reduced the teacher's disciplinary suspension to a warning.[195]

Same-Sex Harassment [New Topic]

The Supreme Court in *Oncale v. Sundowner Offshore Service, Inc.,*[196] held that "same sex" harassment is a cognizable violation of Title VII. Several arbitrators have similarly viewed such misconduct as embraced within a contractual anti-sexual harassment policy.

In one such case a new employee was pretentiously called into an office, where the door was closed and lights turned off. He was then assaulted by a pair of coworkers who tugged at his shorts and encouraged each other to "get him." The perpetrators were initially discharged, but an arbitrator ordered them reinstated without backpay, finding, as mitigating circumstances, the fact that there was no actual sexual act and no intent to cause physical injury, but only "horseplay," which had been tolerated in the past by management.[197]

Another company's sexual harassment policy stated in part:

> Unwelcome sexual advances, requests for sexual favors, and other physical, verbal, or visual conduct based on sex constitutes sexual harassment when . . . the conduct has the purpose or effect of unreasonably interfering with an individual's work performance or creating an intimidating, hostile, or offensive environment.

Interpreting this policy, an arbitrator found just cause to discharge a gay employee who repeatedly related in explicit detail his sexual experiences to other male employees after being told that his coworkers found his remarks offensive. The arbitrator rejected the grievant's claim that he was being discriminated against on account of his sexual orientation.[198]

Fraternization, Intermarriage of Employees, Employment of Relatives, Married Employees

Fraternization between an employee and his or her supervisor may have a serious adverse effect upon the morale within the

---

[195]Fairfield City Sch. Dist., 107 LA 669 (Duff, 1996).
[196]118 S. Ct. 998 (1998).
[197]Coca-Cola Bottling Co., 106 LA 776 (Borland, 1996).
[198]Hughes Aircraft Co., 102 LA 353 (Bickner, 1993).

workforce if it gives rise to the belief that the employee was being accorded preferential treatment. It also creates a risk that a claim of sexual harassment may be made if the relationship should end. Fraternization that involves a sexual relationship during work hours may afford grounds for discharge.[199]

However, antifraternization work rules may be unenforceable if the subject employees are married. Marital status has been accorded varying degrees of protection by legislation in 31 states.[200] The California statute, for example, places marital status in the same protected category as race, religious creed, color, national origin, ancestry, physical disability, mental disability, medical condition, or gender. However, the statute specifically permits employers to reasonably regulate or preclude the assignment of spouses to the same department, division, or facility for reasons of supervision, safety, security, or morale.[201]

So also, a contractual provision prohibiting discrimination based on marital status was not violated by a school district's failure to coordinate the benefits of a married couple who had chosen the same health insurance plan.[202]

An employer's conflict-of-interest rules may extend beyond the workplace and reach an employee whose spouse is employed by a competitor.[203]

Status of Same-Sex Partner [New Topic]

In the absence of statutory recognition of the status of a same-sex partner, an employer need not extend spousal benefits to the partner. Thus, an employer was held not to have violated the antidiscrimination provisions of the collective bargaining agreement when it refused to extend the employee's health insurance coverage to an employee's same-sex live-in partner.[204]

Privacy, Dignity, and Peace of Mind

Disclosure of Information to Employer

The number of challenges to employers' disclosure rules requiring employees to provide "personal" information remains undimin-

---

[199]Wyndham Franklin Plaza Hotel, 105 LA 186 (Dugg, 1995) (employee and her supervisor locked themselves into the banquet office of the headquarters of a hotel during a business conference and proceeded to engage in passionate sexual congress recorded by security cameras).

[200]*Fair Employment Practice Manual* §451:55 (BNA).

[201]Cal. Gov't Code §12940(A)(3)(A).

[202]Elgin [Ill.] Sch. Dist., 104 LA 405 (Briggs, 1995).

[203]Southwestern Bell. Tel. Co., 107 LA 662 (Heinsz, 1996) (employee's wife sold products in direct competition with her husband's employer's products; husband subject to discharge unless wife divested herself of her dealership). See Topic "Moonlighting and Outside Business Interest," *supra* this chapter.

[204]Kent State Univ., 103 LA 338 (Stasshofer, 1994).

ished. A county employer that had disciplined a corrections officer for failing to disclose plans to marry an inmate in the separate state prison system was held to have violated the officer's privacy rights where the county failed to demonstrate a compelling "need to know" about the marriage.[205]

Privacy issues are also implicated when an employer attempts to obtain information about an employee from outside sources, or to publicly disseminate information about an employee. Public employers, in particular, must be concerned about invading the privacy of their employees because public employees are protected by the Constitution against unreasonable searches and seizures.[206]

Arbitrators typically employ a balancing test that weighs the employee's expectation of privacy against management's need to have the information or to otherwise regulate the employee's behavior. As one arbitrator has observed: "The crucial question often will be whether the interest of the company can be adequately served in a manner that is as noninvasive of an employee's rights as is reasonably possible."[207] For example, a city's policy requiring all employees out of work for more than three months to submit to fingerprinting was found to be unreasonable because the employees had already been fingerprinted when they first began work, and the city could not present a compelling rationale for the refingerprinting.[208] In contrast, an arbitrator found that having a handwriting expert examine samples of employees' writings to determine the author of a sexually harassing job evaluation memorandum outweighed employees' privacy rights.[209] But where an employer did not have a preexisting policy requiring off-duty officers to submit to blood tests after being involved in traffic accidents, an off-duty officer could not be disciplined for refusing to undergo such a test.[210]

In the context of disseminating private information, a federal agency violated a police officer's right to privacy when the police chief, in responding to a citizen complaint against the officer, informed the citizen that action would be taken against the officer.[211]

In two discharge cases involving accusations of falsifying employment applications, arbitrators ordered reinstatement because the grievants reasonably believed their criminal records had been expunged. In the first case, the grievant answered no to the question: "Have you ever been convicted of a crime which has not been expunged or sealed by a court?" After the employee was hired, the employer

---

[205]County of Napa, 102 LA 590, 593–94 (Knowlton, 1994).
[206]See also Privacy Protection Act of 1980, 42 U.S.C. §§2000aa et seq.; Privacy Act of 1974, 5 U.S.C. §§552 et seq.
[207]City of Chicago, 109 LA 360, 368 (Goldstein, 1997) (quoting Goldstein & Kenis, "Spying Eyes: Management Rights Versus Employees' Right of Privacy," Labor Arbitration Conference 1997, 100 (Labor Arbitration Institute, 1997)).
[208]City of Chicago, 109 LA 360, 367 (Goldstein, 1997).
[209]Michigan Dep't of Transp., 104 LA 1196, 1198 (Kelman, 1995).
[210]City of El Paso, 110 LA 411, 415 (Moore, 1998).
[211]VA Medical Center, 103 LA 74, 79 (Gentile, 1994).

discovered that the worker had a lengthy juvenile record, an assault conviction, and a driving-while-intoxicated conviction. The arbitrator found that the grievant reasonably considered his juvenile record to fall within the expungement exception because juvenile records typically are not considered permanent criminal records. His assault conviction was also rightfully omitted in light of a statement submitted by the trial judge negating a criminal record. Finally, although the DWI conviction could not be considered a routine traffic violation, in the past the company had taken inconsistent positions on whether traffic violations had to be mentioned in the employment application.[212]

In a similar case involving a public employee, the grievant was found to have been unjustly terminated for falsifying his employment application because the evidence was not "clear and convincing" that the grievant had intentionally lied in order to mislead.[213]

What happens if a candidate for employment who is awaiting trial on criminal charges answers no to a prior-convictions question on the application form but thereafter, before being hired, pleads guilty to a lesser charge? In one such case an employee, who had been terminated when his conviction was discovered, was reinstated because of the absence of a company rule requiring applicants to update the information on their application forms to the dates of their actual hire.[214]

Observing Employees at Work

The National Labor Relations Board has recently ruled that the installation and use of surveillance cameras in the workplace is a mandatory subject of bargaining, notwithstanding an employer's desire to maintain secrecy in the placement of such cameras in the workplace.[215] Prior to this decision, as stated in the Main Volume, a number of arbitrators had upheld the installation of surveillance equipment if recent thefts or other illegal activity in the workplace demonstrated the need for surveillance.

In an analogous context, the installation of surveillance cameras in the corridors of a high school was held not to have violated the privacy rights of students where the cameras were installed to identify students who were spraying perfumes and other fragrances outside the door of a teacher who had a hypersensitivity to these substances.[216]

In a situation where the installation of surveillance cameras was deemed appropriate, an arbitrator found that the company could impose discipline on an employee whose sexual frolics were caught on

---

[212]Freightliner Corp., 103 LA 123 (Galambos, 1994).
[213]City of Minneapolis, 106 LA 564 (Bard, 1996).
[214]Avis Rent-a-Car System, 107 LA 197 (Shanker, 1996).
[215]Colgate-Palmolive Co., 323 NLRB No. 82, 155 LRRM 1034 (1997).
[216]Culver City School Dist., 110 LA 519, 527 (Hoh, 1997).

videotape, despite the fact that the surveillance cameras were not installed for the purpose of detecting such activity. However, the discharge was overturned because the employer refused to permit the employee to have a union representative present at the investigatory interview.[217]

Inspecting Employee Lockers, Purses, Briefcases, or Automobiles

"Reasonableness," as determined on a case-by-case basis under the factual context and applicable contract provisions, continues to guide arbitral decisions regarding the propriety of employer inspections of employee personal items and lockers. Adequate notice that employees are subject to such inspections and a reasonable basis to conduct an inspection have been consistently found to be necessary conditions.

Thus, where correction officers were required to submit to a search of "their person, or automobile, or place of assignment on government property, when such search is required by the Director or Administrator," an officer who had submitted to a routine search on entering the facility was suspended for refusing to permit a search of a personal bag that he had retrieved from his truck after beginning duty. The questioned search had been ordered first by a security officer, then by the acting shift commander, and eventually by the acting assistant administrator, but not the "Director or Administrator." The discipline was upheld in arbitration because the grievant had engaged in self-help, and especially since security issues were implicated, he should have obeyed the order and grieved later.[218]

Can an employer ever justify a nonconsensual search of an employee's residence? One arbitrator thought so. He upheld the discharge of an employee for theft of company property that had come to light when the employee's ex-spouse, who had control over their residence after the employee had moved out, reported the presence of stolen items to the company and asked the company to remove them.[219]

Searches of employee automobiles brought onto the employer's parking lot or premises have prompted many of the disputes. In one case, trained drug-sniffing dogs had been deployed near the grievant's car and had, according to disputed testimony, signaled the possible presence of drugs in the vehicle. Upon being directed to permit a search of his vehicle on pain of discharge, the grievant consented, and traces of marijuana were found. He was thereafter discharged.

The arbitrator opined that the standard for determining whether a search by a private employer was proper, although not identical to that applicable to governmental searches and seizures under the

---

[217]Wyndham Franklin Plaza Hotel, 105 LA 186, 188 (Duff, 1995).
[218]Department of Corrections, 105 LA 468 (Rogers, 1995).
[219]Exxon Co. U.S.A., 101 LA 777 (Baroni, 1993).

Fourth Amendment, required the private employer to show that it "had reasonable cause to search the Grievant's vehicle and did so in a manner which complied with fundamental fairness."[220] However, although he found the conduct of the search with police dogs to be within the general authority of the employer, there had been insufficient notice of the policy regarding searches of automobiles. Accordingly, the arbitrator directed that the grievant be reinstated with backpay.[221]

Reinstatement without backpay was also directed for an employee who had been discharged for refusing to consent to the search of his vehicle to ascertain whether he had brought a firearm onto the company parking lot.[222] A promulgated company policy gave clear notice that personal property of employees was subject to search, and the company had received an anonymous letter alleging that the grievant and another employee were bringing concealed weapons into the premises in their automobiles. Although the arbitrator found the search order to have been proper and acknowledged that "the carrying of a gun onto facility property is a serious matter," he determined that the penalty of discharge was excessive under the circumstances.[223]

No mitigating circumstances were found in the case of an employee who was discharged following a search of his automobile that disclosed what appeared to be an item of company property in his vehicle.[224] The search was prompted by a tip from a coworker that the grievant was stealing company property, and a subsequent observation revealed the grievant carrying a covered object to his car.

Misuse of Electronic Mail (E-Mail) [New Topic]

A public school librarian received a written reprimand after using school equipment to access an E-mail system to send a critical and sarcastic note to 37 other librarians in her state regarding proposed curriculum and class changes. The note came to the supervising school principal's attention after he received a copy from another principal. The librarian claimed that the message was motivated by her need for assistance, but the principal contended that her "editorializing" was improper. The arbitrator, despite finding that the librarian's tone was inappropriate, concluded that there was no clear-cut or blatant misuse of the E-mail system. Rather, he deemed it a situation where an appropriate utilization was intermixed with improper personal opinion. Because the school district admittedly had no rules or regulations concerning use of its E-mail system, the arbitrator found the employee was not subject to discipline because she

[220]Anheuser-Busch Inc., 107 LA 1183 (Weckstein, 1996).
[221]Id. at 1192.
[222]Folsom Return to Custody, Inc., 101 LA 837 (Staudohar, 1993).
[223]Id. at 843. The grievant was the president of the union and had been engaged in heated labor negotiations with the company representative. The arbitrator opined that even though the offense was serious, the employer had improperly considered his union office as a factor in the termination decision.
[224]Tyson Foods Inc., 105 LA 1119 (Moore, 1996).

could not have known that she did not have the right to use E-mail in a "quasi-personal" manner.[225]

Dangerous Weapons on Company Property

Recognition of an obligation on the part of the employer to provide for the safety of employees continues to influence arbitrators to sustain company rules against bringing firearms and other weapons onto the company premises.

However, arbitrators may overturn or mitigate the severity of penalties imposed if a company has failed to consistently enforce the prohibition. It was for this reason that an employer's failure to consistently enforce a "no weapons rule" resulted in the reinstatement without backpay of a firefighter who not only brought a shotgun into the firehouse in contravention of the rule, but accidentally discharged the gun into the floor while in the firehouse.[226]

Despite written rules against weapons possession, where a company had sent a "mixed message" in applying them, an employee who, following a police search related to a protracted traffic stop commencing on company property, had been discharged for having a loaded handgun in his automobile glove box was reinstated. The grievant had credibly testified that the gun belonged to his wife and he did not know it was there. Moreover, the arbitrator found it significant that the company had been lax in its enforcement to the point of even allowing one supervisor to post a "gun for sale" sign and complete the transaction on the premises. However, since the company had committed itself to eliminating guns from its workplace, the company was entitled to enforce its rule prospectively.[227]

Lax enforcement brought about a similar result in another case where an employee/hunter was found to have been improperly discharged for having an unloaded rifle in this truck. The plant was in an area where hunting was a passion of local residents, including, undoubtedly, the majority of the employees at the plant. There had been no other discharges for unauthorized weapons possession on company property during the previous 20 years, and the arbitrator did not find it believable that no other employee had been found to have a gun or bow and arrow on plant property.[228]

Evidence that a discharged bus driver employee had not intended to bring his pistol with him in his personal bag when he began driv-

[225]Conneaut School Dist., 104 LA 909 (Talarico, 1995).
[226]City of Tarpon Springs, 108 LA 230, 236 (Deem, 1996). ("Under normal circumstances I would find that discharge is a proper disciplinary action for even a first offense [because employers are responsible for the safety of his employees]. However, in this particular case I cannot allow the city to make an example of the grievant when they have not put their house in order as it regards this issue").
[227]Luxfer USA, Ltd., 102 LA 783 (Kaufman, 1994).
[228]USS, A Div. of USX Corp., 106 LA 708 (Neyland, 1996). See also City of Tarpon Springs, 107 LA 230 (Deem, 1996).

ing his route did not constitute sufficient mitigation to persuade an arbitrator to reinstate him where a clear rule prohibiting weapons had been promulgated and the employee had failed to take proper corrective steps upon realizing that he had the firearm with him.[229]

In another case, a company published a new rule extending a prohibition against bringing weapons into the facility to employee automobiles parked on company premises, but it failed to comply with a contractual requirement that proposed rule changes be discussed with the union before being issued. The peremptory issuance of the rule had been motivated by the shooting of two employees by a third employee who had retrieved a gun from his car. An arbitrator held that the rule was enforceable as an emergency measure although it did not comply with the contract.[230]

Company Liability for Employee's Damaged or Stolen Property

In addition to the traditional legal remedies,[231] employer liability for lost, stolen, or damaged property of employees may be implied under a collective bargaining agreement. Although recognizing a past practice pursuant to which the company declined to pay "for missing or lost tools where actual theft has not been established or admitted," a recent decision found liability arising from the company's noncontractual requirement that employees provide their own tools and leave them at the plant.[232] The employer's negligence was manifest where it had discontinued furnishing a caged and locked area for the overnight storage of the employees' tools, and the grievant's tools were stolen from the new, unsecured area the company had provided.

Where, as here, an employer requires employees to furnish and use their own tools in performing their work for the employer, to the benefit

---

[229]Bi-State Development Agency, 104 LA 461 (Bailey, 1995). Other arbitrators, however, have found that an employee's innocence of malice may mitigate the penalty; see, e.g., Interstate Brands Corp., 104 LA 993, 996 (Gentile, 1995) (employee who had brought a gun onto company premises intending to sell it to another employee reinstated because "[t]here is a fine line between poor judgment and the willful and knowing violation of a posted and communicated policy").

[230]Packaging Corp. of America, 106 LA 122, 125–26 (Nicholas, 1996) ("While my findings here uphold Union's argument that it is to be advised and be made a party to discussions on a rule change prior to company taking final action, I am nevertheless convinced that such action was necessary and that Company has established a proper foundation for the use of the rule today").

[231]For example, regulations promulgated under the federal Military Personnel and Civilian Employees' Claims Act of 1964 (31 U.S.C. §§240 et seq.) provide that a covered claim is allowable "only" if (1) the damage or loss was not caused wholly or partly by the negligent or wrongful act of the claimant, claimant's agent, a member of claimant's family, or claimant's private employee (the standard to be applied is that of reasonable care under the circumstances); (2) the possession of the property damaged or lost and the quantity possessed is determined to have been reasonable, useful, or proper under the circumstances; and (3) the claim is substantiated by proper and convincing evidence. See 5 C.F.R. §180.104(a).

[232]Litton Precision Gear, 104 LA 151, 155 (Wolff, 1994) (citing 4th edition of How Arbitration Works).

of the employer, and are required to leave those tools overnight with the employer, again for their mutual benefit, the employer has an implied obligation to provide a safe and secure place for the employees' tools. . . . [I]t is also reasonable to imply as part of that condition of employment, that the Company will be liable if the tools are stolen as the result of its negligence.[233]

In contrast, under the Federal Labor Management Relations Act[234] an arbitrator found that claims for property damage to employees' parked cars were too attenuated to qualify as related to employment. He viewed a grievance seeking such compensation as a tort claim falling outside the scope of the grievance procedure.

Union Bulletin Boards

The express terms of a collective bargaining agreement, sometimes informed by company practice, continue to be dispositive of cases involving disputed union bulletin board postings.

When the agreement prohibited "solicitations," an arbitrator found the union's posting of membership campaign materials entitled "Effects of Being Nonunion" and "Why Join the Union" to be in violation of the contract.[235]

The same result followed where a contract provided for the posting of "official announcements and notices concerning meetings of the union, scheduling and results of election, appointments to office, social, educational and recreational affairs," and the company refused to allow use of the bulletin board to provide information about long-term disability benefits. Since the purpose was not plainly within the scope of that detailed contract clause, the company's exclusion was found proper.[236] But a contrary result was reached in a similar case,[237] where the arbitrator found that the contractual listing of specific topics had been expanded by implication because supervisors allowed an additional category of information, hourly pay schedules of village employees, to remain on the bulletin board for seven months, and had removed the material to copy for their own use and then reposted it.[238]

---

[233]104 LA at 155.
[234]5 U.S.C. §7103.
[235]Leggett & Platt, Inc., 104 LA 1048 (Statham, 1995).
[236]Arcata Graphics/Kingsport, 102 LA 429 (Frost, 1993).
[237]Village of Woodridge, 104 LA 806 (Wolff, 1995).
[238]See also Leggett & Platt Inc., 104 LA 1048 (Stratham, 1995) (company-imposed limitations on postings to the categories provided for in the contract approved, but company directed to develop a procedure to ensure uniform administration of posting requests in light of evidence that the same postings had been treated differently in different company facilities).

Chapter 18

Standards in Arbitration of
Interest Disputes

Prevailing Practice—Industry, Area, Industry-Area

A recent fact-finding report[1] for a unit of police officers contained the following observation concerning the inherent difficulties in making comparative wage rate analyses:

> Both parties submitted lengthy lists of communities deemed comparable. The Fact-Finder observes that, not unexpectedly, the City's nominees tend to include departments offering terms less favorable than those available in Willowick. In contrast, the Union's candidates included, in the main, departments providing benefits more favorable than those available in Willowick.

> The selection of representative communities is not easily made.

> This Fact-Finder believes that ideally comparable communities ought to be located nearby in the same labor market . . . be of similar territorial size and population density, draw upon similar resources and tax bases, have a similar mix of commercial, industrial and residential properties with similar need for police protection, and maintain similarly sized Police Departments.

> Unfortunately, developing a list of comparable communities which meets all of these criteria is seldom possible, and the selection process is further complicated because information relevant to disputed issues may not necessarily be available from a community which does meet the criteria.

"Precedent" may be accorded arbitral *stare decisis* treatment and found to be the determinative factor in the selection of an appropriate comparability group. In an arbitration regarding a successor agreement between a police officers' association and the city of Waterville,[2]

---

[1]City of Willowick, 110 LA 1146 (Ruben, 1997).
[2]City of Waterville, 107 LA 1194 (Dichter, 1996).

each party presented a list of municipalities deemed comparable. The cities proposed by the association all had industrial tax revenue bases, while Waterville was a "bedroom community." The association's list had, however, been utilized in a prior wage award. In the successor award the arbitrator noted that the same arguments as to which list was more appropriate had previously been made and considered, and since the budgets of the association-sponsored cities had remained in line with the budget of Waterville and there had been no change in any other material factor, there was no reason to deviate from precedent.

Differentials and the "Minor" Standards

"Internal" comparables may prove more compelling than "external" in a wage increase arbitration when "hazardous duty" is a factor to be considered. Such was the case when the city of Madison firefighters assigned to a hazardous waste emergency response team asked for a premium of 3 percent of their base hourly wage rates.[3] In support of its final offer the city had urged the arbitrator to compare the wages of its firefighters with those of public employees performing the same services in comparable communities throughout the state. But the arbitrator considered "internal" considerations addressed by the union to be more compelling. These included the city's history of offering similar percentage-based pay to its other emergency workers, the higher number of hazardous spills in the area, the greater amount of manufacture and transport of hazardous materials within the region, and the location of the region as an important traffic bridge between other major cities.

Fringe Benefits—When an interest arbitration involves the subject of insurance, arbitrators generally agree that internal comparables are most germane. This is especially so where the contribution rates prevailing in comparable communities lack uniformity. Thus, one arbitrator refused to adopt a police officer association's proposal that its employers pay 100 percent of yearly insurance premiums when the city's two other bargaining units still paid part of the cost.[4] However, he did order an increase in the maximum employer contribution. The arbitrator took into account the fact that the contracts for the other bargaining units would expire during the term of the police officers' contract, and the city's contribution to the cost of its police officers' insurance had been unchanged for four years. "Externalities" were not entirely ignored, however. The arbitrator also considered significant the fact that two of the comparable cities had raised their contribution levels.

---

[3]City of Madison, 106 LA 1059 (Flaten, 1996).
[4]City of Waterville, 107 LA 1194, 1197 (Dichter, 1996).

If There Is No Prevailing Practice

The outcome of a disputed pay rate issue may be determined by a balance of internal considerations, such as the special hardship created by a specific work assignment and the past treatment of the issue by the parties, where no discernible prevailing practice among external comparables exists. In deciding upon the proper increase for "standby pay" for police officers, the arbitrator pointed out that police officers on standby status experienced a special hardship because they had to remain sufficiently close to the station during their lengthy standby shifts to arrive within fifteen minutes from the time of the call-in. Further, the unusual length of the standby status was attributable, at least in part, to the city's having chosen to operate its department with one fewer police officer than it previously had employed. While granting a larger increase than that proposed by the city, the arbitrator did not award the full amount requested by the union. He found its demand to be excessive in light of the past compensation history of the parties.[5]

Cost of Living

Changes in the cost of living as typically measured by the U.S. Department of Labor's Consumer Price Index are often considered in determining the appropriate wage increase but are not normally a controlling factor.[6]

Escalator and Wage Reopening Clauses

A clause in a collective bargaining agreement providing for an automatic wage increase equal to the increase in the cost of living has been held not to survive the expiration of the agreement despite the fact that the parties had agreed to continue the terms of the agreement pending the negotiations of a successor agreement.[7]

Where the financial outlook for an employer or the prospects for a future government regulation or program impacting the issue are uncertain, arbitrators may permit a limited reopener to establish future benefit levels rather than fix the amounts for the duration of the contract.[8]

Ability to Pay

An employer's lack of ability to pay a proposed wage increase is an issue often raised in interest arbitration. In one case, the employer's

---

[5]City of Waterville, 107 LA 1194 (Dichter, 1996).
[6]County of Clay, 107 LA 527 (Dichter, 1996).
[7]Nome Joint Util. Bd., 103 LA 313 (Carr, 1994).
[8]Cuyahoga County Sheriff's Dep't, 102 LA 143 (Strasshofer, 1993).

inability to pay was the event that triggered arbitration. The parties had agreed that the employer would open its books to a union auditor and if, upon inspection, the auditor determined that the wages sought by the union could not be paid, arbitration would follow.[9]

An employer's inability to pay can be the decisive factor in a wage award notwithstanding that comparable employers in the area have agreed to higher wage scales.[10] The city of Detroit had been experiencing recurrent deficits, and the future revenue picture did not appear any brighter. The benefits in the contract were already greater than the average in the community. The arbitrator concluded that the only way to balance the budget was to cut wages by 10 percent.

On the other hand, the entire burden of budget deficits cannot be placed on a union. The Metro Area Express was unquestionably experiencing continuing deficits, but a number of employees had already been laid off, and the arbitrator concluded that cutting wages would have unfairly increased the burden on the employees remaining.[11]

Proof of Inability to Pay

An employer who claims "inability to pay" has the burden of proof on the issue. Obviously, if the financial exigency appears to be continuing and the employer is using its reserves to pay for current costs, arbitrators will temper any wage increase.[12] But even if past dismal financial results support the employer's position, the claim may be discounted if the evidence shows that the employer's fiscal prospects are improving.[13]

Public-Sector Ability to Pay

Disputes over the financial condition of a governmental employer are common.[14] One recent example surfaced in an impasse proceeding between a county sheriff's department and its employees. The county auditor's report showed a general fund balance of $80,924, but the sheriff claimed only $13,677. The fact-finder gave the auditor's calculations greater probative value and found the sheriff could afford to elevate wages to equal those paid in comparable counties.[15]

Wage "Patterns"

Arbitrators look to "wage patterns" that have developed both within and outside a jurisdiction. "Internal patterns" refer to rela-

---

[9]ATE/Ryder, 101 LA 52 (Darrow, 1993).
[10]City of Detroit, 102 LA 764 (Lipson, 1993).
[11]Metro Area Express, 103 LA 1 (Baroni, 1994).
[12]International Falls, 104 LA 323 (Berquist, 1995).
[13]Cuyahoga County Sheriff's Dep't, 102 LA 143 (Strasshofer, 1993).
[14]E.g., City of Detroit, 102 LA 764 (Lipson, 1993).
[15]Cuyahoga County Sheriff's Dep't, 102 LA 143 (Strasshofer, 1993).

tionships among employee units of the same employer with respect to their terms of employment. "External patterns" refer to relationships between the terms of employment of one unit of an employer and those for units of employees of one or more other jurisdictions performing similar jobs.[16] The longer a set of internal linkages is found to have existed, the greater the weight given to maintenance of the pattern.

A well-established internal pattern generally is given greater consideration by arbitrators than external patterns.[17] Exceptions may be found where giving deference to the established internal relationships would result in anomalous disparities between the treatment of the employees in question and those of relevant counterpart units in other jurisdictions,[18] or where there are other compelling or extenuating circumstances. In the absence of an established internal pattern, maintenance of an existing external pattern is given greatest consideration in determining an appropriate wage increase for a unit.

In some cases where the wages paid by the subject employer have failed to keep pace with those offered by the comparable jurisdictions, and thus the subject employer's "rank" has become lower, arbitrators may allow increases during the contract period greater than those offered in the comparable communities in order to allow the subject employees to catch up.[19]

Considerations of Special Interest in the Public Sector

Not all interest arbitration awards issued in public-sector impasse proceedings are binding upon the governmental employer and enforceable in court. When a police union sued the city of Fairbanks during the course of negotiations for failure to comply with the terms of an earlier award, the court decided that legislative approval of collective bargaining contracts was a customary requirement, and a provision of state law to the effect that terms in labor contracts involving monetary commitments were subject to legislative approval was applicable to interest arbitration awards.[20]

---

[16]City of Altus, 105 LA 277 (Neas, 1995) (in order to establish a "pattern," the jobs, as well as the jurisdictions, must be "comparable").
[17]City of West Bend, 100 LA 1118 (Vernon, 1993); City of St. Paul, 101 LA 1205 (Jacobowski, 1993).
[18]City of West Bend, 100 LA 1118 (Vernon, 1993); Oneida County Sheriff's Dep't, 100 LA 581 (Flaten, 1992).
[19]West Claremont Bd. of Educ., 103 LA 1193 (Murphy, 1994).
[20]Fairbanks Police Dep't Chapter v. City of Fairbanks, 920 P.2d 273, 154 LRRM 2791, 2793 (Alaska 1996).

Chapter 19

Arbitration's Place as an Industrial and Public-Employment Institution

[There were no significant developments relating to this chapter.]

Table of Court Cases

References are to footnotes within chapters (e.g., 17: 162 refers to footnote 162 in chapter 17.

A

AFSCME v. Illinois, 529 N.E.2d 534 (Ill. 1988) **2:** 59

Aircraft Braking Sys. Corp. v. Local 856, United Automobile Workers, 97 F.3d 155, 153 LRRM 2402 (6th Cir. 1996), *cert. denied,* 117 S. Ct. 1311, 154 LRRM 2928 (1997) **11:** 8–9

Airline Pilots v. O'Neill, 111 S. Ct. 1127, 136 LRRM 2721 (1991) **5:** 43

Albertsons Inc. v. Kirkingburg, 143 F.3d 1228 (9th Cir. 1998) **13:** 138

Alexander v. Gardner-Denver Co., 415 U.S. 36 (1974) **1:** 6; **3:** 17

Amalgamated Clothing & Textile Workers v. Facetglas, Inc., 845 F.2d 1250, 128 LRRM 2252 (4th Cir. 1988) **10:** 47

Amalgamated Transit Union, Div. 1300 v. Mass Transit Admin., 504 A.2d 1132, 121 LRRM 2894 (Md. 1986) **2:** 64, 66

Amax Coal Co. v. UMW, 92 F.3d 571 (7th Cir. 1996) **3:** 7

American Metal Prods. Inc. v. Sheet Metal Workers, Local No. 104, 794 F.2d 1452 (9th Cir. 1982) **2:** 37

American Postal Workers Union v. United States Postal Serv., 52 F.3d 359 (D.C. Cir. 1995) **3:** 9

Anne Arundel County v. Fraternal Order, 543 A.2d 841 (Md. 1988) **2:** 20

Ansonia Bd. of Educ. v. Philbrook, 107 S. Ct. 367, 42 FEP Cases 359 (1986) **17:** 162

AT&T Techs. Inc. v. Communications Workers of Am., 475 U.S. 643, 106 S. Ct. 1415, 121 LRRM 3329 (1986) **2:** 46, 48; **3:** 12, 14

Austin v. Owens-Brockway Glass Container, Inc., 78 F.3d 875 (4th Cir. 1996), *cert. denied,* 117 S. Ct. 432 (1996) **1:** 6; **3:** 19

Ayala v. Union De Tronquistas De Puerto Rico, Local 901, 74 F.3d 344, 151 LRRM 2298 (1st Cir. 1996) **5:** 41

B

Baltimore County v. Mayor & City Council of Baltimore, 621 A.2d 864 (Md. 1993) **2:** 64

Baltimore Teachers Union Local 340 v. Mayor of Baltimore, 671 A.2d 80, 151 LRRM 2706 (Md. Ct. App. 1996) **10:** 8

Bates v. Long Island R.R. Co., 997 F.2d 1028 (2d Cir. 1993), *cert. denied,* 510 U.S. 992 (1993) **1:** 6

Beadle v. Hillsborough County Sheriff's Dep't, 29 F.3d 589, 65 FEP Cases 1069 (11th Cir. 1994) **17:** 163

Belanger v. Matteson, 346 A.2d 124, 91 LRRM 2003 (R.I. 1975) **2:** 55

Beloit, City of v. Wisconsin Employment Relations Comm'n, 242 N.W.2d 231, 92 LRRM 3318 (Wis. 1976) **2:** 88, 93

Bethany, City of v. Public Employees Relations Bd. of Okla., 904 P.2d 604 (Okla. 1995) **2:** 19

Bevona v. 820 Second Ave. Assocs., 27 F.3d 37, 146 LRRM 2673 (2d Cir. 1994) **7:** 14, 16

B.F. Goodrich v. Betkoski, 99 F.3d 505 (2d Cir. 1996) **14:** 38

Binghamton Civil Serv. Forum v. City of Binghamton, 374 N.E.2d 380, 97 LRRM 3070 (N.Y. 1978) **2:** 57–58, 72

C

N

National Educ. Ass'n-Topeka, Inc. v. Unified Sch. Dist. 501, Shawnee County, 592 P.2d 93, 101 LRRM 2611 (Kan. 1979) *2:* 88

NCR Corp., E & M Wichita v. Machinists and Aerospace Workers, 906 F.2d 1499 (10th Cir. 1990) *3:* 7

New Bedford Sch. Comm. v. New Bedford Educators Ass'n, 405 N.E.2d 162, 108 LRRM 3201 (Mass. App. Ct. 1980) *2:* 99

New Jersey v. State Troopers Fraternal Ass'n, 634 A.2d 478, 145 LRRM 2564 (N.J. 1993) *2:* 97

Newport Mesa Unified Sch. Dist; EEOC v.., 893 F.Supp. 927, 68 FEP Cases 657 (C.D. Cal. 1995) *14:* 4

Newsday, Inc. v. Long Island Typographical Union, 915 F.2d 840, 135 LRRM 2659 (2d Cir. 1990), *cert. denied,* 111 S. Ct. 1314, 136 LRRM 2720 (1991) *11:* 2

New York Bd. v. Glaubman, 53 N.Y. 2d 781, 439 N.Y. S.2d 907 *2:* 51

New York City Dep't of Sanitation v. MacDonald, 627 N.Y.S. 2d 619 (N.Y. App. Div. 1995) *2:* 51

NIDA v. Plant Protection Ass'n Nat'l, 7 F.3d 522, 144 LRRM 2530 (6th Cir. 1993) *5:* 47

Nielson v. Machinists, Local Lodge 2569, 94 F.3d 1107, 153 LRRM 2161 (7th Cir. 1996), *cert. denied,* 520 U.S. 1165, 117 S. Ct. 1426 (1997) *5:* 46

NLRB v. *See name of opposing party*

Nolde Brothers, Inc. v. Bakery & Confectionary Workers Union Local 358, 430 U.S. 243 (1977) *3:* 20

North Adams Regional Hosp. v. Massachusetts Nursing Ass'n, 889 F. Supp. 507 (D. Mass. 1995) *10:* 5

O

Oil, Chem. & Atomic Workers v. NLRB, 46 F.3d 82, 148 LRRM 2461 (D.C. Cir. 1995) *16:* 40

Old Bridge Township Bd. of Educ. v. Old Bridge Educ. Ass'n, 489 A.2d 159, 121 LRRM 2784 (N.J. 1985) *2:* 95

Olmstead v. L.C., 138 F.3d 893 (11th Cir. 1998) *13:* 138

Oncale v. Sundowner Offshore Servs., Inc., 118 S. Ct. 998 (1998) *17:* 172–76

P

Paperworkers v. Misco, Inc., 484 U.S. 29 (1987) *2:* 65; *3:* 8–9; *10:* 10

Paterson Police P&A Local No. 1 v. Paterson, 432 A.2d 847, 112 LRRM 2205 (N.J. 1981) *2:* 76

Patterson v. Tenet Healthcare, Inc., 113 F.3d 832 (8th Cir. 1997) *10:* 12

Pegump v. Rockwell Int'l Corp., 109 F.3d 442, 154 LRRM 2816 (8th Cir. 1997) *5:* 41

Pennsylvania State Police v. Pennsylvania State Troopers' Ass'n, 656 A.2d 83, 149 LRRM 2877 (1995) *2:* 60

Pierce v. Commonwealth Edison Co., 112 F.3d 893 (7th Cir. 1997) *3:* 9

Plumbers Local No. 32 v. NLRB, 50 F.3d 24, 148 LRRM 2833 (D.C. Cir. 1995) *5:* 48

Policeman's & Fireman's Retirement Bd. of City of New Haven v. Sullivan, 376 A.2d 399, 95 LRRM 2351 (Conn. 1977) *2:* 46

Port Huron Educ. Ass'n v. Port Huron Area Sch. Dist., 452 Mich. 309, 550 N.W.2d 228, 158 LRRM 2997 (1996) *2:* 39, 85

Professional, Clerical, Technical Employees Ass'n (Buffalo Bd. of Educ.), In re, 683 N.E.2d 733 (N.Y. 1997) *2:* 19

Progressive Casualty Ins. Co. v. C.A. Reasegurador Nacional de Venezuela, 991 F.2d 42 (2d Cir. 1993) *2:* 51

Providence Teachers Union Local 958
  v. McGovern, 319 A.2d 358, 86 LRRM 2899 (R.I. 1974) *2:* 55
  v. Providence Sch. Comm.
    276 A.2d 762 (R.I. 1971) *2:* 18
    433 A.2d 202, 112 LRRM 2998 (R.I. 1981) *2:* 46

Prudential-Bache Sec., Inc. v. Tanner, 72 F.3d 234 (1st Cir. 1995) *10:* 8

Pryner v. Tractor Supply Co., 109 F.3d 354 (7th Cir. 1997), *petition for cert. filed,* 65 U.S.L.W. 3783 (U.S. May 16, 1997) (No. 96-1830), *petition for cert. filed,* 66 U.S.L.W. 3108 (U.S. July 18, 1997) (No. 97-123) *1:* 6; *3:* 19

R

Racine Educ. Ass'n
  v. Racine Unified Sch. Dist., 500 N.W.2d 379, 143 LRRM 3110 (1993) *2:* 86